A
Philosopher's
Story

Other Books by Morton White

The Origin of Dewey's Instrumentalism
Social Thought in America
The Age of Analysis (ed.)
Toward Reunion in Philosophy
Religion, Politics, and the Higher Learning
The Intellectual Versus the City (with Lucia White)
Foundations of Historical Knowledge
Science and Sentiment in America
Documents in the History of American Philosophy (ed.)
Pragmatism and the American Mind
The Philosophy of the American Revolution
What Is and What Ought to Be Done
Journeys to the Japanese (with Lucia White)
Philosophy, "The Federalist," and the Constitution
The Question of Free Will

A
Philosopher's
Story

Morton White

The Pennsylvania State University Press
University Park, Pennsylvania

Library of Congress Cataloging-in-Publication Data

White, Morton Gabriel, 1917–
    A philosopher's story / by Morton White.

        p.   cm.
    Includes bibliographical references and index.
    ISBN 0-271-01874-7 (cloth : alk. paper) ISBN 0-271-02490-0 (pbk.)
    1. White, Morton Gabriel, 1917–   . 2. Philosophers—United
States—Biography.   I. Title.
    B945.W474A3   1999
    191—dc21   98-39334
    [b]   CIP

It is the policy of The Pennsylvania State University Press to use acid-free paper for the
first printing of all clothbound books. Publications on uncoated stock satisfy the minimum
requirements of American National Standard for Information Sciences—Permanence of
Paper for Printed Library Materials, ANSI Z39.48-1992.

To My Grandchildren

Jenny, Olivia, Alex,
Joe, and Hannah

Contents

1

A Lonely Philistine

Unlike the parents of many Jewish-American boys of my generation in New York, mine were born in this country. My grandparents all came here as adults, but two of them died before I was born, and a third died in the year in which I was born. My parents never told me much about them or about my fourth grandparent, who survived until I was fifteen but with whom I could hardly communicate because she spoke very little English and was very ill. My mother and father, like so many "Yankees" of their generation, were not particularly interested in their origins. I don't know whether there was anyone in that past worth remembering, but I do know that my parents were eager to dissociate themselves from that past. They thought of themselves as Americans, to some extent looked down on their parents as foreigners, and looked forward to a life without pogroms, czars, and emperors. Unlike some of my contemporaries, I was never told much about any real or imagined rabbinical ancestors; I learned only that my father's parents came from Hungary and that my mother's came from a place that moved back and forth like a geopolitical football between Russia and Poland.

My father, Robert Weisberger, was born on the Lower East Side of New York in 1891, the fifth of nine children born there—one of them a half brother. My mother, Esther, was also born there, in 1892, and was one of three children born there—one of them a half sister. My parents were married in 1915, when they began to live at 76–80 Madison Street, which is not to be confused with Madison Avenue; and I was born on April 29, 1917.

The apartment in which I first lived still stands today, a dreary, gray-brick five-story tenement on the corner of Madison and Catherine Streets. In my day it had no electricity and was gaslit; I vividly remember times when the gas ceased to come out of the jets, because the time provided by a twenty-five-cent piece in the meter had run out. I lived in that apartment until I was six years old, in 1923. In that year, when I began elementary school, we moved across Catherine Street to a newer building, which I was taught to call an apartment house as opposed to a tenement house.

Although the move was from a lesser to a greater building, the greater was definitely not grand. The halls of the apartment house were no cleaner than the halls of the tenement house across the street. Indeed, because of the way in which a public dumbwaiter was used, they were much smellier. Instead of reaching in and pulling the ropes in order to get the elevator to come up, and instead of setting garbage pails on the elevator, which then should have been returned to the basement, the residents abandoned the entire principle of the elevator in their haste to get rid of their garbage. When the elevator ceased to ride up and down the shaft, that became a chute into which all the crud was dumped. I can remember the horrible smells that wafted up to us on the third floor, and whenever I was delegated to take out the garbage, I would have to take a deep breath before opening the door to the dumbwaiter and disposing of my bundle in the accepted way. I often came close to fainting during these episodes.

The building at 72 Madison Street not only housed my family, it also housed my father's shoe store on the ground floor. My father had inherited it from his father, who had come to this country in, I think, the 1870s; it was the third and last owned by my grandfather before he died in 1917, the year of my birth. His first had been a cobbler's shop on Water Street, from which he moved to a larger store on the corner of Catherine and Monroe Streets. In my grandfather's time, and in my father's as well, Catherine Street was the main business street of what was sometimes called the "Two Bridges" area because it was bounded by the Brooklyn Bridge on one side and the Manhattan Bridge on the other. When I was a boy, its other accepted boundaries were the East River and East Broadway, the latter being one block from the Bowery, beyond which Chinatown, as I knew it, lay. Therefore during my first twenty-two years I moved, lived, and had my being three or four blocks from

Chatham Square and the Bowery, then the most degraded part of New York, the place of flophouses for derelicts and the home of "Bowery Bums."

"The Store," as we called it, was fairly large by local standards. It was about fifty feet square, and its four walls were lined with shelves that each held boxes of shoes two deep, one on top of another. About two feet down from the ceiling were railings on which stepladders rode, and those railings are forever linked in my mind with the loneliness of my childhood. Living in an alien neighborhood and having two very anxious parents who doted over their only child, I was what would later be called overprotected. At night, after I had quickly finished my homework, I was not allowed outside. My parents were not afraid that I might be stabbed or raped, as a New York child of eight or nine might be today; they were afraid of my being beaten up—and with good reason. Therefore a good part of my night after the evening meal on weekdays was spent playing by myself in the store, which stayed open until ten o'clock at night. I was encouraged to play basketball there until closing time, all by myself. I would take a large carton in which shoes had been delivered by a manufacturer, open its top and bottom, use one of its flaps to hook the box over the ladder railing, and thereby make a "basket" for my ball. Only the entrance of a particularly severe-looking customer would keep me from dribbling around the back of the store, sinking my baskets as I dreamed of becoming another Nat Holman, then the hero of basketball. My ability to play in isolation prepared me to some extent for the lonely subject of philosophy, for my youthful radicalism, for my marriage to Lucia Perry in defiance of my parents' desire that I not marry a Gentile, and for my episodes of academic rebelliousness.

My loneliness continued after I entered P.S. 114 on the corner of Oliver and Oak Streets, undoubtedly one of the toughest New York elementary schools at the time. I was often beaten by bigger (and smaller) schoolmates, who would gang up on me as they did on teachers, too—so often, that there was a period when my parents hired an older schoolmate to accompany me on my walks to and from school. In short, I had a bodyguard at the tender age of seven! I entered P.S. 114 in 1923 and was graduated in June 1928. The reason for this rapid trip through elementary school was that I had skipped several grades, thereby losing the opportunity to make friendships, while I kept leaving classmates who were advancing in the normal way. I am sure, however, that if I had not skipped (or been skipped—that construction was also used), I would have gone out of my mind. The boredom of school was overwhelming, and though I suspect that I was socially handicapped by finally sitting in classes with "guerillas" of fifteen and sixteen when I was ten or eleven, I think my teachers were right in pushing me through elementary school as quickly as possible. I was skipped not because I was a genius. I was skipped mainly because I was more intelligent than average and had received a little more education at home than most of my schoolmates had. I do not mean that my father and mother were scholars, but at least they spoke English and could inform me of things about America that were unknown to my classmates and their immigrant parents.

The subject I learned most about from my father was politics. He was not fascinated by his occupation as a storekeeper, but he was an extremely sociable and affable man who had a consuming interest in the fortunes of the Democratic Party. After I left home, he realized some of his political ambitions by becoming a member of the New York City Council, but in the years of which I now write, he was actively interested in local Tammany affairs, while he held no political office. He made no sharp separation between his life as a businessman and his life as a politician, and so his political cronies were always dropping in to see him at the store. My mother would often complain that so many of what she called political bums congregated in the store that customers who looked into that smoke-filled room would turn away and buy their shoes elsewhere. I clearly remember the summer of 1924, when, in order to keep in touch with the famous Democratic convention at which Alabama kept giving twenty-four votes to Oscar W. Underwood, my father was bold enough to buy a radio and install it in his store, a very unusual thing at the time. It was then that I realized that he might be willing to see his business go down the drain rather than miss the latest episode in the fortunes of the Democratic Party. After I left home, at twenty-two, my father ran in a Democratic primary in alliance with Carmine De Sapio—later the all-powerful leader of Tammany Hall—and in rebellion against the older, Irish leadership. By then I had already moved out on my own, and as a young radical I had come to disapprove of my father's politics, but it was under his influence that I developed an interest in politics and, by extension, in academic politics.

In 1932 my father's interest in the fortunes of Tammany Hall and his losses on the stock market led him to neglect his business, and he went bankrupt. Although the store opened at nine in the morning and closed at ten in the evening, my father spent less and less time in it. He would get downstairs by about 11 A.M., at which time he would visit a local restaurant for breakfast because, he said, he could not eat until he had a walk and some air. This meant that he went to work at about noon, just in time to let his help go to lunch. Often I would hear stories of how his employees had stolen some of the receipts during the morning, and my mother would periodically condemn my father for his waywardness in business, pointing out that he could not expect his unwatched employees to resist the temptation to put a few dollars in their pockets. My father's conduct of his business was very different from that of his immigrant father. I was told that when this grandfather of mine died in 1917, he left an estate valued at $100,000, but that may well be a mythical figure. When he died, a great deal of friction arose among his children, and for reasons that I never fully understood, my father felt himself estranged from his siblings on the matter of the inheritance; my father was not made rich by the terms of his father's will, and he often spoke wistfully of earlier and more glorious times in our family's economic history.

I heard far more about this aspect of our family's life from my mother, who was very bitter about the decline in our economic fortunes. If my life with my father was in the store, my life with my mother was in the apartment. Some of my earliest and most painful memories are of Saturday-morning late breakfasts with her alone, occasions on which all of her venom flowed. In those days she was especially hostile to most of her in-laws and never forgave them for opposing her marriage to my father. She always felt as if she were an outsider in their presence and would often discourse bitterly about the sister-in-law who had warned her before her marriage that my father would come into less money than she was counting on. Under the influence of my mother, I came to have a hostile view of the aunts and uncles on my father's side; I saw little of them and of my cousins, thereby losing an opportunity to diminish my isolation in the slums. With few exceptions, my father's siblings seemed cold, distant, and grasping to me; most of them lived uptown in fancy neighborhoods, while we continued to live in the ancestral neighborhood. I was told that they often criticized my father for continuing to live downtown and for failing to see how much harm that was doing me, but instead of viewing their intervention in my behalf as a favor, I wrote them off as pretentious snobs who could not appreciate the charms of life in the First Assembly District. I was then something of a romanticist about that life, forgetting its filth, my loneliness, and my beatings at the hands of my schoolmates. It was not until I was eleven, when I was sent to a boys' camp—Camp Chicopee—that I came to know my cousins Herbert and James Wechsler. Of all of my many, many cousins on my father's side, only they became and remained my friends in later life. Herbert became a distinguished professor of law at Columbia, and James became the editor of the *New York Post*.

My mother's side of the family was decidedly poorer than my father's. My mother's mother seemed almost destitute to me when I visited her in her flat on Forsyth Street, which was in what was called a rear tenement. It was wooden—a remarkable thing even in those years—and stood behind a brick building that faced Forsyth Street. I well remember walking through the hall of the front building and coming to my grandmother's house after passing through a small dirty courtyard in which there was an unused water pump. Then I would walk up one or two flights to an apartment that was dark and foul-smelling. My visits to this pathetic, broken-down old lady—I don't know how old she was then—were always trying and painfully disturbing. After I became a little older, I'm ashamed to say, I tried my best to get out of visiting her. Her son, Uncle Sam, was a quiet man who worked first as a taxi driver and then as a blocker of women's hats. He was the automobile-driving counterpart on my mother's side of my father's half brother Gilbert, who drove a bus. Gilbert was the son of my grandfather by his second wife, and unfortunately for him, his mother disowned him because he married a Gentile.

Because of the treatment accorded to Gilbert, the relations between Gentiles and Jews were much on my mind during my childhood. I was a lonely, unreligious Jewish boy living in a Gentile environment. I was taken to synagogue on Yom Kippur and Rosh Hashanah; I was taught that the Old Testament God existed; my mother made a feeble effort to keep a kosher kitchen; and I was proud of Jewish prizefighters, like Benny Leonard and Ruby Goldstein, and of Einstein's being the smartest man in the world. But, I was not required to go to synagogue on Saturdays, and my father kept his store open on Saturday. Yiddish was not taught to me, though both my parents would speak it occasionally. I learned a bit of Hebrew in a short course, with the aim of being able to recite a text at my Bar Mitzvah. Before getting this instruction from a private tutor, I was sent to a Hebrew school but had great difficulty in understanding my teacher because he was teaching Hebrew to students who were expected to know Yiddish. My parents and I ate ham at home without compunction, and we ate in restaurants with no concern about whether they were kosher. We knew and liked many Irishmen and Italians, and didn't think of them as horrible except when I received cruel treatment from them in the streets.

My father was much less anti-Gentile than my mother, if that is the correct way of expressing what I have in mind. In later years, when I read Joyce's *Ulysses*, I thought he resembled the Hungarian Leopold Bloom in many respects; he was admired by the Irish and the Italians, and that played a great part in his political success. As a second-generation American he had a great need to demonstrate his patriotism, and I'm sure that "Columbia, the Gem of the Ocean" would bring more tears to his eyes than "Ha Tikvah." I think my mother was more Jewish than my father because she had been brought up in a Jewish neighborhood, whereas my father had been brought up in an Irish neighborhood. When newspapers carried a story of some catastrophe, my mother would immediately ask whether any Jews were killed, and that always angered my father. She would often speak Yiddish in front of customers in order to keep something from them, but my father scrupulously avoided doing so. This was partly because he was more astute politically: he knew it might lose a sale. It was also a product of his being nicer to people and liking them more, which may explain why he almost never used corporal punishment on me, whereas my mother would often slap me in the face when I did something naughty. She was not a particularly good housewife and was a saleslady on only the busiest days in the store. She was alone a good deal of the time after ten in the evening, when my father would close the store and begin his nocturnal politics.

One of the more bizarre and painful stories of my childhood has to do with my relationships with my father's stepmother, whom he called Auntie. For years she lived at 72 Madison Street, one floor below us. There was no elevator in that house, so we were constantly rubbing elbows with her as we went up and down the narrow staircase. In my earliest childhood I greeted her, but as time went on, the "hello"s became feebler and feebler on both sides, for I came to notice that my parents *never* spoke to her. As a result, I am sorry to say, I stopped greeting her. I must add that she was not very pleasant and *looked* like a Dickensian stepmother, and when I heard that she had disowned Gilbert for marrying a Gentile, I came to dislike her even more, under the influence of my parents; they told me she was a bigot—a word they unsuccessfully tried to define for me. They also told me that when my father had been hit by a Madison Street bus in 1923, and when he was lying on the ground in a coma, Auntie was overheard to say: "It serves him right." Her point was that God was punishing my father for encouraging Gilbert in his waywardness, and from that time on there was *never* a nice word said by my parents about Auntie within my hearing. Indeed, when my mother became nervous about my marrying Lucia, my mother said that Auntie (by that time dead) had hurled a curse upon her and my father that was now being carried out. They had encouraged Gilbert to marry a Gentile; therefore God was answering Auntie's prayers by having me marry a Gentile!

From this the reader may rightly infer that my parents were not highly educated. They were intelligent but did not read very much. They had not gone to school beyond the eighth grade, and like so many American-born children of Jewish immigrants they had lost a good deal of the love of learning and culture associated with European Jews. If my parents had such a love, it was manifested only in their conventional desire that I become a lawyer or physician. My parents rarely read books, and I was never encouraged to read them. Newspapers were a very different affair; they abounded because of my father's interest in politics. Every night he would buy three papers, which were delivered by a newsboy who came by the store with early editions of the next morning's *New York American*, the *Daily News*, and the *Daily Mirror*. My father and mother both had good voices, and my father had been given violin lessons in his childhood, but in spite of the fact that I was somewhat musical, I was never asked or encouraged to take up an instrument. My father himself played the piano by ear and would sing sentimental old-time ballads to his own accompaniment whenever he came near a piano in someone else's house—we never owned a piano. But I never heard a concert or a recital until I entered the College of the City of New York at fifteen in 1932. Painting was absolutely out of my parent's ken and mine. I was, in short, a young philistine whose childhood "culture" was a compound of politics, journalism, jazz, restaurants, baseball, and movies. I was a child of the streets and the store. My father had been a boyhood friend of the comedian and singer Eddie Cantor; he also knew Jimmy Durante, who came from our neighborhood. Every Sunday night, when my father closed his store at six o'clock, we would all go to an expensive restaurant for dinner, often to a Lower East Side place called Manny Wolff's on Forsyth Street. It was then one of the most popular political speakeasies in New York, and there we often saw our mayor, Jimmy Walker. The place was an old-fashioned steak-and-chop house that was guarded by a delightful Jewish doorman known as Silk-Shirt Sammy. I was allowed to have a short beer with my meals at Manny's when I was about ten, an infant *bon vivant* who astonished his classmates with reports of what and whom he had seen in Manny's, including Joe (Socks) Lanza, the gangster who was so powerful at the Fulton Fish Market. I was also permitted to go to restaurants by myself at a tender age. Sometimes it would be a place in Chinatown; often it would be a place on Park Row called Solomons, well known by virtue of its advertisement that read "Be Wise, Eat at Solomons." There I would go, all by myself, and have myself a lonely dinner, served by friendly waiters who would tell me what I could eat. As part of his lore about restaurants my father would tell me stories about Lindy's, a restaurant that was a nearby haunt of my father's before it moved uptown and became immortalized by Damon Runyon under the name Mindy's.

Movies also played a great part in my lonely life. On Park Row, then covered by an elevated and only a little more reputable than the Bowery nearby, there was a theater called the Venice, which was owned by a bizarre creature called Mazie Gordon, "Queen of the Bowery." She has been immortalized in a *New Yorker* profile by Joseph Mitchell, who has recorded, among other things, her ministrations to Bowery bums. She sat in the ticket taker's box, her peroxide-blonde hair and gold teeth shining as she took your money. Occasionally she would enter the theater to throw out a snoring drunk or to fumigate the place with some horrid-smelling spray. Mazie was a friend of my father and mother, and I was always welcome in the theater, along with my bodyguard, even though both of us were below the age at which children could legally enter the theater unaccompanied by an adult. I can remember going to the Venice every day for months on end, since they offered a new feature every day. I would go there soon after school closed and after I had quickly finished my homework.

My Runyonesque contact with politicians, cops, movies, gangsters, and speakeasies was jolly, and I learned a great deal about the world from it, perhaps more than I learned at school. I can remember little of what I learned there besides the rudiments of arithmetic and writing. I knew how to read before I went to school, but I can't remember reading a complete book before I was eleven, having seen few books at home. There was a public library on East Broadway between Catherine and Market Streets, but I seldom borrowed books there. Because my education was so different from that of, say, John Stuart Mill, some readers might think that I gained so much experience in Manny Wolff's, the Venice Theater, and my father's store that I should have been glad not to have been learning Greek as a baby. They might also think that while Mill prepared himself for an early nervous breakdown, I became a knowing, sociable participant in the urban world of the twentieth century. What such readers would not see is that although my childhood was probably more cheerful than John Mill's, and filled with experiences that he never had, I was very isolated—ethnically, religiously, socially.

I really didn't have a friend until I left my neighborhood to go to high school at age eleven. Although my parents had friends, my passionate yearnings for friendship were never satisfied. I was constantly being told that I was different from my playmates, that *they* could go out and raise hell but that I, as the representative of a locally important family, had to present a different face to the world. I was the son and grandson of well-known Jewish merchants in our village—for it *was* a village—and Jews who live among Gentiles, I was told, must be dignified, respectable, and never in the least suspect of doing anything that was perfectly all right for an Italian janitor's son to do. In short, I was expected to keep up appearances of superiority in a Gentile world. I *had* to be the first in my class, and I was when I was graduated from P.S. 114, but upon my graduation several things happened that epitomized my isolation.

My parents decided that a party should be given in my honor, but not a single child was invited! It was a party attended by all of *their* friends, who caroused into the night. They were celebrating not only my graduation but the fact that I was the valedictorian and the youngest graduate. But the graduation had been marred by a strange incident. During the Spring before, the American Legion had offered a prize for the best essay on Americanism. I entered the contest, and I produced a piece that was voted by a committee of teachers to be the best. One of the teachers had reported this to my father and had congratulated him on my success, but soon afterward my father was told by another teacher that the principal of the school had decided that it would be impolitic to have a Jewish boy be both valedictorian and winner of the most distinguished prize at the graduation of a class that was almost entirely Italian. For this reason, the principal reversed the decision of the committee and awarded the prize to another boy.

My father was furious and proceeded to do something that horrified me. He forced me to go to the principal's office with him for a confrontation. In my later radical days I would have applauded this, but as a scared child of eleven, I was appalled. The confrontation has remained in my mind for all these years with utmost clarity. My father led me into the room and introduced himself and me to the principal—a tall, tough, ruddy Irishman. "Morty," my father asked me, "who won the prize for the best essay on Americanism?" "I did." The principal angrily contradicted me, but my father persisted, like a lawyer. "Morty, how do you know that you won the prize." "Because my teacher told me." "And wasn't it announced in the school assembly last week?" "Yes," I said in another frightened response. After that the principal furiously insisted that I hadn't won and my father that I had, and they almost came to blows. We finally left the office, my father very flushed and I very miserable about the whole thing. The upshot was that the principal stood his ground and I had to make do with my honor as valedictorian.

I want to add another story that vividly illustrates my father's tendency to force me into confrontations. One night during the period I am talking about, I was set upon by a gang of four or five of my supposed friends. A neighbor came into my father's store—it was a busy night—to tell my father what was going on, at which point my father abandoned his customer and rushed out onto Catherine Street with an open shoebox in his hands. He managed to save me from a pretty severe beating, but he also did something bizarre and unforgettable. He forced me then and there to square off with the toughest of my tormentors in order to show them that I could handle myself in a fair and square fight, and to impress upon me that *in such an encounter* I would have to defend myself without his help. While he held my other attackers at bay, I was required to give a good account of myself in the manly art of self-defense. The reader will see a connection between the two confrontations I have described and certain confrontations in which I found myself later in life. Sticking up for one's rights, as my father called it, was an important part of my life in imitation of his.

I hope I do not give the impression that I was a self-righteous little prig; but I was upset by my father's latitudinarianism even though I loved his sweetness and his easygoing way with people who did not try to bully him. He was the most popular man in the neighborhood, and I was proud of that. But his work habits and his politicking made for a limited family life. He and my mother loved me, but my life was very different from that lived by other children. My mother used to tell a story that probably epitomized her situation and mine. One night, when I was about five years old, my father was very late for supper. I was playing with a little friend but was aware of my mother's concern, so I turned to him, according to my mother's story, and said: "Jack, I think you'd better go home now. My mother is worrying about my father, and I have to worry with her." My poor mother continued to worry about my father for about a half century, but she remained loyal and devoted to him to the end, as he did to her.

My parents made me feel that I could do no wrong so far as they were concerned, that even my marriage to a Gentile would in the end be accepted by them, as it was. I knew that I could ask for their help whenever I needed it, that I could always turn to them for moral support and for whatever limited financial support they were able to give me. Even in the days when I was a student radical and therefore really crazy from their point of view, they helped me financially and let me have my way, confident that I would land on my feet. I cannot exaggerate how important this was to me; more than anything else it saved me from becoming a complete victim of the slums. Having said that, however, I must also say that my parents did nothing—as they could have—to get me out of those slums, where I witnessed so much filth, degradation, and ignorance and could rely on little but my own inner resources and their support to nourish my desire to make something of myself. On top of that, they were far less devoted to the intellectual life than were the parents of many of my Jewish contemporaries: they lacked the respect for books that immigrant students of the Talmud or immigrant socialists had. Notwithstanding that, they helped me survive my surroundings on Catherine and Madison Streets without becoming a gangster, a pool shark, a song-and-dance man, or a shoe salesman; they made me feel that I could and should do better than that, and I tried to justify their confidence in me. In the jargon of today, they helped me develop self-esteem, and through their willingness to tolerate my becoming whatever I wanted to become, they helped me climb out of the gutters of Catherine Street.

However, they could do little to help me plan for my schooling when it came time for me to go to high school in 1928, so I decided on my own to apply to DeWitt Clinton High School. The main thing my parents did then was to veto the idea of my applying to Townsend Harris High School, where bright New Yorkers could complete the four years of high school in three. Had I gone to Townsend Harris I would have entered college at fourteen instead of fifteen, and that seemed as unwise to my parents then as it does to me now. So, for some reason I can't remember, I picked DeWitt Clinton, which was then uptown on the West Side of Manhattan. I entered it in the fall of 1928 but did not remain in it very long, because my parents decided that a boy of eleven should not travel alone by bus and subway to such a distant place, especially when there was a high school on the Lower East Side, namely, Seward Park High School. Their idea was that I should transfer to Seward Park, but that plan faced one serious obstacle. Seward Park was a three-year high school that began in the tenth grade, and since I had just been graduated from the eighth grade, I was eligible only for admission to a high school that began in the ninth grade. To be sure, Seward Park Senior High School was connected with Seward Park Junior High, which consisted of grades seven, eight, and nine, but the rules also forbade me from entering Seward Park Junior High in midstream.

By now the reader has heard enough about my father to realize that rules rarely fazed him. To him no rule seemed to be beyond politics, and he was better at that than one might infer from his unsuccessful effort to persuade my elementary school principal to restore my American Legion prize to me. Consequently, he went to the board of education and made a personal appeal on my behalf. As he recounted the story, he was at first told by the superintendent that the thing was impossible. Rules were rules. But as the interview approached its end, my father looked at him and said: "Dr. Veet, weren't you once the principal of P.S. 1?" That was the trump card, to be held just so long. "Why, of course," said Dr. Veet. "How did you know?" the superintendent asked. "Because I was a student in your school," my father replied, adding that his father had owned the shoe store on the corner of Catherine and Monroe Streets, the location of the store preceding the one I knew. "Why, of course, I remember your father," the superintendent said. "You had three brothers, didn't you?" "That's right, Superintendent," my father replied, seeing the ice melting. "Well, now, you know that this is one of our strictest rules, but seeing that your boy is only eleven, I think we can make one of our very rare exceptions." "By the way," the superintendent continued, "do you ever see the governor?" The reference, of course, was to Al Smith. "Why I saw him only the other day," said my politically shrewd father, only too aware of a school superintendent's interest in maintaining good relations with someone who knew Al Smith. There followed some happy reminiscences about the good old neighborhood, and my father was given a document that admitted me to the ninth grade of Seward Park Junior High School.

Seward Park Junior High School was next door to its allied senior high school, which in those days was on Hester Street facing Seward Park itself, one of the great centers of the Jewish Lower East Side. It was where Trotsky had spoken to great crowds before the October Revolution, and across from it on East Broadway stood the building of the Yiddish newspaper, the *Forward*. In recent years, when I have driven from my old neighborhood to Seward Park, the distance seemed like nothing, but the park was a world away during my childhood—a world of strolling rabbis, pretzel vendors, lox and bagels, Jewish delicatessens, socialist orators, chess-playing denizens of the park, and all the other elements of a ghetto about which I knew little even though I could get to it by walking a long block on East Broadway from Catherine to Market, a short one from Market to Pike under the Manhattan Bridge, and another long one from Pike to Rutgers Street. When I was eleven, the shadows of the Manhattan Bridge formed the boundary between my part of the Lower East Side and this other world. Pike Street, which lay just beyond the bridge, was definitely Jewish, for we made our annual pilgrimage to a synagogue there after the disappearance of one that stood closer to us on Henry Street between Catherine and Market.

The year 1928 marked my entry into the Jewish world. In that year, after I was hit by an automobile while playing ball in the street, my frightened parents sent me to a camp in the Poconos where the sons of many rich Jews went, and a few months later I entered a junior high school attended mainly by what someone once called "Jews without money." There I had to compete with children who were much more imbued than I was with a love of learning, and I was no longer automatically the best student in my class because I knew what a primary election was; I was also introduced for the first time to girls, since Seward Park was coeducational. My P.S. 114 was not; the girls in my neighborhood were sent to P.S. 1, by my time a school for girls alone. Of course, there *were* girls in my neighborhood, but I realize with amazement that I can't remember a single one of them. I played with Italian boys who were my schoolmates, but I seemed to have come close to Italian girls only when they bought shoes in my father's store. I was shy of girls in general, and I also labored under some feeling that I ought not to play with Gentile girls, whether Italian or Irish. There were, as I have said, a few Irish left in our neighborhood, but they rarely attended the public schools; they usually went to St. James's parochial school on James Street. I knew some Irish boys who lived on Catherine Street but hardly any Irish girls; my parents, in spite of being good friends with many Irish people, somehow insulated me from their children. Whatever lay behind this was probably at work in my parents' later disapproval of my marriage to a Gentile.

My ninth grade in Seward Park Junior High School left me with only a few memories worth setting down. I can remember being told by a classmate that "Morton" was a sissy name and that I should use "Mike" instead, so everyone called me that during all of my high school years. I can also remember that my contact with this new part of the world encouraged me to visit some of the many settlement houses in it. Before I was eleven, I knew only the Jacob Riis House on Henry Street; it was named for the famous author of *How the Other Half Lives*, in which he described the conditions of New York slums at the turn of the century. But by the time I was twelve, I had begun to visit the more famous Educational Alliance on East Broadway and Jefferson Streets, and the Madison House on Madison Street. There I played a lot of basketball, and I joined various clubs that were supervised by earnest social workers whom we regarded with a mixture of appreciation and contempt because of their uptown ignorance of what our downtown lives were really like. Many of them seemed to us like the "rubbernecks" who were guided through our streets by megaphoning bus drivers and who regarded us almost as animals in a zoo. Still, our social workers did much to Americanize us, to use a popular verb of the time, and many an East Side boy of my generation met his first white Anglo-Saxon Protestant in the person of a social worker. They were not all Jane Addamses, but they were, for the most part, decent people, dedicated to the ideals that guided Jane Addams's life.

It is worth saying something about my lack of contact with Protestants in my early childhood, especially since I later married one. In my earliest years

I knew nothing about the great schism in the Christian world. In the streets I learned that the Irish and the Italians were both Christians, and that they often hated and feared each other. But I did not know that there was another division within the Christian world until I went to high school. In my eleven-year-old mind a Christian was a Catholic. Across the way from where I lived, there was something called the Five Points Mission, run by Protestants, and on the corner of Oliver and Henry Streets there was a semi-abandoned Protestant church built for sailors, as there was on the corner of Market and Henry Streets. But I never knew anyone who attended them. I knew the *word* "Protestant," since it was a term of abuse in the mouths of my Irish friends; but so far as I was concerned, it was like the word "dragon," the name of a fearful, nonexistent thing. There must have been Protestant teachers in my school, but I had no way of knowing who they were.

Upon entering the tenth grade, I had to begin senior high school in a building even further from my home because Seward Park High School was then in the process of moving from its old buildings on Hester and Essex Streets to new quarters on Grand Street. While the new building was going up, I was required to begin my tenth grade in an annex of Seward Park High School on Ridge Street; I believe it was P.S. 22. Once again I was at school with the children of immigrants—this time immigrants from Central Europe and Russia rather than from Italy—and had the advantage of my "Yankee" parentage only when it came to speech. Little did my teachers realize, however, when I was once again made valedictorian, that I was not the most reliable of public speakers. At commencement I began to deliver my memorized address and—horrible thought—I forgot my lines in the middle of the speech. Fortunately a prompter came to my rescue after what seemed like a millennium. There, in front of what seemed like a thousand people, I had fallen into silence in the middle of a sentence. I could see my parents and my Uncle Sam wincing and sweating with me until I finally recovered myself in the middle of a quotation from the writings of David Starr Jordan—why I was quoting *him* I don't and shall never remember. I left the platform in a state of shame that had a severe effect on my later life. After a career of lecturing and public speaking, I have never freed myself from a fear of large audiences that began with that youthful mishap. To this day I approach public speaking with feelings that must have originated in that moment of terror.

While in high school I came in contact with the children of immigrants whose appreciation of learning, as I have said, was greater than what I had known in the store, the streets, or P.S. 114, but that did not fire me with great intellectual enthusiasm. I was brighter than many of my classmates and informed about a side of American life of which they knew little, but as yet I was not a great reader, and I had no serious intellectual ambition. I was a lonely, unreligious child who knew little about what is sometimes called the spiritual life, little about books, and much about movies, sports, restaurants, prizefighters, baseball players, and politics. My parents were better educated than their neighbors, but their formal education was slight, and their interest in religion or affairs of the mind was slighter. They saw to it that I had a goodly supply of what later came to be called "street smarts," but they did little to prepare me for an intellectual life. They rarely read books, and we had few in our apartment; they knew nothing of art, music, philosophy, or science and therefore told me nothing about the things that came to mean most to me in later life. Indeed, they had a philistine hostility or indifference to such things, which I shared before I entered college—a contempt for the life of the mind except insofar as the mind figured in politics, law, or medicine, the professions that they held in high esteem and hoped I would enter. Nothing was further from their minds or mine than a life as a philosopher or scholar.

2

City College
A New World

Once again my educational plans were not carefully laid in preparation for a major step. My parents knew little about colleges, and when my father went into bankruptcy in 1932, he could not afford to send me to a college that charged a tuition fee. The crash of the market and the depression had hit us very hard, and I can remember the deep melancholy into which I fell when I saw the store closed up, its windows covered with the whitewash that signified the suspension of operations. The creditors had taken over, and the whole family was in darkest gloom. At last some settlement with the creditors was made, a brother of my father with considerable business experience managed to buy back the fixtures, and the business was opened again. I toyed with the idea of applying to Cornell and also to Columbia, where my cousin Jimmy Wechsler had just finished his freshman year, but soon realized that that was out of the question financially. It occurred to me at that time to wonder why my father had been so extravagant in his manner of celebrating my Bar Mitzvah two years before. He had in fact laid out what for him was an enormous sum in 1930 in order to imitate the style of celebrations that some of his more affluent relatives had financed. He gave a banquet that approached in splendor one given, I believe, in honor of a son or nephew of Andrew Geller, the shoe tycoon who was my father's first cousin. Geller was the richest man linked by blood to my family, the owner of shoe factories and a string of shoe stores throughout New York. How idiotic, I thought, for my impecunious father to imitate Geller and then not to have a nickel for my college education. However, such reflections and regrets availed me nothing, and therefore I entered the College of the City of New York in the fall of 1932, at the age of fifteen. I consoled myself with the thought that the most distinguished intellectual figure produced by my family, Herbert Wechsler, had been an alumnus of City College, and that he was already launched on his dazzling career in the law. My parents consoled themselves with the thought that I was, after all, very young to be leaving town. In fact I think they would have opposed my leaving town even if I had been much older and even if they could have afforded to send me to an out-of-town private college. They did not want me out of their sight.

For my part, I yearned to be out of their sight. I had heard about the fun of college life, and I knew very well that there was not much of it on St. Nicholas Heights, where City College stood. My rah-rahing would have to take place in Lewisohn Stadium, rooting for a seventh-rate football team. And I was not to dine in the clubs of Cambridge, New Haven, or Princeton that I later heard about. Instead, I was obliged, as most of my college mates were, to eat in what were called the "alcoves" on the lowest floor of the main building of City College. There we brought lunches that we carried from home in greasy brown paper bags; there we played and watched Ping-Pong endlessly; there we engaged in interminable debates on the views of Marx, Engels, Lenin, Kautsky, Trotsky, and other revolutionaries. Consequently, I was once again incarcerated in an all-male institution after briefly experiencing some of the pleasures of knowing girls in high school, where I had eyed a few with pleasure but with little success. One of them was the daughter of a Russian immigrant who ran a candy stand on Allen Street, under the elevated; another was the daughter of a Greek who served as a janitor in a Wall Street office building. I lost touch with both of them when I entered college, at a time when I was even more eager to know girls. Moreover, I was thrown in with young men who were often two and three years older than I and who claimed to be in touch with mysteries that I would do no more than think about in frustration. The girls they knew and to whom they might introduce me were also seventeen and eighteen, and likely to be indifferent to a short boy of fifteen.

My first year in college was not intellectually stimulating, and I did not do well in my courses. I had little interest in a so-called Science Survey course, and a course called Introduction to Mathematical Analysis left me cold even though it was taught for part of the time by the distinguished mathematical logician E. L. Post—a man who, according to some of my logician friends, may well have been the most original thinker ever to teach me. Post had lost an arm and was extremely nervous and impatient as he talked to the blackboard, busily trying to explain the elements of calculus to freshmen upon whom he wasted his logical fastidiousness. As I recall, he was forced to abandon us because of illness in the middle of the first half of the yearlong course. Later I learned that he was subject to bouts of mental illness, and I believe that he later committed suicide. Had I been taught by Post when I was more interested in logic, I might have learned something from him, but at fifteen I had no interest in logic or mathematics, just as I had no interest in natural science. Then, as now, my interests were more verbal than mathematico-logical, more directed toward human matters than toward numbers and electrons. True, I once mastered the rudiments of physics while teaching it during the Second World War, and I learned the elements of mathematical logic because of its connection with philosophy. But I never kidded myself into thinking that I could become a distinguished logician or even a philosopher of natural science who could speak with the kind of authority about science that I think such an occupation requires.

Though I was not especially gifted in mathematics, I have always had an interest in, and I think some talent for, analytical thinking. I think I might have done well in the study of foreign languages, but was never properly launched in that direction. When I came to college, I began to develop an interest in English literature, but I decided that I would learn from professors of that subject nothing that I could not learn by myself. I was good at history, but in my youth I found it insufficiently dialectical; it did not give enough scope to my penchant for close reasoning. Finally, I had some idea that I wanted to study law; and I think it was this, combined with my desire to use whatever analytical powers I might have in nonmathematical subjects, that sent me in the *direction* of philosophy. I say "in the direction" because I had absolutely no notion of what philosophy was. On the other hand, I had some good reasons for wanting to study law, a very tangible subject whose outlines I thought I knew something about.

At least three things propelled me in the direction of law. First of all, I wanted to prepare for a profession, since it was already clear to me that I couldn't bear the idea of becoming a shoe merchant. Second, I had reason to believe that my father's political influence might help me if I were to become a lawyer. It was common for sons of political fathers to be appointed assistant district attorneys, or even to judgeships if they were lucky, though I was fully aware that such plums came only to the sons of fathers who could buy them, as my father could not. Third, my legal cousin, Herbert Wechsler, had already become a model for me, even though I hardly knew him. His intellectual exploits and his academic success were such a common subject of family talk that I admired and envied him enormously. Besides, I couldn't abide the prospect of becoming a medical doctor—a path that was taken by so many boys of my background.

My aversion to medicine and the shoe business, and my interest in the law, were soon joined by a developing interest in humane subjects; and by the time all of these agents were at work together, I was even more definitely on the road to philosophy. One of my friends had praised a course in philosophy he had taken, and that led me to register in the course Introduction to Philosophy. The lectures were given by a popular but shallow teacher, Harry Allen Overstreet, who later became the author of a few best-sellers. One of the books he assigned was Bertrand Russell's *Proposed Roads to Freedom*, which introduced me to the theory of socialism and Communism. In a course in government, which I took because of its presumed link with law, I read other things that combined with Russell's book to make me even more interested in Marxism. Meanwhile I had been admiring the activities of Jimmy Wechsler, who had already become well known as a young campus radical. I was also listening to alcove talk about Communism and going to radical demonstrations; and, of course, I was the son of a lower-middle-class merchant who had just lost all of his money. All of these things combined to make me think that I could kill several birds by studying philosophy. I could solve the problems of the world while I had fun and learned how to earn a living. My view, insofar as I can remember it—and I run the risk of making it more articulate now than it really was—was that ethics was the most important philosophical subject because it was a guide to life, personal, political, and social. I reasoned, however—and here I am sure that I am not inventing—that one cannot think profoundly about moral problems without being trained logically, and therefore I concluded that I had better study logic.

With this in mind I took a course based on a famous text by Morris Cohen and Ernest Nagel, *An Introduction to Logic and Scientific Method*. Occasional lectures in the course were given by Cohen himself, and I discovered to my great surprise that I liked the course and did very well in it. Receiving an A settled the question of my major. I read everything philosophical I could get my hands on; I went on to take advanced courses with Cohen himself and with Ernest Nagel, who, although he was primarily an instructor in philosophy at Columbia, taught one course called Advanced Logic at City College. With Cohen I also took a course in philosophy of law and another one called Philosophy of Civilization. The latter was divided into two parts. One was devoted to the study of all volumes, except the first, of Santayana's *Life of Reason*, the other to systematic questions in the philosophy of history along the lines of Cohen's later Carus Lectures, *The Meaning of Human History*.

Cohen and Nagel had great influence on me at City College; but since I shall have more to say about Nagel when I come to describe my graduate days at Columbia, where he taught me again, I shall confine myself to writing about Cohen here. He was a man of great learning, and he was a giant at the college. He symbolized the ambitions of all City College students who wished to succeed as scholars. He had himself risen from poor immigrant origins; he was a friend of the jurists Holmes and Frankfurter; he was a political liberal; he was interested in logic; he was learned in the history of philosophy, science, and law. He was, however, notorious for his capacity to put down students who had the courage to lock horns with him; and it was his ruthless "logic" that first attracted but later repelled me. Very soon I was appalled by what seemed to me to be the sophistry of some of his put-downs; I was made angry by the logic-chopping with which he would bully some of his students. When I came to know Cohen a little better, I came to like him more, partly because I could detect more warmth in him than I could see or feel while being bullied. He was a decent and basically kind man who had undergone great hardship as he climbed the academic ladder; and he must have sincerely felt that his students, coming from a background like his own, would learn best if they were put through his somewhat heavy-handed version of Socratic dialectic. He often said that his main aim was to dissolve his students' prejudices, to remove intellectual obstacles in the way of their getting at truth, to lead them out of the desert. Therefore he often said that he was not eager to indoctrinate them in any way. The fact is, however, that he had no original positive philosophical doctrine to impart to them. Most of what he published on his own, before his pious children began to turn many of his unpublished manuscripts into works that did him no great honor, was negatively critical in nature; and his criticism was usually directed against doctrines that were popular with some of his students. He set himself up as a destroyer of Marxism, of logical positivism, of psychoanalysis, of pragmatism, and of what he called nominalism; and in my youth I was drawn to all of these doctrines, particularly positivism and Marxism.

In those days positivism was entering the American philosophical world mainly through the writings of Rudolf Carnap, who exerted great influence on Cohen's former student Nagel. From Nagel some of us had learned something about positivism, and we felt, as Nagel did, that Cohen's attacks on it were often misdirected and that they reflected a serious misunderstanding of what the positivists were saying. Cohen's tirades against psychoanalysis also seemed less than profound, and his antipathy to Marxist doctrine seemed prejudiced and lacking foundation in a firm grasp of Marx's writings. Many of us shared the philosophico-political views of Cohen's student Sidney Hook. Hook, already an established philosopher when I was an undergraduate, frequently entered the lists against Cohen, defending an amalgam of Deweyanism and Marxism and attacking his former teacher's views on both of these philosophies.

Behind all of our sympathy with Marxism there lay of course the economic chaos of the times, the threat of Hitler, and the frustration and poverty we all knew in our homes. I need not rewrite the history of that sad and dismal period to explain what I mean. For about a year before I graduated, I was drawn to Communism but never took the plunge of becoming a member of the Young Communist League. Through lack of courage, innate skepticism, or a philosophical distaste for the crudities of Marxist dialectic, I could not bring myself to sign up. Yet for about one undergraduate year I sympathized with the Stalinists and was led to think that the least I could do for the cause was to resist what I took to be Cohen's unfair attacks on the doctrine of historical—as opposed to dialectical—materialism. I can remember one occasion on which Cohen had delivered an attack on historical materialism in a class full of young Marxists bristling with tension and hostility. At one point Cohen asked for questions, and about a dozen hands went up. Soon there was a sharp exchange about whether Cohen had fairly criticized a passage in Marx's *Critique of Political Economy*. Then something unheard of happened, at least unheard of in those days: a student in the back of the lecture hall produced a copy of the book and rudely asked Cohen to cite the passage he was talking about. I can still see that blue volume slowly moving down from the upper rows of the amphitheater to the lowest one, and then being pushed into the hands of our embarrassed lecturer. He nervously fumbled through the pages without success, and the ringing of the bell ended one of the more dramatic and saddening classroom confrontations of my life. For me it rivaled the upsetting occasion when a boy in P.S. 114 yelled an obscenity at a teacher in the middle of a class. Even in the most radical college in the United States, a confrontation like that between Cohen and his students was unheard of. And when I had attended one of the toughest schools in New York City, it was just as unthinkable for a student to shout an obscenity at a teacher.

I believe that my period at City College was one of the turning points in my life. It was there that I began the study of philosophy, which became my career; it was there that I became interested in some of the intellectual topics that have been of concern to me for more than a half century. In spite of my reservations about Cohen as a philosophical thinker and in spite of my great distaste for the way in which he treated some of us in his classes, I think that were it not for him, I should never have begun the serious study of philosophy. He taught me that philosophy should go beyond the quadrivium of logic, metaphysics, ethics, and epistemology, and therefore deal with fundamental aspects of civilization like law, politics, education, religion, and history; and it was his interest in the history of American thought that probably sparked my own. However unoriginal he was, his learning and his interest in critical discussion were of great value to generations of New York boys. He may not always have called attention to the right errors in the right way, and he may not have replaced error by creative philosophical insight, but he performed a great service in teaching his students the value and importance of philosophy.

3

Graduate Student
and Young Marxist

James T. Farrell, Meyer Schapiro, and Others

I was graduated at nineteen from City College in the spring of 1936, and soon afterward I again took a big educational step without much prior planning. I had thought seriously, as I have said, of becoming a lawyer, but when the time came to apply to law school, I developed cold feet. My philosophy and my radicalism led me to think that I would not be happy as a lawyer, so I appealed to my parents to let me take a year off in which I could think about my future. I was, after all, only nineteen, and my education had so far not cost them a cent. I would have been willing to let them finance me at law school on the theory that I would one day be able to pay them back, especially if I struck it rich; but I didn't think that I could ask them to finance a graduate education in that mysterious, poorly paying subject, philosophy. That is why I contemplated becoming a dropout for a while. Soon, however, something happened to change my plans. I was walking down Broadway from City College to Columbia in September of 1936, when I met a City College classmate—I forget his name—who had recently entered the graduate school at Columbia. Knowing that he was just as poor as I was, I wondered how he was financing the thing. He told me that he was able to get a loan from the university and that once in the graduate school he hoped to get scholarships or to get a research assistantship that would be financed by the National Youth Administration (NYA). I was intrigued by his scheme and began to think I would do something similar. Nagel was at Columbia, and I knew on the basis of my contact with him at City College that I could learn a great deal more from him. Furthermore, I had already become friendly with two contemporaries who were to have great influence on me, Albert Wohlstetter and Lawrence Kegan, who were already in graduate school studying philosophy; and I had been coming down to Columbia in my last year at City College, occasionally listening to lectures given by Nagel in courses well beyond the level of his course at City College.

After some consultation with my parents, I applied for admission to Columbia and was accepted as a student in the graduate school for 1936–37. It may sound surprising that all of this—application and admission—was accomplished so quickly, but that's the way it happened. I was loaned enough money by the university to cover my tuition, and since I would live at home, my parents could supply me with pocket money, and I thought I could manage. My father had made something of a financial recovery and could afford that expense. True, I would not be bringing money into the family and would instead still be a dependent, but it seemed to me that I was justified in accepting further support of the kind I needed. I vowed to myself to pay the money back—something I did many times over in the years to come. In this way I was launched on my professional career—on a financial shoestring and with a prayer that I would like my studies and some day get a job teaching philosophy. In those depression days the prospects of earning a lot of money as a lawyer were not very rosy, and therefore I was not making a choice between poor philosophy and rich law. Those were the days in which lawyers were driving taxicabs.

My first years at Columbia were so rich and exciting by comparison to anything I had previously known that I find it difficult to recount all of my experiences there. By comparison to City College, of course, Columbia was a cosmopolitan, affluent place. There I came to know a little better what Protestants were, and there for the first time I caught a glimpse of an aspect of American life that I never knew on Catherine Street, in Seward Park, or at City College. Columbia was in those days still living on the material capital of an earlier generation. Nicholas Murray Butler, its ancient president, was still at the helm; the buildings were ugly but comfortable and well appointed (at least by comparison to those at City College); and Columbia undergraduates and faculty still had some sense of social superiority. Toward Harvard, of course, a good deal of resentment and envy was felt—and the intensity of those feelings seemed to increase over the years as Columbia went downhill financially and intellectually. Toward City College, on the other hand, the predominant attitude was one of contempt and condescension. Jewish boys whose parents could afford to send them to Columbia often expressed those feelings toward their City College contemporaries. Often Columbia Jews—especially those on the faculty—were German in origin, the descendants of those who had come to America during an earlier wave of immigration, so their English, their dress, and their manners were far more refined than those of City College men of poor Polish or Russian origin. For many of us the contrast was epitomized in the very different persons of our City College professor Morris Cohen and our Columbia professor Irwin Edman. One was a tough argumentative logician, the other an elegant writer of popular books and essays. One knocked you out in the classroom, the other was cruelly called the Santayana of the Bronx by City College alumni who were stung by his condescension toward them. I shall never forget how humiliated I felt after Edman told me that I ought to learn how to conduct myself at lunch. I was, he said, given too much to shoptalk and therefore likely to be boring. He told me how Oxford dons never discussed philosophy at lunch—a great falsehood, as I was to learn when I visited Oxford.

Edman was a witty, facile writer of popular books, such as his *Philosopher's Holiday*; but he was cursed by extreme ugliness and by what I think was albinism. He would occasionally invite me into his office in Philosophy Hall, guide me to a place in the room where my back would be against a wall, put both of his hands on my shoulders, and roll his albino eyes at me in a disconcerting way as he talked about whatever it was that supposedly led him to ask me into his office. I don't think he was trying to seduce me, but I was certainly not seduced by him. Nor was I seduced by his philosophy, which was an unoriginal compound of Dewey's and Santayana's ideas, as were the philosophies of most of his colleagues. He gave a well-attended course of lectures in philosophy of art that I never took, but at one point he needed an assistant to teach a section in it for undergraduates and offered the job to me—to my great surprise. Being impecunious and somewhat flattered to be asked to teach the class, I accepted. I can't remember much about it except that after a few meetings with five or six Columbia undergraduates, I was invited to Edman's office for one of our eyeball-to-eyeball sessions. He asked me how the section was going, and I made the mistake of replying candidly. I said the students were not very bright and not reading the assigned work—one of the books they were supposed to read was Dewey's *Art as Experience*, about which I, as a Dewey scholar, could be expected to know something. To my surprise and distress, Edman said that my reaction to the students might have arisen from the fact that I had never taken the course and, worse, from the fact that I was not coming to the lectures during that very term. It was true that I had never taken the course and that I was not attending it while I was his so-called section man, but Edman had never asked me to come to his lectures, and more important, my complaint about the students had absolutely nothing to do with Edman's lectures: I had said that they were not very bright and that they weren't reading the assignments. But Edman found it hard to accept either of these statements of mine, and our session ended abruptly.

This episode did not help me as an aspiring philosopher at Columbia, for it fueled Edman's distaste for my views and for me. It strengthened his inclination to regard me as a mere logician, as a bookworm, as lacking the charisma necessary for a good teacher, as one who engaged in too much shoptalk at lunch. Indeed, he once compared me with the dullest but perhaps the kindest man in the Columbia Department of Philosophy, Horace Friess. This led me to pen the following bit of verse:

From I to M

Bubble, Bubble, you must bubble,
Talk less of toil, still less of trouble,
Bubble like French champagnes,
Piano, piano, on heady campaigns,
When lunch comes, let logic cease,
Above all—remember Horace Friess.

Edman's likening me to the dreary Friess, his resenting my criticism of his students in aesthetics, his harping on my lack of Oxford manners, and his view that I was crude and too City College, so to speak, in my interests led me to be very surprised when, in 1944, he liked the outline of a book I had mentioned to him: "Your general idea for a book sounds like an excellent one and what is more a really publishable one. Let's talk about it soon after I get back" (from Williamstown, Mass., where he had been spending the summer). The book I outlined was my *Social Thought in America*, about which Edman later spoke to his friend Ben Huebsch of Viking Press. In this same letter to me Edman reported that he had enjoyed himself while recently serving as a visiting professor at Harvard but said in answer to a question of mine that he was not transferring permanently to Harvard. When I had asked Edman whether he was leaving Columbia for Harvard, I did so because of a widely spread rumor that Harvard had invited him after he had supposedly wowed the place on his visit there. In his reply he said nothing to scotch this rumor: he simply denied that he was transferring to Harvard, while bypassing the question whether he had been offered a permanency. But, when I joined the Harvard Department of Philosophy in 1948, I learned that it had never made an offer to him and that a number of my Harvard colleagues had been outraged not only by the rumor but also by the fact that he had done nothing to prevent its spread through the profession. In his reply to my letter, Edman not only indicated that he was not moving to Harvard but also took the occasion to say that he would stay at Columbia, whose philosophy he thought was superior to Harvard's.

At that time, Columbia philosophy was living on the spiritual capital of an earlier generation. John Dewey no longer taught there, having retired at seventy in 1929, but there was nobody in the department who came close to replacing him as a philosopher of worldwide reputation and distinction. His name was still listed in the catalogue, and occasionally he would come in to pick up some mail or to visit with some of his former colleagues. His ideas continued to dominate the Department of Philosophy, and I think that many a foreign student may have come to Columbia under the misapprehension that Dewey still taught there. His political liberalism was officially shared by Columbia philosophers, but I felt that most of them were not very liberal as human beings. A parvenu snobbishness pervaded the atmosphere of the department, and this was most evident in the treatment its supposedly liberal professors accorded their New York graduate students who came from City College. No professor except Ernest Nagel ever invited Lucia and me to dine at his home, even after I became a member of the teaching staff.

Like me, many City College philosophy students who came to Columbia worked with Nagel, hoping to learn logic and philosophy of science from him. However, it was a measure of the Columbia department's poor judgment or philosophical prejudice that when I entered graduate school in 1936, Nagel was, at the age of thirty-five, still a lowly instructor, even though no one in the department rivaled him in intellectual power. Nagel had studied modern logic on his own, he was enormously industrious, and he gave very useful courses in mathematical logic and the philosophy of mathematics. His views were close to those of the logical positivists, but they were also influenced by an attachment to certain aspects of Dewey's thought and by a conviction that the philosophy of science should be conducted in a manner less formalistic than that preferred by some positivists. Nagel's views were enriched by a considerable knowledge of the history of philosophy and science that he had acquired after coming from Czechoslovakia to the United States as a boy; and it was extraordinary to think that he could have read so much in spite of having to teach high school mathematics in this country before he could get a job in a college or university. He was in touch with the most advanced currents of European philosophical thought, and his most important contribution to his students' education was introducing them to those currents of English and Continental philosophy. Often when a distinguished visiting philosopher of analytic or positivistic inclinations came to New York, Nagel would invite his best students to his house for a session with the visitor. Whenever a student wished to consult with Nagel about a philosophical problem or about a problem connected with his professional career, Nagel's door was always open. I marvel now at his ability to find time for that, for the assiduous preparation of his lectures, for his omnivorous reading, for publishing many articles and an incredible number of thoughtful book reviews. Not only was he an encyclopedic reader, as Cohen was, but unlike Cohen he was a *careful* encyclopedic reader. Nagel was an excellent expositor of the fundamentals of formal logic even though he was not creative in it, and, curiously enough, he did not lecture very much in those days on the subject of his main scholarly interest, the philosophy of natural science. However, he was working on the theory of probability in a way that received expression in his pamphlet, *Principles of the Theory of Probability*, published in the *International Encyclopedia of Unified Science* in 1939. Under the influence of Nagel I published my article "Probability and Confirmation" in the *Journal of Philosophy* in 1939 and wrote my M.A. thesis, "Peirce's Theory of Probability," for which I received a degree in February of 1938.

Nagel's courses were the only ones from which I learned anything of value while I was at Columbia preparing to write my thesis. I listened to lectures by other philosophers, like Herbert Schneider and J. H. Randall Jr., but I did not learn anything of great value from them. Most of my peers took a year's course with Randall on the entire history of philosophy, a course that could be taken for credit in lieu of a qualifying general examination, but my closest friends and I couldn't be bothered with it—out of arrogance or wisdom. Instead, we boned up together for about a week and easily passed the daylong examination that entitled us to go on to write the thesis. Although my teachers at Columbia showed some approval of my work when they awarded the fellowships I was soon to be given, the only one of them besides Nagel for whom I felt any intellectual respect was Randall. He was, in spite of his unpredictable outbursts of sarcasm, a well-read person who respected scholarly ability but who made his students uneasy because he did not know how to communicate his decent and generous feelings toward them. By contrast, his colleague Herbert Schneider did not strike me as very distinguished, though, as things turned out, he became the official director of my Ph.D. thesis because he specialized in the history of American philosophy.

Although I learned little from Randall or from Schneider, Randall struck me as the brighter and deeper of the two. Both of them were specialists in the history of ideas under the influence of their teacher Woodbridge, author of a book on Plato called *The Son of Appollo* and of another book called *The Realm of Mind*. (The latter was once listed in a French philosophical journal as *The Realm of Wind*, much to the delight of graduate students who thought that the French had given it the title it deserved.) It was to Woodbridge that Randall dedicated his remarkably precocious book on the history of ideas, *The Making of the Modern Mind*, published in 1926, when Randall was about twenty-seven years old. I attended a number of Randall's courses—one of them, as I recall, was pompously entitled Aristotle for English Readers and another was called Leibniz and Whitehead—but I cannot remember a single thought that came to me by way of Randall's instruction. He was remarkably loyal to his teachers Dewey and Woodbridge, and also to Santayana, but he was extremely hostile to logical positivism and to analytical philosophy in general, losing no opportunity to put down in a ruthless way any student who showed signs of sympathy with those movements. Randall's lecturing was accompanied by weird mannerisms and by periodic puffs on large cigars that kept going out. I also recall his habit of compulsively stroking his shoulders as if to remove dandruff from them, as well as a cackling laugh that would fill the room when he thought he was making an especially good point. But I find it hard, as I drag my mind back fifty or so years, to recall a distinctive philosophical method that I associate with Randall, or a profound philosophical proposition that he originated, defended, or attacked in an interesting way.

Although Randall was often nice to me, he did not know how to be unreservedly nice; there was always some little knife that he had to throw or twist after he had been generous to someone. His capacity for causing pain was evident to me toward the end of my relationship with him. Some time in the late forties he had asked me to collaborate with him on a study of American thought during the Second World War, thereby indicating his good opinion of me in pretty clear terms. But after I began to teach at Harvard, I received a perfectly nasty letter from him that ended my friendship with him. It was about the manuscript of an essay of mine, "Toward an Analytic Philosophy of History," that was scheduled to (and later did) appear in Marvin Farber's volume *Philosophic Thought in France and the United States*, which was later published. For a while I wondered how Randall could have gotten hold of my manuscript, but Farber thought that Randall may have served as a referee for a publisher to whom the whole volume had been submitted. In any case, Randall insinuated that I had tacked to some philosophical wind in order to win my appointment at Harvard in 1948, since I had read a part of the paper there when I was being looked over by the Department of Philosophy. Randall did say that publication of this paper would vindicate those of his Columbia colleagues who, unlike him, had opposed my promotion there, but the letter was so distasteful that I could not bring myself to answer it, and I returned it to Randall. Later, when I mentioned the letter to someone who had taught in the Department of Philosophy at the University of Washington while Randall had been visiting there—Randall had written to me on Washington stationery—I was told that Randall had been drinking heavily that term and probably had written the letter while drunk.

My relationship with Randall's colleague Schneider never approached friendship even though he was the official director of my Ph.D. thesis. How that came about and how I came to write that thesis, *The Origin of Dewey's Instrumentalism*, reveals something about Columbia in the thirties and forties as well as something about me. Why didn't I write a thesis in the philosophy of science, in which I was much interested at the time? First of all, I was affected by the peculiarly sour attitude of Nagel himself toward his own subject. Rarely have I known a man who could turn his nose up so disapprovingly at the mention of so many famous philosophers who shared his interests. Dewey, Russell, Carnap, Broad, Wittgenstein—all of them were seriously deficient in his eyes. Dewey didn't know enough about natural science; Russell was not familiar with the latest work in logic; Broad was "too thin"; Carnap was too formalistic; Wittgenstein was too obscure; and so on. Every philosopher of science was condemned, was caught coming or going. In addition, Nagel had an unfortunate tendency to dissociate himself from his best students, either because he was driven to hate what he himself stood for when he saw it expressed in the work of his students, or because he was afraid to support them in the face of the strong antianalytic bias of his Columbia colleagues. For whatever reason, Nagel did not encourage or inspire his best students to try their hands at logic or at systematic philosophy in their theses. He knew, I think, that he was not enough of a logician to direct a thesis in serious mathematical logic; and he may have been fearful that his students might embarrass him by producing a less than world-shaking thesis in systematic philosophy. His lack of courage and his excessive caution quickly communicated itself to those who had some instinct for survival in that atmosphere, and the result was that many who might have written daring philosophical theses were led to the comparative safety of historical theses.

This, of course, fitted in with the predominantly historical tendency at Columbia, encouraged by Schneider, by Randall, and by the gray eminence of the Columbia department, F.J.E. Woodbridge, who was still alive but very old while I was taking courses. I took a pointless course on Locke from Woodbridge, who met students in his apartment while dressed in bathrobe and slippers. A vastly overrated mind was Woodbridge, not to be put in the same class as Dewey—and yet many Columbia philosophers who had studied with both of them thought that respectively they were the Plato and Aristotle of their time and place.

All of these elements of the Columbia scene had something to do with my writing a thesis on Dewey, but I do not mean to imply that I went into the history of philosophy unwillingly or without a positive taste for it. Since I had a serious interest in historical research, that interest, together with a sense of prudence, led me to choose the history of philosophy as the area in which I would write my thesis. I should remark, however, that I began by planning a full-scale critical examination of Dewey's logical theory, prompted in great measure by the appearance of Dewey's *Logic: A Theory of Inquiry* in 1938. This was in keeping with my belief that his writings in what *he* called logic were the key to his philosophy. My historical sense—if that is the right phrase—led me to think that I should study Dewey's development from his early idealism to his instrumentalism, and it was my excursion into the earliest Deweyana that made it officially necessary for me to become the student of Schneider, the acknowledged Columbia specialist in the history of American philosophy. The operative word here is "officially" because in spite of my polite acknowledgment of his aid in the preface to my thesis, which was published by the Columbia University Press in 1943, I wrote the thesis without much aid from Schneider. I was burrowing into early articles and books by Dewey that Schneider certainly did not know as well as I came to know them.

In *The Origin of Dewey's Instrumentalism*, I followed Dewey's development only up to 1903. I stopped there because I had written enough in my discussion of these early years for a coherent book that could earn the Ph.D. And since I *had* to publish my thesis according to the rules then existing at Columbia—and *might* have had to publish it at my own expense—there was a premium on keeping it short. Fortunately, it later won Columbia's Woodbridge Prize, and that covered a good part of the cost of publication. The book is still cited occasionally, so it may continue to be of some use. Yet I sometimes wonder why I hadn't been as bold in my thesis as I had been in some of my other juvenilia.

To me it is now a little startling to think that I was publishing articles and reviews in 1939, 1940, and 1941, before I defended my thesis in the spring of 1942—articles and reviews that were very different in spirit from *The Origin of Dewey's Instrumentalism*. Some were in analytic philosophy; some were politico-philosophical pieces that appeared in the *Partisan Review*. As I now look back at some of my first publications, I am struck by the fact that my present combination of intellectual interests was formed at a very early age. In 1939, as I have indicated earlier, I published my article "Probability and Confirmation"; and in the same year Albert Wohlstetter and I jointly published an article called "Who Are the Friends of Semantics?" in the *Partisan Review*, a sharp attack on the popular semantics of Stuart Chase, S. I. Hayakawa, and Count Korzybski. In the next couple of years I published reviews of Richard von Mises' *Probability, Statistics, and Truth* and of Quine's *Mathematical Logic*. In 1940 I published a criticism of Sidney Hook's *John Dewey* in the *Partisan Review* under the title "From Marx to Dewey"—an ironic allusion to the fact that Hook, the author of a book called *From Hegel to Marx,* was then shifting his political allegiances from revolutionary Marxism to liberal Deweyan philosophy as he moved to the right.

When I compare my very safe thesis with my very unsafe Marxist journalism in the late thirties, I ask myself why I was not as daring in my thesis as I was in my articles and reviews, why I didn't write a systematic thesis. I think it was in part due to Nagel's unwillingness to encourage the writing of such a thesis, and in part due to my eagerness to get out from under the control of my teachers. I reasoned that if only I could get free of them quickly, I would be able to do what I really wanted to do without having to please *anybody* like Nagel, Randall, or Schneider. Therefore I chose to do a respectable, modest thesis that they would accept rather than a possibly exciting one that they might not accept. Of course, the more daring one that I see in my mind's eye would probably have turned out to be a dud, but I like to think that it might have been more lively than the thesis I did write even though it would have been less likely to withstand later scholarly scrutiny. I fully understand what Dewey meant when he wrote to his friend Arthur Bentley that he thought my thesis "was good, but not tackling the 'funda-ment.'"

While writing my thesis I kept admiring Harvard for abandoning the requirement that Ph.D. theses be published. Without question the Harvard system allowed a young philosopher to try being creative in a way that was rare at Columbia in my graduate days there. On the other hand, I am convinced that the great thing about the Columbia system, by contrast to the Harvard system, was the fact that graduate students at Columbia did not have to take final examinations and to write term papers in their courses. As my Western friend Henry Aiken used to say, you could get a Ph.D. in the Columbia Department of Philosophy by driving a team of horses across 116th Street (then it was open between Broadway and Amsterdam Avenues). But Columbia's relaxed standards permitted young philosophers to range widely in their interests—as my pieces between 1939 and 1942 show—and I am eternally grateful for that opportunity. True, Columbia was—partly because of this freedom—turning out a lot of inferior Ph.D.'s who could not be trusted to teach the staple philosophical courses, whereas Harvard Ph.D.'s, forced as they were to take courses with grades and also pass a fiendishly demanding set of preliminary examinations in those days, could be more relied on to teach the elements of philosophy respectably. And yet a serious philosophy student, who didn't have to be *forced* to jump over a demanding set of hurdles, found it heavenly to be able to read whatever he wanted to read and to let his mind roam freely, as one could at Columbia in my time.

There were several young people who did roam freely with this kind of academic license. In the late 1930s there gathered around Nagel a number of very able students, among them, as I have said earlier, Albert Wohlstetter, later a well-known writer on nuclear warfare who taught for a while at the University of Chicago, and Lawrence Kegan, who became an economist. Both of them had graduated from City College a year or two before me: Wohlstetter in 1934 and Kegan in 1935, I believe. In the winter of 1935–36 I first met Lawrence in the Reading Room of the New York Public Library. He was sitting next to me, poring over a philosophical work that caught my eye, and after falling into conversation we found that our interests were remarkably similar. We were not only interested in philosophy, but also in logic, Marxism, T. S. Eliot, James Joyce, and a million other things of the kind that eager young New York intellectuals then found time to learn about. Lawrence introduced me to his friend Albert, who, like himself, was studying philosophy in the graduate school at Columbia. He too was a very bright polymath. They were both about three years older than I, and they were more lively and more learned than any young men I had ever met at City College. Lawrence lived in the Bronx with his widowed mother. Albert lived in the seventies, west of Broadway, just up from the Ansonia Hotel, as I recall, and his house became a gathering place for all of his friends.

Albert also lived with a widowed mother, but the same enormous apartment that housed them also housed a divorced oldest brother who was an auctioneer, a bachelor older brother who later became a tycoon known as "Wall Streeter Charlie Wohlstetter," a divorced sister, and a spinster aunt who taught high school. What a ménage! It was by my standards a luxurious apartment, comparable to some of those in which some of my uptown cousins lived. Occasionally Albert's friends would be asked to dine there, and I can remember with amazement the night that one poor boy ate all of an artichoke, not knowing that the leaves were to be left behind. In spite of the seeming affluence of Albert's family, however, he didn't have any more pocket money than the rest of us. His family disapproved of his having left the Columbia Law School in his first year there for graduate work in philosophy; he was thought to be a sort of intellectual bum who should not be encouraged in his peregrinations. Many of his peers and teachers also found his widely ranging interests suspect, and he was wrongly thought by them to be a shallow dilettante. Their view was a result of their underestimating his depth and powers of logical analysis, although at one time that view seemed to be confirmed by the fact that he never completed his Ph.D. thesis and left philosophy without having done as much as I think he could have done in it. I ceased to be close to Albert in the 1940s, but I shall always be immensely grateful to him and to Lawrence Kegan for their intellectual companionship in the late 1930s.

Prompted by our joint interest in philosophy and radical politics, Albert, Lawrence, and I, along with a number of friends and fellow students, formed a club in which we studied logic, philosophy, and political economy together. We saw ourselves as a sort of junior Vienna Circle in New York, cooperatively working on all the ideas that excited us. Sometimes our interest in combining logic and politics even led to futile efforts to "axiomatize" parts of *Das Kapital*. But we didn't work all the time. There was time for girls, for parties, for museums, and for concerts when we could afford them. We bought a community phonograph and records, which we passed round; we were devotees of the modern dance, and some of us were even courageous enough to take lessons in it from a student of Doris Humphrey; we went to foreign and avant-garde movies when we could afford them. Our lives in those few years between 1936 and the outbreak of the Second World War were much happier than one might think if one concentrated on the fact that we were all poverty-stricken graduate students without jobs.

Despite my gloomy prospects I became unbelievably happy when I met Lucia Perry in September of 1938. We met through Albert and his girlfriend, Roberta Morgan, who had been Lucia's roommate at Vassar and who was then sharing an apartment with her on East Fifty-second Street. They introduced us in front of the circulation desk at the Columbia library while all of us were waiting for books. By the winter we were much in love and seeing each other all of the time. Albert, Roberta, Lucia, and I gave rousing parties on Fifty-second Street, and I can remember the jolly night on which I parodied Eliot as we staggered down Lexington Avenue near Fifty-second Street: "Oh the moon shone bright on Mrs. Morgan and on her organ." Mrs. Morgan, Roberta's mother, was the dignified wife of Professor Edmund Morgan, a distinguished teacher of evidence at the Harvard Law School.

Albert and I had similar problems so far as our girls were concerned. We were both penniless Jewish New York scholars and were courting comfortable Gentile Vassar alumnae. Roberta's father, as I have said, was a Harvard professor; Lucia's father, who had been dead for about a dozen years, had been a Harvard graduate who, before his untimely death, had headed a large industrial firm, and her mother was a Vassar alumna. Neither Albert nor I, therefore, were exactly great catches for our girls. He was condemned for not having a job of any kind—whereas I ran into difficulties created by my parents on religious grounds. For a reason I cannot recall, Albert was at one point anxious to keep his relationship with Roberta from his family, but he was eager to have the family meet her before he announced their plan to marry. So one night all four of us went to dinner at the Wohlstetter apartment, pretending that Lucia was Albert's girl and Roberta mine. In the end each of us married the right person, but before I come to some events that preceded my marriage, I want to say a little more about our intellectual gang's interests and activities between 1936 and 1940, the year in which I was married.

By the time I entered graduate school in 1936, I had abandoned my yearlong sympathy with Stalinism but remained a Marxist. Those who were not up on the details of such matters would have called me a Trotskyite, and many did on the assumption that any Marxist to the left of Stalinism was a Trotskyite. But such people would show their ignorance of the finely separated political splinter groups that flourished in New York in those days. Through Albert and Lawrence, I was introduced to a group known as the Fieldites, so called because they followed a man by the name of B. J. Field—not to be confused with the Stalinist Noel Field, with whom B. J. Field had no kinship. B. J. Field was the American leader of a group called the

League for a Revolutionary Worker's Party, and all I can now remember about the league's doctrine is that according to it the Soviet Union had returned, or was about to return, to capitalism, whereas the Trotskyites held that Russia was at worst a degenerate workers' state. This meant of course that the Trotskyites were more sympathetic to the Soviet Union than the Fieldites were, and that the Fieldites were further to the left. I was never a member of that league; once again I followed my wise or timorous practice of being a sympathizer or fellow traveler. Their headquarters were a little north of Union Square, somewhere in the teens and a little to the west of what was then called Fourth Avenue. They met in a bare loft that was one long flight of stairs up from the street. This dimly lit place with its one table and a dozen or so chairs was the scene of very informative lectures by Field on Marx's economics and of his very lucid denunciations of Trotskyism.

Meanwhile, uptown at Columbia, a distinguished and handsome admirer of Trotsky held forth. I mean Meyer Schapiro, by all odds the most brilliant figure in the faculty of arts and sciences. When I first came to Columbia, I was so overwhelmed by Meyer that I registered for a course in Romanesque sculpture with him and audited one on illuminated manuscripts even though I was not a graduate student in fine arts. While pursuing my degree in philosophy, I also sat in on his more popular course on modern painting, which was made easy by the fact that graduate students could then get their degrees at Columbia without having to take letter grades in their courses, that is to say, merely by attending lectures. This, as I have suggested earlier, encouraged all of us wandering polymaths to partake of any intellectual feast that caught our fancy—so much so that Albert and Lawrence were Schapiro's NYA assistants in his class on modern painting, where they would furiously take notes of his machine-gun delivery, which was interrupted only by the noise of a little device that he snapped as he said "Next slide, please" to the man who ran the projector. How I wish that Meyer had turned those notes into a book! Never did so much erudition combine with so much sensibility. Meyer had a considerable interest in philosophy, having been a student of Dewey's and a close friend of both Ernest Nagel and Sidney Hook, and he could discourse with a great deal of knowledge and gusto about pragmatism and positivism.

It was on the Columbia campus in about 1940 that Meyer introduced me to his friend James T. Farrell, who became a good friend of mine. Jim thought well of my review of Sidney Hook's *John Dewey* in the *Partisan Review* for January and February 1940, and I was thrilled to be praised by so eminent a literary man. He encouraged me by taking my work seriously and was intrigued by my familiarity with Irish-American life. After all, my father had been a friend of Al Smith, about whom Jim once thought he would do a book, and I had taken enough beatings from young Irishmen to think of myself as a specialist on their way of life. So in 1953, when asked by Jim's publisher to write an appreciation of his work for a pamphlet about him, I could honestly and sincerely write that I had been reading him with excitement and appreciation ever since Studs Lonigan pounded his way into my consciousness with all the significance he had for a boy living on the streets of New York in the thirties. I said that I was overwhelmed not only by his kindness but also by his interest in my work and by the encouragement he gave me, that he was not only a great novelist and a generous friend but an inspiring figure in our cultural life, an enemy of both philistinism and snobbism who effectively fought against the devastating effects of Stalinism in both literature and politics. I added that he had done more to explain and defend moral ideals and spiritual freedom than most of the philosophical illiterates who complained about his "materialism" and his "determinism."

Columbia excited me because I could see a good deal of Jim, who was then living on 110th Street near Broadway, because Nagel was teaching me and my friends a lot of philosophy, because Schapiro was encouraging us in our Marxism while holding forth on modern painting, and because gifted young people were all teaching each other. For example, I learned an enormous amount of history from Benjamin Nelson, the brilliant medievalist who could discourse so remarkably on the history of usury and who had a considerable interest in philosophy. I knew him for about forty years, I admired him enormously as a scholar, and I treasured his friendship. He pushed through or ran around the ends of conventional academic lines with the speed and power of a great running back, loping from medieval studies to philosophy, from history to sociology, from sociology to psychology, with ease and with purpose. He was about six years older than I and was already a legendary figure when I came to Columbia in 1936. I recollect that we first met at a lecture given by Otto Neurath, and that we had dinner together afterward in a Chinese restaurant on upper Broadway. We laughed a lot about Neurath's *Index Verborum Prohibitorum,* as he called it, because it seemed to contain so many words we were in the habit of using freely.

Ben, like Meyer Schapiro, was one of the great talkers in New York at that time. One night Ben, my boyhood friend Gerry Rosenbaum, and I had left a party near Columbia and had entered the subway station at 116th Street at about two in the morning—it was possible to do that sort of thing without anxiety in those days. They were deep in learned conversation, while I was nervously pacing up and down the platform on the lookout for the train. Gerry, who had had a little too much to drink, was leaning up against the wall of the station; and while Ben was speaking to him, Gerry's head began to droop forward. Seeing this while taking my eye off the track for a second, I rushed to the pair, fearing that Gerry was about to collapse and that Ben would need help in dealing with him. But Ben grandly and characteristically waved me away with his left hand, pushed his right hand up against Gerry's chest, and kept his interlocutor in an upright position so that he could finish his point before the train arrived.

Ben Nelson's friend Paul Goodman would often visit Columbia while on vacation from Chicago, to which he had gone under the aegis of Richard McKeon, as had a number of other City College and Columbia boys—for example, William Barrett—in the years just before I came to Columbia in 1936. Paul had studied with Cohen well before I had, and we often argued about the merits of Cohen's philosophy, Paul maintaining more respect for the views of our former teacher than I could manage. I can remember Paul reporting a conversation with Cohen about Carnap, whom Paul knew at Chicago. It seems that in spite of Paul's hostility to positivism he was praising Carnap to Cohen, who, Paul thought, underestimated Carnap. One day Paul said: "But, Professor Cohen, he is such a virtuoso!" to which Cohen characteristically replied: "Yes, but is he a composer?"

In those days—the late thirties and early forties—Elizabeth Hardwick was a graduate student in English at Columbia; she had not yet started to publish but was already displaying the brilliance that was to make her such a distinguished literary critic. She was a good friend of my friends Robert Snyder and George Justin, both of whom became movie producers. George, in spite of his mocking remarks about the logicians' "p implies q," would audit Nagel's and Schapiro's lectures and would join me and my philosophical friends in discussions of just about everything. Another of my nonacademic friends was Fred Tropp. I came to know Fred when I was a camp counselor at Camp Swago in the Poconos, where I had gotten a job in the summer of 1936. Fred agreed to rent a room with me on Morningside Heights in the fall of 1939 because he wanted to live closer to northern New Jersey, where he had taken a job as a chemist in a paint factory. At the time, Lucia was living in an apartment on West 114th Street, just behind the Columbia library, and I wanted to be near her after I had left my parents' apartment on Madison and Catherine Streets.

Fred and I first rented a room in a so-called residence club near the corner of 112th Street and Broadway, perhaps the seediest place I have ever lived in—and that is saying a lot. Often we would read in the newspapers that some diamond thief who had pulled off a job downtown had stopped off at our "club" to hide away before getting out of town. Our room was in a large apartment that had been broken up. Next door was a common kitchen that we seldom used and a common bathroom. All over the place were monitory signs: "Turn off the lights," "Turn off the gas-jets," "Turn off the faucets," "Quiet," and "Jiggle the toilet-handle if the water runs too long." In the hall was a pay telephone that rang constantly. Finally we decided to get the hell out of that trap and to rent a room in a brownstone on 109th Street near Broadway. It was shown to us by the owner, who said his name was Kreis; "Just like Jesus Kreis," he added. The place was kept tidy by two middle-aged ladies who always wore black and who drifted through the place like a couple of nuns. George Justin, who had not yet made the big break from his parents' home, would pay us a small fee in order to come up on weekends so that, as he said, he could smoke cigars and read the Sunday paper in peace.

In those days Morningside Heights was not only the gathering place of the assorted teachers, friends, and fellow scholars I have just described, it was also the place where I really got to know my cousin Herbert Wechsler. In 1936 Herb was on the faculty of the Columbia Law School, teaching, as I recall, criminal law and federal jurisdiction. Many of my former City College classmates went to his lectures and were enthusiastic about them. This pleased me greatly, since, as I have indicated, Herb was my great model. However, my ability to follow him was questionable, for here I was, only seven or eight years younger than he, and an impoverished graduate student, while he was already a luminary on the Columbia faculty, ensconced in a posh office in Kent Hall. He was always impeccably dressed and very impressive for one so young. I would sometimes bump into him as he walked from Kent Hall past Philosophy Hall, on his way to the Faculty Club with his older colleague Jerome Michael, also a specialist in criminal law. Michael had some interest in philosophy, sparked and encouraged by the Thomistically minded Mortimer J. Adler, with whom Michael had collaborated on a book called *Crime, Law, and Social Science*. Michael became very sympathetic to Thomism, and I believe Herb was somewhat taken with it. Through Adler it had gained a foothold at the University of Chicago under the powerful academic sponsorship of its president, Robert Hutchins, and so in New York it was reported that Chicago was where Jews converted Protestants to Catholicism.

By the time I had come to Columbia in 1936, Richard McKeon's departure for Chicago had left the Columbia philosophy department with no comparable spokesmen for the medievalism then encouraged at Chicago, but Michael and Herb Wechsler were said to defend something like it in their Law School classes. A friend who attended those classes told me that Michael and Wechsler had taken him to lunch in an effort to counter what they regarded as the corrupting positivistic influences on him, and he concluded that Michael was philosophically silly, whereas Herb was exceedingly bright and not a card-carrying Thomist. Encouraged by that report because I was as far from Thomism as any young philosopher could be, I asked Herb to appoint me as his NYA assistant. Only if I got some such financial aid could I continue with my graduate studies past the first year, but I feared that Herb might worry about the nepotistic implications of such an arrangement. Instead, he turned out to be as cooperative as he could be, and in this way began a series of favors for which I shall always be grateful. He appointed me as his NYA assistant and asked me to prepare a report on Kant's philosophy of law, which I duly completed and submitted to him. I can't remember anything about that report, but I'm sure it couldn't have been very good, since I was not and never have been a Kant scholar. Still, it may not have been altogether worthless, and I don't think that Herb felt that I was getting my fee for nothing.

Shortly afterward Herb tried to get me a teaching fellowship at the University of Chicago through his friend Hutchins, but that fell through, I am happy to say in retrospect. It seems that Hutchins had a slush fund that he could use for proselytizing either at Chicago or at St. John's College in Annapolis, but in his mind St. John's needs were greater than mine, so I didn't get the fellowship. I can well remember a long conversation with the philosopher William Barrett, then an assistant at Chicago, about the cost of living in Chicago, so there was probably a moment when I thought the thing was in the bag. Later I suspected—probably wrongly—that a hostile review of Mortimer Adler's *Art and Prudence* that I published in a radical students' magazine edited by Jimmy Wechsler might have had something to do with my failure to get that fellowship. Adler's book was published in 1937, so I infer that my review, entitled "St. Thomas and Mae West," must have appeared while Herb's negotiations with Hutchins were going on.

What I have said about Herb Wechsler so far does not cover his great accomplishments as a legal scholar in the years following those I am now talking about. Even by the time I became his NYA assistant around 1937, he had made an impressive legal name for himself. He had entered the College of the City of New York at the age of fifteen from Townsend Harris High School and finished first in his class at Columbia Law School in 1931 at the age of twenty-two. He then taught for a year at Columbia and returned to teaching there after serving as clerk to Justice Harlan Fiske Stone. In 1940 he and Jerome Michael published *Criminal Law and Its Administration*, said to be a classic in the field.

During the late 1930s, while Herb Wechsler was teaching at Columbia, his Communist brother, Jimmy, and Jimmy's wife, Nancy, were living in an apartment on Amsterdam Avenue while Nancy was going to law school; and so I got to know them quite well during those years. I can remember long arguments in which I voiced all of the usual anti-Stalinist complaints to no great avail. Yet there came a time when they saw the light under the influence of more persuasive people, and I like to think that my persistent arguing with them in earlier years might have softened them up. In any case, deep as our political differences were in those days, our friendship was never in the least threatened. The fact that Jimmy had asked me in his Stalinist days to review a book for him, as well as the fact that I had agreed to do it, shows that neither of us was as fanatical as some of our friends were. I suppose that the bond created by being the only Marxists in our family was strong enough to resist the fierce differences that separated Stalinists and anti-Stalinists.

Such intellectual liberalism—I think "sanity" may be a better expression—did not prevail among other radical acquaintances of mine. I learned this not only when Stalinists refused to greet me on the street but also when some of them, recalling my youthful affiliations a few years later, questioned my suitability for an academic post in 1946. I also encountered this fact of radical life when I began to slide away from the Fieldites toward the end of the thirties. Some time in the spring of 1940 I came to feel that there was something mad about them, that they were not really doing anything to improve anyone's lot, and that in certain respects they were quite as dogmatic as the Stalinists and the Trotskyites. One day, screwing up my courage while three of them and I were walking together—the spot on my road to Damascus was in front of the same Chinese restaurant on upper Broadway where I had once eaten with Ben Nelson—I said that I was fed up with the whole business, that they were doing nothing to prevent the world from being destroyed, and that they were all out of their minds, or words to that effect. I also said a few more concrete things of a political nature, I am sure, but I can't remember them. In any case, I was solemnly told by my condescending friends that we should all have a long, careful discussion of the matter. I agreed, and since the closest place to which we could go was the flat that Fred Tropp and I lived in on West 109th Street, we all went there. I can remember nothing about the substance of that discussion, but I clearly remember one procedural matter: it was decided that the four of us could not have such a discussion without appointing a chairman! The chairman was appointed, we talked endlessly, and at the end I was a new man, an ex–Fieldite sympathizer.

4

Husband, Father, Teacher

Readers of what I have said so far will not find it altogether surprising that I married a Gentile. I had not been raised in a very Jewish home; I was a philosopher; I was an atheist; I was a political radical; I was very much in love with Lucia, and she was in love with me; and the world seemed to be going to hell in so many ways that it seemed like madness to let anything stand in the way of our being married after we had lived together long enough to know that we would be happy together. We felt from the start that we would face trouble with our parents, and we did. However, as so often happens in such situations, Lucia's Protestant mother took it better than my parents did. By every conventional standard Mrs. Perry, who used a lorgnette(!), should have given us more trouble, since her daughter was stooping very low indeed to marry me, a jobless Jewish intellectual. Yet Mrs. Perry gave her unenthusiastic assent, whereas my parents were exceedingly uneasy about the match from the start and continued to be so for a long time. During a brief interval they grudgingly accepted the idea, so the wedding was scheduled for September 4, 1940, in the Vassar Club, which was then housed in what was once the New Weston Hotel at Madison Avenue and East Fifty-second Street; it was to be attended only by family and a few close friends. But some time in August my mother developed a change of heart. She complained that it would be "the end of her life," that she had hoped I would marry a girl who would be a daughter to her, since she had never had one, that I could not be happy with Lucia, and so on. Unfortunately, my father, who was at first not adamantly opposed to the marriage, became one of my mother's instruments in the campaign to stop the wedding, even though I had expected better of him. My mother had also conscripted her brother in the campaign to change my mind, and one day I was so nasty to the poor man about his intrusion into my affairs that he and I never saw each other for the rest of his life. Throughout this stormy period I could not help recalling my parents' admirable behavior when my Uncle Gilbert had married a Gentile, but here they were showing their colors in a remarkably ironic way. I tried all sorts of arguments on them and even enlisted the aid of Herbert Wechsler. My father had enormous respect for Herb, and Herb did help to calm him down, but since Lucia and I were not prepared to budge an inch, my parents were firmly told that the wedding would take place on September 4 as scheduled. They declined the invitation to attend, and that precipitated a decision by Lucia and me to get married immediately, feeling that we did not wish to risk any dramatically obstructive gestures before the wedding day. Therefore we drove up to Yonkers on August 29—accompanied by my roommate, Fred Tropp, who would serve as a witness—and were married by a justice of the peace with the improbable name Eustace J. Farley.

Our elopement was of course kept secret from Lucia's mother as well as from my parents, and on September 4 the official ceremony took place as planned. As I recall, Jimmy and Nancy Wechsler were there to "represent" my side of the family, and Lucia's sisters, Virginia and Celia, came, but I can't remember any other attendants besides Lucia's mother and the minister. He was a Baptist, probably because Mrs. Perry had been born a Baptist before adopting her husband's Episcopalianism. She decided that if the minister stayed after the ceremony, there would be no champagne, in deference to his predictable teetotalism; but champagne was kept in readiness on the chance that he would leave. Naturally we all prayed that he would leave, and God responded by sending him away. A good time was had by all, and the married couple left the New Weston in a Pontiac coupe for Virginia Beach.

When Lucia and I were married, my finances were not exactly in great shape. I was on a Columbia University fellowship that yielded me $1,000 for the year 1940–41, but Lucia was working as a psychiatric social worker in the Social Service Department of the Presbyterian Hospital, and that made it possible for us to manage comfortably. We lived in a three-room apartment on the corner of Broadway and 109th Street, just next door to the house in which I had lived the year before; we had a large living room, a tiny bedroom, and a kitchenette in a renovated eleven-story building called the Manhassett, which ran from 108th to 109th Streets on the west side of Broadway. It was divided into two separate apartment houses, one having an entrance on 109th Street, the other on 108th Street. After living on the 109th Street side for one year, we moved to a larger apartment on the 108th Street side in September of 1941 because Lucia's then unmarried sister Celia came to live with us. She shared the expenses with us, so we were able to rent an elegant place with an enormous living room that looked out over Broadway from the tenth floor.

The apartment was very big, the walls were very thick, and there was plenty of space in which to give lively parties for our friends. I can remember one attended by Jim Farrell, his wife at that time, the actress Hortense Alden, Dwight Mcdonald, Paul Goodman, Ben Nelson, Jimmy and Nancy Wechsler, Elizabeth Hardwick, George Justin, Albert and Roberta Wohlstetter, and several others whose names I can't recall. But I can recall Dwight Macdonald sidling up to me in a corner of the living room and asking me: "Why the hell is that Stalinist Wechsler here?" I replied that for one thing he was my cousin and that for another the party had no line. I should add that although Macdonald and his fellow editors had published pieces by me on popular semantics, on Sidney Hook, and on Jacques Barzun in the *Partisan Review* for 1939, 1940, and 1941, I was not in any sense a member of what was called the P.R. crowd. I had once met William Phillips at the New York Public Library to discuss his editing of my piece on Hook, and I had also met P.R.'s other editor, Philip Rahv, but I did not really know them. At that time Dwight Macdonald was the only one in the group whom I knew and liked, but even Dwight was not exactly a friend. I can remember his complaining to me about my "arthritic" style in "From Marx to Dewey," and I can remember his telling me that Sidney Hook had complained about P.R.'s assigning Hook's *John Dewey* to me for review—a "mere boy" of twenty-three when it appeared. I can also remember Dwight's asking me later to write for his magazine *Politics* and my reviewing Croce's *Politics and Morals* for him.

Other *Partisan Review* people I knew at one time or another in the late thirties and early forties were Mary McCarthy and F. W. (Fred) Dupee. Mary had been Lucia's classmate at Vassar, and we would occasionally bump into her at parties but never knew her very well. Dupee taught at Columbia for a while when I was there as a graduate student and instructor in the years between 1936 and 1946, and he and I would occasionally have lunch together at the cafeteria of the Union Theological Seminary. Much later, when he was a visiting professor at Harvard, I would see him occasionally without really getting to know him. However, I liked him, as I liked Macdonald, without ever having had the opportunity to discuss ideas in a serious way with either one of them. One of the few bonds I had with them and their fellow editors was our joint opposition to Stalinism, but that was not a basis for serious exchange about the intellectual matters that concerned me most at the time, and I confess that in my youthfully arrogant way I did not think of them as deep thinkers.

Lionel Trilling was a *Partisan Review* contributor whom I hardly knew while I was in New York. He was at Columbia when I was there, but I didn't really get to know him until I was about to leave Columbia. Why, I ask myself, did it take that long for me to get to know someone I liked very much when I did get to know him? One possible explanation comes to mind. In 1941 I had published a sharp attack on one of Trilling's friends—Jacques Barzun—in a review of his *Darwin, Marx, Wagner* that appeared in the *Partisan Review*. So I speculate that close friends of Barzun were not likely to feel cordially toward me and therefore did not want to have much to do with me. I recall that my Columbia philosophical colleague James Gutmann—a good friend of the Trillings and of Barzun—was apoplectic about my review. According to Meyer Schapiro, Gutmann had said to him that one of my more damaging quotations from Barzun had been taken out of context, whereupon Meyer replied that *no* context could have justified the statement I had quoted. In 1941–42 I went on a traveling fellowship at a stipend of $2,000 per annum from Columbia, but because we could not travel to Europe in that wartime year, Lucia and I drove from New York to Mexico City and back. Needless to say, I did not learn much philosophy on the trip, but it was exciting and illuminating to someone, like me, who had never been out of the United States. In Mexico City we stayed in a hotel on the Avenida Insurgentes where some German tourists lived, and I can remember my horror at seeing parked motorcycles flying swastikas. I also remember my surprise at seeing articles on German metaphysics in the daily newspapers. One day we were amused to attend a concert at which Prokofiev's *Peter and the Wolf* was accompanied by a Spanish narration. I can also remember our trying to get into a recital given by the violinist Szigeti, and having the man at the box office tell us that we should buy our tickets from the scalpers hovering around his window. When we finally managed to get in at an exorbitant price, we had the unusual experience of seeing a great violinist break a string while playing. He was playing a César Franck sonata with his accompanist, Andor Foldes.

The most amusing incident of the trip came when we tried to see the wife of Diego Rivera at the suggestion of Meyer Schapiro, who wrote me on August 16, 1941: "I am enclosing a letter to Frieda Rivera, . . . she has remarried Diego Rivera. . . . I have just learned from a friend that the Riveras are living in the San Angel quarter of Mexico City, opposite the San Angel Inn." In pursuit of Frieda, Lucia and I drove out to Rivera's house, which had a high picket fence around it. A Mexican manservant came to the gate, and I tried, in my broken Spanish, to say that I wanted to see Senora Rivera. He left, and then, to our surprise, a beautiful young blonde came to the gate. When I explained that I wished to see Frieda Rivera, the blonde said simply: "Frieda doesn't live here any more."

Meyer had also written: "I know several young painters now in Mexico— a Chilean, Matta Echaurren, his English friend, Gordon Onslow-Ford, and a former pupil of mine, Robert Motherwell; they are all surrealists and will have a lot to tell you about their work." Unfortunately, we got to see none of them. We went to Matta's house, but he was away; he was renting it to a man who hunted iguana with eagles and who showed us his eagles tethered in the yard. I can't remember the iguana hunter's name.

After we returned to New York from our Mexican trip, we entered the most critical year of our lives up to then. On December 7, 1941, Pearl Harbor was attacked; in the spring of 1942 I finished my Ph.D. thesis; and on July 17, 1942, our Nick was born. Nick was what was called a "pre–Pearl Harbor" baby, a child who won me a draft deferment because he was conceived earlier than babies whose fathers might have been regarded as draft-dodging impregnators of their wives! He was a joy to behold and brought us much happiness. He also made my parents happy, so happy that they forgot the unpleasantness of two years before. They came to like Lucia, and she was, of course, capable of letting old wounds heal. It was a joyful time for our family even though the world itself seemed to be sliding downhill at a great rate.

Our joy, however, was not complete, if only because my future as a teacher was hardly secure. I had won my Ph.D. that spring before Nick was born, but the only job to which I could look forward was a part-time one teaching philosophy in the evening session of City College, and even that evaporated before the summer was over. While Lucia, Nick, and I were on a short vacation in Connecticut, I received a depressing postcard. It was mailed on September 15 by someone at City College; this person informed me that I would probably have no courses to teach, and that turned out to be an understatement. He wrote: "Since we spoke last . . . about your getting at least 9 hours, the talk about drafting 18–20 yr. olds has sent them to war jobs, and Evening Session Registration figures have been drastically affected. . . . Your elective course . . . had only 5 students. Most probably you . . . will have *no* courses to teach. In all of 12 courses scheduled, only 67 students registered! . . . Sorry, but the war is getting all of us." Getting us indeed. I was the father of an infant son but was unemployed. Fortunately, I was almost immediately rescued by unexpected news from the Columbia Department of Philosophy. One of their young instructors who had no children had been drafted, and therefore there was an opening for me. I accepted the job with an enormous sense of relief; it was the first full-time job ever offered to me. When I began to work in the fall of 1942, I was asked to teach two sections of a freshman course called Contemporary Civilization, a history of Western thought and institutions. It was not a course in philosophy, but many-sided New York philosopher that I was, I was not daunted by that. I was sorry that I could not teach pure philosophy, but beggars couldn't be choosers. Indeed, one term after I had started to teach C.C., as it was called at Columbia, I began to teach elementary physics at CCNY. When my evening session job in philosophy collapsed, I had begun to take a "refresher" course designed to teach the elements of physics to humanists who might be required at any moment to stop teaching their own subjects. I took this course at what was then the University Heights branch of New York University, and at the same time listened to graduate lectures on mechanics at Columbia. Soon afterward I was asked by Hyman Goldsmith, a friend who taught physics at City College, whether I would be interested in an instructorship in the Department of Physics, teaching elementary classes. I accepted the job at once.

As a result, I found myself, in the spring of 1942–43, continuing with my eight hours a week at Columbia as a teacher of Contemporary Civilization, and adding fifteen or sixteen hours a week of physics to my heavy schedule. I do not know how I kept myself from going mad that spring, rushing back and forth from Columbia to City College. Luckily, my teaching in physics was not intellectually strenuous; and by the time I had done all the problems in the textbook, I had lost my fear of misinforming the young. Early in the game I resolved that I would be perfectly honest with the students by making clear that I was not a professional physicist. Therefore, I was under no pressure to perform like Einstein, and I think that my own need to study the problems very carefully and my interest in logical exposition may have made me a better teacher of some students than many high-powered physicists would have been.

I can recall two amusing things that were connected with my ignorance of physics. Once I had been discussing a hard problem with a very bright City

College student and had persuaded him that a solution he had proposed was incorrect; but a minute after he left the room, I realized that I had been wrong and that he had been right. So I pushed out through a crowd of milling students in the hall, running to catch up with him in order to tell him of my latest discovery. At last I did catch up with him on the campus and puffed the truth out to him. Never were a student and a teacher more pleased by a confession. The other story had to do with my teaching of laboratory classes at City College. I soon discovered that someone who learns his physics from a book, and who has no experimental training to speak of, can often be surprised by what happens in the laboratory. In labs on mechanics untoward results are not likely to be very serious in their consequences, but not so in classes on electricity, where expensive equipment may be ruined if a badly constructed circuit is plugged into the main line. What to do? My solution combined caution with progressive education. At the beginning of the term I quickly found out who the best student was and appointed him monitor of the laboratory class. "Check your circuits with Goldstein before plugging in" was my formula; in that way I headed off expenditures for repairs that would have caused me great embarrassment.

When my physicist colleagues at Columbia learned that I was moonlighting in physics at City College, they appealed to me to teach physics for them instead. So I resigned my extra job at City College and made do with my job at Columbia. By 1943–44, registration in philosophy at Columbia was also starting to fall dramatically because of the draft, so I became a full-time teacher of physics at Columbia while officially maintaining my title as instructor in philosophy. At Columbia many professional physicists were working on defense projects, and the Department of Physics was eager to hire people who would be able to teach elementary courses. They would not only hire a philosopher but even undergraduate Columbia physics majors to teach the Navy V-12 students. And so the undergraduate Harold Brown, later a member of the Carter cabinet, and the undergraduate Robert Jastrow, later the director of the Goddard Institute, were both colleagues of mine on the staff teaching elementary physics at Columbia. My closest friend on the staff was Martin Klein, later a distinguished historian of physics at Yale.

One of the most noteworthy things I remember about teaching at Columbia was connected with what I later learned was a secret research laboratory in the basement, just below the room in which supplies for the elementary physics laboratory were kept. In that room in Pupin Hall was a red bulb, and we were told that if ever that bulb should light up, we were to race out of the room at once. To this day I don't know why, but I suppose there was fear of radiation or explosion. I often wonder whether I shouldn't have been wearing something more than my cloth vest when I was teaching physics at Columbia, and I also wonder whether any physics student of mine has ever blown up something by using misinformation received in my classes.

I continued to teach physics until 1945, the year in which our son Steve was born. He arrived on April 16—another lovely child. When we brought him home, we asked Nick where Steve, his brother, should sleep, and Nick answered: "On the doormat." I am happy to say that their later relations do not seem to confirm the dire predictions that our psychoanalytically minded friends embroidered around Nick's answer. And although we did not have Steve sleep on the doormat, I came to think that my years of teaching at Columbia amounted to my doing just that in the Department of Philosophy. I think that I imparted some physics to my students but, of course, no philosophy, and I certainly ran the risk of becoming a dilettante. Perhaps I was stocking my brain in a way that would come in handy later, and perhaps that was a better way to be spending my late twenties than in teaching philosophy. In any case, I was able to learn a lot of philosophy in wartime New York without teaching it, as the next chapter will show.

5

G. E. Moore and Alfred Tarski

Fresh Foreign Air in the Forties

During my years as a graduate student and young instructor at Columbia from 1936 to 1946, I was lucky enough to come to know the distinguished thinkers Alfred Tarski and G. E. Moore. Getting to know them more than made up for my failure to teach philosophy and my failure to learn much from any of my Columbia teachers except Nagel.

My contact with Tarski began by way of W. V. Quine, whose Harvard course on mathematical logic I attended in the summer of 1938. On the strength of my work in that course, Quine recommended me for a fellowship in the Harvard Department of Philosophy for the year 1939–40—a fellowship I did not accept, because I had already met Lucia and wanted to be near her in New York. When I told Quine that I had instead accepted a job as a paper reader in philosophy at City College, Quine advised Tarski, who was to be a visiting professor in the same department, to appoint me as his assistant. Tarski had been attending the Congress for Unified Science in Cambridge, Massachusetts, when war broke out in 1939, and had been in this country without a job until City College invited him to give an introductory course in mathematical logic, along the lines of his well-known textbook, in addition to an advanced course in the logical theory of relations. Tarski asked me to read papers in both courses, and as it happened, I taught his introductory course for a month while he was ill.

Tarski had some very provocative philosophical ideas, and they served to encourage my growing doubts about certain tenets of logical positivism—doubts that Quine shared with Tarski when they criticized Carnap during a seminar at Harvard in the fall of 1940. In 1944 Tarski wrote me a long letter in which he challenged the positivistic view that a sharp distinction may be drawn between the ways in which we test the truths of logic and those of natural science. In this letter, which I reprinted in the *Journal of Philosophy* in 1987, Tarski said that he was ready to reject certain logical statements in exactly the same circumstances in which he was ready to reject physical hypotheses. He argued that we reject scientific theories if we notice their disagreement with statements reporting experiences but that no such experience can compel us to reject a theory, because too many additional hypotheses are also involved in the prediction, hypotheses about initial conditions, about the circumstances of our experiment, and about the instruments used. For this reason, Tarski observed, we can almost always save the theory by surrendering or altering these other hypotheses instead of the theory that is ostensibly under fire. Tarski went on to say that although we are rarely moved in such situations to change the axioms of logic, certain experiences might make us change even those axioms. In other words, he saw no difference "of principle" between the axioms of logic and physical theories in this respect. Related views were later defended by Nelson Goodman in his paper "On Likeness of Meaning" in *Analysis* for October 1949, by Quine in his paper "Two Dogmas of Empiricism" in the *Philosophical Review* for January 1951, and by me in my paper "The Analytic and the Synthetic: An Untenable Dualism," which had appeared in the volume *John Dewey: Philosopher of Science and Freedom* in 1950.

I have said enough about Columbia philosophers in the forties to make it easy to understand why my contact with Tarski and with G. E. Moore was so exciting. Although Quine and Nagel had prepared me to some extent for what was going on in British and Continental analytic philosophy, it was something else to meet Tarski and Moore in person. They represented two influential, though opposing, strains of analytical thinking. Moore was preoccupied with the analysis of concepts expressed in ordinary language, whereas Tarski was a militant advocate of formalizing language and constructing systems with the help of mathematical logic; but since they were both giants compared to the New York philosophers I knew, the disagreements between Tarski and Moore made contact with them extremely exciting. They sent shafts of brilliant light into the hazy atmosphere created by all of my teachers at Columbia except Nagel. True, I admired the foggy but deep

Dewey, and I was still carrying Marxist intellectual baggage that prevented me from fully appreciating the analytical views of Moore and Tarski, but I was ready and eager to partake of what they had to offer, because I was so philosophically estranged from my nonanalytic Columbia professors and so depressed by the negativism of Nagel. By contrast to him, Moore and Tarski believed wholeheartedly in the value of their philosophical work, and that was very exciting to a neophyte.

I described Moore's effect on me in a talk I gave at Columbia and on the BBC just after his death in 1958. I said there that Moore was the most distinguished and most admirable philosopher I had known up to then, and that I wanted to focus on his personality as a teacher and as a source of inspiration to young philosophers. I reminded my audience that Moore, in spite of his ferocity in argument, was a man of deep and delicate feeling, as anyone could tell by listening to him sing Brahms and Schubert while accompanying himself on the piano. I went on to report Moore's writing me in 1945: "Now that our younger son is living with us, I have the pleasure of constantly playing duets with him. I think you get to know music better if you play it yourself, however inadequately, than if you merely hear it." And I used this as a point of departure for saying that Moore would have said something similar about philosophy—that you get to know *it* better by playing it yourself than by merely listening to others, recording them, and playing the records back to yourself and your students.

This was a transparent allusion to my philosophical education in the heavily historical Columbia department, to its view that doing philosophy required great learning in the history of science and of philosophy, technical expertise in logic, and an aptitude for delivering wise sayings. But Moore, I added as I thumbed my nose at my former teachers in the audience, was deficient in all these respects. I pointed out that Moore did not share Marx's view that philosophers should stop interpreting the world and start changing it. Indeed, because Moore was less interested in interpreting Marx's material world than in analyzing concepts, he deviated from every New York philosophical tendency of that day, from logical positivism, from materialism, from naturalism, and from pragmatism.

In explaining what he meant by philosophical analysis Moore was typically content to use a homely example to illustrate what he had in mind. Suppose, he said, we want to understand what it is to be a brother. Moore thought our problem was that of analyzing the concept or attribute of being a brother and that the correct answer to our question should be formulated as follows: "The concept or attribute of being a brother is identical with that of being a male

sibling." This, however, committed Moore t[o]
things as concepts or attributes, which, like Pl[a]... *that there are such*
objects; and it implied that Moore was not a mat... *eas, are not physical*
a materialist believes that only material objects... *r a naturalist, since*
distinguishable from a materialist, believes that on... *nd a naturalist, if*
Clearly, Moore held, the concept of being a star is... *ural things exist.*
therefore different in kind from material or natural ... *star, and it is*
believing this, Moore obviously differed from the Marxia... *By virtue of*
were so active in New York during the thirties and forti[es]. *terialists who*

Moore also differed in a fundamental way from logical ... *nsivists, but his*
disagreements with them differed from those of Tarski. Whe[n] ... *Tarski veered*
from positivism in the direction of an empiricism like John... *ruart Mill's,*
Moore was a throwback in some respects to Kant. Moore belie[ved that] the
result of a philosophical clarification, like "Every brother is a ma[le]," is an
analytic necessary truth because it is true merely by virtue of the m[e]anings of
the terms "brother" and "male," but he thought that the statement "Every
cube has twelve edges" is a *synthetic* necessary truth, since it must be true and
since the meaning of the term "cube" as used by an ordinary crapshooter does
not contain the meaning of the phrase "has twelve edges." Like Kant, Moore
believed that such a synthetic necessary truth is not supported by experience,
and in defending this view, Moore came into sharp conflict with logical
positivists, who said there were no synthetic necessary truths.

Moore's views not only came into conflict with the materialism, naturalism, and positivism of New York in the thirties and forties, but they also came
into conflict with William James's pragmatism of an earlier generation.
According to Moore, James mistakenly held that the attribute of being true
is identical with that of being useful, since Moore held that the meaning of
"true" as applied to a theory is not expressed by saying that the theory is useful
even if it should be the case that all and only true theories are, as a matter of
fact, useful. Moore held that usefulness may be a criterion of truth but that it
is not identical with truth. Bertrand Russell, who criticized James in a similar
way, once offered the following illustration. Russell said that the presence of
a book's title in a library catalogue would be a criterion of whether it is in the
library, if in fact all and only books in the library were mentioned in the
catalogue, but, he said, it would not follow that the phrase "is a book whose
title is in the library catalogue" *means the same* as the phrase "is a book in the
library."

The views of Moore that I have summarized were not the only ones that
separated him from his Columbia colleagues and most other New York

philosophers of the time, alone show why he represented a way of
thinking that young Ne… philosophers knew little about in the 1940s.
Even though I often fo… elf disagreeing with Moore, I thought that he
provided me with on… most refreshing episodes in my philosophical
education. I went o… in my memoir of him that he was living proof of
the importance of … y, clarity, integrity, and careful thinking in philosophy, that he neve… ed anything that he did not believe was true, that he
never said that … ement followed from another unless he was absolutely
convinced th… did, and that he never said that he understood an
expression w… he didn't. I added that these qualities meant more to me
when I be… to stand on my own philosophical legs than all of the
machinery … *Principia Mathematica*, than all the learning of the learned, than
all of the wisdom of the ancients. And they appealed to me not because I
accepted Moore's doctrines but because I was enchanted by the spirit in
which he enunciated them. In my memoir of Moore I said that while some
might not agree with my high estimate of him as a philosopher, no one could
deny that he possessed in the highest degree those moral and intellectual
qualities that every great philosopher should have. And I concluded by
saying: "Once I heard a man say after a sharp exchange with Moore: 'I hate
Moore's mind.' I can only say that I had many a bout with Moore that I lost,
but I never came out of one with any doubts about how I felt about Moore *or*
his mind. I loved them both." When I finished my lecture, a member of the
Columbia Department of Philosophy came up to me and asked in apparent
consternation: "Who made that statement about Moore's mind?" I did not
answer the question, because the person who asked it was the very person
who had made the statement fifteen years earlier! But I *looked* at that person
in a way that I am sure he understood.

In explaining my admiration for a philosopher whose views I often
rejected, I said that he seemed to provide a young philosopher with a method
in philosophy even though Moore shied away from talking about method.
The late William Frankena wrote me after seeing Moore in 1949: "One bit of
conversation was about Keynes' *Two Memoirs*. I asked Moore if he knew at
the time that he was having such an influence on Keynes, etc. He said,
approximately, 'No, I didn't. I used to hear them speak of "The Method"
sometimes, and understood that it was regarded as mine, but I never did know
what it was.'" Moore may never have known what the method of his
philosophy was as viewed by the so-called Bloomsberries, but Moore was
unusually agnostic on such matters. It fitted in with his dislike of philosophical pomposity. Anyone who listened to his lectures could not fail to observe

a few characteristic moves and a few characteristic gestures and grimaces. You watched him begin by disentangling the different senses of the expression in which he was interested, and then, after he specified the sense with which he was concerned, he would consider the various proposals for analyzing it. Almost all of them, it seems in retrospect, he found defective. "*Surely,* the word so-and-so doesn't *ordinarily* mean such and such," he said, as he wrinkled his nose. Or then there was that characteristic conversation stopper as he wagged his head violently: "I shouldn't have thought anyone could possibly say that *that's* what we ordinarily mean by that expression!" Because he was so cautious about saying that one expression meant the same as another, Moore seemed to be left with a set of *unanalyzable* concepts in one hand, and in the other a set of concepts about whose analysis he was never certain. The result was that one of the greatest philosophical analysts of our age found it hard to point, in all honesty, to a single successful analysis of an important philosophical idea even while stimulating more than one generation of philosophical analysts.

Moore was not only immensely stimulating but extremely kind to me. After he left Columbia for England, I thought it would be useful for me to have some kind of testimonial from him, since I was not at all sure of staying on at Columbia once the war was over and would therefore be looking for a job once again. So I wrote to him on April 8, 1945, that although I was scheduled to return in the fall to the teaching of philosophy—as distinct from physics—I might be leaving Columbia. "For this reason," I went on, "I wonder whether I might ask you a very great favor. If you feel that you are in a position to do so, I wonder whether you would write a testimonial in my behalf. Since, at the moment, there is no place in particular with which I am negotiating, it would be most useful if this letter could be addressed to Ernest Nagel. If it were so addressed it could be used not only at Columbia, but also at other schools. I could then avoid troubling you more than this once."

On May 15, 1945, Moore replied:

86 Chesterton Rd.
Cambridge
May 15/45

Dear White,

Here is a testimonial. I have written it in the form of a letter to Nagel, because I thought this was what you must mean by saying it should be addressed to Nagel. But perhaps I was wrong. If so, it can be easily altered by omitting the "Dear Nagel" & the "as you know." So I hope that in any case it may serve your purpose. I don't think I'm good at writing testimonials, though I feel more pleased with this one than I usually am with those I write. I hope you will like it, & that it may be useful to you, if ever you want to use it.

In his letter Moore praised my philosophical ability, my acuteness and persistency in argument, my sanity, my clarity, and my anxiety to get things as clear and correct as possible. I was deeply touched by the letter, and I am sure that it helped me in the job search that I was about to begin. It also bucked me up by counteracting the different estimate of my powers that my Columbia colleagues had formed when they decided to let me go.

In reflecting on my years at Columbia, I realize how much the war had indirectly shaped my intellectual life. I might never have taught the history of Western thought and institutions at Columbia if the war had not arranged events as it did, and I certainly would never have taught physics were it not for the war. I would never have learned the logic I learned from Tarski if the war had not brought him to these shores; and when the war brought G. E. Moore to this country from Cambridge University, I came in contact with a variety of analytic philosophy about which I would have learned little if I had not seen and heard it defended by Moore himself in his inimitable way.

While learning from them, of course, I was personally protected from the devastating effects of the war itself. At the time, I felt less guilt about not serving in the armed forces than I would have felt if I had been more in favor of the war. The remnants of my Marxist pacifism continued to influence me heavily until I later realized the absurdity of my politics and learned more about the horrors of the Holocaust. By then, however, the war was drawing to a close, and I continued to be deferred because I was teaching physics to naval students at Columbia. When the war was over, I soon faced the end of my employment there as a retreaded philosopher, to use a phrase of the time, and was forced to look elsewhere.

6

Castoff

When I told Moore that I might use his testimonial at Columbia, I was not at all sure that I would have the opportunity to do so. And I was right. Sometime during the academic year 1945–46 I was informed that I could not expect to remain in the Columbia Department of Philosophy. My senior colleagues had begun a general deck-cleaning operation in which people who did not meet the standards of the Columbia department were urged to relocate themselves in the labor seller's market that followed the end of the war, to take jobs that were opening up. I was of course extremely disappointed to be let go. By the end of the academic year 1945–46 we were the parents of two little boys, since Steve had been born in April. Once again the arrival of a child heralded an academic crisis, but this time I had a little more time in which to find a new job.

I also had time in which to reflect with sadness on my failure at Columbia. It had awarded me a University Fellowship, a Cutting Traveling Fellowship, and the Woodbridge Prize for my dissertation. The dissertation had been well received in the philosophical journals; I had published articles and reviews, not only in professional but also in general periodicals that were more highly prized than professional journals by some of those who had my fate in their hands—for example, Edman. Furthermore, I had been a good student of

Nagel's and had even won some kind of favor from Randall, who was so fickle and peculiar in his relationships with students. True, I was to be counted an analytic philosopher, and such an affiliation was not widely prized at Columbia in those days; but I was also a historian of ideas and a specialist on Dewey, who (I later learned) had written to his friend Bentley in 1945 that "White's . . . briefer articles and reviews . . . are headed in the right direction. Probably I should cultivate acquaintance with him, intellectually speaking. He has more stuff in him—not stuffed in him—than most of the younger men who are writing." Why, then, did Columbia let me go?

In trying to answer that question I can only speculate. First of all I think some of my senior colleagues just didn't like me. Period. In those days I found it hard to accept the fact that some people didn't like me, but time has made that much easier. Furthermore, I now think—though I once did not—that one should not support a person one really dislikes for a job in a small department of philosophy. My impression was that I did not hit it off personally with either Schneider or Edman in spite of the latter's interest in the plan for my *Social Thought in America*. Randall, I had some reason to believe, was cordial to me; so hopeful was I that Randall would go to bat for me that I would often discuss his attitude with Nagel, who would keep me abreast of developments by saying, in effect, that at Monday's departmental meeting Randall had not yet come through with support, at Tuesday's meeting he hadn't, and so on, day after day. I did not have the courage to ask Nagel whether *he* had done anything to lead a charge for me, because Nagel always gave the impression to his students that he was about as influential in the department as the woman who operated the elevator in Philosophy Hall. One simply didn't *expect* him to forward the professional aims of anyone even though he was by that time a permanent member of the department, so I could not help thinking that Nagel never lifted a finger to keep me at Columbia. Despite his willingness to give me strong support for positions elsewhere, and despite the fact that he may have liked me, I thought he could not overcome his distress over the fact that I did not see eye to eye with him on a number of key philosophical issues. I thought that he disapproved so much of my published work that I have never dedicated a book to him. I was happy, therefore, to be one of the editors of a *Festschrift* for him; in that way I could express my gratitude to him without running the risk of his sneering about a book I had dedicated to him.

At the end of the academic year 1945–46 I was very depressed about the prospect of leaving New York even though I was also set up by the great interest in me displayed by other departments of philosophy. After it became known that I would not stay at Columbia, I received actual offers, or feelers that could have been turned into offers, from New York University, Reed College, the University of Washington, the University of Minnesota, and the University of Pennsylvania. Sidney Hook was the chairman of the Department of Philosophy at NYU when their offer was made, but the prospect of working under Sidney, who was said to be a tough boss in spite of his theoretical sympathy with the proletariat, led me to decline the one job that would permit me to remain in New York. Lucia had no fear of leaving the city for distant places, and she encouraged me to feel as she did. I contemplated several of the offers from outside of New York, thinking that our whole family would greatly benefit by a departure from the metropolis.

One of my links with several of the places I was dealing with was Henry Aiken, who had recommended me to his alma mater, Reed College, and to the University of Washington, where he had been teaching in 1945–46 before accepting a permanent position at Harvard. In 1944–45 Henry had been brought to Columbia by Irwin Edman, who had come to know him at Harvard. I can remember the first day I had lunch with Henry in a cafeteria on Broadway near 116th Street. We began to talk of our philosophical views and tastes; and he told me that his favorite philosophers were Hume and Russell, so I immediately asked him how Irwin Edman had ever come to like him. He laughed uproariously, and that was the beginning of a long and very important friendship in my life. Henry was the first professional philosopher I met after my graduate-student days with whom I could range with pleasure over so many of my interests: philosophy, literature, politics, and music. He was also the first far westerner I had ever known well, a man of enormous energy and capacity for pleasure and alcohol. He was very handsome, very attractive to women, half Jewish, born in Portland, Oregon, and reared in Ogden, Utah. Lucia and I took to him and his wife immediately, but they were having grave marital troubles, and one night, Henry reported to us in despair, he came home to find a note telling him that she and their children had left for good. We comforted him as well as we could and saw a lot of him to help cheer him up. He left Columbia to our disappointment at the end of his one year there to take up his appointment at the University of Washington in the fall of 1945, but that was far from the end of my friendship with Henry.

As soon as he went to Seattle, he became active in a campaign to bring me there. However, he ran into some difficulty that is worth reporting because it illustrates a general phenomenon of the times. He wrote me on December 2, 1945, that a certain P., whom he called "a dyed-in-the-wool red," had the idea, via M., a New York comrade of P., that I was a Trotskyite and hence unacceptable. Two weeks later Aiken reported that P. was trying to get more dope on me from his New York Stalinist friend. Soon after that the New York Stalinist wrote as follows to *me*, though I hardly knew him: "From time to time, my old friend, Dr. P., of the U. of Washington has asked me what I knew of various candidates for philosophical positions. I suppose it is difficult to pick out the right men at a distance of 3,000 miles, and that any scraps of information would be of value. Some time ago he mentioned your name, among others, and I told him what I knew about you which wasn't much— that you were brilliant and that I had a high respect for your scholarship. If I had known anything else about you I would have told him that but I didn't. Now P. writes me again, and I want you to know that I am sending an air mail recommending you for the position highly, and without qualification. I have no reason to think that my endorsement will have much, or any, weight, but in view of gossip which is always so easy and delicious, I want to make my stand clear."

On December 17 Aiken wrote me, confirming that M. had indeed written to P., "absolving himself of any knowledge of or concern about your politics. Whatever he had said in his earlier letter was, I take it, simply taken up by P. and magnified into something out of all due proportion. P. is sometimes inclined to do that. However, M. did praise your powers and work to P. . . . He also said that he was writing you a letter about this matter. I hope by the way that this thing can drop, as I don't want, even indirectly, to be the cause of hard feelings between P., M., and you."

The matter did drop because I immediately lost interest in the Washington job and began to look with more favor on the possibility of going to the University of Pennsylvania, from which I had had an inquiry on January 11, 1946. However, there were also Marxists in the Pennsylvania Department of Philosophy, only they were anti-Stalinists, and they sought assurance from a New York friend of mine—I think Meyer Schapiro—that I was also anti-Stalinist! Meyer found it easy to give this, so I once again passed a political test. On February 8, I received an offer of an assistant professorship from the University of Minnesota at $3,500 a year; and on February 13, Pennsylvania made the same offer to me. I accepted Penn's offer on February 16, and on February 19, after receiving my word that I had closed with Penn, the president of Reed College wrote: "[I]t was the unanimous view of the council that we should offer you a position on the faculty at Reed College. After receiving your telegram that you have accepted a position at Pennsylvania I shall not make the offer that I had hoped you would find most attractive."

Once the die was cast in the direction of Philadelphia, I was much relieved. In November of 1945 I had been given a contract by the Viking Press for the book that was to become my *Social Thought in America;* and when my decision to go to Penn was made, I plunged into this enterprise with renewed energy. In the spring of 1946 I gave a course in the adult-extension program at Columbia entitled American Ideologies of the Twentieth Century. It was based on the book I was writing, and so far as I could gather, the course went well. I gave it in the evening, mainly to a group of students who worked in the daytime; and although there was almost no classroom discussion, I felt that I was reaching and teaching them. I recall, however, that when the course ended, I rushed away from the lectern in a fit of sadness after I had said my last word to the class. My ten years as a graduate student and instructor at Columbia were over. The castoff therefore thought—as Henry Adams might have put it—that he should slip away quietly. Lucia, who was listening to the lectures, joined me afterward in my office, and we both went home to prepare for life in Philadelphia. When Ben Huebsch heard that I was going to the University of Pennsylvania, he told me a Philadelphia story I had never heard before. A man goes to a ticket counter in New York's Penn Station and says to the ticket agent: "I want to go to Philadelphia," to which the ticket agent replies: "Sir, you don't *want* to go to Philadelphia; you *have* to go to Philadelphia."

7

At Penn with Nelson Goodman

While I was agonizing about which job to accept after I left Columbia, the University of Pennsylvania commended itself to me mainly because it was close to New York and in "no mean city," as one writer described Philadelphia with the help of Saint Paul's phrase. That proximity to New York was attractive to me for several reasons. My parents had become very fond of Lucia and very attached to Nick and Steve, and I knew how lonely they would have felt if all of us had departed for the Middle West or the West Coast in the days before frequent flying. In addition, the University of Pennsylvania had a strong philosophical tradition. Its central figure was Edgar A. Singer Jr., once an assistant of William James at Harvard and in 1946 an emeritus professor at Penn. Singer had been a well-known member of the American philosophical profession, but he assumed the status of a deity in his own university, where his position resembled that of Woodbridge at Columbia. I realized how intensely devoted to him Singer's students were when in May of 1946, before I formally joined the department, I received a copy of a letter that had been loyally sent by its members to P. A. Schilpp, then editor of the Library of Living Philosophers, a series of volumes of essays on the views of eminent contributors to the subject. "We feel," they declared, "that a volume devoted to the work of Edgar Arthur Singer, Jr. is necessary for the completion of any adequate account of contemporary philosophic thought. Through his own work in such volumes as 'Mind as Behavior,' 'On The Contented Life,' and 'Modern Thinkers and Present Day Problems,' and numerous articles which have appeared and are appearing in philosophic journals, he has made, if not the most significant, certainly one of the most significant contributions to the history of thought." In a covering letter I was told: "Pressure should be applied on [Schilpp] from all directions." I must confess that I thought the description of Singer's importance was, to say the least, exaggerated, but it was a touching tribute to an admired teacher.

The chairman of the Pennsylvania department was a bright and genial philosopher who was only a few years older than I was. He was trying very hard to build up the department and was extremely nice to me in the earliest days of our acquaintance. As soon as I agreed to sign on, he made me feel that I would have a considerable say in the operations to rebuild the department. I was heartened to find him responsive to my proposal that Nelson Goodman be invited, and Nelson joined the department in the same year as I had. Some in the department, however, tried to combine their Singerism—which I never fully understood—with an attachment to a non-Communist variety of Marxism. One professor and a graduate student in the department were the prime movers in an effort to push the department in the direction of what they called "experimentalism." Dewey, of course, had used this word in description of his own philosophy, but although the Pennsylvania experimentalists were respectful of Dewey, they regarded his version of experimentalism as deficient in a way that I cannot remember.

In addition to trying to improve the faculty, the chairman at Penn was very active in encouraging graduate students of philosophy. When I first came to Pennsylvania there were a number of very able people in my classes who have gone on to become members of the teaching profession. One of the graduate students in a class of mine was Sidney Morgenbesser, later a professor at Columbia. Noam Chomsky of MIT and Hilary Putnam of Harvard were undergraduate students in my logic course of 1947–48; and in that year Putnam was also registered in a course of mine in the philosophy of the social sciences. In 1946–47 I taught a logic course based on Hilbert and Ackermann's text; in 1947–48 I concentrated on more philosophical aspects of logic by using Carnap's *Meaning and Necessity*. In 1946–47 I gave a seminar called "Analysis, Positivism, and Pragmatism," which was attended by several graduate students, who presented their own papers after I gave some lectures to get the seminar started. That course was the first version of one that I gave at Harvard under the title "Problems of Analytic Philosophy," later to become the basis of my book *Toward Reunion in Philosophy*.

In my earliest days at Pennsylvania I was exceedingly happy. I was at last on my own as a philosopher and a teacher, and I was benefiting enormously from contact with Nelson Goodman. He was thoroughly dedicated to his philosophical work and a very original mind who encouraged me to think through things for myself. I was especially interested in his highly instructive views on contrary-to-fact conditional statements; and we talked a great deal about meaning and analyticity in a manner that is reflected in a three-sided correspondence in which he, Quine, and I engaged in 1947. Ever since those days I have been reading publications of Goodman's, from which I have learned much, and in 1956 I dedicated *Toward Reunion in Philosophy* to him and Quine. Some people find him too fussy and thorny, but I have never found him so. Some philosophers resent his condemnation of certain philosophical moves by appealing to his "philosophic conscience," but I have often found his censoriousness instructive and challenging.

In 1946–48 Lucia and I thanked our lucky stars that Goodman and his wife, Kay, were at Penn with us, both for personal and intellectual reasons. Together, Nelson and I opposed some of the more aggressive moves that the Singerians had begun to make, especially when they came up with the idea of an Institute for Experimental Method that was to "supplement" the work of the Department of Philosophy. In effect this was to be a philosophical enclave within which a student could get his Ph.D. by helping to celebrate and perpetuate the work of Singer and his disciples. Nelson and I thought it a great mistake to give one philosophical position a privileged sanctuary in the university, since allowing a graduate student to get a degree within this institute would prevent any professor who was not a member of the experimentalist crowd from examining the student. He or she could take all courses and qualifying exams within the fold of the institute, and thereby avoid all contact with any heathen philosopher. To make matters worse, most members of the Department of Philosophy would have been unable to give courses in the philosophy of science, since that was the main preserve of the projected institute. In that case Goodman and I would have been cordoned off and prevented from having contact with students who specialized in the philosophy of science, often the best students.

As a result of my alliance with Nelson against the experimentalists, I was regarded as a renegade by the Singerian socialists. After all, they had checked my political reliability with a friend whom they thought they could trust, but here I was selling out to the capitalist class and its epistemological lackey

Nelson Goodman! For the first time in my life, in spite of all of my previous New York experience with leftism, I felt politically trapped in a department of philosophy. I had known Stalinists, Trotskyists, Fieldites, and other members of left-wing groups in New York, but I had never encountered political ideologues who were so determined to dominate a department. I had met something like this, of course, when my Fieldite friends had scornfully disapproved of my political waywardness, and I had had my political credentials tested while I was under consideration in Seattle and Philadelphia, but I never dreamed that any such thing would happen in a department of which I was a member. As a result, my experience in Philadelphia led me to think that all party thinking, all sectarian loyalty of the kind demanded by Marxism, was an abomination.

My experience in Philadelphia may also explain why, in my paper "The Analytic and the Synthetic: An Untenable Dualism" of 1950, where I reported certain agreements among Goodman, Quine, and myself, I wrote, trying to be mildly witty while I had my recent experiences in mind: "I hesitate to name too many names, but I venture to say, under the protection of the academic freedom which still prevails on such matters, that some of my fellow revolutionaries are Professor W. V. Quine of Harvard and Professor Nelson Goodman of the University of Pennsylvania. As yet the revolution is in a fluid stage. No dictatorship has been set up, and so there is still a great deal of freedom and healthy dispute possible within the revolutionary ranks."

Goodman and I were relieved to see the plans for an experimentalist institute collapse, but we had to face another unpleasant development. One of the Singerians, a graduate student, submitted as his Ph.D. dissertation a typescript that bore his name and that of a professor as authors. It was a practice in some scientific departments of the university to allow this kind of collaborative thesis, but not in the Department of Philosophy. Therefore the candidate and his mentor were asked to indicate the part of the joint work in which the candidate had made his own contribution to knowledge, since the readers of the dissertation did not want to be put in the awkward position of deciding whether the mentor was capable of writing an acceptable Ph.D. thesis. All of this created a great deal of embarrassment and tension, since it was exceedingly unpleasant to have to treat a colleague in this way. In the end, the candidate named a specific chapter as his, he was examined on that, and he was passed, but the episode left a very unpleasant taste. I was terribly depressed by it. I had come to Pennsylvania with high hopes; I had learned a lot there; I was happy there for a while; I had wanted to collaborate with my chairman in his effort to build a good department; and I liked him as a person.

But I refused to be steamrollered by an effort to take over a department as one might take over a local of a union. My life at Pennsylvania was also made miserable by Lucia's becoming seriously ill in the fall of 1947. She went into a hospital, and I was forced to take care of the two boys by myself for four months. It was a very, very difficult period for me.

We lived in a suburb called Elkins Park, northeast of Philadelphia, having bought a house there after an unpleasant experience in Swarthmore. We had liked one house in that college town, but just before we were to make an offer for it, the real-estate broker volunteered that we should be especially pleased by the fact that it was in an area where neither Negroes nor Jews were acceptable. He meant that neither he nor any other broker would show houses there to them. Upon hearing this, we immediately broke off negotiations and turned toward the northeastern suburbs, where, we were told, such things didn't happen, because Jews were already living there in large numbers. That was indeed true, and they were often businessmen, lawyers, or physicians. In spite of not being accustomed to their style of life, we found them very friendly and some of them were extremely helpful to us while Lucia was ill. I shall never forget the generosity of our neighbors in Elkins Park, especially Lawrence and Barbara Blumenthal. And I shall always remember my contact with Goodman at Pennsylvania as a critical, stimulating, and profoundly instructive chapter in my philosophical development.

As I reflect on what I have said about my days in New York and Philadelphia, I realize that I have sometimes spoken about the impact of pure academic politics on my career and sometimes about the effect of what might be called real, or outside-world, politics. I think I was the victim and witness of both during this early period in my life. Pure academic politics was primarily at work when I was let go by Columbia, where the decision was in great measure based on doctrinal philosophical disagreements with me and on what were thought to be personal flaws of mine. A majority of my senior colleagues at Columbia disapproved of my analytical orientation and found me too aggressive, too harsh, too brash, too abrasive, too outspoken. By contrast, when the Stalinist philosopher in Seattle almost removed me from the running for a job there, his objection to me was based on what I've called real politics. That sort of objection could also be based on religious prejudice, as when Bertrand Russell was denied a visiting professorship in the Department of Philosophy at the College of the City of New York in 1940 because of his publicly expressed views on sex, marriage, and morals. As a lowly paper-reading assistant in that department, I was assigned the errand boy's job of going downtown to a historian of education at Teachers College to get a signed document in which he attested to the fact that eminent British scholars do not usually get M.A.'s and almost never get Ph.D.'s. Such a letter was thought to be necessary in order to deal with a question raised by a New York judge who asked why Russell, who did not have a Ph.D., was invited to teach at CCNY when so many Ph.D.'s in philosophy were out of work! In the end, Russell was prevented from teaching at CCNY by a tricky move on the part of the supposedly liberal mayor of New York City, Fiorello La Guardia, who simply used his line-item veto to rid the budget of the job that Russell was to fill.

I find it ironical that in spite of my childhood hope that I would escape from my father's politics by becoming a professor, I have been enmeshed in politics throughout my academic life—so much so that in later years I came to think that I would never have survived in the academy if I had not been born across the street from the Downtown Tammany Club and raised by one of its members. What I learned at my father's knee prepared me for much that I had to contend with when I moved from the mean streets of New York to the supposedly pure air of the Ivy League and the Institute for Advanced Study.

8

Social Thought in America and Philosophical Thought in New York
Some Differences with John Dewey and Ernest Nagel

If partisanship is treason to philosophy, as Santayana once said, it would seem that most, if not all, philosophers are traitors to their subject. Since philosophy generates so much disagreement, philosophers inevitably divide into parties. James Madison wisely said in Federalist Number 10 that "as long as the reason of man continues fallible, and he is at liberty to exercise it, different opinions will be formed" not only on points of practice but also on those of speculation. The most frivolous and fanciful distinctions, Madison continued, have been sufficient to kindle the unfriendly passions of men, as I learned in my days as a young radical and rediscovered when I failed to get certain jobs because of my views. I realized that when you criticize a person's ideas, or anything else to which he or she is closely attached, the person will strike back in some way—no matter how big he or she is or how small you are. I had known something like this on Catharine Street, of course, but for some reason I had forgotten it by the time I entered the halls of academe. I knew in my childhood that a big man would go after a small one if the first thought that the second had gotten too big for his breeches, but I was naive enough to think that it would not happen in the noble world of the university, where big men were really big.

Yet it did happen after I published two things that I had begun to work on seriously while I was at Pennsylvania, my *Social Thought in America* and my article on the concepts of value and obligation in Dewey and Lewis, the latter publication having been partially incorporated in the former. Both of these works appeared in 1949, but they were very much in progress before I went to Cambridge, Massachusetts, in 1948 and therefore represented what might be called my pre-Harvard thinking. They elicited negative reactions from two figures who had heavily influenced that thinking: John Dewey and Ernest Nagel. Dewey, of course, had much to complain about, since I had directly criticized some of his ethical views in my book, but his reply was printed posthumously in 1990, more than forty years after I had criticized him in print. That reply, though temperate, did not mask Dewey's disappointment at the fact that I did not agree with him in ethics. On the other hand, Nagel had a very different axe to grind. Even though I had not criticized his views, he had reservations about my book that were prompted in part, I think, by a need to keep a former student in his place, to keep him small enough for his breeches.

The main general theme of *Social Thought in America* first appeared in an article I had published in 1947 while still at Penn—"The Revolt Against Formalism in American Social Thought of the Twentieth Century." I say there why I linked several thinkers as opponents of formalism by delineating what they objected to in their different but related ways. Dewey, I said, attacked formal logic in his earliest writings; Veblen attacked the use of deductive method by classical political economists; Holmes said that the life of the law has not been logic but experience; Beard said "that law is not an abstract thing, a printed page, a volume of statutes, a statement by a judge," and added that F. W. Maitland was a great scholar because he was "emancipated from bondage to systematists." After saying that these American thinkers had rebelled against formalism, I admitted that it was very hard to give an exact definition of "formalism." Using an idea of Wittgenstein's, I said that the term as applied to movements in different fields might not retain precisely the same meaning but that there was a strong family resemblance between Holmes, Dewey, Veblen, and Beard, who called upon social scientists in all domains, asked them to unite, and urged that they have nothing to lose but their deductive chains. This attack on formalism, I continued, was associated with two important elements in the thought of these men—"historicism" and what I called "cultural organicism." By "historicism" I meant the tendency to explain facts by reference to earlier facts; by "cultural organicism" I meant the tendency to find explanations and relevant material in social sciences other than the one in which the scholar worked. I said the historicist reaches back in time in order to account for certain phenomena, whereas the cultural organicist reaches into the entire social space around him. Holmes was a learned historian of the law and one of the heroes of sociological jurisprudence, Veblen an evolutionary and sociological student of economic institutions, Beard an advocate of the view that political instruments are more than documents, James Harvey Robinson a student of how society comes to be what it is, and Dewey an "evolutionary" and "cultural" naturalist. All of them insisted upon coming to grips with *life*, *experience, process, growth, context, function*. They were all products of the historical and cultural emphases of the nineteenth century, following, being influenced by, reacting to its great theorists of change and process—Darwin, Hegel, Maine, Marx, Savigny, Spencer, and the historical school of economics.

Social Thought in America appeared late in 1949. Although it is primarily a work in intellectual history and although it is read mainly by historians, it is also a philosophical work insofar as it critically analyzes the methodological and ethical views of the figures it deals with. In it I treat the social context of those views, and that is not usually done by historians of philosophy. Furthermore, *Social Thought in America* could not, in my opinion, have been written by a historian without considerable philosophical training. The elder Arthur Schlesinger, who liked the book, once said to me that he thought it could have been written by a historian—by which I suppose he meant a historian trained in the conventional way—but I don't think that is true. Writing *Social Thought in America* required more philosophical training than an ordinary historian usually has, and a kind of interest in social history that philosophers rarely have. I think therefore that whatever success the book achieved was due in great measure to my having had little competition from historians or philosophers. The dearth of competitors in the English-speaking world was perhaps connected with the fact that the philosopher A. O. Lovejoy, America's distinguished historian of ideas, trained no students who produced anything as good as his *Great Chain of Being*, and with the fact that Isaiah Berlin's splendid contributions to the subject have not stimulated many British philosophers to work as brilliantly as he in the history of ideas. Because both of them had produced outstanding work in philosophically oriented intellectual history, I was very happy to receive a favorable review of *Social Thought in America* from Berlin in the leading British philosophical journal *Mind*, and to receive a very encouraging letter from Lovejoy after the book appeared. On November 20, 1949, he wrote me:

I have received a copy of your *Social Thought in America,* and, though its provenience is not indicated, I assume that I owe it to your kindness. I have now read it not only with interest but with enthusiasm. The analytical exposition seems to me clarifying and the critical comments almost always searching and just—sometimes erring, if at all, a little on the side of leniency. It is a capital contribution to the history of ideas in America in the generation which has now (with the exception of Dewey at 90!) passed from the scene. My only serious grievance is over your introduction of the term "Formalism" as a general designation for the movement, or group of ideas, with which you deal. It doesn't seem to me to describe clearly or precisely what it was your five authors were chiefly revolting *against;* it is not free from ambiguity; and, like most similarly general and vague words ending in *ism,* it is likely to degenerate into a catchword—or in this case rather, into a term of abuse—. However, I cannot, I confess, suggest a substitute; but, I think, better no label than an obscure or a misleading one.

Best thanks for the volume. I hope it will be widely read.

Charles Beard, who died before my book appeared, was quite enthusiastic about the main theme of my book as presented in my article. After I sent him a reprint of the article, he wrote me on May 24, 1947: "Reading your excellent paper has evoked a flood of memories—memories of ancient days and the men with whom you were good enough to associate me. I think that you have hit on the formula that really warrants bringing us together. . . . Among the memories called forth by your paper is that wonderful sentence in Holmes' dissenting opinion in the Lochner case (1905): 'General propositions do not decide concrete cases. The decision will depend on a judgment or intuition more subtle than any articulate major premise.' Like a flash of lightning that declaration illuminated for me then, the dark heavens of juridical logic."

In my reply to this letter I expressed my gratitude to Beard and used the occasion to ask his help in finding materials that would illuminate his attitude toward the First World War and his resignation from Columbia in 1917. To this Beard replied that he was sorry not to be able to help me, that I should consult files of the *Times* and other New York papers, and that his memory of the affair was very dim. Beard's reply surprised me, and it ended my brief correspondence with him. However, when my book appeared, soon after Beard's death in 1948, I received a charmingly encouraging letter in the summer of 1950 from Mary Beard, his wife and collaborator.

Mrs. Beard said that she wished to pay me belated homage for my *Social Thought in America* but confessed that when she read my remark that Beard had "inordinately" denied his reliance on Marx by attributing certain ideas to Madison about the role of economics in history, perhaps playing safe thereby, she laid the book aside for some time. After she returned to it and finished reading it, she said she was "intensely happy" about what she called my noble enterprise in dealing with the "Revolt Against Formalism," adding that my final pages completely clarified my evaluation for her. She then invited Lucia and me to visit her in New Milford, Connecticut, and said: "There is no other person in the throng of my husband's friends and acquaintances in the gilds of learned societies with whom I would like so much to talk." I cannot find a copy of my reply to Mary Beard's letter, but her next letter indicates that Lucia and I must have agreed to drive to her place in New Milford from our summer cottage in West Cornwall, Connecticut. Unfortunately, we never did get there, and I cannot remember why.

My relations with John Dewey were as cordial as my relations with the Beards before my book appeared. I had begun corresponding with Dewey on November 26, 1941, when I wrote him at the suggestion of my thesis adviser, Herbert Schneider, that I would value any help he might offer me. Schneider had given him a copy of the manuscript of my dissertation and had reported to me that Dewey had taken exception to one point of mine in a footnote. I wrote Dewey that I would appreciate hearing his objection, and so he invited me on November 29 to come to talk with him, remarking that "the matter of footnote on p. 38, as I recall it, was not very important intellectually, but concerned a matter of biographical fact." My visit to Dewey on December 11 was brief but most enjoyable. He lived close to the Dalton School in New York, and stuck on the door of his apartment were all sorts of messages and drawings from children at the school. After I knocked and was invited to enter, we got right down to business about the footnote, had a brief conversation, and I left after promising to send him a copy of the book after it appeared. When I sent it to him, I inscribed it somewhat as follows: "To Professor Dewey, but for whom this book could not have been written."

Dewey wrote me next on October 31, 1944, after I had sent him my review of Felix Kaufman's *Methodology of the Social Sciences* in the *Journal of Philosophy*. Dewey congratulated me on it, told me that what I had said needed to be said, and that I had "pretty well hit the nail on the head." In 1945, I sent him a review of Richard Hofstadter's *Social Darwinism in American Thought, 1860–1915* and received an illuminating comment from him about how Darwin's work had affected him. Dewey wrote that it was difficult to recall the influences that affected his development, because changes in his views took place slowly and cumulatively, and he remarked that he didn't ever realize the valuable element in Darwin till other influences had made him see that what he had arrived at committed him to naturalism and that Darwin's *general* position concerning man gave the coup de grâce to "extra & supra-naturalistic views."

In 1948 I sent Dewey a copy of the *Sunday Philadelphia Bulletin Book Review* that contained a notice by me of the Briefer Version of Ralph Barton Perry's *Thought and Character of William James.* In my review I remarked that William's brother Henry had not joined "that long line of literary misinter-preters from Lewis Mumford to Julien Benda who have painted William James as the ideologist of opportunism and private gain, the high priest of American smugness." Dewey wrote that he had enjoyed the review and took his own swipe at Benda, author of *Le trahison des clercs:* "I am glad to see you coupled Mumford with the French traducer—who ought to be an authority on treason." Then, after receiving my article on the revolt against formalism, Dewey sent me a telegraphic postcard, thanking me "for the reprint of your interesting and clear article"; and I responded in August 1947 to his obviously unconsuming interest in my article by asking him a question about Veblen, much as I had asked Beard one about his resignation from Columbia. I reminded Dewey that in 1906 Veblen had published an article called "The Place of Science in Modern Civilization," in which he attacked something he called "pragmatism" by saying that "[p]ragmatism creates nothing but maxims of expedient conduct. Science creates nothing but theories. It knows nothing of policy or utility, of better or worse." I went on to say that someone had called Veblen's essay "a protest against Dewey's pragmatic theory of knowl-edge," and so I wondered what Dewey's reaction would be to such a remark. I received an informative and cordial reply from him that should have great interest for historians of American thought. Dewey wrote:

Hubbards, Nova Scotia
Aug. 16 '47

Dear Mr. White,

Yours of the 11th just reached me here where I shall [be] till the end of this month. I have to answer your letter largely on the basis of impressions and somewhat hazy recollections. First, you have probably gone over the literature of the first decade enough to be aware how supposedly critical accounts of pragmatism reacted to the suggestion of "practicality" in the word pragmatism, being, among other ignorances, quite ignorant of Peirce's statement about the Kantian suggestion of the word. It is my belief that Veblen had little or no personal acquaintance with my writings, but I have no factual evidence on that point. But you may have heard that academically as well as personally Veblen was aloof; I do not think the fact that we were at Chicago at the same time meant a thing to him in the way of knowledge of my views. He was as near the academic iceberg as anyone. I probably should have paid some public attention to his article; it didn't help that I didn't, but I was rather disgusted with that kind of criticism and except in a few cases ignored it. To come to your specific question, I do *not* believe there is any disparity of at all a fundamental character between our views; I certainly learned a lot from him. But of course he had little vogue in those days and I think that probably his preoccupation with "business" as practical (as he understood practice) disposed him to take an antipathetic attitude toward pragmatism as a justification of American devotion to business. Of course philosophically there is a difference between us in that he made a distinction between theory and "practice" that I do not think is justified, agreeing with Justice Holmes that in the long run theories are the most important of all practical matters—but that point is so definitely "philosophical" that I am reasonably sure it didn't influence either of us with respect to attitude taken to the other one.

> Sincerely yours,
> John Dewey

I should have said that I expect we shall be in N Y City most of the time thru September and shall be happy to see you; 1158 (corner 97th St) 5th Ave., Phone At 9, 6392. I give the no. as we may be out of town off and on.

This letter of Dewey's was quite different from one that he wrote me on November 6, 1949, after I had sent him *Social Thought in America* and "Value and Obligation in Dewey and Lewis," both of them critical of his views in ethics. To my disappointment, he merely acknowledged receipt of these publications without saying anything about their contents. That letter of acknowledgment was the last letter I had from Dewey, so I concluded that he had not read my two things or had not thought them worth discussing. I was very surprised, therefore, when I learned upon reading the last volume of his *Collected Works*—published in 1990—that in a previously unpublished piece written in 1950 he *had* paid attention to my criticisms. When I read it, I was sorry to think he had not said in a letter what he said in that posthumous piece, "Comment on Recent Criticisms of Some Points in Moral and Logical Theory"; but because I thought the issue between us was important and because Dewey's views were then being actively revived, I published an article called "Desire and Desirability: A Rejoinder to a Posthumous Reply by John Dewey" in the *Journal of Philosophy* in 1996.

In several of his writings Dewey had maintained that the relation between a thing's being desirable and its being desired was like that between its really being red and its looking red. He seemed to accept Peirce's view that the relationship between an apple's really being red and its looking red may be expressed by saying that the statement "This apple really is red" is synonymous with "If a person with normal vision looks at this apple in normal light, it will look red." According to this Peircean analysis, we cannot infer that a thing *is* really red merely from its looking red, since a thing that is not red might look red to an observer who did not have normal vision or who did not look at the thing in normal light. Imitating this Peircean analysis of real redness, Dewey went on to say that "This apple is desirable, i.e., ought to be desired" is synonymous with "If a normal person considers this apple under normal conditions, he will desire it." According to this analysis of an ethical statement, the apple might be desired under *ab*normal conditions or by an *ab*normal person and yet *not* be desirable, that is, *not* be something we ought to desire. But this favorable consequence of Dewey's analysis, I thought, was not enough to show that it was correct. I objected that "ought to be desired" does not mean the same as "is desired by a normal person under normal conditions" by analogy to Peirce's statement that "really red" means the same as "appears red to a normal person under normal conditions."

Briefly stated, my main objection was that if a moral statement that a thing *ought to be* desired were synonymous with a statement that it was desired by a normal person under normal conditions, then the presumably nonmoral statement that a thing appeared or looked red to a normal person under normal conditions would be synonymous with the moral statement that it *ought to appear* red. In other words, Dewey was in the awkward position of saying that the descriptive statement "It is really red" is synonymous with "It ought to appear red," where the "ought" in the latter is the moral "ought." This, I said, would make every statement about the real color of a thing synonymous with a moral or ethical statement, which seemed absurd. I knew that Dewey would disagree with what I had said about his view, but I did not learn until forty years later how he defended himself against my criticism.

While writing his reply to me, Dewey had evidently been discussing my views with Sidney Hook, his "bulldog," much as Thomas Huxley was Darwin's. Hook had himself tried to answer my criticisms of Dewey's ethical views in an article he contributed in 1950 to a *Festschrift* for Dewey that he edited: *John Dewey: Philosopher of Science and Freedom*. Hook had sworn almost complete allegiance to his master, agreeing with him in ethics *and* in logic, whereas I was a more selective admirer of Dewey who found some of his logical views more congenial than his views on moral obligation. By contrast, Hook's more positivistic friend Ernest Nagel was not as devout a follower of Dewey; Nagel wrote me that although he liked my criticism of Dewey's ethical views, he had serious reservations about other aspects of *Social Thought in America*.

My relations with Nagel, however, were very different from my relations with Dewey. For many years Nagel had been my teacher and my colleague, whereas I never knew Dewey very well. He was a distant famous figure whom I knew mainly through his writings, whereas Nagel had taught me as an undergraduate and as a graduate student, and I regarded him as a good friend. During the forties, Lucia and I lived in the same apartment house with the Nagels on West 108th Street; we often joined each other for dinner; we went to concerts and movies together, and were very congenial. Nevertheless, my relations with Ernest had always been covered by a cloud of ambiguity. When I went to Harvard in 1948, he seemed very pleased; but when I sent *Social Thought in America* to him in 1949, he wrote me a letter that confirmed some of my worst suspicions. He began the letter of October 28, 1949, with praise, with his telling me how well written the book was and how much he enjoyed reading it, but then he signaled that he was about to let loose at me by writing: "I think too highly of you, and believe our friendship is equal to the strain of frank exchange of opinion, to want to conceal from you that I expected more from the book and in consequence I've read it with a measure of disappointment, in spite of the many excellent things I've found to applaud in it."

There followed a division of what he called his negative comments into three parts: animadversions on my notion of antiformalism, on the book's unevenness in what ideas it picks out for detailed criticism, and on my failure to state my own position in social theory clearly. He also remarked that Bertrand Russell and Morris Cohen were liberals but not antiformalists, implying that this showed that my main thesis was false. After that he felt compelled to point out that I should not be too pleased that some of our friends seemed to like the book more than he did, writing: "By the way, I met Jim Farrell at the Dewey dinner last week, and he was most enthusiastic over your book, though when we began to talk about it (I could do so only diffidently, since at that time I had not read more than a few chapters) he was giving me *his* views on the men and period you discuss rather than a disciplined judgment on your discussion. When I last talked to Meyer [Schapiro] he had not had time to read more than a few chapters of the book, one of which (chap. XI) he liked very much." Finally, to remove some of the sting of what he had written, Ernest concluded the philosophical part of his letter by remarking: "I think your piece on Dewey and Lewis was excellent, and I hoped to write you more detailed comment on it."

Rereading my exchange with Nagel almost a half century later, I see that I said many things that I would no longer say, but I do not feel very differently about Nagel's effort to take me to the woodshed when I was thirty-two and he was forty-eight! It seemed to me then, as it seems to me now, that he was to some extent rationalizing his decision not to support me at Columbia. Here is my wounded but outspoken response.

November 1, 1949

Dear Ernest:

I have received yours of October 28, in which you report your disappointment with my SOCIAL THOUGHT IN AMERICA. In a way I feel complimented, because disappointment implies high expectation and high expectations are flattering. But I cannot hide my own disappointment with your criticism, for I had expected something more helpful. Please allow me to run the risk of offending that you took in being so candid with me. I would not have been "bored" with the details you elected to suppress. I assure you that I would have studied them hard and carefully. As it is, I can only reply somewhat dogmatically.

1. *On anti-formalism.* I made clear that it was very difficult to formulate this as a doctrinal agreement on a set of propositions which they all believed and which could be labeled "the thesis of anti-formalism." On the other hand, I find it hard to see why Dewey's early antipathy to formal logic (the "fons et origo malorum" in philosophy), Veblen's attitude toward deductive economics, and Holmes' "life of the law is not logic" attitude, cannot be joined as anti-formalist in an almost obvious way. Moreover, I should have thought that they reflect

a temper that could hardly be assigned to the early Russell. Imagine Russell talking about logic in that way at the turn of the century! And even if Russell and Cohen participated in similar views on certain points, that would not affect my point. I don't say that no one else participates in this feeling, and so I cannot help thinking that your remark about Cohen and Russell is irrelevant. I might add that the essay in which I advance this view was published over two years ago, and I'm sorry that I didn't know your attitudes earlier. I had the impression from your silence that you disapproved, but I wish you had taken the occasion to be candid then. I might have had the benefit of your criticism and tried to meet some of your objections. I am pretty sure, however, that if you had dismissed the idea wholesale then, I would not have assented, for I'm firmly convinced of the basic correctness of my view. But there's no point laboring that. Some day we may be able to talk it out at length.

2. *On the omission of Dewey's logic and Beard's isolationism.* I omitted a detailed consideration of Dewey's logical theory for two reasons. First of all, I don't think that the details of the *Logic* or the *Essays in Exp. Logic* form part of liberal American *social* thought in the sense in which I was considering it. I gave whatever I took to be relevant in my Chapter IX. Secondly, I made it clear that I was limiting myself to work through the twenties. Only in the case of some of Beard's later work on the philosophy of history do I violate the decision to avoid coming up through the thirties. The *Logic* appeared in 1938.

I avoided discussing Beard's isolationism because that could only be done systematically by coming up to the book on FDR (1948). And besides, I believe that Beard's isolationism is a matter of detail by comparison with the broad ideas I do discuss. When Beard is thought of as a liberal of the first generation in the 20th century his isolationism does not usually figure. It's rather the economic determinism, the attitudes toward history and civilization, the Madisonianism that count.

3. *On what I think a social theorist ought to do.* I think he ought to do more than limit himself to the exhortation to be scientific and I assume you do too. When you say that you share my weariness with social philosophies that simply recommend intelligence, I gather that you too want social philosophers to do more. Where we must disagree, then, is in *what* we expect them to present over and above the recommendation to be intelligent. I think this should consist in presenting us with what Dewey calls a political technology. I think that presenting a political

technology falls somewhere between telling us to be intelligent and to vote for Al Smith. It should announce social ends (of varying degrees of generality), and then proceed to formulate ways and means of reaching them, and retaining them as long as they are satisfactory. In any case, it ought not to discourage this activity with palaver about "fixed ends" and rigidity. Now if you think Dewey has presented such a technology, I am wrong. I don't think he has, and he himself admits that he hasn't (Schilpp volume). Moreover, I think he has discouraged others from doing this with dubious philosophical arguments that are parts of what I call (forgive me) his anti-formalism.

Now I am not denying the difficulty of the problem. It is the central problem of social ethics. But I don't think Dewey can be defended by arbitrary definitions of the "task of the philosopher." Dewey has a broader conception of the task of the philosopher than those who limit it to methodology and analysis. I have simply recorded what I think is a failure; a failure that he handsomely admits and which he does not justify by making distinctions between the tasks of philosophy and social science. But I want to repeat that there is ambivalence in his writings; sometimes it's a failure he admits and on other occasions it's failure which he defends as part of his opposition to formulating panaceas and fixed ends.

I am trying to think these problems through positively. I have spent most of my adult life accepting certain political views that I now reject and others that I now hold with diminished confidence. On my Guggenheim I will try to carry out what I criticize Dewey for not carrying out. If I fail I may see the folly of criticizing others (though, of course, that needn't follow), but I cannot forsake the job as impossible, as unphilosophical, as unnecessary, or silly.

As you see, I don't accept the validity of your criticism. . . .

I am sure that these were not the only serious reservations you had about the book and I would like to know the others. In that way my future work will be helped. Now, I have the feeling that even if I did commit the errors of omission of which you speak, even if these omissions could be fairly criticized in the light of the task which I explicitly set myself, they would not make up a major criticism. Of course they justify disappointment on the part of someone who looked forward to discussions of these points. On the other hand your criticism on the score of my theory of these men as "anti-formalists" is more serious. If I am wrong here, my thesis is undercut in a fundamental way. But, as I have said, here I am not convinced and unrepentant.

That I have not written *the* last word or my last word on this subject, I know quite well. And here I take some consolation in a moving letter from John Stuart Mill to Theodor Gomperz:

> "That you must be dissatisfied is inevitable, for nobody ever does anything of much value unless his standard of excellence is much above his present powers of execution; but, if one gives way to discouragement, this disparity is always increasing, for self-culture raises one's standard always higher and higher, so that unless one keeps one's powers of execution in such full exercise as makes them also grow *pari passu,* one is driven to absolute despair."

I have taken my chances and have disappointed someone whose opinion I respect greatly but whose criticisms in this instance I cannot accept without protest.

> As ever,
> Morty

To this letter Nagel replied on November 3, 1949, in a way that should have mollified me more than it did; he proposed, with tongue in cheek no doubt, that I come to live in New York, and then wound up saying something about my father's political doings:

> Some of our best talks took place when we had a common roof over our heads on 108 Street. How about moving into this chateau—I hear there is a vacancy in the offing?
> According to some reports in the papers, your father cannot help being the next councilman for his district. How about having him get the rents lowered in Columbia apartments?

Shortly after this exchange with Nagel I complained to Jim Farrell that Nagel had caviled about my book and that although I had once profited "from such treatment at the hands of a stern teacher," I had come to find it "wearying." Jim replied quickly: "I agree with what you say about Ernest. At least, to the extent to which I know and understand him. I thought about your remarks, and after doing this, I came to the conclusion that the word *cavilling* is accurate. It seems to me that he does a great deal of intellectual cavilling. I imagine that if you had put in the things he said he missed, he would have found other things which he would like to have seen in the book."

Before saying something further about my exchange with Nagel, I want to add a few comments on the expression "the revolt against formalism," especially because Nagel and my more sympathetic critic Lovejoy both expressed reservations about it. Lovejoy's reservations seem to me different from Nagel's, both in content and in the spirit in which they were conveyed to me. If I had merely said that Dewey had attacked formal logic, that Veblen had attacked the use of deductive method in economics, that Holmes had said that the life of the law has not been logic but experience, that Beard had criticized formal-juridical approaches to the Constitution, and if I had *not* tied these views together into a so-called revolt against formalism, Lovejoy would not, I gather, have complained. He seems to have thought that the individual views of my men *were* significantly linked but *not* successfully characterized as attacks on something that could be labeled formalism. But by confessing that he could not suggest a substitute for the expression "revolt against formalism," he at least left open the possibility—as Nagel had not—that another general expression might be found that would more effectively convey how the various attacks leveled by my men were linked to each other.

Some readers of my correspondence with Nagel may think that he was a gentle, avuncular critic of my book instead of what William James would have called a stingy one, who could not bring himself to go all out for anyone or anything. My own view, based on many years of experience before and after this correspondence, is that the Jamesian characterization is closer to the truth and that there was something about me or my work that put Nagel off. Of course I know of glowing recommendations of me that he wrote to certain colleges and universities, since he sent me copies of them to show me how strongly he supported me (in places other than Columbia, I should add). Yet in 1956, after my *Toward Reunion in Philosophy* appeared, Nelson Goodman wrote me: "Hear that Steve [C. L. Stevenson, author of *Ethics and Language*] and Ernest [Nagel] rather actively dislike your book. Not too surprising." Goodman was not surprised by these reactions because I had explicitly attacked Stevenson's views in ethics along with views in the philosophy of science to which Nagel subscribed.

My attacks on these views reflected my doubts about both positivistic ethical theory and the positivistic distinction between analytic and synthetic statements, but Nagel never seemed to understand my doubts about the latter. As early as 1947, he had written to me on this subject in response to a letter in which I had reported to him on the triangular correspondence of Goodman, Quine, and myself mentioned earlier. I have no copy of my letter to Nagel, but here is what he said in reply:

> What you wrote in your own last letter about the three-way correspondence with Van and Nelson left me very puzzled indeed. Doubtless I don't understand the points involved—I sometimes get the feeling that the revolt against the distinction between analytic and synthetic is a private trade secret in a closed circle to which I have not been admitted—but from the little I know about the matter I think there is a lot of shooting over nothing. When I last saw Peter [Carl Hempel] in the city he told me something about Nelson's criticisms—Peter did not recall them very well . . . and I was not impressed. Put me down as a reactionary if you will—I guess I do belong now to the older generation—but I find in some of Nelson's stuff a *Spitzfindigkeit* which, while admirable in many ways, has the danger of losing the forest for the trees. Some day soon, if you think you won't be wasting your time, you must sit down with me and explain what is what from scratch.

It was (and is) clear to me that Ernest did not like the idea of my sharing "private trade secrets" with Van Quine and Nelson Goodman, because the little he knew of those "secrets" pointed to a growing difference between me and him. He had probably begun to fear that I was breaking some cords that had tied me to him as my teacher; and I suspect that he continued to be critical of me for that and related reasons until the end of our friendship in 1975. For example, in May 1962, after I had read my paper "The Logic of Historical Narration" at a conference at New York University, I was provoked by Nagel into a sharp exchange with him that led my witty Harvard colleague Donald Williams to speak of Nagel as having been in a state of "rancorous disarray" while attacking my paper.

Some years later, in 1975, I applied for a research grant from the John Dewey Foundation—of which Nagel and Hook were two of the three directors—and was offered $3,000, a laughably small amount by comparison to the $20,000 I had asked for. I was told later that Nagel was opposed to offering me anything but that Hook's "compromise" solution was that I be offered $3,000; I wrote to Nagel, who was secretary of the foundation, that I would not accept the foundation's grant. I was not surprised, of course, when the letter in which I spurned the foundation's money went without a reply from Nagel, but I was sorry that I had no further contact with Nagel during the remaining years of his life. I report this with sadness, but, as I have said, my relations with him in my forty years of contact with him before 1975 were always affected by uncertainty and doubt. I really never knew how I stood with him even though he taught me much and we had many pleasant times together. I thought highly of him as a philosopher, but I did not think he was what Justice Holmes used to call a "big fellow." He could be mean at times, and I think that he came close to hating his chosen subject and wishing that he had been a scientist or a mathematician. He was a very intelligent man, a well-read man, and a penetrating critic at times, but a less than generous one. Even Lucia, one of the most gentle and sweet-natured persons I have ever known, thought this about him, and when the affair over the grant from his foundation ended, she said to me: "Forgive him and forget him."

I tried to follow her advice in later years, but I feel compelled to express my feelings on a matter that has long troubled me. No other teacher, senior colleague, or supporter of mine ever treated me as ambiguously as Nagel did during my long association with him, and so I hope the reader will understand why I could never in all sincerity dedicate a book to him. After I left Columbia, he would often tell me how lucky I was in not having stayed at Columbia, but though I think he was right, that was not only because of the limitations of his *colleagues*, as he suggested. To have worked under the watchful eyes of Ernest Nagel himself might have been the death of me intellectually, as my mother would have said. Had I been kept on at Columbia as an untenured assistant professor with my future at his mercy, God only knows what would have happened to me.

In 1954, eight years after I had left Columbia, I wrote to Isaiah Berlin in reply to a request that I help him soothe the feelings of its Department of Philosophy after his failure to keep an engagement to come there for a visit: "Unfortunately my relations with that University—at which I was trained— are not very good. In part because of my critical remarks on John Dewey in *Social Thought in America* . . . ; in part because of my having gone to Harvard after they had exiled me to the University of Pennsylvania—an unforgivable step because of Columbia's deep . . . jealousy of Harvard. So you see I can do you nothing but harm in that part of the world. They control the *Journal of Philosophy* and the *Journal of the History of Ideas* and neither of these journals reviewed my *Social Thought in America*." Randall of Columbia, an editor of both of these journals, after enthusiastically accepting my article on the revolt against formalism for publication in the *Journal of the History of Ideas*, predicted that my book would be a "landmark in American studies." But readers of Randall's two journals never learned from any reviewer whether that prediction was true or false, perhaps because Randall felt that I had swerved too far from Columbia's canonical Deweyanism.

9

In Praise and Defense
of a Distinguished Publisher
B. W. Huebsch

Having described some intellectual reactions to *Social Thought in America*, I want to say something now about the generous support given to my work by B. W. Huebsch, the New York publisher who did so much to bring the book into existence. In turning to what Marx might have called the forces of production by contrast to the more celestial sphere in which my book's philosophical critics and I operated, I want to say that Huebsch's behavior toward me was far more helpful and kind than what I had met in the intellectual world. Yet in spite of his decency, honesty, and goodwill, he and his reputation could not escape being affected by the contentious atmosphere of New York in the forties. Neither philosophy nor literature could fail to be influenced by the polemics of a period in which liberalism, Communism, pragmatism, and positivism often did battle with each other on political and personal levels.

Unfortunately, Huebsch was able to bring out only my *Social Thought in America* because I later wrote books that a trade publisher like him would find hard to accept. My contract with Viking for *Social Thought in America* gave them an option to publish my next book, but that turned out to be *Toward Reunion in Philosophy*, which was far too technical for them. Still, my connection with Huebsch, however brief, was a very happy one. While I was writing *Social Thought in America*, I had a delightful time with him, eating and drinking at good New York restaurants as his guest, smoking his splendid cigars, enjoying conversation with him, and profiting by his wise counsel. I first met him when I was twenty-eight, and then he was a tall, heavyset gray-haired man of about seventy, with conspicuously bushy eyebrows that drooped over the top frames of his thick eyeglasses. He was an imposing figure as he marched up and down Madison Avenue from Forty-eighth Street— where Viking had its offices in those days—wearing a handsome camel's-hair overcoat and carrying a walking stick that reminded me of Stephen Daedalus's. I was proud to be able to say that James Joyce's American publisher was also mine.

My dealings with Huebsch began in the fall of 1945, when I talked with him about my plans for a book. Later I sent him a statement that was very much like my statement about the revolt against formalism in an earlier chapter. Soon after Huebsch received my outline, he sent me a contract with Viking for the publication of my book; I signed it and received an advance of $500. Thereafter Huebsch's letters to me were cordial, and almost fatherly. When he heard that I was leaving Columbia for the University of Pennsylvania, he wrote: "I learn with pleasure of your new assignment and I hope the post may give you every opportunity"—but understandably asked a question that he was forced to ask on many occasions while I delayed the completion of my manuscript: "What are the chances of work on our book?" And in November of 1946, just after I went to Penn, Huebsch wrote me: "I was disappointed when I learned from Irwin [Edman] that you had called me, for I should have enjoyed seeing you again or even talking to you on the telephone. It was a satisfaction to hear from him, and now to have you confirm it, that you are content in your present situation. It is good to know that you are sticking with the book and that you will probably have the manuscript ready in June." Though I had to write Huebsch in March 1947 that I would be unable to deliver my manuscript in time for it to be published in 1947, I offered him evidence in May of work done on it by sending him a reprint of my paper on the revolt against formalism in the *Journal of the History of Ideas*. Upon receiving it he thanked me and expressed the hope that he would see me in New York after his return from Europe in the middle of August. Then, in his polite but persistent way, he wrote in September: "I hope to learn that you were able to carry out your intention to devote the Summer to our book. Did you finish it or are there still obstacles to be met?"

Pricked by this query, I wrote on September 11 that I had ten chapters "in almost final form" and that things were looking up. I ended my letter by saying:

> I am quite disgusted with myself for delaying this ms. for so long (the contract called for completion by June, 47) but I assure you that the delay was caused primarily by events I could not foresee when I made the agreement—chief among them my transfer of post. This turned my plans topsy-turvy, but I think I'm out of the forest now [I did mix my metaphors!], and utterly sure I can bring the matter to a close within a reasonable amount of time. I will try to make that more precise when I see you. Meanwhile my most sincere thanks to you for your patience and for your willingness to support this project on the little evidence I presented two years ago. I feel that the draft I have now is stronger evidence of the likelihood of my presenting you with a *good* book. I have been very heartened by the response to the article I put forth as a feeler; especially by Beard's response as well as that of others interested in some of these questions.

Within a month Lucia fell ill and entered the hospital, and I was once again in the forest from which I thought I had escaped. At that point Huebsch showed his generosity and decency by writing on November 11, 1947, that he was sorry to hear my news and that under the circumstances I had better drop all thought of my obligation to Viking until my affairs were in a normal state. Huebsch's letter of November 11 came soon after I read my paper to the Harvard Department of Philosophy and about a week before I accepted an invitation to join the department. To cheer me even more, Lucia came out of the hospital early in 1948, and I was able on March 22 of that year to write Huebsch: "Some of my personal problems have ironed themselves out very well and I have been able to work regularly on my book for you. The next time I see you, I hope to have a good deal of material which I'd like to show you." Huebsch wrote on March 25 that he was glad to hear of Lucia's recovery, and on June 16 he commented favorably on a part of the manuscript I had sent him, saying that it was a pleasant foretaste of the book and that I was writing something peculiarly appropriate to the time.

After arriving in Cambridge in August, I wrote to Huebsch at the end of September 1948:

> I'm writing to report that I think that I've just about come to the point where I would appreciate some advice and assistance from you on

how to finish my book. What I mean is that there are two ways of bringing it to a close. The most firmly formed part of the book is that on the *historical* development of these different modes of thought which I've been writing on. It is mainly an *account* of the growth of an outlook in different fields of social and philosophical thought with less of an emphasis on *critical* analysis by myself. This critical material I had thought of saving for the second part of the book. But now that I come to the critical part I find that if I decide to go into *it* in detail commensurate with the amount I've given to history in the first part, I shall have a very large work on my hands. The second alternative is easier; it would involve a kind of critical concluding chapter or two in which I state my attitude toward this whole way of liberal thinking in the social sciences and political philosophy. At the present moment I would be inclined to take the second way because of my desire to bring the book to a close and to begin on another. What I am writing to ask you is whether I might send the ms. on to you as soon as I get it typed (so that I'd have more than one copy) and then come down to discuss it with you.

I realize that you may not be home yet but I would appreciate whatever comments occur to you. I realize that you may not be in a position to answer my question without seeing the ms. and so I will do my best to get it to you shortly.

I hope that your trip to Europe was enjoyable and I look forward to hearing something about it when I see you. I note with pleasure that we are fellow members of the Independent Voters for Norman Thomas.

The reader should take special note of the last sentence about Independent Voters for Norman Thomas, since it figures significantly in what I say later about the politics of Huebsch while defending him against some false accusations.

To my September letter Huebsch replied on October 14, 1948, saying that he leaned toward the proposal to make the conclusion an expression of my own attitude toward the ideas surveyed in the body of the book. And on May 19, 1949, after congratulating me on having won a Guggenheim fellowship a month or so earlier, he wrote something I now reread with sadness. He said that he was glad about my winning the award for my sake "and, as well, for [his] because it makes the companion volume to the present one more of a certainty than it might otherwise have been. I need hardly repeat here that our interest in your career does not arise out of the hope of publishing a single book which, at best does not imply a project of commercial importance, but because of the belief that we would be rewarded from several points of view by a sustained relation with your literary achievements." I reread this with sadness because I did not reward Viking in the manner contemplated by Huebsch.

After I sent him the final manuscript of *Social Thought in America*, he wrote with typical cordiality: "You did not say anything about an Associate Professorship but Irwin Edman mentioned Monday night that he heard that you had received that. Is he in error or are you open to the congratulations which that advancement invites?" Huebsch went on to say that the manuscript seemed to be in excellent shape and that "the writing is clear, unambiguous and inviting." With a good editor's eye he also remarked: "I ran across one word which you may want to change, namely 'obscure' where . . . you refer to 'Morris, the obscure American idealist.' Those who don't know Morris will be uncertain whether the word connotes 'little known' or 'cloudy.'" In a telephone conversation with Huebsch I said that I meant to use "obscure" in both senses and would let it stand.

After writing in the preface to the book that "without the kindness and interest of B. W. Huebsch of The Viking Press I would never have begun it," I received a letter on May 25 in which he said: "Your recognition of my small share in this enterprise is entirely too generous, yet it pleases me that you feel as you do about it and I thank you warmly." And when I reported in July 1949 that in trying to present a manuscript that was not messy, I had engaged someone to retype it and therefore had to ask him reluctantly for a further advance, Huebsch sent me a check for $500 but stipulated that such balance as might not be earned by the book should be applied as an advance against royalties on any other book by me that Viking might publish later. Fair enough. It was clear that Huebsch hoped that there would be another such book, and I hoped so as well.

Social Thought in America was published in the fall of 1949, and a good deal of my correspondence with Huebsch after that focused on various reviews of the book and on letters to me about the book, which I would occasionally send to Huebsch. On November 18, 1949, he wrote me that he had seen the favorable *Herald Tribune* review by the philosopher Charles Frankel as well as Donald Adams's extract from the book in the *New York Times Book Review*. Huebsch also wrote that "Jim Farrell seems to have been exerting himself on behalf of the book to good effect" and in his next letter, on December 15, told me that I would be pleased—as I was—by Richard Hofstadter's notice in the *New York Times Book Review* and by Arthur Schlesinger Jr.'s review in the

Partisan Review. On January 3, 1950, Huebsch wrote that the lawyer Jerome Frank was just as much interested in my book as his review in the *Nation* would imply, and that he had expressed a desire to meet me. Continuing to convey his pleasure at the reception of my book, "Ben," as he now signed himself, wrote a letter to me on February 10, 1950, that bore on his politics. The Holmes to whom he referred in it was of course not Justice Holmes (who died in 1935) but the liberal minister John Haynes Holmes. And the "last line" of Arthur Schlesinger's to which Huebsch referred was one in which Arthur had complained that Viking had allowed the book to appear without an index—a mistake for which I must take some responsibility and one that I rectified in a later edition.

> Here are the *Partisan* and *Saturday* reviews which you had not seen up to the 6th; Schlesinger is more than good—except for his last line! The others are duplicates of reviews in our file. Too bad that there was none in the B.O.M.C. News, for that circulates in vast numbers. I look forward to seeing the Isaiah Berlin review since that man has been sold to me in a rather big way, as I told you.
>
> I suppose that the real sale will begin when we get adoptions (including that for your own class!) but thus far we have disposed of something under 1200 copies. These recent reviews, especially in the *Partisan*, ought to open new channels.
>
> The Norman Thomas lunch was the most effective of such celebrations that I have ever attended. The programme was imaginative and interest in the proceedings never flagged. Holmes was the ideal chairman and Norman spoke with his usual fervor. The thing lasted for about three hours and everything was so harmonious that not even Jim Farley's participation, with a brief speech, sounded a false note.

On June 8, 1950, Ben wrote me about a favorable review by Lewis Corey but expressed the "wish that it were being printed in the *Reader's Digest* instead of the *Antioch Review*." And since I had sent him a copy of a letter I had received from Mrs. Charles Beard, Ben wrote me the following on October 31, 1950: "It must have afforded you great satisfaction to get such unusual praise of your book, and from so keen and able a person. I hope that you were able to accept her invitation for the contact ought to be profitable from several points of view."

After I sent Huebsch the manuscript of the book that I later published as

Toward Reunion in Philosophy, I received a letter from him that I reread now with some pain, since it meant the end of my literary association with him.

June 10, 1954

Dear Morton,

Although you led me to suspect that your manuscript entitled "From Existence to Decision" might not be what we call a trade book, that is to say for the literate public in general, I did not have to read long to discover that you have written for the scholar and the student. You suggested that it might be more appropriate to a University Press, and I am confident that your opinion is right; also what with your standing and connections you will have no difficulty in arranging its publication.

Since the book is obviously one with which we could not do as well for you as a publisher who commands an academic audience, I should not be too sorry at having to decline the opportunity were it not for the fact that our option on your further output now terminates. I trust, however, that you may be able to arrange for the publication of the present manuscript without committing yourself to subsequent manuscripts. In other words, I hope that you may be free to offer us whatever you may have that is not for the strictly academic public so that you may continue with the Viking Press in a manner which I think we both had in mind when you started with us.

I hope that your trip is working out as happily as you planned. I start off on mine tomorrow to return in the early Autumn.

Sincerely yours,
Ben

P.S. Please drop a line to this office to state how the manuscript should be disposed of.

I was disappointed that Viking could not publish the book, but I continued on friendly terms with Ben. In October of 1954 I wrote him about the death of his good friend Edman, and he replied by saying, among other things, that it took Edman's death "to make me aware of how completely I had allowed myself to become dependent on his being for spiritual and intellectual sustenance." Most of my later exchanges with Ben had to do with reviews, inquiries about possible translations, and similar matters. In 1955 we corre-

sponded about an Italian translation to be done for the publisher *Il Mulino*
and also about a paperback edition to be brought out by Beacon Press. In
November of that year Ben wrote to thank me for a copy of my *Age of
Analysis,* and in January of 1956 sent me a letter that showed his continuing
interest in publishing anything of mine that might be handled by a general
publisher.

> You will receive, or may already have received, a letter from Victor
> Gollancz, now in New York City, containing a suggestion of a topic for
> a book to be done by you if you should like the idea. Gollancz happened
> to see your "Age of Analysis" in my office; its presence, he said, recalled
> the regret that he felt at having declined the British rights in the series
> in which it appears.
>
> Gollancz asked me about you and in the course of my remarks I
> reminded him gently that I had offered him and he had declined "Social
> Thought in America." However, his mind immediately got to work,
> hence his, and now my, letter to you. My purpose in particular is to say
> that if you hold Gollancz's proposal to be good, you bear in mind my
> continuing interest in whatever part of your production lies within the
> operations of a general publisher.

After 1956, when Ben was eighty, my correspondence with him diminished rapidly. In the autumn of 1957 I tried to cheer him up after hearing that
he had broken his knee in Italy, and added that the Beacon Press, in an
informal report on my *Social Thought in America* in their paperback edition,
had mentioned sales of more than five thousand. Ben answered that I "should
be well satisfied with the Beacon Press's report on sales. Judging by a comparable series of our own, it strikes me that Beacon has done satisfactorily."
A year later Huebsch asked me once again whether I was at work on any
book that might be of interest to Viking, and went on to say that the English
publisher George Weidenfeld had inquired about publishing a book of mine.
Huebsch wrote that he didn't know the origin of Weidenfeld's interest and
wondered whether it might have been stimulated in part by Isaiah Berlin.
Weidenfeld was probably referring to my book of essays, *Religion, Politics, and
the Higher Learning,* which he published in England after Harvard had
brought it out in this country, so I wrote to Ben on October 10, 1958:

> Unfortunately, I do not have anything on the fire that I can show to
> you. The book that Weidenfeld must have had in mind is a volume of

essays by me which the Harvard Press will be bringing out in 1959. Given the habits of the American trade publisher, I decided that this book was a University Press book because of the technicality of some of the essays. On the other hand it may well be a possibility for an English publisher, and I shall suggest to the Harvard Press that they keep Weidenfeld in mind. Thank you very much for letting me know of his interest. I met him in Boston when he was here last year and we have many common friends, among them Isaiah Berlin.

On February 27, 1961, I had a very nice note from Ben in which he reported that he had retired from active work, but his last letter to me was firmly and clearly written by hand on August 27, 1963, on the stationery of the Athenaeum Court Hotel in London. A year later he died at eighty-eight. I had the greatest admiration for him and regret that I could not have continued as one of his authors until the end of his days with Viking. Later I shall describe the tension I felt between writing books like *Toward Reunion in Philosophy* and books like *Social Thought in America*, but now I must add a postscript to the present chapter that I wish I did not have to add.

After writing what I have just written, I had occasion to read Diana Trilling's memoir, *The Beginning of the Journey*, where she says or implies that Huebsch had been "an ardent longtime Communist," and asks: "Was Marshall Best [of Viking Press] also a Communist sympathizer?" as if she had said or implied in the previous sentence that Ben Huebsch had been a Communist *sympathizer* rather than a Communist. That ambiguity in labeling Ben Huebsch is of no great concern to me here because I firmly believe that he was neither a Communist nor a Communist sympathizer during the years in which I knew him. However, Diana Trilling says he was one or the other in order to explain why, in 1949, when the Hiss-Chambers case dominated the front pages of the newspapers, Viking Press did not try to revive interest in her husband Lionel's anti-Hiss novel about the case, *The Middle of the Journey*. Since 1949 was also the year in which *Social Thought in America* appeared, I was then in close contact with Ben. As I have said, I had written him in September 1948 that we were both members of Independent Voters for Norman Thomas, and in 1950 Ben wrote to me about a Norman Thomas celebration he had attended with pleasure. Readers who are old enough to remember or who are versed in American political history will know that in 1948 a Communist or a Communist sympathizer wouldn't have been caught dead voting for Norman Thomas and therefore against Henry Wallace; nor would such a person have enjoyed attending a celebration of Thomas in

1950, as Huebsch had. I became a Voter for Thomas at the suggestion of Jim Farrell; in his letter below, "Meyer" refers to Meyer Schapiro, another anti-Stalinist who was supporting Thomas. Farrell wrote:

June 1, 1948

Dear Morty:

    I don't know if I've written you about it, but we are starting to organize a committee of independent voters for Norman Thomas. Meyer has come in on it. Have you made up your mind? If so, please let me know so we can put your name on the list, in the event that you care to join. . . .

    My love to all of you.

Jim Farrell

A notation I wrote on Farrell's letter reads: "Answered 'Yes' by phone to both questions."

Naturally, I do not know the details of Ben Huebsch's entire political history. He was born in 1876, and at some point in his early life he might have given support to the Communist-run International Publishers, as Diana Trilling says he did, or perhaps signed a document that was also supported by Communists; but she goes much further. She accuses him of being a Communist or Communist sympathizer in 1949 who was hostile toward Lionel's novel and who tried to discourage a British publisher from republishing it. She says that Fredric Warburg's book *An Occupation for Gentleman* supports her view, but Warburg says nothing there about Huebsch's alleged reluctance to sell him British rights to Lionel's novel.

As it happens, on May 30, 1950, Lucia and I had occasion to write a joint letter to Diana in which we both praised and criticized a piece of hers in the *Partisan Review* on the Hiss case. We were highly critical of the following passage in her piece: "Ideas are not to be separated from the acts to which they might lead; and whether or not, in any particular instance, they do actually lead to acts is irrelevant. They might lead to acts; they often do lead to acts; they must therefore be judged as if they were acts. The Communist idea must be judged as a Communist act. And similarly, the idea of tolerance of Communism must be judged as an act of tolerance of Communism." We wrote her that much as we admired some parts of her article, we strongly disagreed with what she had said in the paragraph just quoted. On June 6,

1950, Mrs. Trilling replied to us at length. She began by saying that Lucia and I had written very generously to her and that she appreciated what we had said enormously; she also said that our criticism was very cogent and that she wished that it had been made in time for her to have corrected herself. She admitted that ideas and acts "are significantly separable," and added that although she was referring "to the moral, not the legal sphere," she did not say so and therefore her text could be read as an argument for "dangerous thoughts legislation"—something she certainly had not intended. In the light of what she said in that letter, I like to think that she would, if she were alive today, be as willing to retract her statements about Ben Huebsch's politics in the late forties as she was to revise her statements in 1950 about the relationship between a Communist idea and a Communist act. For I am certain that Huebsch was not a Communist or Communist sympathizer when I knew him and equally certain that Mrs. Trilling gives no evidence to show that his support of Norman Thomas in 1948 or his favorable comments about him in 1950 were a camouflage for secret Stalinism. I should add, however, that I do not associate myself with those who would regard Mrs. Trilling's criticism of Huebsch in 1993 as a piece of latter-day McCarthyism, since there was a good deal of Stalinist corruption in literary and academic life in the late forties that deserved to be attacked. But it is one thing to say that the sort of behavior Mrs. Trilling ascribes to Huebsch was common at the time and another to say that *he* engaged in it. I am sure he did not when I knew him.

This concludes my recollections and reflections on certain features of New York intellectual life in the late forties. They continued to affect me in my earliest years at Harvard, and I look back with sadness at manifestations of them in Ernest Nagel's criticism of my *Social Thought in America* and in Diana Trilling's maligning of Ben Huebsch. When I went to Harvard in 1948, I hoped that I would be escaping that sort of thing, and in great measure my hopes were fulfilled during my earliest years in Cambridge.

10

Entering the Harvard Department of Philosophy

In the second of my two years at the University of Pennsylvania, a plan to bring me to Harvard, like the plan to bring me to the University of Washington, was conceived by Henry Aiken soon after he had joined the Harvard department in 1946–47. We had been friends ever since we had met at Columbia, and I was greatly indebted to him for the encouragement he provided after the lukewarm support of my Columbia teachers and my disappointing experiences at Penn. Aiken was a protégé of the retired Harvard moral philosopher Ralph Barton Perry, who seems to have regarded him as his spiritual son. Perry, a widower when I met him in 1948, had been married to the sister of the art collector and critic Bernard Berenson, and Aiken, who was part Jewish, part Gentile, had many intellectual qualities that Perry might have hoped a child of his would have. Aiken was deeply interested in the philosophical questions with which Perry was most concerned, and he held views in ethics that were close to Perry's, so it was not surprising that Perry played a decisive part in bringing Aiken to Harvard as a permanent member of the Department of Philosophy.

Aiken began his campaign to bring me to Harvard by persuading his colleagues Quine and Donald Williams to support me. Quine may not have needed much persuasion, since I had done well in his course on mathematical logic in 1938 and in 1947 had agreed with him on several key philosophical issues. Williams, then chairman of the Harvard department, wrote to me in mid-October 1947, inviting me to give a paper to what was called the Philosophy Colloquium, and about a week later I came to Cambridge and delivered a quickly prepared version of the piece on the philosophy of history that I was about to publish in Marvin Farber's volume *Philosophic Thought in France and the United States*. When I arrived in Cambridge to give my talk and to be interviewed for a job, the air was its frigid, damp, raw New England self, and I was exhausted after several hours on the train from Philadelphia to Boston. In spite of that, it seemed wise to consult carefully with Aiken about what I was to say on the next day, so I spent a good part of the night going over the lecture with him to be sure that it would represent me to the department in the best possible light.

Anyone who reads the published version of that lecture and can remember the composition of the Harvard philosophy department in 1947 will see that the style and substance of my paper might have offended some of its members. It contained a fair amount of logical jargon by the standards of American philosophy in the late 1940s, and I feared that it would not be admired by Harvard philosophers like Raphael Demos and John Wild, or even by the more analytical C. I. Lewis. Lewis, although he had once been a distinguished logician, was not very hospitable to much use of symbolic logic in philosophy, and I thought that my logical machinery might have clanked too much for him; indeed it might have seemed especially incongruous in a paper on the philosophy of history, with all its evocations of Hegel and other majestic figures. Still, since the paper was the only one I could produce at the short notice I was given, I brought it with me and read it to the Philosophy Colloquium late in the afternoon of October 25. I can recall little of the discussion that followed, but I think that almost all members of the Harvard department participated, and I suppose that by the relevant standards it went well, since I was ultimately offered an appointment.

I was not allowed to go away immediately after I had read my paper. Partly out of a desire to show me hospitality and partly because they wished to find out more about me, the department members invited me to a dinner at the Faculty Club and then grilled—there is no other word—me for as long as they could. Since I was scheduled to leave Boston on a midnight sleeper, the department used the opportunity to examine me for what turned out to be a total of almost eight hours. After Aiken and Quine managed to detach me from their colleagues and to drive me to South Station, Quine, who had little love for those colleagues, suggested that it might be unwise to join such a department even if it should invite me. I confess that I was not as outraged by its performance as Quine was. Among all the questions asked during the evening, I can remember only one, which was raised by Lewis; and that was whether I thought there was some grand Hegel-like pattern in history. Aiken later said that that was Lewis's way of trying to find out whether I believed in God and that he was indirectly conducting a religious test. I believed that was an exaggeration, but I had no way of knowing whether it was.

Shortly after my lecture, Harvard offered me an assistant professorship at an annual salary of $4,500. In response to that offer, Pennsylvania offered me $5,000 and a promotion to an associate professorship with tenure; and therefore I was forced to choose between a permanency at Pennsylvania and the insecurity of an appointment at Harvard without tenure. In deciding to leave Penn, I reasoned that it would be good to leave a place where Lucia had been ill and where I had experienced such unpleasantness in my dealings with some colleagues. True, I would be leaving the intellectual stimulation and companionship that Goodman provided, but in exchange I was acquiring Quine as a colleague. Furthermore, Pennsylvania was not a first-rate university in the years 1946–48; it was a sleepy, defensive, economically down-in-the-mouth place. Of course, Philadelphia could boast of distinguished museums, of a famous symphony orchestra, of a few good restaurants, and of being only ninety minutes by rail from New York, but Harvard was Harvard, in those days still a place that scholars rarely turned down or left.

I think it fair to say that Lucia was vindicated when I was invited to Harvard. I can clearly remember having scoffed at such a possibility a few years earlier, saying that Harvard was not liberated enough to ask a complete outsider like me to come there; but she, the daughter of a Harvard alumnus, had a far rosier picture of it, and she insisted that it was a more liberal place than Columbia. When the invitation came, she seemed to be right; in fact, I think she *was* right, except for some grave doubts created in both of us by what happened there in the spring of 1969. At that time certain unpleasant features of the place—hidden or submerged in our happiest years there—manifested themselves in the lurid light that broke upon the Yard when President Pusey ordered his famous "bust" after University Hall had been occupied by students.

When I first came to Harvard, the permanent members of the Department of Philosophy were Clarence Irving Lewis, Henry M. Sheffer, Raphael Demos, Donald Cary Williams, John Wild, Willard Van Orman Quine, and Henry David Aiken. Sheffer had long since given up active research and was subject to severe emotional illness. He published very little but was still famous because Russell and Whitehead had said in the second edition of *Principia Mathematica* (1925) that the most definite improvement in logic since the first edition of 1910 was due to Sheffer. He continued to teach his own brand of advanced logic course, using, I was told, an idiosyncratic notation and fulminating against logicians he called "marksians," that is to say, those who approached the subject too formalistically. In any case, the subject of logic had long since left him behind, and he was in many ways a pathetic figure. He was an extremely sweet man, and very generous to me when I came there. He would often invite me out to lunch, usually at the Howard Johnson's that was then in Harvard Square, and reminisce charmingly about Royce, James, Santayana, and his friend Morris Cohen. Sheffer was a notorious punster. Harry, as he was called, probably produced his greatest pun when the U.S. Department of Agriculture wrote to the Harvard Department of Philosophy, asking that it recommend some philosophers for employment. When Harry heard of this, he snapped: "That's putting Descartes before the horse!" Demos once reported another of Sheffer's unforgettable puns to me. Upon entering a staff room in Emerson Hall many years earlier, while the philosophers Harry Wolfson, Horace Kallen, and Sheffer were talking with each other, Demos exclaimed: "Ah! three lights." To which Harry Sheffer responded immediately: "Yes, three Israelites."

In my first year at Harvard, poor Sheffer collapsed and was unable to teach his classes. They were taken over by his former pupil Paul Henle, who was visiting Cambridge from his post at the University of Michigan while on a Guggenheim fellowship. Henle loyally taught Sheffer's classes and graded the blue books. Henry Aiken was also very fond of Sheffer and would go to his room in the old Ambassador Hotel just sit there with the poor man while he sat with his face to a wall and groaned loudly. I vividly remember this groaning on a day when I went to lunch with Sheffer and Lewis while Sheffer was ill. Lewis, who was familiar with the ways of his almost lifelong friend, paid no attention to Sheffer's peculiar noises throughout the meal and kept up a conversation with me alone. It was clear to Lewis that Sheffer wanted merely to *be* with people and not talk with them during these episodes, but I did not know that and tried unsuccessfully to make conversation with Sheffer. Soon I got the point and tried to disregard him, except for an occasional furtive glance at the painful spectacle he presented.

Lewis, a very different sort of person, was about sixty-five when I came to Harvard. He was at that time the most famous philosopher in the department and had published his Carus Lectures, *An Analysis of Knowledge and Valuation*, two years before, in 1946. He was a tall, spare, dignified New Englander who sometimes used a pince-nez; he was therefore dour in appearance but capable of a charming smile and even a loud chuckle at times. I learned quickly that Lewis was very different from G. E. Moore, although I had naively supposed that they would be more like each other because of the similarity of some of their philosophical views. Unlike Moore, Lewis was unwilling to converse straightforwardly about philosophical matters. I remember trying to discuss some points in his Carus Lectures with him, but instead of being able to engage him in the kind of lively discussion I used to have with Moore in New York, I met with a frosty response. On the other hand, Lewis would almost always respond in a clear way in letters to me about reprints that I sent him. He was often frank and decisive in these letters, very different from what he was in his published writings or in his conversation. In spite of disagreeing with him on several questions of philosophy, I thought he was a distinguished and impressive figure.

I disagreed with Lewis on two fundamental questions in ways that I discussed in two of my earliest papers: "The Analytic and the Synthetic: An Untenable Dualism" (1950) and "Value and Obligation in Dewey and Lewis" (1949), two papers that I had no hesitation in publishing while I was Lewis's junior colleague at Harvard. My feeling free to do this illustrated one of the more refreshing things about Harvard in contrast to Columbia. A junior colleague who challenged a senior colleague at Columbia or who challenged the reigning ideas in the Department of Philosophy would take his professional life in his hands, but this was certainly not the case at Harvard in 1948. Perhaps the tradition of James, Royce, and Santayana, with its encouragement of philosophical disagreement, explains this; I don't know. But the fact is that I was not afraid to challenge Lewis and felt to some extent encouraged to do so. I thought it ironical that the Columbia Department of Philosophy was supposed to be *the* liberal department in the country, whereas the Harvard department was the home of two likely Republicans, Lewis and Williams, and of Quine, who was, rightly or wrongly, thought by some to be a fellow traveler of the Republicans.

My disagreement with Lewis on the analytic and the synthetic concerned his view that the analyticity of a statement like "All squares are rectangles" depends on whether the criterion you have in mind when you say that something is a square *includes* the criterion you have in mind when you say that it is a rectangle. Lewis held that the answer to the question "Does your schematism for determining application of the term 'square' include your schematism for applying 'rectangle'?" is determined in the same general fashion as is the answer to the question "Does your plan of a trip to Chicago to see the Field Museum include the plan of visiting Niagara to see the falls?" According to Lewis, one either sees the inclusion of plans and therefore of criteria in mind, or one does not, and that is the end of the matter. In my view at the time, such an appeal to intuition was not satisfactory; I was eager, as Quine was, to find a criterion for analyticity that was clearer and therefore more useful in settling debates about whether one concept includes another. But while I was not altogether happy with Lewis's approach to analyticity, I praised his approach to the problem in my paper by contrasting it with the approach of certain logical positivists, saying that unlike them he recognized the need to clarify the notion of analytic in a natural language as opposed to a constructed, artificial language. I also criticized two views that had frequently appeared in the literature of logical positivism. According to one, analytic statements such as "All men are animals" are those whose denials are self-contradictory; according to another, attributing analyticity to "All men are animals" amounts to saying that if we were presented with something that wasn't an animal, we would not call it a man. After criticizing these views for various reasons, I went on to say that I believed, with Quine and Goodman, that the difference between an analytic statement and a synthetic statement was one of degree rather than of kind, and that this view was consonant with the kind of gradualism to be found in some of Dewey's writings. My basic concern, which I did not fully express in the paper, was to show that if analysis is a fundamental task of philosophy and if the result of an analysis is expressed in an analytic statement, then a philosophical statement is re-moved only in degree from a scientific generalization. This would be true, for example, if one measured the degree of a statement's analyticity by determin-ing how reluctant one would be to surrender the statement.

Since I want to communicate the flavor of my relationship with some of my Harvard colleagues, I want now to quote the whole of a curious note Lewis sent me soon after I had presented him with a copy of my paper on the analytic and the synthetic. He wrote: "I have just glanced through your discussion of analytic and synthetic and have an equally superficial and corrigible reaction: namely, I agree with you that the answers to the questions concerning this distinction depend on the meanings assigned to 'analytic' and 'synthetic.'"

This was Lewis at his frostiest, but he could behave differently. In my paper "Value and Obligation in Dewey and Lewis," I pointed out that Lewis held that what is right and ought to be done does not depend on empirical knowledge alone, but that since he sharply divided all truths into empirical and analytic statements, he seemed forced to hold the strange view that the statement "It was right of Brutus to stab Caesar" must be analytic, true by virtue of the meanings of its terms. I never received any comment about this from Lewis, but when I made essentially the same point almost fifteen years later in an essay entitled "Pragmatism and the Scope of Science," Lewis wrote to me in 1963, after his retirement:

> As you know, I am a most dis-agree-able person, but I find that I fully agree with everything you have said about pragmatism; including [your] observation of my present predicament with respect to ethics. I am hoping that my waning energies are going to allow me to finish a book which will accomplish a little on that point. If you should reread Dewey's "Supplementary Essay" (8 pages) to Morris Cohen's collation [of Charles Peirce's essays] *Chance, Love, and Logic*, I think you might guess a little the drift of that. (Emphasis on pp. 302–04). I have always misdoubted any claim I could make to be classed as a pragmatist but think I have followed out some of Peirce's most basic thoughts.

Leaving aside the unpredictable Sheffer, the department was in 1948 divided into three factions. At one extreme, Quine, Aiken, and I were empiricist, agnostic or atheistic, and relativist in outlook. At the other, Demos and Wild were religious, metaphysical, and traditional. In between were Lewis and Williams, who feared that Quine, Aiken, and I would, if we had our way, fill the department with positivists. This was ironical in light of the fact that Quine and I had sharply criticized logical positivism, whereas Lewis and Williams, in spite of their negative attitude toward Carnap—the foremost representative of logical positivism—shared his fundamental views on the analytic and the synthetic. Lewis once told me that he thought the positivistic Vienna Circle was "a bunch of phonies," and, like Williams, seemed disturbed by their doctrines and by the fact that they were foreigners. Lewis was torn between his pragmatic theory of knowledge and his absolutistic ethics, and at times I felt that he did not want the department to be taken over by foreign phonies or their American followers, who, he feared, might raze the temple of moral philosophy and replace it with something alien that he abhorred. The fears shared by Lewis and Williams may explain why they often supported the appointment of second-rate devotees of traditional philosophy. It may also explain why Lewis did not look with favor on the appointment of Goodman, his most distinguished pupil and an expert in applying logic to philosophical problems. And it certainly explains some of

Williams's xenophobic outpourings, for example, the following one published in 1950:

> During the last century, an immense immigration from Catholic Europe, steeped in an ancient and authoritarian ideology fundamentally hostile to Puritanism, science, and capitalism, built a broad popular basis for the cult of improvidence. During the last fifteen years, thousands of able and assertive refugees, thinkers and teachers fleeing from tyranny or poverty in Europe, have discoursed a babel of unsympathetic doctrine such as no nation ever had to accommodate before. Meantime, the bohemian intellectuals, rootless writers and talkers of whatever origin, congregated in the big cities and universities, have cultivated a precious disdain for the common intellectual life which Franklin, Jefferson, Emerson, and Mark Twain were content to share and celebrate.

One of the most conspicuous features of the department was its psychological instability. Perhaps this is endemic to departments of philosophy, but the one I belonged to at Harvard in 1948 had more than its share of fickleness and lunacy. I have mentioned Sheffer's emotional troubles, but there was also Aiken, who, though shrewd and sensitive, was absolutely unpredictable at times, just as Wild and Williams were. This unpredictability was much on my mind after I entered the department and contemplated my prospects there. I felt confident of the support of Aiken, Sheffer, and Quine, and I hoped that it would continue. But what about the others? I knew that the one other assistant professor in the department had been appointed as a doctrinal counterweight to me at the junior level, and in spite of assurances that there were permanencies waiting for both of us if we made the grade, I doubted whether I could get anyone besides Aiken, Quine, and Sheffer to support me, given the philosophical prejudices of their colleagues.

In my first year at Harvard two things happened that seriously affected the outcome of whatever competition might have been in the offing. One of them was the divorce of my rival at the junior level. It occurred in 1948 before our first year of teaching at Harvard began, and it did not sit well with Williams the agnostic Puritan, with the more religious Demos and Wild, or with Lewis the strict moralist. I am sure that it seriously hurt my rival's chances with them, though it may have led Aiken and Quine, themselves divorcés, to sympathize with him even though they were in sharp philosophical disagreement with him. The other event that more seriously influenced the outcome of the competition was my having received an offer from

Michigan State University during the spring of 1949; I was asked to come there as head of the department.

This offer had been precipitated by recommendations of me by the philosophers Paul Henle and William Frankena, who were both visiting Harvard on research fellowships in 1948–49. Frankena was then a member of the University of Michigan department (not to be confused with the department that made me my offer); and Henle was at Northwestern, having gone there from the University of Michigan, to which he was to return later. Frankena and Henle had considerable influence at Michigan State, which made me a very generous offer. My salary was to go far beyond what I was earning at Harvard, and I was asked to become a czarlike chairman of the department. The dean at Michigan State, however, was a crusty, tough old man to whom I took an immediate dislike. I recall his pointing out with pleasure that there would be no blacks living in or near the university community and telling me that I would have the power to fire a number of members of that department—power that I did not relish. I also recall his unnerving statement that he would not make his offer in writing, because young academics from the East had a way of taking such letters to their deans and using them merely as devices for getting themselves promotions.

His statement had an effect that was the opposite of what he had intended. As soon as he made it, I could contemplate nothing but using his offer as a way of bettering myself at Harvard. I had published a respectable amount for my age, and I thought that I deserved tenure at Harvard, if only because I had served two years as an assistant professor at Penn and had been offered tenure there when I had been invited to Harvard. All of this, plus Lucia's small inheritance—which served to make us feel independent to a degree beyond what its amount really justified—led me to take a gamble. I candidly informed my chairman—Williams—that I had had an oral offer that I was prepared to accept if Harvard did not meet it. Of course, I was going out on a limb in saying that I would go to Michigan State if Harvard did not come through with a promotion to tenured rank, for what would I do if Harvard did nothing and the monster dean reneged? Fortunately, the department re-sponded by recommending to Harvard's provost Paul Buck that I be pro-moted, provided that this would not prejudice my rival's chances when the time came to consider him three years hence. Lewis, I was told, insisted on this proviso.

The next step was for the provost to recommend the promotion and to lay his recommendation before an ad hoc committee appointed by President Conant, a committee usually composed of members of the Harvard faculty who were not members of the department making the recommendation and of outsiders who were in the field of the candidate or close to it. Although I was not supposed to know about the composition or the deliberations of this committee, I did learn who was on it and did hear about some of its deliberations. If my memory serves me, some of the inside people were the philosophically minded physicist P. W. Bridgman, the historian of ideas Crane Brinton, I. A. Richards (the co-author with C. K. Ogden of *The Meaning of Meaning*), and C. I. Lewis. Lewis's presence constituted an exception to the rule that members of the recommending department not serve on an ad hoc committee. Stephen Pepper, the Berkeley philosopher, was also one of the outside people; and another was Isaiah Berlin, who was visiting Harvard from Oxford as a lecturer in Slavic studies.

The committee voted favorably on my nomination. I think I was helped by the breadth of my interests and the speed with which I had made friends outside of my department, especially among people in American history, like the two Arthur Schlesingers—Sr. and Jr.—and Perry Miller. I had already published a chapter of my *Social Thought in America* in the *Journal of the History of Ideas,* and that paper, I knew, had pleased the Schlesingers and Miller. I had come to know the elder Schlesinger and Miller personally when I occasionally examined for the interdepartmental Committee on American Civilization. (I was later to become a member of that committee.) Young Arthur Schlesinger and Perry became good friends of mine early in my stay at Harvard, and since they were very well known in Cambridge, they introduced me to a number of people whom a new assistant professor would otherwise not likely have met that soon.

By the middle of the winter, Lucia and I were being invited out a good deal, and in a short time we came to have a wide circle of acquaintances. I can clearly remember a dinner party at the house of Jack Sawyer—then a junior fellow, later president of Williams College and of the Mellon Foundation—where I sat next to some faculty wife who said to me: "What's this I hear about your leaving Harvard? I must talk to Paul Buck and see to it that he does something about that." Elder statesmen like the retired Ralph Barton Perry and Kenneth Murdock, then chairman of the Committee on American Civilization, were both cordial to me. And because the Department of Philosophy was then very isolated in the university—for good and bad reasons—my interest in American thought, my publication, and my quickly formed friendships earned me a reputation beyond what I deserved, and being liked by Isaiah Berlin did not hurt, to put it mildly. Unlike most of the members of my department, I had an interest in history, literature, and politics. I was also known for my contributions to nonscholarly periodicals such as the *Nation*, the *Kenyon Review*, and the *Partisan Review*. Rightly or wrongly, all of this played a part in my early success at Harvard, although it had gotten me nowhere at Columbia. I doubt whether I was a prophet at Harvard, but I certainly was without much honor in my home town.

In addition to making many friends outside of the Department of Philosophy in my first year at Harvard, I got to know some of the brighter students who have since attained distinction. Burton Dreben, while a senior in Harvard College, and the historian Cushing Strout, then a graduate student, attended my seminar on the philosophy of history, which was audited by Jack Sawyer and by the historian Bernard Bailyn. I got to know Hao Wang, the distinguished logician who was then also a junior fellow, and at one point planned a monograph with him on the problem of a priori knowledge, a monograph that never got beyond the earliest stages of planning. I taught lecture courses on American philosophy, the philosophy of social science, and nineteenth-century empiricism, which last course consisted of a commentary on Mill's *Logic*. I tutored Thompson Clarke, later a professor at Berkeley, and had as a student in my classes my future colleague Hilary Putnam, who had come to Harvard in 1948 as a graduate student after receiving his bachelor's degree at Pennsylvania that year. I appointed Putnam the paper reader in my course on American philosophy.

At first I did not try to play a prominent role in the teaching offered by the department. If I had tried, I would not have had much success, because Lewis commanded epistemology, Quine and Sheffer took charge of logic, Aiken was the master of ethics, and Williams and Wild divided the field of metaphysics. Of course, I might have set up shop as a philosopher of science, but for a variety of reasons I drew back from that. Teaching physics during the war did not lead to my becoming seriously interested in physics, perhaps because I never got beyond teaching its elements, and therefore I came to think that any work of mine in the philosophy of science would suffer from my ignorance of advanced physics. However, I thought my powers as a historian of ideas and as a philosopher of history might lead to a contribution that would be more memorable and of more general interest than anything I would ever do in the philosophy of physical science. Therefore I decided to lecture on the philosophy of history, which most of my philosophical colleagues regarded as a very peripheral discipline indeed, and to do research in the history of American ideas, a subject in which most of my colleagues had no interest at all.

In spite of my peripheral junior position in the department, I am sure that

I was regarded as too aggressive by some of my colleagues, since I was forthright in meetings and did not hesitate to express my opinions at a time when senior professors were not giving their juniors much of a say and the administration was urging departments to abandon this tradition. The senior members of my department went to the other extreme by allowing assistant professors to participate even in the discussion of tenure appointments, a step that was well beyond what the administration required. I recall that my fellow junior colleague and I took part in a discussion about whether Rudolf Carnap should be appointed to the department, though, I later discovered, our votes were not taken into account by the administration. That discussion issued in a favorable vote just before my Michigan State offer came, with the result that Carnap's name and mine were both submitted to the ad hoc committee of which I have already spoken. One of my more vivid memories was the firm opposition of Lewis to Carnap, but Lewis was voted down in a departmental meeting. Such defeats were partly responsible for his feeling that the younger wing of the department—Aiken, Quine, and I—were ganging up and forming a dangerous clique.

Although I was certainly regarded as pushy, I had the distinct feeling that my candor in department meetings was also earning me some good marks from my colleagues. I feared their fickleness, but by winter a majority of them surmounted whatever prejudices they might have had concerning me and recommended me for promotion. I was never told exactly how people voted, but I believe that Aiken, Quine, Williams, and Sheffer were all strongly for me. I suspect that Lewis went along, but with less than enthusiasm; and although I think that Wild liked me, he and Demos must have been far less receptive to my philosophical credentials than Lewis was. All of this is speculation, but I would not be surprised if, once a majority voted for me, the department closed ranks and made a unanimous recommendation to the administration and its ad hoc committee.

Immediately after the meeting of the committee, Lucia and I ran into Isaiah Berlin in Harvard Square, and he was good enough to say "You're in" as soon as we met. When we all repaired to Schrafft's Restaurant in Brattle Square, Berlin treated us to one of his machine-gun accounts of what had taken place. He told me that the committee had rejected Carnap, which made me feel very embarrassed after hearing that they had accepted me; after all, Carnap was a world-famous philosopher, and I was nobody. It seems that only Isaiah and Richards voted for him. Lewis, I surmised, had probably led the charge to torpedo Carnap, but Carnap was so distinguished a philosopher that I thought it was a great mistake.

It seems that I got by the ad hoc committee in spite of one dangerous moment that was hilariously described by Isaiah. He told me that President Conant, who chaired the meeting, had informed the group that Ralph Barton Perry had once said to him that you could not tell whether a man was going to be a good philosopher until he was more than thirty-two years old, and at the time, I may have been a bit short of that. Discussion of this bit of numerology was proceeding seriously over sherry at the president's house, Isaiah said, when a maid came in to announce that luncheon was served. At that point the discussion broke up for the meal, but when the committee reconvened for business afterward, the objection did not count against my promotion, though it did seem to affect the time of my promotion. I was told soon afterward by the administration that I was to be promoted to the rank of associate professor with tenure, to take office not in the approaching year, 1949–50, but in the year following, 1950–51, by which time I would certainly be thirty-three years old! When this word came to me, I broke off my negotiations with Michigan State and prepared myself to remain at Harvard until my retirement.

About a year later, on January 7, 1950, almost a year after my promotion had been approved, I wrote to Isaiah Berlin in reply to a letter in which he had asked about the department's progress toward nominating a philosopher in place of the rejected Carnap, since Conant was consulting members of the ad hoc committee by mail on this question and Isaiah was confidentially seeking my opinion on it. In my letter to him I wrote: "Here is the situation. Quine, Aiken, and I continued our struggle in behalf of Goodman until the very last moment, until it seemed absolutely hopeless. The rest, led by Lewis, were obdurate in their opposition." I went on to say that part of the reason for this "was a real fear lest Q., myself, and G. (Aiken to a lesser degree because of his not being interested in logic) would overwhelm the department with our interest in technical matters, our empiricism, and our free-thinking. (I almost said 'free drinking.' Although Goodman is a teetotaller, Williams in one of his irresponsible moods said that he was opposing G. because he didn't want to add to the 'cocktail set' of Q., A. and myself!!) I sincerely believe this loses us the opportunity of getting one of the most original minds in American philosophy at the moment. But I really think it would be almost impossible to get him over Lewis' adamant opposition."

My offer from Michigan State was not the last such offer to play a part in my career at Harvard. On February 24, 1950, I received a letter from Paul Henle—the same Paul Henle who had so much to do with bringing about the offer to me from Michigan State—informing me that he was about to recommend me for the chairmanship of the Department of Philosophy at Northwestern University, since he was leaving that post to return to the University of Michigan. Soon I received an invitation from Northwestern, which I took seriously but finally declined after speaking with Provost Paul Buck. On April 5, 1950, after talking with me about my future at Harvard, he wrote me that beginning July 1, 1950, my salary would be $7,000 per annum; that beginning July 1, 1951, it would be advanced to $7,500 per annum, then the maximum salary in the associate professor rank; that sometime during the year 1953–54 the matter of my promotion to a full professorship would be considered; and that if I continued to do work of distinction, I would be recommended to the governing boards for promotion as of July 1, 1954. Then, on the basis of our earlier talk, he said that he was happy that with the assurances given in his letter, I would remain at Harvard.

During my earliest years at Harvard I had received much encouragement and support from Buck, who, as an American historian, was especially interested in my work in American intellectual history. Most likely he had received laudatory reports about me from his friends Perry Miller and the two Schlesingers, so on more than one count he was well disposed to the idea of pushing me up the academic ladder. In those days he was a very vigorous administrator who favored the idea of encouraging younger scholars at Harvard, even at the expense of antagonizing those who felt that age and seniority were to be given great weight. Once a man was a permanent member, Buck had virtually complete power over his salary and rank and was free to decide, without consulting the man's department or his chairman, whether to push him or hold him back. The chairman of a department was not much more than a secretary. He lacked power to promote or to recommend raises even though he was the budgetary officer of his department. From the dean he would get a list of salaries of permanent members as fixed by the dean, and he was sworn to keep this secret from the other members. In McGeorge Bundy's time as dean this tendency became even more pronounced because Bundy tried to keep even the chairman ignorant of what other permanent members earned. Bundy replaced names by numbers in the section of the budget devoted to permanent members' salaries, but he may not have realized that secretaries like our dear Ruth Allen knew all our numbers and would pass her knowledge on to the chairman. I always had doubts about the wisdom of giving so much power to the dean, but I was certainly the beneficiary of it in Buck's time. He did everything in his power to encourage me, to the point of creating consternation in some of my colleagues and sometimes embarrassing me.

The most conspicuous example of this was the occasion on which he promoted me to the rank of full professor ahead of my colleague and patron Aiken. In Buck's letter to me of April 5, 1950, he had written that my promotion to a full professorship would be considered in 1953–54, but I had not extracted that statement as a condition of my declining the Northwestern offer and I had not produced any other offer that prompted his recommendation in 1952–53 that I be made a full professor. Yet Buck called me in one day in the fall of 1952 to tell me that he was about to recommend my appointment to a full professorship to begin in the coming year, 1953–54, when I was to be a visiting member at the Institute for Advanced Study. I don't know what prompted this decision, perhaps some idea that the Institute would make me an offer. In response I said that I was honored but that I was deeply concerned about whether my colleague Aiken was to be promoted to a full professorship, and that I hoped he would be, since I would be very embarrassed and pained to jump over him. Buck said that his treatment of Aiken was none of my business, and that in his opinion I deserved a promotion but that Aiken did not, particularly since I had by then published two books, *The Origin of Dewey's Instrumentalism* and *Social Thought in America*, whereas Aiken had published none. When I pointed out that Aiken had published many articles and was a very popular teacher, Buck spoke as though the articles were not enough—a really absurd point of view, and one that was no longer controlling in later years—and as though Aiken's teaching, for all of its popularity, was of little import. After a while I ran out of things to say and left his office with mixed feelings. I was pleased to be promoted but dreaded the prospect of facing Henry after he had received the news of my promotion. On Saturday, January 17, the *Crimson* announced the news, and on Monday, January 19, I received a touching letter from Henry:

> I want to offer you my sincerest congratulations on your promotion to a Professorship. *No one* in American philosophy could deserve it more. Your development as a philosopher is a source of never-ending delight and gratification to me.
>
> I want you to believe that I mean this with all my heart. The friendship which you and Lu have given me is one of the things I most cherish in my life. If, by *any* chance, some malicious person should indicate the contrary, in view of subsequent events, reread this letter, and let it be a token that such gossip is false as hell.
>
> Ever yours,
> HDA

I never knew what "subsequent events" Henry had in mind; but I was told later that he had been terribly upset, and maybe he had told some people on the intervening weekend that he was going to resign. In any case he did not resign then, though he did several years later, after a history of up-and-down relationships with Harvard. When I received his letter, I felt great admiration for him and great sadness about the whole business. I wished that I had been able to persuade Buck not to do what he had done. Should I have declined to accept the promotion until such time as Henry received one? But Buck spoke as though this might never happen, and indicated that the time of Henry's promotion—if it were ever to come—was none of my business. Fortunately, however, Buck's successor as dean—McGeorge Bundy—recommended Aiken's promotion in the following academic year, 1953–54. Henry wrote me while I was in Princeton: "I was, of course, very gratified by the Dean's call the day before Christmas. It was very gracious of him to let me know in this way. It still has to go through the governing boards, but I suppose there isn't much likelihood of it being held up there. The appointment won't be announced, I gather, until early spring. Via the grapevine I hear that some of the younger historians are also to be promoted, Arthur and Oscar among them." The "Arthur" and "Oscar" referred to were Arthur Schlesinger Jr. and Oscar Handlin, both of whom went up to full professorships at the same time as Henry. In the same letter, Henry told me that my appointment as chairman of the Department of Philosophy had been announced the previous week on the floor of the faculty.

By the end of five years at Harvard, then, I had moved from assistant professor to professor and chairman, but I was hardly under the illusion that this was evidence of greatness. A chairman at Harvard, as I have said, was little more than a glorified secretary, and the fact that I came to be chairman at a relatively young age was more of a reflection on some of my older colleagues than it was a recognition of any great talents of mine for leadership. Nor was becoming a full professor at thirty-six a measure of my intellectual distinction when one thinks of the majority of my colleagues. I was quite aware that I had come to the department at a relatively low point in its history and that my scholarly candlepower may have seemed large only because of the dimness of some of my colleagues. Nevertheless, I felt in my early years at Harvard that my department was being subjected to unfair criticism by those who compared it invidiously with the department to which some of its great members of the past had belonged. I gave vent to some of these feelings and thoughts in an article I was asked to write for the *Harvard Alumni Bulletin* that was called "Harvard's Philosophical Heritage."

I began my article by pointing out that because Harvard philosophy, like that of Cambridge and Oxford, was becoming more analytic in tendency, aged students of Royce, James, and Santayana, and many scholars in other fields complained that the department of my day lacked the wisdom and the literary distinction of the department at the turn of the twentieth century. However, I went on, it would be a mistake to suppose that Harvard philosophers in the middle of the twentieth century had completely abandoned the traditional interests and humane concerns of Royce, James, and Santayana. And, I continued, if they did not show this by writing big fat books, that was partly because the philosophical article had become a more common means of scholarly communication, much as it was then in science and mathematics. This deflationary tendency, I pointed out, was a feature of midcentury British and American philosophy, and it represented a far cry from the writing habits of Royce, who, when he was once asked to write an article, replied that he could not do so, because he was "doing his thinking in book lengths." I also suggested that maybe the worries of the rest of the scholarly world about its own abandonment of the literary blockbuster as a means of communication had ironically led it to resent the philosopher's abandonment of a practice that it itself had been compelled to abandon.

Then I shifted my attention to the view that latter-day philosophers, unlike those of the golden age, were too preoccupied with technical questions. The effort to distinguish between both generations in this way was a mistake, I said, prompted perhaps by the fact that alumni remembered the old pundits only from their popular lectures and their more popular books and so did not realize that they too were much concerned with technical questions. They were not Sunday supplement scholars, I went on, but serious thinkers who worked on difficult problems of logic and metaphysics that had baffled their predecessors from Plato to Hegel. Royce, I pointed out, had encouraged Lewis and Sheffer to work in logic, and the pragmatism of Peirce and James encouraged reflection on the procedures of the natural sciences. The logical and pragmatic tradition of Harvard combined with the positivism of Vienna and the analytic tradition of Cambridge, England, to turn the attention of a younger generation toward a tighter, more scientifically oriented, less monumental conception of philosophy. But, I said, this did not mean that everyone in the Harvard department of my time was a logician or a pragmatist. Like the earlier department, we valued doctrinal diversity, and even those of us who were not logicians or pragmatists believed that the main instrument of philosophy was careful reasoning and therefore tried to avoid irrationalism and obscurantism.

I concluded my essay in a way that clearly reflected a tension in my own thinking. On the one hand I admired Quine's work in semantics and his use of logic in philosophy, but on the other I was a historian of ideas and a philosopher of history who did not agree with Quine's statement that philosophy of science was philosophy enough. That is why I ended my essay by dissociating myself from philosophers who conceived their subject so narrowly as to rule out the study of several other questions. And, with the growing interest in the work of the later Wittgenstein in mind, I said that a broader view of philosophy was developing within the very tradition that had once made so much of the logical analysis of science. I wound up by writing:

> Instead of maintaining, as some positivists have, that the only type of language worth studying philosophically is the language of science, a number of philosophers have come to believe that there are many important uses of language which are not scientific and which may be studied with profit. This view is becoming more and more popular among the youngest generation of American philosophers and it may turn out to be the medium whereby philosophy will regain close contact with the humanistic tradition. For once it is recognized that the problem of knowledge is not the only problem in philosophy; once it is recognized that there are other modes of human activity which demand philosophical analysis and description, philosophy will cease to be equated with logic and the theory of perception. They will undoubtedly continue to be central subjects and no philosopher will risk the study of any other subject without a firm grasp of their fundamentals, but they will cease to constitute the essence of the discipline as they do for so many today. Esthetics, the philosophy of education, the philosophy of history, and philosophy of religion, political philosophy, and jurisprudence will flourish as serious philosophical concerns and not be regarded as "soft subjects," fit only for lesser minds. When this happens on a larger scale in American philosophy, we shall have witnessed a new chapter in the development of the subject.

11

W. V. Quine

Teacher, Colleague, and Friend

Although my interests in the philosophy of history, the history of ideas, and other humanistic subjects were far removed from those of Quine, and although I disagreed with his well-known remark that philosophy of science was philosophy enough, he had other interests and views that I applauded, and he certainly was the Harvard philosopher I respected most. I had known him longer than I had known any of the others, having first met him in the summer of 1938, when I took his course on mathematical logic at Harvard while still a graduate student at Columbia. It was an exciting and instructive experience, but I was forced to drop the class just before the end of the session because my money had run out and I had to leave Cambridge. I find in my files a hand-transcribed copy of a letter dated August 8, 1940, from Quine to Y. H. Krikorian, then chairman of the Department of Philosophy at the College of the City of New York, in which Quine recommended me for a job there. He wrote: "In the course he did brilliant work—the best of all the fourteen students, indeed, even though there were several exceptionally able and well-trained men among them. Outside circumstances compelled him to drop out shortly before the end of the course, but he was clearly headed for an A+."

On October 31, 1940, I wrote to thank Quine for writing his letter and to ask him for yet another letter of recommendation, this time to Queens College in New York. I also told him that I had asked the *Philosophical Review* to let me review his *Mathematical Logic* for it, and that the editors had informed me that they had not received a copy of the book. After expressing his hearty congratulations to me on my marriage to Lucia in late August, Quine replied that he would write to Queens and that his publisher had, at his urging, finally sent a review copy to the *Philosophical Review*. I soon got hold of the book and published a very favorable notice of it.

I am sure that Quine and I were in touch with each other between 1940 and 1945, but I find no letters between us dated earlier than May 4, 1945, when I wrote him a long philosophical screed that raised a question that was once again broached in the correspondence between Quine, Goodman, and me in 1947. My letter had to do with the paradox of analysis as propounded by C. H. Langford in his paper in *The Philosophy of G. E. Moore*. The paradox begins by assuming the correctness of an analysis expressed, for example, by the statement (1) "The attribute of being a brother is identical with the attribute of being a male sibling." Since this statement is assumed to be true, we may replace the expression "the attribute of being a male sibling" in it by the expression "the attribute of being a brother" without changing the meaning of (1), in which case (1) would have to be regarded as saying the same thing as the trivial statement (2) "The attribute of being a brother is identical with the attribute of being a brother." The question, then, is whether we can analyze the notion of identity of attributes in a way that would eliminate the paradox.

In his reply to my letter of May 4, Quine considered the possibility that we might give an adequate analysis of what it is for two attributes to be identical by defining what Carnap had called the conceptual equivalence of the expressions "brother" and "male sibling," and yet not be able to dispel the paradox of analysis. Quine wrote to me on May 7:

> I don't know that defining identity of attributes on the basis of conceptual equivalence would dispel the paradox of analysis; maybe the "brother" and "male sibling" of your example *are* conceptually equivalent in Carnap's sense (and in a sense adequate to purposes of indirect discourse, translation, etc.). If so, maybe we have to resort to psychological considerations and say "Yes, 'A brother is a male sibling' *is* trivial and equivalent to 'A brother is a brother,' and even psychologically trivial for one who understands all three terms, but it can be informative, as revealing a definition, for one who understands 'male' and

'sibling' but not (God what a dumb cluck) 'brother'." But I recognize that in throwing out these vague remarks I haven't come to grips with the problem. I'm interested in seeing what further you do with it.

I mention this letter of Quine's not only because of its interesting philosophical remarks but also because of the encouragement he gave me when he said: "It was good to hear from you. And pleasant to be asked questions which, despite belonging to the most disputatious reaches of semantics, are not such that I have to preface my answers in the fashion 'I must first make certain distinctions. If you mean by etc. etc.' to a length double that of the questioning letter. So pleasant that I am sitting down immediately to pound out my answers."

Soon after Quine finished pounding out his answers to me, I began in the fall of 1946 to teach at the University of Pennsylvania. And soon after that, Nelson Goodman and I teamed up in an effort to bring Quine to Penn, but to no avail. On April 2, 1947, Quine wrote me that Harvard had responded by offering him what he called "a bright financial future"; and he added: "I'm very grateful to you, as to Nelson, for your valiant efforts in my behalf." On May 25, 1947, I sent to Quine from Philadelphia the manuscript of a note I later published in *Philosophy and Phenomenological Research* under the title "On the Church-Frege Solution of the Paradox of Analysis"; it dealt with an aspect of the problem I had corresponded with Quine about earlier. Quine replied on June 3, making reference to something I had attributed to Goodman in my note, so I sent my note to Goodman, along with Quine's letter of June 3 and a reply to it that I had written on June 5. On June 8 Goodman formed a triangle by sending a letter to Quine and me, and our correspondence, reprinted in an appendix, continued until July 8. I was encouraged to think of writing a paper like "The Analytic and the Synthetic" by a remark Goodman made on July 5 about my letter of July 3: "Morty's letter convinces me more strongly than ever that he is the man to do a survey article on the whole problem. If Van feels the same way, perhaps he will help me urge it." On July 7, Quine wrote: "I think it would be a swell idea to talk Morty into doing a survey article on all this."

Although Goodman and Quine helped stimulate the writing of my paper on the analytic and the synthetic, part of what I said there had been developing in my mind for a few years under the influence of Dewey and Tarski, as I have indicated earlier. In my paper I did not concentrate on formal logical statements of the kind that Tarski discussed in his letter to me in 1944 but rather on statements like "Every man is an animal," which have traditionally been called essential predications. However, I was influenced by the view on formal logical truths outlined by Tarski and by the gradualistic writings of Dewey, and therefore was drawn to the idea that there is no fundamental difference between the way in which we support essential predications and those of natural science. Tarski wrote me after the appearance of my paper in the volume honoring Dewey on his ninetieth birthday: "I read your article in the book on Dewey with real interest and found once more that your and Van's [Quine's] views on the problem of the analytic and the synthetic are very close to my own." I found this reassuring, since I had acknowledged my gratitude to Tarski in that paper. One of its chief concerns was a problem discussed at length in my correspondence with Goodman and Quine—that of providing a criterion for synonymy. We talked at length about the view of some philosophers that "man" is synonymous with "rational animal" but *not* synonymous with "featherless biped" even though the latter denotes the same class of individuals as "man" denotes. Although all of us agreed that no such criterion was available, Quine and I may have been more inclined than Goodman to say that we could understand the expression "is synonymous with" well enough to seek a criterion for it. Goodman was not so inclined, for reasons that he gave in some detail.

In the spring of 1948, after I had been appointed to an assistant professorship at Harvard, I wrote to Quine:

> Forgive me for waiting so long, but I do want you to know how much I appreciate your help in connection with the recent appointment at Harvard. Thanks for your support and for your help on that fateful day when I came up to read my paper (prepared in 5 days, incidentally, for that was about the notice I got) in Cambridge. I shall never forget our little interlude . . . at your apartment, especially my imploring you and Henry to stop plying me with liquor if you wanted me to be coherent at the dinner-table! Thanks for *complying*.
>
> Little did I dream, as the saying goes, in the summer of 1938 when I took your course at Harvard, that I would ever be your colleague. I look forward to a happy and profitable association with you up there.
>
> Naturally I shall miss Nelson and sincerely hope that he will be able to get himself the colleagues here he deserves. But, as I said to him this afternoon, I can't imagine being with anyone who would be more like Nelson philosophically than yourself. I remarked that I would probably know as much about his views in Cambridge as I did in Philadelphia! I

do hope, of course, and I am sure you'd agree, that it would be wonderful to have him in Cambridge too.

My years at Harvard between 1948 and 1954 saw the deepening of my association with Quine. This was evident in January of 1954, when he wrote me a letter from Oxford about teaming up two of our courses. (In his letter the reference to Lucia was made because she had audited his course Philosophy of Language, and the Donald in the letter is Donald Williams, then our chairman.)

> I have thought lately that it might be fruitful if you and I were to team up our courses, making better use of our congeniality of outlook. If your Analytical Philosophy has tended to be a bit less technical than my Phil. of Lang. (a point on which Lucia could advise), then how about my *citing* your course as advised preparation for mine? (I also cite Phil. 140—Ded. Logic. Both prerequisites would be advisory rather than mandatory, simply because of Jakobson's occasional good student and such.) *From a Logical Point of View*, though insufficient for my course, would be the nucleus of it; additional main topics could include the nature and function of logical regimentation of language, and the theory of spurious relative terms (hunting unicorns) and propositional attitudes, such as I developed last spring. I would warp away from your coverage as much as possible without violence to *From a Logical Point of View* and make as much use as possible of the students' knowledge gained from your course (on which I would want briefing). In recently proposing my program to Donald I listed Phil. of Lang. for the spring term, so, if you are doing Analytical Phil. the fall term, we can institute the scheme forthwith in case the idea seems sound to you.

On January 13, 1954, I said that I was flattered by Quine's proposal that we link our courses, but warned him that I would cast a pretty large net in Philosophy 154 (Problems of Analytic Philosophy). I wrote, as I anticipated what I would do in my book *Toward Reunion in Philosophy* (1956):

> I'm very flattered that you should want to cite Philosophy 154 but I do hope that it's not a mistake from a logical point of view. I should say that I try to cover a pretty wide range of subjects, including some in ethics. But it is true that I introduce the students to certain things that are treated in FLPV and that many have said that they were helped in your

course by what they had imbibed in mine. I can't give you a very clear picture of what I plan to do next Fall because it depends on how the book I am working on comes out. In that I try to deal with the notions of existence, necessity, and value with a view to showing the connections between them. Value is treated not only as a subject of interest to students of ethics but also to students of existence and necessity insofar as notions like analyticity, synonymy, clarity, acceptability of a certain kind of quantification, resemble the notions of good and right. (I hope this doesn't frighten you!) And then, of course, there is some effort made to connect this with the theses that logic and epistemology are "normative sciences."

We might discuss bibliographical details as well as topical details if you should be in the country at the end of the summer (if *we* are; we sometimes think of dashing off somewhere if I get done what I want to get done). In any case, let me say that I accept your proposal in principle and would be willing to alter my own course to suit some general scheme that was acceptable to both of us. It seems to me a rare opportunity to educate people jointly. Maybe (not next year) we could even give a joint seminar some day on problems that exercise us both.

We never did give that joint seminar; would that we had given it. Later I heard that Van was not keen on giving seminars, and I can recall his saying sardonically that they provided a platform for students who were less interested in the truth than in scoring points against the teacher or each other. He struck me as not liking sharp oral exchange even though he was capable of punishing remarks about those with whom he might tangle. I can remember how devastating he could be in meetings of the department (or after them). Once, after Henry Aiken had mysteriously announced that some student should be "appraised" of the fact that he was not doing well, Van intervened to say in his inimitable way: "And he should be apprised as well." Yet, in spite of his extraordinary sharpness and quickness in exchanges like that, Quine could be warm and even gentle to those he liked, whereas those for whom he felt intellectual or moral contempt fared very differently at his hands. After one acrimonious meeting of the department at which Demos and Wild did not behave very well, Van bitterly reminded me of his advice in October 1947 that I not join the Harvard department.

I can also remember an unpleasant occasion on which Quine expressed what I thought was excessive contempt for a Harvard philosopher's mind— not the mind of a then extant member of our department but that of Josiah

Royce. Quine, Burton Dreben, and I were having lunch at the Faculty Club in the spring of 1969 (about a month before the "bust" concerning which I have a lot to say later on), and, for some reason, the name of Royce entered the conversation. It seems that Quine had read Royce's *Spirit of Modern Philosophy* as an undergraduate at Oberlin College and had not come away from the book with any great admiration for its author, our famous predecessor—or perhaps I should say our once famous predecessor whom William James once called the Rubens of philosophy. Van said without qualification that reading Royce was like going through muck. At the time, I was reading Royce for my course on American philosophy and for my forthcoming book *Science and Sentiment in America,* and I thought "muck" was a little much even though I was hardly a follower of Royce. I said something that led to a sharp, though polite, exchange between Van and me at the table, and when I went back to my study, I wrote him a letter in which I tried, as it were, to give Royce a break by calling attention to some ideas of his that resembled Van's. I realize that what follows may be daunting to some readers, but I reproduce it for the happy (or unhappy) few who might be able to follow it.

March 7, 1969

Professor W. V. Quine
Emerson Hall 201

Dear Van:

In the hope that it will lead you to think that reading Royce is not merely a matter of going through muck, I call your attention to a passage on pp. 302—303 of his *Religious Aspect of Philosophy* (2nd edition) which bears a striking resemblance to a passage on p. 44 of *From a Logical Point of View.* The former passage reads:

> "In short, the popular assertion of an external world, being an assertion of something beyond the data of consciousness, must begin in an activity of judgment that does more than merely reduce present data to order. Such an assertion must be an active construction of non-data. We do not receive in our senses, but we posit through our judgment, whatever external world there may for us be. If there is really a deeper basis for this postulate of ours, still, at the outset, it is just a postulate.

"All theories, all hypotheses as to the external world, ought to face this fact of thought. If the history of popular speculation on these topics could be written, how much of cowardice and shuffling would be found in the behavior of the natural mind before the question: 'How dost thou know of an external reality?' Instead of simply and plainly answering: 'I mean by the external world in the first place something that I accept or demand, that I posit, postulate, actively construct on the basis of sense-data,' the natural man gives us all kinds of vague compromise answers."

In the light of this, maybe those who write Ph.D. theses about you will be very interested to know that you read *The Spirit of Modern Philosophy* in college, for on p. 382 of that book (footnote 1), Royce quotes part of the above passage from his *Religious Aspect of Philosophy*.

Also, you may be interested to know that in Lecture V of the second volume of *The World and the Individual* Royce distinguishes between "the perfectly literal statements of how the facts of nature are known to behave" and statements reflecting the "extremely ideal ways in which science finds it convenient to conceive facts." This distinction, of course, is not unrelated to your distinction between convenient myth and literal truth on p. 18 of *From a Logical Point of View*.

In a much more speculative vein I would suggest that Royce's notion that to be is to be "the embodiment" of what he calls "the internal meaning of an idea" (*The World and the Individual*, passim ad nauseam) is not altogether unrelated to the view that to be is to be the value of a variable. Since an idea is a sign for Royce, he, like you, uses a formula that begins with, "To be is" and ends with a semantical expression. To be is to be the external meaning (*Bedeutung?*) of a sign which a person intends to use in a certain way and which therefore has internal meaning (*Sinn?*). To be for me is to be a thing of which I mean to speak (*Spirit of Modern Philosophy*, p. 406).

I could go on and cite passages that repudiate a sharp distinction between the analytic and the synthetic, but I will spare you those.

So: positing physical objects, distinguishing between convenient construction and literal truth, a semantical approach to ontological commitment, an aversion to a sharp distinction between analytic and synthetic—not bad for a mucky idealist. Perhaps you can now see what I meant by saying that reading Royce helps me understand how better philosophers might have come to their views. Who knows, maybe your

teacher at Oberlin wrought better than he (or you) knew when he put
The Spirit of Modern Philosophy in your hands!

Yours ever,
Morty

As I reread my letter, I regret some of its tone, but I think it conveys
something about Quine that I believe, namely, that he could be excessively
off-hand in dismissing the ideas of some people and that he had no
sympathetic interest in the history of philosophy or the general history of
ideas. Although his *Mathematical Logic* is a model of punctilious citation of
past achievements in logic, he never had the sort of interest in the history of
thought or in questions of general human concern that his teacher Whitehead had or that Russell had, and therefore his position in the history of
twentieth-century philosophy ironically resembles that of his bête noire
Lewis because of the narrowness of his focus. It is true that Quine's interests
have ranged beyond logic and philosophy. But his study of linguistics,
psychology, and geography never brought him great influence in literary or
political circles. He is certainly not a public philosopher, but he has always
been generous toward me even though I have strayed from philosophy in
ways that do not mean much to him.

When Quine wrote glowingly of my work in his course in 1938, when he
supported me for a fellowship at Harvard, when he supported my appointment to the faculty there, and when he proposed to me in the fifties that we
"team up our courses," he boosted my morale enormously. While he was
producing his articles and books in logic and the philosophy of language, I do
not think he was much interested in the philosophy of history or the history
of American thought, but he was all for my producing and trying new ideas,
for writing. It didn't seem to matter to him that I was interested in such odd
creatures—from his point of view—as Beard, Holmes, and Veblen in my
Social Thought in America, or that Lucia and I were working on *The Intellectual
Versus the City: From Thomas Jefferson to Frank Lloyd Wright*. Yet the only
comment I can remember his making about my work on American thought
was his writing that I had made "the *bon mot* of the year [1947]" when I wrote:
"Antiformalists . . . call upon social scientists in all domains, ask them to
unite, and urge that they have nothing to lose but their deductive chains."

So far as I can remember, my conversation with Quine about Royce was
the only unpleasant one we ever had, excepting, perhaps, one that we had
over a controversial Ph.D. thesis. Our most important philosophical agree-

ment centered on our doubts about the analytic and the synthetic. I was led to agree with Quine about that, in part because he opposed what I called epistemological dualism in a manner that I applauded. As an undergraduate I had become familiar with Duhem's view that we test systems of belief rather than isolated beliefs, but Duhem did *not* include logical principles in the systems tested by experience. And because I was, from my earliest philosophical days, sympathetic to John Stuart Mill's empiricism, I was attracted to the Quine-Tarski view that logical principles are included in such systems and might be rejected if these systems came in conflict with experience.

In spite of our considerable epistemological agreement, Quine and I did not agree very much in political philosophy. Indeed, Quine's conservative political views perplexed many logicians and philosophers who admired him greatly as a thinker, for example, Tarski and Carnap. They accepted the fact, without making much of it, that Quine was a political conservative, and that was certainly my attitude until events at Harvard in the spring of 1969 brought our political differences to a head. He writes of that period in *The Time of My Life*: "Feeling ran high in the faculty between a radical caucus at one edge, which backed the vocal students, and a conservative caucus at the other edge." Strictly speaking, Quine's remark is true, but he fails to point out that between those two edges there was a centrist, moderate, or liberal caucus that did *not* "back" those students. Quine was a member of the conservative group, and I was active in the centrist group. He correctly reports that personal relations among faculty members deteriorated during the spring of 1969 and that there was, to say the least, a loss in rapport and fellow feeling on the faculty, which I try to describe in a later chapter. Happily my admiration for Quine and my friendly feelings toward him survived those events at Harvard in 1969. It would seem that our friendship underwent a strain that our philosophical agreement overcame. By contrast, my philosophical disagreements with Nagel seemed great enough to overcome our considerable political agreement and to destroy our friendship. This may show that the three of us took our philosophy more seriously than we took our politics, but it also may show that Quine and I felt a greater temperamental affinity than Nagel and I felt. Nagel was a naysayer who found it hard to like many ideas in philosophy, whereas Quine and I, for all of our opposition to distinguishing sharply between the analytic and the synthetic, were more optimistic and affirmative in our attitudes. It is no accident, as my Marxist friends used to say, that Quine's autobiography was entitled *The Time of My Life*. And I am both happy and proud to have been his student, his colleague, his friend, and his admirer since 1938.

12

A Gamut of Harvard Teaching

From Hard-Core Philosophy
to Ideas of Man and the World

My earliest teaching at Harvard reflected my two main interests, analytic philosophy and the history of ideas. In the early fifties I launched my systematic courses called the Problems of Analytic Philosophy and the Nature and Function of History as well as a historical course in General Education called Ideas of Man and General Education of the World in Western Thought. These became staples in my teaching after I had received tenure, for I started then to shed the courses that had been foisted on me when I was, as I used to say, low man on the departmental factotum pole. I began the gradual transformation of my offerings from those that I *had* to teach when I did not have tenure to those that I *wanted* to teach when I did have it.

In my years of servitude, so to speak, I gave Philosophy of the Social Sciences in the fall of 1948, but stopped giving it after my *Social Thought in America* appeared, since a lot of what I had to say on the subject was in that book and I didn't want to repeat its contents in future classes or make up a new course. My course of 1948–49 on nineteenth-century empiricism I abandoned after two years, and I taught a course in American philosophy in 1948–49, 1949–50, and 1951–52 that I did not teach again until my last year at Harvard in 1969–70. The latter course was rarely taken by graduate students in philosophy, who were either uninterested in it or unable to fit it into a schedule that was tightly packed with requirements for their degrees. At no time did I teach American intellectual history of the kind Lucia and I deal with in *The Intellectual Versus the City*, since I did not think it would be appropriate to do so in a department of philosophy; and after 1952, I stopped teaching any courses in what I jokingly called "Americanology," for I had become tired of serving as Ralph Barton Perry's successor in the interdepartmental program on American civilization. I had not lost interest in the history of American thought, but I found it difficult to teach the subject to students whose training was mainly historical or literary rather than philosophical. While serving on the Committee for Higher Degrees in American Civilization, I was appalled at the philosophical weakness of students I had to examine jointly with colleagues in history, literature, government, and fine arts; and I felt very sorry for them. Although they were primarily trained in history and literature, they were required by a pretentious program to speak about the philosophy of C. S. Peirce with as much competence as they were required to demonstrate when talking about metaphor in *Moby Dick*. I sat through some very dreary examinations and some heartrending ones, in which very able literary students would understandably quake when I asked them to distinguish the pragmatism of Peirce from that of James or Dewey. After a while I asked the chairman of the committee to stop encouraging students of American civilization to take American philosophy as one of their four fields of oral examination, and I ceased to take the active part in the program that the elder Arthur Schlesinger and Perry Miller had hoped that I would take. I did not give up thinking about, and doing research in, American intellectual history, but from that point on I used my right hand to prepare lectures in philosophy, while my left wrote the history of American ideas with an eye mainly to publication.

Although most graduate students of American civilization found my historical courses *too* analytical, most graduate students of philosophy found them *insufficiently* analytical. And there was another problem to be faced in the case of philosophy students: many of them avoided my course on the theory of historical knowledge in spite of the fact that it *was* analytical. Why? In great measure because the topics that I dealt with, such as historical explanation, were not the central concerns of philosophers and not likely to be asked about in the preliminary examinations that students would take at the end of their first year. The result was that most of the courses I was forced to give in my first year at Harvard were out in left field, so to speak, and if I had continued to teach them and only them, I myself would have been out in left field as a professional philosopher.

Consequently, when I achieved tenure and security, I decided to flex my philosophical muscles by teaching a course in analytic philosophy while simultaneously satisfying my historical interests by joining Aiken to teach Humanities 5, a course aimed at Harvard and Radcliffe freshmen. Like other courses in General Education at the time, it was pretentiously entitled Ideas of Man and the World in Western Thought, and in one of the descriptions that I find in my papers—I am not sure whether this was used in the catalogue—Aiken and I said: "This course will be concerned with major attitudes, ideas, and problems arising from man's reflection on science, the arts, morals, and religion." When proposing the course to the Committee on General Education, my colleague and I wrote: "We want to introduce the student to the history of philosophical ideas conceived as vital components of western thought rather than to the history of philosophy as a purely technical discipline." Aiken taught the first term of the course, which was concerned with ancient Greek thought. It was very courageous of him to venture into a field in which he did not specialize, but he did so with his usual gusto and had the students in a pretty elevated state by the time I came on in a more subdued manner in the second term. Aiken was loudly applauded by several hundred students after each lecture, and when I gave my first lecture in the second term, I too received applause. Since I didn't like what I took to be the perfunctory quality of the clapping, I took my life in my hands and said that while I appreciated it very much, I preferred not to be applauded. Typically, and with a good deal of friendly humor on the part of some, the students proceeded to hiss and boo!

My part of the course concentrated on philosophical works such as Locke's *Second Treatise on Civil Government,* Hume's *Dialogues Concerning Natural Religion,* Kant's *Fundamental Principles of the Metaphysic of Morals,* Hegel's *Introduction to the Philosophy of History,* and Mill's *On Liberty.* In other words, I focused on the works of great modern philosophers in which they treated matters like politics, religion, morals, and history rather than matters like perception, necessity, and knowledge, though I tried to show how their views on the former subjects were related to their views on the latter. I also contrasted the philosophers' discussions of these subjects with those offered by Dostoyevsky, Marx, Kierkegaard, and Freud, not exactly figures in the history of philosophy as conceived by professional philosophers. The course became very popular and at one point registered something like seven hundred students, but it was exhausting to give, and soon Aiken dropped out, to be succeeded by Rogers Albritton. Later I was succeeded by Stanley Cavell, who had been an assistant in it when I first gave it in the spring of 1952–53.

I think "Hum 5," as it was called, performed a very valuable service for many undergraduates, for many graduate students, and for the Department of Philosophy itself. It provided a course in the humanities that could be followed with understanding by students who did not take very well to what was provided in more literary elementary courses in General Education. It also provided employment for philosophy graduate students who taught discussion sections in it, and it helped somewhat to restore the department to a position in the university from which it had been removed by self-appointed custodians of Harvard culture who kept complaining about the excessively technical orientation of the department. No longer could it be said with truth that we were not doing anything to tell students in Harvard College and Radcliffe about the eternal verities, not doing enough to continue the habits of our revered predecessors James, Santayana, and Royce. The course also prodded me into dealing with a part of intellectual history I had never taught before and to develop some views about the relationship between philosophy and general culture in the West. Giving it made me feel less guilty about abandoning other courses that my philosophical colleagues had expected me to give as a so-called service to nonphilosophers. I thought that I was rendering so much to the Caesar of service in Humanities 5 that I could, with a good conscience, teach the philosophy of language, epistemology, and analytical ethics.

The course called Problems of Analytic Philosophy resembled my Pennsylvania course Analysis, Positivism, and Pragmatism. As textbooks I used Bertrand Russell's *Problems of Philosophy*, G. E. Moore's *Ethics*, A. J. Ayer's *Language, Truth, and Logic*, and Gilbert Ryle's *Concept of Mind*. I also assigned papers by Quine, Tarski, Frege, Carnap, Lewis, Schlick, Nagel, Waismann, Hempel, and Stevenson as well as several things by Goodman, Quine, and myself. I began my lectures by acknowledging that the phrase "analytic philosophy" was vague and difficult to define, and that I might just as well have called the course the Philosophy of Russell, Moore, Wittgenstein, Carnap, and a Few Others with Whom They Have Succeeded in Communicating. I divided these philosophers into three groups: one associated with the earliest analytic philosophy of Russell and Moore; another with orthodox logical positivism; and a third with postpositivistic analytic philosophy as represented by the later Wittgenstein, by the Oxford philosophers of language, and by Goodman and Quine. I used Ayer's book as an example of orthodox positivism, and because Wittgenstein's posthumous *Philosophical Investigations* was not yet available (it appeared in 1953), I cited Ryle's book as an example of work done under the influence of some of Wittgenstein's later ideas. I discussed ontological, epistemological, and ethical problems while admitting that there were dangers in ranging so widely. I also distinguished three main methodological strains in analytic philosophy: one best represented by those who tried to analyze ordinary language and the actual procedures of science, a second that used the logical method called the "rational reconstruction of science," and a third that tried to relieve what Wittgenstein called mental cramps and to study the use of language outside of mathematics and natural science.

At times I thought that I talked so rapidly and tried to cram so much into the course that I may not have encouraged as much give-and-take as I should have liked. Nevertheless, I think the course went well. It introduced many students to philosophical ideas that they were not likely to learn much about in courses given by my colleagues, and I think it stimulated a number of able young philosophers to develop their own ideas, often very different from mine. In my grade book, where I wrote brief comments about students in courses other than my mammoth Humanities 5, I proudly find the names of many who have since become notable members of the philosophical profession, though not all of my comments about them may be called prescient in the light of what has happened since then. I continued to give this course or something like it for a number of years, and I often gave a follow-up seminar that allowed more intensive discussion of the same topics. The seminar met in the evening in my house at 28 Coolidge Hill Road in Cambridge because that encouraged a degree of informality that was not typical of classes in Emerson Hall.

I worked extremely hard preparing my lectures, but as soon as I began to speak with a confidence that carried me through my fear that I would repeat my catastrophe as a high school valedictorian, I would take courage and leave my notes by going to the blackboard or by pacing back and forth in the front of the room. When I returned to my notes, I would usually be able to find the place from which I had digressed; but sometimes when I had left them in a state of excitement, I would try desperately—sometimes without success—to pick up my carefully prepared thread. I don't think my students realized how hard I found it to give lectures; that was one reason why I insisted that they carry the ball in seminars and read their own papers to the class. In seminars I felt obliged only to comment on their papers and to moderate the discussion that followed. I didn't treat the seminar as the occasion for more lectures by me.

I confess that I do not altogether understand why I felt as I did about lectures. Of course, my adolescent lapse during my high school valedictory speech doesn't explain it, though it may have had something to do with it. I think that other things were involved. One was a concern about my English. Although my parents spoke well by comparison to most of our immigrant neighbors, they nevertheless spoke the language of New York streets, and the same was true of me for longer that it should have been. I made grammatical mistakes; my intonation was objectionable; and my earliest English probably sounded like an amalgam of that spoken by Eddie Cantor, Jimmy Durante, and Al Smith. When I went to City College I became self-conscious enough to know that I didn't speak well, but I didn't meet many people there who spoke better than I did. In any case, I was not pleased with my way of speaking. That did not bother me very much until I went to Philadelphia, where I could hear how different my speech was from that of most others around me, but my uneasiness in Philadelphia was as nothing compared to what I felt when I went to Harvard. There I was also much concerned, as any young lecturer would be, lest I say something obviously false or make a logical mistake, and I was very concerned lest I sound dull or boring. I certainly was not indifferent to the possibility that I was boring. The *Harvard Crimson* once said in its Confidential Guide to Freshman Courses that everybody in Quine's elementary logic class was bored and that the professor was more bored than anybody else! Knowing Quine, I'm sure that wounded him deeply; and I know how I would have suffered had it been said about me, even by silly undergraduates. I was very thin-skinned, and later one of the pleasures of leaving Harvard for the Institute for Advanced Study was the thought that I would never again have to face a sea of undergraduates such as I used to face in Humanities 5. I liked many of them individually, but when I viewed them en masse from the podium, they frightened me. I always felt easier in small groups where I could see the reactions of every student and therefore be able to alter my delivery or my argument so as to achieve more intellectual rapport and to be more persuasive. Former students of mine have often expressed surprise upon hearing that I was anxious in large lecture classes, saying that they never sensed it while listening to me. They have also spoken about my effectiveness as a teacher and seemed to think that was incompatible with my feeling as I did. I believe they labored under a false supposition in my case: I was often petrified in my large classes.

Although I was a decent teacher, I did not enter the academic world with a passion to teach but rather with the hope that entry into it would give me an opportunity to think, to write, and to advance knowledge in an interesting way. Teaching was a comparatively easy way of earning my living while I tried to do these things, but the desire to teach was not my ruling passion. I am glad, of course, to have been thought by some to be a good teacher, especially since teaching was not an occupation that I loved altogether for its own sake. When I left Harvard in 1970 for a life of research without teaching, some of my colleagues said that it was ironic that I, a person devoted to teaching, should be giving it up. Little did they know.

When I first transferred to the Institute for Advanced Study, I was invited on a number of occasions to give courses by the Department of Philosophy at Princeton University—professors at the Institute who agreed to do that were required by the Institute rules to do it without being paid by the university— but I always declined to do so. This was partly because I didn't relish teaching and partly because my last few years at Harvard were so hectic as to prevent me from getting as much writing done there as I had wanted to get done, thereby creating a backlog of unfinished work. Besides, the luxury of not teaching at all was something that I wanted to savor to the last drop. That is not to say that lecturing at Harvard (in the years before the chaos of the late sixties) interfered with my publishing things. As a matter of fact, one of the advantages of lecturing then was that my anxiety about public speaking led me to write out lectures that could be transformed into manuscripts for books. Although I did not read lectures to my classes, having them in written form on the lectern gave me courage; I knew that I could always depend on them if my mind were to go blank. Moreover, three of my books were based on notes that I used in teaching.

Teaching provided me with opportunities to test my ideas by defending them against able young minds. In exchange for this, I like to think, I imparted something of value to those minds in my classes; I also tried my hardest to help students—especially graduate students—in more practical ways. In doing so, I was reacting to some extent against what I regarded as a stepmotherly attitude toward me on the part of most of my Columbia teachers. At Harvard one could not fail to be aware that graduate students were at the lowest rung of the local social ladder, far below the undergraduates, who were often much better off. And since graduate students had to find jobs after receiving their degrees, I wrote an enormous number of letters of recommendation for them in the twenty-two years I spent at Harvard. In addition, I wrote such letters for undergraduates, who sometimes would ask that fifteen copies be sent to the different law schools or medical schools to which they were applying: this, mind you, before the days of the word processor and the photocopier.

While giving courses at Harvard, I think I acquitted myself pretty well for someone who did not gladly teach and who ran the gamut in his teaching. I derived enough benefit from teaching there for twenty-two years to dedicate my book *Pragmatism and the American Mind* as follows:

> To
> My Students at Harvard University
> in the Years 1948–1970
> In Grateful Recognition
> of How Much They Taught Me.

13

An Extraphilosophical Galaxy

My interests in the philosophy of history, law, religion, and education, as well as my work in the history of American ideas, made it useful for me to know something about a variety of subjects, so I came to know several people who worked in them. And since I was lucky enough to find a number of these people interesting as human beings, my life at Harvard was made more exciting and enjoyable when I became friendly with them during my first years in Cambridge. Among such people Arthur Schlesinger Jr. was one of the best friends I had. He was exceedingly generous, warmhearted, and bright. In the fifties, many Harvard people were critical of his outspoken attacks on Stalinism, but as an anti-Stalinist I had no sympathy with their criticism. Many Harvard professors disliked him because he knew and said that Harvard was in many ways provincial and complacent, but coming as I did from New York, I knew what he meant. I remember saying to Mary McCarthy that he reminded me of a now nonexistent restaurant in New York that described itself as "A Little Bit of Paris in New York," because he was a little bit of New York in Cambridge. Anybody who was invited to his house in the fifties discovered that it was one of Harvard's openings to the outer world. All sorts of interesting visitors to Cambridge would turn up at Arthur's house, and I met several of them there, among them Edmund Wilson, Senator John F. Kennedy, and Adlai Stevenson.

In 1948 Lionel Trilling wrote me, after I had told him that I was going to Harvard, that Arthur would be one of the good people for me to know there, and Lionel was absolutely right. On June 14 of the same year Arthur wrote in acknowledgment of something I had sent him: "Thank you for sending me your thoughtful review of Laski [Laski's *American Democracy*, reviewed by me in the *Philadelphia Bulletin*] which I would otherwise have missed. I did not miss, however, your brilliant article on the revolt against formalism, and I am looking forward to making your acquaintance in the fall." We did meet that fall, and for me that was the beginning of a long and valuable friendship. I cannot begin to recite all of the kindnesses I received from Arthur. He wrote to magazine editors, urging them to get me to review for them; he wrote to publishers, urging them to get me to write books for them; he wrote letters introducing me to friends of his abroad; and he was, I am sure, one of those who encouraged Paul Buck to send me up the Harvard ladder. When my *Social Thought in America* appeared, Arthur published a very favorable notice of it in the *Partisan Review* and praised it whenever he got a chance to do so.

I can remember only one serious intellectual issue on which Arthur and I disagreed: the worth of Reinhold Niebuhr's philosophical and theological views. He was a great admirer of Niebuhr, along with so many other Cambridge people, like Perry Miller, McGeorge Bundy, and Judge Charles Wyzanski. Their admiration for Niebuhr was based on political agreement with his liberalism and personal fondness for him, but often, I thought, that admiration was transformed into unmerited praise of Niebuhr's views of human nature and his attacks on rationalism. My own views about Niebuhr were very different, and I expressed them in print on a number of occasions, most notably in an essay, "Original Sin, Natural Law, and Politics," which became the epilogue of the paperback reprint of my *Social Thought in America* after a briefer version of it appeared in the *Partisan Review* in 1956. Much of that essay was directed at those whom I labeled "Atheists for Niebuhr."

In January of 1961 Arthur Schlesinger and several other Harvard people moved to Washington to join the Kennedy administration, so I saw much less of him. On December 29, 1963, I was in Washington for a philosophical meeting, and a little later recorded in a journal the following reaction to a visit with Arthur after the assassination of Kennedy:

On Friday and Saturday I lunched with Arthur, this time in a sad period after Kennedy's murder. The first lunch was with Arthur and Isaiah Berlin at the Occidental Restaurant on Friday, the second on Saturday with Arthur alone at the "Sans Souci." It was at the second ironically named place that he told me of his views and confusion about the future. Also about some past events.

Just after the assassination, he said, he submitted his resignation to Johnson. But he was then called in immediately, and solemnly and earnestly asked to stay on. The new President told him that *he* (Johnson) needed him even more than Kennedy had, "because Kennedy knew everything that you know," whereas Johnson didn't. Arthur said he realized that Johnson needed him as "liberal symbolism"—as Kennedy did not—but was impressed by the earnestness of the request and its apparent sincerity, so he decided to stay.

But as things have turned out, Arthur said, he sees that he is being shelved, since he hasn't been called in on anything of importance for three weeks. He has therefore decided to leave soon. But what to do now? He has been asked back to Harvard but evidently the History Department wants him to come back soon because it must fill his post with someone else if he doesn't come—presumably by an American historian. And although Arthur does not exclude the possibility of coming back at *some* future date, he does not wish to come back soon and will therefore say "no" if forced to come back this fall.

I asked him what the other possibilities were. He replied that first there was the possibility that he might take time off to do a memoir of J.F.K. This is being urged upon him by "Jackie" and "Bobby" and he feels that as an historian he has a certain obligation to do so. Then Richard Goodwin has urged him to team up with him to do a column in which they try to keep alive J.F.K.'s ideals and principles and act as a rallying point for those who wish to keep up pressure from the left, I suppose, on the Johnson administration. Yet Arthur thinks that he is first and foremost a writer of *books* and worries about whether he has enough energy to write columns *and* books. There are also a number of other invitations—like one from the Stanford Center and one from Princeton and the Wesleyan Institute—of an academic sort. I was bound to throw cold water on the Stanford idea, pointing out how remote and quiet that was for one of his temperament. And although I understood his feeling that Harvard was dull, in the end I felt that he should resume his duties as a professor there.

It is really sad to see this gifted man torn by conflicting ideas—at age 46—of what he should be, but I can deeply sympathize with him. He is enormously ambitious and very talented, but scattered. He wants to be scholar, courtier and the glass of fashion—and I can feel for him. I do not know what he will do. We left the "Sans Souci" in a government car and went to his house, where I said "Hello" to Marian for five minutes before being driven to the airport in the limousine. Pointing to the car and chauffeur he said, pathetically but whimsically: "I don't see how I'm going to be able to give this up." It is really sad and I feel very sorry for him.

In his conversation Arthur made clear that he felt closest to Bobby Kennedy among all the contenders for the nomination for the Vice-Presidency. He seems to be through with Stevenson and feels that Bobby is the most sincere liberal of all—e.g. by comparison to Humphrey and Stevenson. . . .

I do hope that this very warm-hearted, bright, good-natured guy can solve some of his problems. I felt, more than I ever have, that he has been on the whole the most interesting and attractive man I have known during my years at Harvard. He is occasionally superficial and too quick to come to conclusions, but he comes closest to being a "big man" than anyone I've known in my Harvard days. I often recall how Lionel Trilling predicted (in 1948) that we would get along very well. Trilling was absolutely right. I hope Arthur comes back, but I doubt that he will.

Another notable figure in my Harvard days was Robert Oppenheimer. I first met him when he was an overseer of Harvard College and chairman of the Committee to Visit the Department of Philosophy. Although I found some of his ways peculiar—especially his tendency not to look you in the eye when talking to you—I liked him. As Chairman of the Visiting Committee he was responsible for arranging a meeting with the department and giving a dinner after a day of consulting and conferring. At the time, Donald Williams was chairman of the department, so it fell to him to give a summary of our activities during the year and a statement of where we were and where we were going. In those days the department was constantly wrangling about whether we should have more balance in the department—more idealists, more realists, more theists, indeed, more of anything that would stem the tide toward analytic philosophy and what was indiscriminately called "positivism." With this in mind, Williams made a speech at the meeting of the department and the Visiting Committee in which he went on at great length about how the department needed more philosophers who had philosophies, meaning, of course, that we needed fewer analytic philosophers. As I listened to this, I became angrier and angrier, for it seemed to me not only silly but also unfair to level such an attack on that occasion. I felt compelled to speak out, and I did so heatedly. I said that although variety was an important consideration in forming a philosophy department, intellectual excellence was much more important. I added that if, in an effort to bring a man to Harvard who was, say, an absolute idealist or a Thomist, we would have to dig down to number fifty on a list of philosophers arranged in accordance with their excellence or intelligence, then we should not invite number fifty no matter how much variety he would bring. As soon as I finished, Oppenheimer said something like "You think, I suppose, that bringing an idealist here now would be like bringing an alchemist into the chemistry department." "Exactly," I said, concluding that Oppenheimer was terrific.

Oppenheimer made his crack about philosophy, chemistry, and alchemy even though he did not particularly admire or understand analytic philosophy. He said what he had said because he too thought that Williams was being silly, and also because he was given to siding with the young. However, in the course of his wide-ranging education he had picked up some Sanskrit and a taste for Indian philosophy, so when he talked about philosophy, he was likely to be fuzzy and, ironically, to share Williams's desire to appoint people who would speak movingly about man's condition and the cosmos—someone like Whitehead, whose student Oppenheimer had been when he was an undergraduate at Harvard. In fact, Oppenheimer's tendency in that direction attracted the more traditional wing of the department so much that they once proposed that we suggest to President Conant that he bring Oppenheimer to Harvard as a university professor. This was a very exalted appointment, attached to no department and made by the president without his needing approval by the faculty or any part of it. The rank had been created primarily to bring famous wide-ranging scholars like Werner Jaeger and I. A. Richards to the university, and most of the Department of Philosophy went along with the idea of inviting Oppenheimer to take such an appointment. They thought that he might strengthen our offering in the philosophy of science because, unlike so many philosophers who taught that subject, he was a distinguished scientist. President Conant was enthusiastic about the idea and approached Oppenheimer, but he declined and decided to remain as director at the Institute for Advanced Study.

When I first went to the Institute as a visiting member in 1953–54, I got to know Oppenheimer better. My first trip there was made possible by a grant from a director's fund that he had at his disposal and that he used for bringing visiting members who would not fit easily into the Schools of Mathematics and Historical Studies, then the only two schools at the Institute. When my friend Perry Miller was appointed as a member for the year 1953–54 and asked by Oppenheimer to recommend someone else with an interest in American intellectual history, Perry supported me strongly. When I came to the Institute, I saw something of Oppenheimer and came to like him more. It seemed to me that he postured less than he did when he was running the Harvard Visiting Committee, and he seemed more friendly and less pretentious on his home ground, where he didn't try to demonstrate that he was a universal genius. Oppenheimer the man was more in evidence in Princeton, and he was far more attractive there than the quirky darting figure I had met in Cambridge.

In April of 1954, when the academic year ended at the Institute, Lucia, the boys, and I drove from Princeton to Washington for a short vacation, and the morning after we arrived, we were amazed to see a picture of Robert on the front page of every newspaper. The so-called ordeal of Oppenheimer had begun; a "wall" had been put by Eisenhower between Oppenheimer and the nation's scientific secrets. After we returned to Princeton, we saw little of Robert that spring because the hearings about him were going on. We felt very sorry for him, and wrote him a note in which we expressed our support; Lucia wrote a comforting note to his wife, Kitty, who was thought by many to have lured him into the radical movement and to have been a major factor in his downfall.

In the year 1956–57, Oppenheimer came to Harvard to give the William James Lectures under the joint sponsorship of the Departments of Philosophy and Psychology. That was the first time such joint sponsorship was ever offered to a James lecturer, since the two departments usually alternated in their choice of lecturers and would normally pick scholars in their respective fields. When the appointment of Oppenheimer was announced, it was attacked by right-wingers among the alumni, and as chairman of the Department of Philosophy I was often called upon to speak out publicly in defense of it. The lectures were given in Sanders Theater and were all packed—right through the last of the six. Students and nonphilosophers on the faculty, like I. A. Richards, loved them and applauded wildly, whereas the philosophers were on the whole disapproving. Oppenheimer did not confine himself to physical relativity but, characteristically, went into the epistemological and metaphysical aspects of relativism and by doing so in a sloppy way offended several of the philosophical *pros*. However, I remember little about the content of the lectures, partly because as chairman of a sponsoring department I was preoccupied with more mundane things like the condition of the public address system and the blackboard, and partly because I found the lectures disconcertingly obscure. I recall that after the first lecture Oppenheimer came up to me and said: "I could see that you did not like that; but I think you will like what I have to say next time."

I found this sad and embarrassing, of course, but I was distressed by the fact that some of the Harvard philosophers of 1957 were so hostile to Oppenheimer. Unlike those who had sought earlier to have him appointed as university professor, they resented his intellectual arrogance, and some of them felt that he was too much of a cold warrior and too eager to dissociate himself from his youthful radicalism. For my own part, I defended him not as a philosopher but as an intellectual force for good, and I wrote a favorable review of his book of essays *The Open Mind* in the *New Leader*. I liked him and remained loyal to him during his troubles even though I was quite aware of his limitations, especially of his arrogance and his pretensions to omniscience. I can remember one particularly amusing example of this. He and Kitty were our guests for dinner in 1953, along with two English historians, the late James Joll and Asa Briggs (now Lord Briggs). For some reason, the subject of Gödel's incompleteness theorem came up, and Robert began to pontificate about it in a mistaken way. When I protested and allowed myself to say that Robert was wrong in what he had said about the theorem, Kitty seriously declared: "Robert is *never* wrong!" and Robert did nothing to disown her foolish remark, probably because he feared what the effect of doing so would be when they got home. I admired Oppenheimer, just as I admired Arthur Schlesinger Jr., even though I knew that my views of them were not shared by a number of people whose opinions I respected. Of course different things motivated their critics, but there was one that seemed to operate in both cases—a smallness of spirit that is too common among academic people. Arthur and Robert were both brilliant; both of them were very much in the public eye; and both of them were influential. They were therefore fair game for envious people who liked to aim at bigger people.

Another force for good at Harvard was a professor of American literature, Perry Miller; he was very different from Oppenheimer and Schlesinger, having been born in the Middle West to a New England family, and trained at the University of Chicago. He was a tall, heavy, boisterous man who liked to drink; and he had a great fund of goodwill and sentiment that could always be drawn upon by those he liked. He and his wife, Betty, did not have children, and younger faculty people were often treated by them as if they were their children—generously and affectionately. Like the younger Schlesinger he liked my article "The Revolt Against Formalism in American Social Thought of the Twentieth Century" when he read it in 1947. And since he was, like so many Harvard humanists, very critical of the Harvard Department of Philosophy in the late forties because it was so unhistorical in its interests, he welcomed the addition of an intellectual historian to the department. I was told that he had supported me strongly to the administration when it had solicited his opinion at the time of my promotion to associate professor.

Lucia and I first came to know the Millers well in Tokyo in 1952. I can remember a Cambridge party at which I told Perry that I was going to Japan—that must have been in the winter of 1951–52—and he reported that he had once been asked to go under the same auspices but had declined. I asked him whether he would like to go that coming summer, and when he said that he would, I told the Stanford philosopher John Goheen, the American director of the Tokyo seminar. Within a week Perry was invited. He accepted immediately, and so the Whites and the Millers were in Tokyo together in the summer of 1952. Perry was a great hit with the Japanese. He would put his great big arm around their little shoulders when he talked to them, and soon he was known as "Papa-san." Sometimes he would speak to them in pidginlike English. "I, you, meet here—unnerstan?"; "You come; you stay; I come; unnerstan?"—and so on with hilarious effect. He loved to drink with the Japanese, but since he found it hard to put down as much sake as he would have liked, because of the tiny cups in which it was served, he would supplement his sake with quart after quart of beer.

Soon after our happy summer together in Tokyo, and at the beginning of our stay together in Princeton—in September of 1953—Perry dedicated his *Roger Williams* to Lucia and me. After the academic year 1953–54 we became very good friends of the Millers and saw them often. In 1962–63 both of us were members at the Institute once again, but by then Perry was seriously alcoholic. It seems that he would leave the Institute by bus to buy his liquor in town and then bring it back to his office at the Institute, where he would drink a bottle a day. When he left his office at the end of the year, his file case was full of empty bourbon bottles. Perry died in December 1963, after a very sad few months during which he and his wife had been separated. He came to our house for lunch on the day of President Kennedy's funeral, and he sobbed as he watched it on television. He was dead a couple of weeks later.

Perry Miller was remarkable for uniting enormous powers of industry with a very graceful style; he was like a great big elephant who could dance a minuet. As a historian of ideas he was able to discern subtle threads of feeling that ran through poetry, fiction, and theology, but in my opinion he lacked the capacity to understand difficult philosophical ideas. When I was working on my chapter on Jonathan Edwards for *Science and Sentiment in America,* I thought I would see what Perry had to say in his book on Edwards, especially on the subject of free will. Alas, it turned out as I feared it would: he had no dialectical skill at all. It reminded me of a dreadful evening at his house in May of 1956, when he attacked my article "Original Sin, Natural Law, and Politics." I wrote afterward in a journal: "Once more I had the feeling that Perry's logical powers are virtually nil. I concluded that his adverse judgment on the piece was that of a man who was personally attached to Niebuhr and temperamentally attached to his doctrine, but incapable of defending him from the kind of attack in my article." At the end of my description of this exchange, I wrote: "I will never again discuss with Perry a serious question involving subtle—or even unsubtle—logical analysis without remembering the dreadful hour and one half of today." Yet, in spite of all his admiration for the religious Niebuhr, Perry spoke out eloquently during the crisis over religion at Harvard in 1958. When a group of us waited on Pusey, it was Perry who made the most devastating remark to our chief. He said: "Mr. President, what worries us most about the atmosphere at Harvard today is the pietistic fallout." That remark was omitted from the Minute on the Life and Services of Perry Miller in the records of the Harvard Faculty of Arts and Sciences because a member of the committee that prepared the minute objected that it might give offense to Pusey.

Perry Miller, Arthur Schlesinger, and visiting overseer Robert Oppenheimer all helped to make Harvard an exciting place for Lucia and me in the fifties. They were not only good scholars but lively, intelligent, civilized men with whom we had many enjoyable times. When Arthur left—as it turned out, permanently—to join the Kennedy administration, when Robert stopped visiting Cambridge, and when Perry died, Cambridge became a very different place for us in the sixties.

So far I have spoken only about more worldly forces for good at Harvard who did not teach in my department, and therefore I have omitted mention of Harry Austryn Wolfson, the learned historian of philosophy. Nobody could have been more different in background or temperament from Perry Miller, Arthur Schlesinger, and Robert Oppenheimer. Wolfson was almost exclusively devoted to his scholarship and utterly removed from the Harvard society in which Miller and Schlesinger traveled. I got to know Wolfson in 1947 through my Columbia friend Ralph Marcus—a historian of Hellenistic times and translator of Josephus who had left Columbia in the forties to take a professorship at the University of Chicago. Marcus brought us together when, while I was at the University of Pennsylvania, he and Wolfson were attending a meeting in Philadelphia, but I did not really get to know Wolfson until I came to Harvard. He was a professor of Semitic languages and literature who gave courses on ancient and medieval philosophy under the auspices of the Department of Philosophy. He had been at Harvard from the time he had entered it as an undergraduate; he had been a student of Santayana and a protégé of the philosopher James Haughton Woods and of George Foote Moore, the great historian of religion. He spoke English with a Yiddish accent that reminded me of one of my grandmothers, and we were united by his having lived as a boy on the Lower East Side before going to Scranton, Pennsylvania. For years Wolfson's mother had lived on Henry Street, near Rutgers Street, which was close to my neighborhood; and he had a brother—a dentist—who lived in Knickerbocker Village, where my parents had lived during the last years of their lives. Wolfson was therefore a link with my childhood, and he loved to reminisce about the East Side as it was when he was a boy there. His East Side, of course, preceded mine by twenty-five years or so, but they were sufficiently alike to make reminiscing about them especially enjoyable in the distant precincts of Harvard Yard.

For several years I lunched at the same table with Wolfson in the Harvard Faculty Club; indeed it was usually called "Wolfson's Table." Whenever Wolfson heard it referred to in this way, he insisted that its original name was "The Table of the Timid." Originally, he said, it was the first table that one came to upon entering the dining room, so many timid scholars—especially foreigners—would sit down at it immediately in order to avoid parading down the long aisles of the dining room in search of another table. The fact is, however, that most of these scholars came to it because of Wolfson's charm and continued to do so long after its location in the dining room had changed. Once a writer in the *Harvard Alumni Bulletin* called it "The Legendary Table of Scholars" and said that it was a gathering place of those "significant in the realms of thought." All of the regulars, especially Sam Thorne, the legal historian, and Van Quine, had a good laugh at that. Some of them were significant in the realms of thought, but their table talk certainly didn't show it. I can remember one man who said that he had been afraid to come to our table because of its allegedly high level of conversation, but when he finally did, he found us talking endlessly about some awful cowboy movie that Wolfson had seen the night before.

In 1963, I contributed the following appreciation of Wolfson in celebration of his seventy-fifth birthday; it appeared in *Mosaic*, a publication of the Harvard-Radcliffe Hillel Societies:

In 1935 Harry Austryn Wolfson delivered a lecture at the College of the City of New York when I was an undergraduate there. I do not remember what he lectured on—probably on his favorite, Spinoza—but I do remember the spell he cast upon me. He simply overwhelmed me. I had already been taught to admire great scholarship in the history of philosophy but had never before been exposed to the real thing: a dazzling display of Latin, Greek, Hebrew and Arabic, an impeccable command of the text on which he discoursed, a prodigious knowledge of its background and its impact on the philosophical tradition. To me Wolfson became a symbol of awesome scholarship, philological accomplishment, and devotion to learning. I saw him as a scholar's god, to be admired by mortal philosophers and historians, but never to be approached.

Fifteen years passed and I had the good fortune to become Wolfson's colleague on the Harvard faculty. He was, in his majesty, taking time off from studies in Jewish and Mohammedan thought to lecture to students in my Department on ancient, medieval, and modern philosophy, but I was still too overcome by my boyhood vision of his magnitude to try to get to know him. Moreover, Emerson Hall was not his permanent habitat: he merely visited it on periodic excursions from his real home, Widener Library. It was only when I had the further good fortune to have my office translated to that Cambridge version of Solomon's House in Bacon's *New Atlantis* that I really came to know Wolfson. Not only did I enter the house, but at last I got to know Solomon himself. Soon I enjoyed the pleasures of a daily walk with him from Widener to what is rightly called Wolfson's Table at the Faculty Club, of summer foraging with him at the Wursthaus and the Waldorf Cafeteria when the Faculty Club shut its doors, and of talking with him about the condition of man, to say nothing of women and children. At last I had the opportunity to see that my boyhood hero was not only immensely learned, but truly gentle, charming and warmhearted. I saw that he combined the way of science with the way of wisdom in the tradition of those philosophers he admired most. And then the fun began, as he reminisced about Europe, the Lower East Side and Scranton, Pennsylvania; offered bits of shrewd advice that so many of us treasure; reflected on Harvard in the good old days and Harvard in the bad old days; and gave other touching signs of his humanity.

In this year of celebration others will speak more fully and more authoritatively of Harry Wolfson and his work, for I am a mere neophyte in the cult. As a comparative newcomer to his world, it is hard for me to believe that he—the first to enter the library and the last to leave it, the first to get a point and the last to forget it—is seventy-five. I wish him new joys as he begins the next quarter of a century, chasing down ever more references in the stacks, deepening our knowledge of the history of philosophical thought, and brightening the lives of his friends.

Wolfson, I once thought, was a kind of Jewish G. E. Moore because of his simplicity, purity, and dedication to his intellectual work, but after getting to know him better, I saw that he possessed a shrewdness and knowledge of the world that Moore lacked. A Jew who had lived in a small Russian village, or at Harvard in the early years of the twentieth century, was bound to have learned more about man's limitations than a cloistered English don in the same period. Wolfson rarely spoke in detail about his early academic years, but I gathered that they had been extremely hard. He was not bitter about them, but he certainly never forgot them, nor was he unwilling to venture generalizations about the lesser qualities of human beings he had encountered during those years. Wolfson spoke often about the ingratitude of people, and he warned me that they would not only be ungrateful to me but that those for whom I did a lot would be most ungrateful to me. They would, he added, come to resent my favors to them, especially if they thought they richly deserved them. I have a notion that it was Wolfson who first called my attention to a related thought in the writings of Hobbes, the philosopher— Wolfson once told me—whom he admired most among those he had studied carefully. Hobbes writes in chapter 11 of his *Leviathan*: "To have received from one, to whom we think ourselves equal, greater benefits than there is hope to requite, disposeth to counterfeit love; but really secret hatred; and puts a man into the estate of a desperate debtor, that in declining the sight of his creditor, tacitly wishes him there, where he might never see him more. For benefits oblige, and obligation is thraldom; and unrequitable obligation perpetual thraldom; which is to one's equal, hateful."

Wolfson could often be surprisingly revealing about himself. Once he told me that after finishing a large and important book—I can't remember which—he made the mistake of not going on at once to another scholarly project. The result, he said, was a curious symptom: he was unable to swallow. He saw all kinds of physicians and psychiatrists to no avail, but then the symptom disappeared when he launched another large project. The most revealing story of all had to do with his great disappointment about not having become a famous literary man—a novelist or a poet. That, he said, was what he had wanted to be, and therefore he counted himself a failure in spite of all the scholarly honors and awards that had come to him in his old age.

I do not wish, however, to give a misleading impression. Although Wolfson would often unburden himself and talk about ancient wrongs and man's failings, his main effect upon me was one of refreshment and encouragement. He would warmly praise many people—for example, Arthur Schlesinger Jr.—"How dot fellah can write! He's ah genius." Wolfson was a source of great pleasure and wisdom, and after I left Harvard, I missed him as much as I missed any other former colleague. It was a great tribute to Harvard that it made possible my friendships with people as different as Harry Wolfson, Perry Miller, and Arthur Schlesinger Jr. And I can say the same thing about Harvard's making it possible for me to get to know President James Bryant Conant.

Although I was not close enough to Conant to call him a friend, he was a powerful source of support to me. Conant was a very intelligent, thoughtful man who had a serious interest in the philosophy of science and a genuine desire to see Harvard philosophy improve. And I was happy to learn from him that he was interested in some philosophical ideas that I shared with Quine. Writing to me in the fall of 1952 about my article "The Analytic and the Synthetic," Conant said: "I have read it with great interest and also Professor Quine's 'Two Dogmas of Empiricism.' I had his reprint and had read it before but not as understandingly as I should have. With the aid of this rereading and your article I think I understand better the controversy between you and Professor Quine on the one hand and logical empiricists on the other." Conant concluded his letter by saying: "Perhaps sometime before Christmas you and he would have an evening free and I could have the benefit of your counsel for a couple of hours. I will take the liberty of seeing if we could arrange such a meeting after the first rush of October is over and after I have tried out my views about the nature of the 'real' world on the class."

Conant was referring to a class in the philosophy of science that he was giving in our department in the fall of 1952–53. And since he was quite sincere in his proposal that Quine and I come to talk philosophy with him, we soon received invitations to come to his house for a meal. It was quite extraordinary for a Harvard president who was a chemist to read two technical articles in philosophy and then to take a couple of hours discussing them very sensibly with the authors. I think that when Harvard lost Conant, it might well have lost the last president who could do that sort of thing. I was so saddened when I read in January 1953 of his resignation—to take effect

the following year, when he would go to Germany as high commissioner—
that I wrote him a letter expressing my sense of loss. To this he replied:

January 23, 1953

Dear Professor White:

Thank you so much for your kind note—much too kind. I am quite
sure that my being the President of Harvard is far less important for
the future of this University than you imply. The professors make the
institution and in the long run remake the president! One of the
comforts I take on leaving Harvard is the strength of the Philosophy
Department. I am sure that you and the colleagues of your age will in a
few years restore the reputation of the Harvard Department of Philosophy to the position which it held forty-five years ago. I do regret that I
shall not be staying to see this accomplished.

As I am writing Professor Quine, I am deeply indebted to the
Department for the privilege of giving a course these last few months.
I shall look back on it as one of the most pleasant parts of my twenty
years of service. For your assistance and your participation in the
invitation, please accept my most sincere thanks.

Sincerely yours,
James B. Conant

The reader may now see why I enjoyed Harvard so much in the earliest
years of my teaching there. New York had launched my philosophical career,
but it was at Harvard that I began to breathe more freely, especially because
I ranged beyond the social confines of the Department of Philosophy. I came
to know congenial colleagues in other subjects, interesting students like
Susan Sontag and David Souter, and distinguished neighbors in the Boston
area like Robert Lowell and his then wife, Elizabeth Hardwick, whom I had
known in New York. I also made very brief contact with Billy James, son of
the Harvard philosopher, with Evelyn Whitehead, widow of the philosopher,
and—strangely enough—with the present king of Nepal.

The strikingly handsome Susan Sontag came into my office sometime in
the 1950s while I was chairman of the Department of Philosophy, asking that
she be allowed to become a graduate student in philosophy instead of English.
It was within my power as chairman to accept her, and I did so readily after
an interview in which she displayed great intelligence and a prodigious

amount of learning for one her age. Since I was chairman at the time, the meeting must have taken place between the fall of 1954 and the spring of 1957. My recollection is that she had been an undergraduate at the University of Chicago—a fact that might help explain her impressive range of reading. I can also recall being struck by her great intelligence when I met her once at the sociologist David Riesman's house. I was discussing the trials and travails of Robert Oppenheimer with her and her husband, and she seemed to me to be especially acute and sensitive on the subject. Although I thought her husband was excessively hard on Oppenheimer, Susan seemed less demanding and more generous toward him.

As I look through my Harvard grade book I find that she never took a seminar or a lecture course with me but did take a so-called reading course in connection with a planned Ph.D. thesis that she never wrote. I also remember several lengthy discussions with her that prompted my writing a number of strong letters of recommendation about her. I wrote to the Department of Philosophy at the City College of New York and to the department at New York University; I spoke of her excellent teaching as an assistant in my Humanities 5 course and said she was extremely well read and very acute, as she certainly was. I spoke of her command of Anglo-American analytic techniques and of her familiarity with Continental philosophy, of her insight and her maturity. In short, I went all out for her and predicted that she would be very sensitive to the needs of students. The chairman at City College said my letter persuaded him to offer her an appointment, as did President Harold Taylor of Sarah Lawrence College when I recommended her to him. He wrote: "On the basis of our conversation and your letter, I invited Miss Sontag to accept the appointment for next year. She seemed delighted with the prospect and I must say that I am too."

These letters were among the many that I wrote for her or received from her between June 1958 and February 1963. She wrote me from Paris in June of 1958 to say that she would, when she returned to Cambridge, Massachusetts, like to talk about a manageable thesis topic and about getting some teaching work because she was strapped financially. She also said some very perceptive things about Oxford, allowing that she didn't take to philosophy there very well and to life even less. She discovered, as she put it, how American she was in failing to appreciate the cracked high voices, the deadpan witticisms, and the virtuoso debating maneuvers of the dons, though she added that John Austin had taught her that all the epistemology she had cherished was wrong. In ethics, political philosophy, and the philosophy of religion, she went on, the mannered tones of the British said nothing to her.

All of this was in part consonant with what the Oxford philosopher Herbert Hart had written me on December 18, 1957, about Susan's attitudes toward Austin, Berlin, and Hampshire.

> Sir Isaiah has been in good form all this term and the knighthood sits as lightly on him as any cocked hat—to which he likens it himself. His lectures, a vast panoramic survey of political philosophy from Aristotle onwards, have attracted huge numbers: car-loads from Cambridge are said to come over. Among his most formidable critics is Miss Susan Sontag. She is right in thinking that he is a bit careless of the detail, but she is wrong if she thinks there were not shafts of great insight and illumination. She has, I think, enjoyed her term here though she professes to think very little of everybody except Austin, whose sense data lectures have sent her into raptures. . . . She has been to Stuart [Hampshire] for tutorials and is critical though appreciative. She complains that there is too much frivolity, too many jokes; but I think she will end up an *aficionada*.

As everyone knows, of course, Susan did not end up in that way. She left philosophy and became the distinguished writer she is today, but I believe she would have become just as distinguished in philosophy had she chosen to follow that path.

My relations with my former student David Souter were very different from my relations with Susan Sontag if only because I knew Souter as an undergraduate at Harvard, whereas Sontag was a graduate student. Souter was a student in Humanities 5 when I taught it; he was registered in my course on the philosophy of history in the fall of 1960–61; and in that same term I tutored him while he was writing his senior thesis on the legal philosophy of Justice Holmes. Souter was a very agreeable and very bright young man, and I remember his being extremely polite and especially well groomed when he came to his tutorial sessions with me. When he was nominated to the Supreme Court, many people asked me what I thought of him, and I usually replied that he was very intelligent and decent but that of course I knew nothing of his legal ability. On one such occasion a distinguished lawyer grumpily remarked to me that admirable as those qualities were, they did not constitute a basis for nomination to the Supreme Court. I agreed that they did not constitute a sufficient condition for such a nomination, but, in my nonlegal opinion, they certainly constituted a necessary condition that has not always been satisfied.

All of my correspondence with Souter dates from a period well after I had taught him. A letter I wrote to him on August 29, 1976, helps me date the occasion on which I revived my acquaintance with him. While staying in a cottage in Vermont, I kept hearing references to Attorney General David Souter on a New Hampshire radio station. So I called his executive assistant in Concord and, by piecing together with her a number of facts, concluded that the attorney general was indeed my former student. I then wrote him about my discovery and received an answer from him.

Souter wrote on September 9, 1976, that his being attorney general was connected with a peculiarity of New Hampshire politics. The attorney general in that state, he said, is not elected but is appointed by the governor, whose action may be confirmed or vetoed by an executive council of five. Since this constitutional scheme produced his appointment and since he was not a politician, he said his appointment "was unusual even within the realm of peculiarity" he had mentioned and promised to tell "the rest of the story" of his political career when Lucia and I might come to Concord. He also recollected that the last time we had met was in the spring of 1964, when he was in his first year at Harvard Law School. He was a tenant of Betty Miller's in her house on Agassiz Street in Cambridge, and he had on his desk a memento of his time there—a little wooden statue of St. Yves, the patron saint of lawyers, given to him by Betty after Perry died. "So," he said, "on the most uncivilized days here in my office Cambridge is never too far away." He concluded by saying it would be fun to see me again, graciously adding that he owed me much and hoped he would see us for lunch in Concord some day. When I acknowledged his letter on September 20, 1976, I said I was delighted to hear that he was the real David Souter, but I never did take lunch with him in Concord, and our correspondence broke off until I congratulated him in October of 1990 on his appointment to the Supreme Court.

After I wrote to him on that occasion and sent him a copy of my *Philosophy, "The Federalist," and the Constitution,* Souter replied with his usual charm: "I count your letter of October 15th among the most happy dividends of the recent disruption in my life, and I am planning for the day, probably next summer, when I can do justice to the book you have so kindly inscribed and sent to me. Although I have done a fair amount of reading in and about the Constitution over the years, the new job seems to whet the old thirst, and it will gratify me to be your student again as I read your latest work." Then, referring to his statue of St. Yves, he wrote: "In the rush to get to work here after confirmation, I failed to bring the lawyers' patron saint with me, but I will get him down here at the earliest opportunity. Coming here is like walking toward a tidal wave, and I will need all the help I can get." Finally, he expressed his desire to have the lunch we had been planning since the seventies. Unfortunately, I haven't been to Washington since Souter's elevation to the Supreme Court, but I must say that his role on the Court since then has increased my pride in having taught him.

When Lucia and I lived in Cambridge, we did not profit only by getting to know people who were officially connected with Harvard; we also got to know Robert ("Cal") Lowell and revived our friendship with Elizabeth Hardwick. One day in the fall of 1954 we ran into Elizabeth at a concert of the Boston Symphony Orchestra in Sanders Theater at Harvard, where she introduced us to Cal. He was then teaching at Boston University, and they were living in Boston. A datebook of mine tells me that we went to their place at 33 Commonwealth Avenue on December 14, 1954, for dinner; it also shows that we had been at Sanders Theater on November 29, probably the day we bumped into Elizabeth. When we knew her in New York in the late thirties and early forties, we liked and admired her very much; we also came to like Cal and would enjoy seeing both of them from time to time at their place in Boston or at ours in Cambridge.

When I finished a story about a trip across the Atlantic that I thought of publishing, I sent it to Cal and Elizabeth, and received the following reply. The reference to "the Santayana" below is to a review I had written of a book about the philosopher, and my "crack at Natural Law" was my article "Original Sin, Natural Law, and Politics," published in the *Partisan Review* in 1956.

December 3, 1956

Dear Mortie:

How refreshing to see that you can write this sort of prose with the same intelligence and strength as your PR crack at Natural Law. I think you need have no fears about the tone and the interest.

My suggestions are about the same, I think as Elizabeth's. 1) You should write it as yourself, Morton White, in such and such a year on such and such a ship. You needn't tell much about yourself, but here and there let there be a touch of your humor, a quick hard thought or a reply. 2) A few more particulars, descriptions of the ship, colors, overcoats etc.

It's an indulgence and an impertinence for me to give you advice, for

I feel in most things your pupil and a tyro. What I like about your piece is that it has a point. . . . I find nothing comes harder to me, for I have a strong touch of our old New Englander's disease, the intuitive mumble, the perceptive, never completed sentence. Also, as I already knew, you can write straight prose, the kind Robert Graves admires.

Many thanks for the Santayana. It's strange to have something deepened in our feeling four years after his death. I would like to write him a fan letter and Christmas message.

You and Lucia always make us feel more alive. I am thankful that we are friends and neighbors.

Affectionately yours,
Cal

I wasn't a close friend of Cal's, but I do think that his use of the word "affectionately" was meant sincerely, and I felt the same way toward him. But it wasn't always easy to deal with his antics when he was in one of his upset states. One night he came to a party at our place without Elizabeth and met my Harvard colleague Bob Hightower, a professor of Chinese. They had known each other when Cal was married to Bob's friend Jean Stafford, and Cal greeted Bob warmly. I recall his saying that Bob was getting to look more and more like Joyce, adding how appropriate that was for a Hightower—the allusion of course being to Martello Tower at the beginning of *Ulysses*.

The dinner took place without incident, but after dinner Cal began to speak about Kant—why I can't remember—and asked me whether I had a copy of *The Critique of Pure Reason*. As the reader will see, I should have denied that I did, but how could a respectable professor of philosophy say that he didn't own a copy of that book? Well, I brought out the Kemp-Smith English translation and gave it to Cal. Taking it in hand, he immediately went to the chapter entitled "The Antinomy of Pure Reason" and began to intone some of the contents of the double pages: "The world has a beginning in time, and is also limited as regards space," followed by "The world has no beginning, and no limits in space; it is infinite as regards both time and space." Then he went on to the other antinomies, sometimes making brilliantly comical comments as he went through them, but sometimes commenting in pure philosophical gibberish and asking me what I thought. Cal's Kantian monologue went on for about an hour; people became very nervous; it was impossible to stop him. When he finished, the party was about over, and people began to look for their coats in an embarrassed effort to escape.

Of course he was not like that in his more normal states. But when he was like that, he must have been a difficult person to live with, as I am sure Elizabeth learned. She had not changed much since our New York days. She was still lovely looking and could still be devastating about pretentious people, especially about those at Harvard. Being married to a Lowell gave her entrée into Boston high society, but this did not prevent her from publishing a savage piece about some of the people she had met there. One of the members of Cambridge society whom she knew but did not skewer in her article was Billy James, the painter and son of the Harvard philosopher of the same name. I can remember our joking sympathetically about him, both of us laughing, as Isaiah Berlin did, about his references to "Dad" and "Uncle Henry." Billy James was then an elderly gentleman, always dressed impeccably and always very pleasant on the few occasions when I met him. He had a pronounced stutter that became worse when he was nervous, and he would introduce himself at cocktail parties by pointing to his chest and saying "J-j-james." Often he would have in tow his large wife and, according to some wit, would nudge her along as if he were a tugboat and she a large liner.

One day in the fifties, I believe, James and I met during a Harvard meeting of the Eastern Division of the American Philosophical Association. Since my department was the host, I had to carry out some administrative duty in the lobby of what was then called the Allston Burr lecture hall. To my surprise, I saw James there, looking at a bulletin board, and we had a cordial chat. Sometime later he wrote to me, and we agreed to have lunch together.

95, IRVING STREET
CAMBRIDGE
MASSACHUSETTS

April 6, 1959

Dear Morton White;

You once admitted that you might find time to lunch with me.

Such a meeting, *à deux*, will be pleasant in this house because of associations that go with it but, if it would be more convenient for you, Church Street, Chez Dreyfus, would be OK. I suggest any day of the week beginning April 13 or beginning April 20 with the exception of Saturdays. Perhaps you can't escape.

I have been reading, with delight, your *Age of Analysis*. In spite of my defective intelligence I emerge with affection for certain philosophers. They turn out to be Bergson, Whitehead, and my father. You will tell me which ones you favour.

Sincerely yours,
William James

I was of course delighted to have this letter and especially so to have one on a letterhead that might have been used by the great philosopher himself. I noted with special interest the British way of putting a comma between "95" and "Irving Street" as well as the British spelling of "favour." I replied by telephone and was invited to have lunch at 95, Irving Street on April 13, 1959. I had of course noted James's remark about his "defective intelligence," but I was not prepared for another self-deprecatory remark he made after we had both consumed a couple of excellent Martinis. He said to me, as I recall, "I know why you've come here. It's not b-b-because of me; it's because of *them*"—and he pointed at the wall on which portraits of his dad and his Uncle Henry hung.

I want now to tell about an earlier visit with Billy James's friend Evelyn Whitehead, the widow of Alfred North Whitehead. Since I came to the Harvard Department of Philosophy after his death, I had never met her husband, but on November 16, 1949, I was taken by my colleague Harry Sheffer to meet her in her apartment at the Ambassador Hotel in Cambridge. She was almost completely blind and used a cigarette holder that consisted of a circular loop attached to a small stick or rod. She would put the cigarette through the loop and would hold the rod so that it and the cigarette formed a capital *T*, with the cigarette as the horizontal bar. At one point she asked Sheffer to light her cigarette while her head was tilted downward; and when he struck the match the flame flared upward and came so close to her face that she screamed, "Harry, you're burning my nose!"

During the conversation Sheffer mentioned that I knew G. E. Moore, and this prompted Mrs. Whitehead to talk about an occasion when Moore had visited the Whiteheads in this country. It was during the Second World War, while Moore was in Cambridge to give a lecture at Harvard. "Poor Moore," she said (she constantly referred to him in that condescending way). "He sat down as soon as he came into the room, and he was very tight." At this point Sheffer interrupted, saying, "Oh Evelyn! You mean 'tense,' don't you? I'm sure Moore wasn't drinking." "Of course, Harry, I meant 'tense.' Moore sat down after coming into the room and said, before he entered into any further conversation, that he was a pacifist and that both of his sons were." Her point was that Moore, knowing that the Whiteheads were certainly not pacifists, felt compelled to announce his differences with them in this militant way.

I cannot remember anything else about my visit to Mrs. Whitehead, and I must say that I did not take to her. Some years later, in 1959, after Moore had died and I was preparing a talk about him, I wrote to Mrs. Moore: "I have heard that when Moore came to visit the Whiteheads while lecturing at Harvard he said, before he entered into conversation with them something like the following: 'I am a pacifist and both of my sons are.' As you were not there I know that you are not in a position to confirm the story at first hand but I wonder whether this does accurately express Moore's views and those of your sons at the time."

In reply, Mrs. Moore wrote to me:

Feb. 5/59

Dear Mr. White,

Your letter has just come. I am afraid the story is apocryphal. It sounds improbable, as it seems to me to show an aggressive and provocative spirit wh. was quite alien to Moore—except in philosophical argument. He would, no doubt, answer a direct question truthfully, but he would never wittingly hurt people's feelings. Besides, and more important, I don't think Moore ever was a pacifist. I know that, in the 1st World War, when I was a convinced pacifist, Moore could not make up his mind one way or the other, and said that he wd. join the Army if ordered to do so, because "if one can't make up one's own mind, one ought to obey the Government of one's country." Luckily, his age-group was never called up.

We both thought there was more excuse for the 2nd World War, though we may have been wrong. It is true that both our sons were, and are, pacifists.

Yours in haste,
D. Moore

The reader can see that Harvard was a place where I met a number of extraordinary individuals. Let me add something about another one of them, the then crown prince, now the king, of Nepal. Lucia and I were first introduced to him by our friend Robert Bates, a great mountain climber who taught English at Exeter.

When we were first introduced to the crown prince at the Bates house, he struck us as a handsome, unpretentious, genial, conversable, friendly young man. He was accompanied by someone who was a professor of literature, I believe, in Kathmandu and who struck us as though he were a bodyguard as well. The professor paid little attention to me when I was introduced to him as a fellow professor, indeed a professor of philosophy at Harvard, but for some reason he lit up when he discovered that I was the editor of *The Age of Analysis*, which, he proudly informed me, was available in Kathmandu. That led to a brief exchange between him, the crown prince, Lucia, and me; and when we learned that the prince was at Harvard as some sort of special student, we asked him and his companion to our house for dinner. We also invited our next-door neighbor, the Harvard professor of Sanskrit, Daniel Ingalls, and his wife. I remember the evening especially because it was the only occasion on which we entertained a king-to-be but also because of a memorable exchange that took place between our royal guest and the scholar of Sanskrit. Dan Ingalls spent a good deal of the evening urging that Nepal should encourage the study and preservation of its ancient languages and traditions, but Shah Dev, as we called him, did not respond enthusiastically. He seemed to be for modernization in all of its Western forms—science, technology, industry, economics, mathematics, the whole bit. He was joined by his professorial bodyguard, as both of them turned their backs on ancient philosophy, poetry, religion, and whatever else it was that Ingalls had urged them to revere and protect. Indeed, it was then that the bodyguard revealed the reason for his admiration of my *Age of Analysis*: it was a showcase in which I had displayed samples of the sort of philosophy that he seemed to prefer to the sort that Ingalls was urging the prince and him to preserve. The attitudes expressed by our Nepalese guests led us to think that they would also have great respect for the democratic political society that often accompanies the Western institutions and ideas they were praising. We also hoped that the crown prince would, on his accession to the throne, be a powerful force for democracy, but we have been told by some who should know that our hopes have not exactly materialized.

This chapter, which summarizes a small part of the story of my life in Cambridge, may seem like an exercise in name-dropping to some, but I include it primarily as a way of showing how exciting and interesting to me Harvard was in the fifties. Up to the writing of these lines, I have met only one king. In my earlier years I had to make do with meeting lesser celebrities such as Al Smith, Jimmy Walker, and Eddie Cantor, who were known to my father. But my father never introduced me to a Lowell, a James, or a future justice of the Supreme Court. To meet them I had to go to Harvard, where I found a world that was very different not only from the Lower East Side of New York but also from City College, Columbia, and the University of Pennsylvania. However, as the reader will later see, Harvard could show a less glamorous side to me, just as God did when he showed his back to my namesake Moses.

14

Some Questionable Forces for God at Harvard

Dr. Pusey and Dr. Niebuhr

During my first decade at Harvard I did not confine myself to pure philosophy or to historical scholarship. I found it hard to imitate Moore or Wolfson—one fixed intently on such matters as perception, free will, and the good, and the other devoted exclusively to studying what great philosophers had said about such matters. My experience in the shadow of the Downtown Tammany Club and among New York Marxists and Deweyans made it difficult for me to live the life of a completely detached philosopher or historian of ideas. My attitude toward religion and my taste for intellectual exchange on matters of general concern prompted me to take an active part in a controversy about the Harvard chapel that erupted in the fifties. Several things led me to defend the right of Jews to be married in Memorial Church: my disagreement with President Pusey's views on the nature of religion and education; my fear that Harvard would cease to be a place where atheists and agnostics could express themselves freely; and my Deweyan idea that a philosopher should participate in such a debate.

My entrance into the controversy over the chapel was indirectly connected with my disappointments in the world of real politics. The more I shed the Marxism of my youth, the more I focused on dealing with political and intellectual ills that I knew more about. Since I could quickly see the results of my action on the university scene, I thought it was an arena in which I could accomplish something of practical value without suffering as my father had in his dealings with the Democratic Party or as so many of my contemporaries had while they were members of the Communist Party or of other leftist groups.

Although I was very happy during most of my twenty-two years at Harvard, I spent a number of less than happy days there after the end of Conant's administration in 1953 and at the beginning of Pusey's. When I had written to Conant to express my sadness at his resignation, I did not know who his successor would be. After I learned that it would be Nathan Pusey, I read his essay "Religion's Role in Liberal Education" and was filled with disappointment and anxiety. Although many Harvard liberals were pleased to learn that he had stood up to Senator Joe McCarthy while he was president of Lawrence College in Wisconsin, and although I too applauded that, I was deeply worried by his views on the role of religion in education. In his essay Pusey began innocuously enough by saying that anyone who goes to college is faced with the burning question, "What shall I do with my life?" But soon I was startled to find him saying that when we ask this question, "whether we are conscious of it or not, we have begun to think religiously, and have begun to ask of God." Pusey admitted that there was a widespread feeling in university circles that religion, especially organized religion, was hostile to the pursuit of truth, and he conceded that religion in our great universities could hardly be regarded as a disinterested force in the service of truth. But this fact of history, he went on to say, should not prevent us from observing "the failure of recent educational practice to prepare men in terms of heart and will and mind to prevent the strife, misunderstanding and willfulness that now arise, or constructively and resolutely to cope with them once arisen." A time had come again, Pusey announced with increasing fervor, "to make the attempt that religion makes, to seek once more for an education that will address itself to the whole person—not any less to minds, but also to hearts and wills." This reference to hearts, wills, and the whole person was followed by Pusey's sermonic declaration that educators should be concerned for "the ability, and the desire, in the strain and stress of life, to walk humbly, constructively, prayerfully, and hopefully with God." And soon after Pusey's message reached God it became very Christian: "Without faith, without some glimpse of the meaning of Christ, there is much evidence to suggest one must always face life and all crises in terms merely of his own temperament." Education, Pusey warned, cannot turn away from its responsibility to help people find meaning in life, to help them develop trust, awareness, and concern. But whence will these come, Pusey continued in ministerial tones, "if we focus attention on anything less than God's truth or fail to feel its sustaining strength?"

Because this sort of talk alarmed me for many reasons, I decided to give voice to my views in an article called "Religion, Politics, and the Higher Learning," published in December 1954 in a Harvard magazine called *Confluence*, edited by Henry Kissinger. Although in the article I made no explicit reference to Pusey or to his views, I was aiming at those views, and people in Cambridge and elsewhere knew that very well. I said, to begin with, that we must distinguish between teaching students *about* religion and teaching them *to be* religious, and that whereas the first task was appropriate in a secular college like Harvard, the second was not. I also said that religion was not simply a matter of feeling and willing as opposed to knowing, and that it was a mistake to think that religious instruction was simply instruction in feeling and willing that could be mechanically added to intellectual instruction to help train "the whole person." In passing I said that the distinction between teaching students to be religious and teaching about religion was analogous to the distinction between teaching students to be Communists and teaching them about Communism.

In my article I noted that many religious intellectuals tended to ask the question "Should I be religious?" rather than the question "Does God exist?" A traditional sort of religious thinker might try to defend his belief in God's existence by offering arguments for it, I said; and if such a thinker appealed to faith, he might offer arguments for believing that faith was defensible. But, I went on, a large number of religious intellectuals of the time did not feel obliged to defend any substantive theological beliefs, possibly because they believed that being religious, by contrast to believing in God, required no such defense. However, I thought that it did, and that those who advocated that undergraduates in a secular college should be taught to be religious had a special obligation to tell us what being religious was. I remarked that the twentieth century had seen many attempts to tell us what it was, all the way from Pusey's view of religion as feeling and willing rather than knowing to my own view that religion is a total way of life that is simultaneously cognitive, aesthetic, moral, and even political. Religion is a species of poetry according to Santayana, a variety of shared experience according to Dewey, ethical culture according to some, and insight into human nature according to those I called "Atheists for Niebuhr." My own view was that a religion is not any one of these things taken by itself but rather an organic union of all of or most of them. Accordingly, I said, no seriously religious person can adopt a religion made up of the liturgy of Roman Catholicism, the ethics of Judaism, and the theology of Protestantism; each of these traditional religions is a whole that contains a particular liturgy, a particular ethics, and a particular set of dogmas that cannot be united as we can eclectically unite furniture of different styles or periods while decorating a house. A religion, I said, binds statements, feelings, tastes, customs, attitudes, and actions to each other. Therefore I concluded that "[t]o teach people to be religious . . . we must do something which is beyond the function of an undergraduate college simply because it involves inculcating a total appreciation of and belief in historical religions treated as the vast, all-embracing structures that they are. But are we prepared, I asked, to lecture as advocates in Judaism 7, Catholicism 8, and Protestantism 9?"—meaning: "Are we prepared to inculcate all of these religions at Harvard?" In my view of religion and of being religious, I went on, it would be impossible to teach students to be religious without teaching them to accept a particular religion. But in that case, I asked, *which* religion should be taught at Harvard in the middle of the twentieth century? And if we cannot pick *one* religion to teach, can we teach three or more incompatible religions?

The reception of my article was on the whole very favorable. It was mentioned by *Time* magazine in its issue for January 24, 1955, so I received a fair amount of mail about it, most of it sympathetic. Robert Oppenheimer liked it very much; so did Reuben Brower of the Harvard English department. Judge Charles Wyzanski praised it, and so did Brand Blanshard, Howard Mumford Jones, David Riesman, Ernest Nagel, Philip Rahv, Harold Cherniss, and many other people of different religious backgrounds and philosophical persuasions. I had struck a resounding note that many people had been waiting to hear from someone on the Harvard faculty. Robert Oppenheimer wrote me on January 11, 1955: "I read it and liked it immensely, and without reservations. I hope someone else will read it too; it is a brave job." By "someone else" Oppenheimer meant Pusey, of course. Ernest Nagel wrote me on April 3: "I do not recall whether I wrote you about your *Confluence* piece. If I did not, I want to say now that I thought you did a very clever job (or am I wrong that it was aimed in part at your Prexy?) and that I enjoyed it very much."

The article *was*, as I have said, aimed at Pusey's views. I tried my best to indicate to him that I disagreed with him sharply on the question of religion at Harvard, and I had another opportunity to do so after he published his annual report for the year 1954–55. There too Pusey delivered himself on religious instruction at Harvard. He wrote, for example:

If it was only yesterday that theology was simply "tolerated" within universities as a harmless survival from an earlier day which it would be needlessly embarrassing to expunge, today it is almost universally acknowledged that the study of religion rightfully belongs, and that this is so because religion's concerns make valid claims upon us all. In view of this changing attitude toward religion, it becomes even more important that the subject be given expert attention within the university by scholars of the highest competence who can study theology fully because they do so as committed men.

Soon after reading this, I spoke before the Hillel Foundation at Harvard on December 3, 1956, and criticized this statement of Pusey's in a talk that later became an article I published in *Confluence* in the summer of 1957 under the title "Religious Commitment and Higher Education." There I addressed the following two questions: "Can a teacher give instruction—excellent instruction—*about* a given religion without being committed to that religion? Can a scholar successfully study a given religion without being committed to that religion?" I answered both questions in the affirmative, saying that we can understand a statement without accepting it, understand a style of literature without admiring it, understand the motives of Napoleon, Caesar, or Stalin without sharing them. I said that a non-Aristotelian could effectively expound Aristotle, that a professor of English who did not agree with Emerson's transcendentalism could lecture informatively about it, that a Byzantinist need not belong to the Greek Orthodox Church, and that an anthropologist could study the Zunis without being one of them. Coming closer to home, I mentioned two great Harvard scholars: the Protestant George Foote Moore, who had produced profound studies of Judaism, and the Jewish Harry Wolfson, who had brilliantly illuminated the philosophy of the church fathers.

It was not long before the whole issue of religion at Harvard under Pusey came to a head, in the spring of 1958. One of the main precipitants was a long article in the *Harvard Crimson* by William Bartley, then a student of philosophy, later a teacher of it before his death. The article quoted me favorably at several points—so favorably and so often that I was wrongly thought to have instigated it. In the course of his mainly philosophical discussion of the role of religion in education, Bartley reported as follows on the views and actions of George Buttrick, preacher to the university:

> In 1955 . . . Professor Buttrick refused to permit a Jewish student to be married in Memorial Church by a Rabbi. This month he re-affirmed the "Protestant Christian" tradition of the church and his conviction

that "it would be intellectually dishonest for Christian and Jewish marriages to be carried on beneath the same roof." Deploring the use of shifting altars at M.I.T.'s chapel, Buttrick praised Brandeis University's decision to build three separate chapels. Acknowledging that there should be some official place at Harvard where Jews might marry and worship, Buttrick suggested that a synagogue be built—"at the initiative of the Hebrew Community"—on University property in the Yard. As an indication of his own tolerant spirit he said he would ask to be allowed to contribute the "first $100 toward the building."

Bartley's article appeared on March 28, 1958. On Wednesday, April 9, the following letter from Pusey appeared in the *Crimson*:

To the Editors of the *Crimson*:

The *Crimson*'s recent article on Religion at Harvard and the subsequent editorial would lead your readers to believe that a fundamental change has been made in the role of the Memorial Church at Harvard and that this change has been brought about by the present Preacher to the University. Such is not the case.

Harvard's historic tradition has been a Christian tradition, and although Memorial Church is not considered as affiliated with any one denomination it has always been thought of as a house of Christian worship. This was made explicit both in the architecture and symbolism of the present building and in Dean Sperry's words: "Wherefore unto the King Eternal, Immortal, Invisible, the only Wise God, we dedicate this Church in the service of Christ."

Occasionally in the past people of other faiths have requested the private use of the Chapel for non-Christian services, such as marriages or funerals. In all such cases the University Preacher and his predecessors have made clear that the Corporation feels that the Memorial Church is a place of Christian worship. So far as I know the only isolated exceptions to this rule occurred without authorization, or when there was no Chairman of the Board of Preachers.

The Corporation has always felt that the many churches in the vicinity of the Square and other places of worship in the Boston area would be preferred by those who are firmly attached to one religious persuasion or another. For those who do not feel they want to use such places of worship and yet still prefer a non-Christian service, Harvard has always been willing to provide facilities in Phillips Brooks House or elsewhere in the University.

In response to Pusey's letter, the faculty was in an uproar. Arthur Schlesinger Jr. and I quickly gathered together a number of faculty members who shared our outrage at Pusey's letter. According to my datebook we met on Monday, April 14, 1958, at the Faculty Club, to which I brought the draft of a letter to Pusey. It was revised and then signed by the following: Arthur Schlesinger Jr., Philip LeCorbeiller, George Williams, Myron Gilmore, Samuel H. Beer, Robert G. McCloskey, I. B. Cohen, J. K. Galbraith, and me. The letter was then circulated throughout the faculty for additional signatures. It was headed "NOT FOR RELEASE TO ANY NEWSPAPER" because some members of the group preferred that way of stimulating the president and the corporation to act. The letter read:

> Dear President Pusey:
>
> We, the undersigned members of the faculty of Harvard University, wish to reaffirm the spirit of William James' "True Harvard," a Harvard which should be as free and tolerant in religious matters as it is in all others which affect the lives of civilized men. And if, unhappily, there should be any legislation of the Corporation which is incompatible with this spirit, the corporation should rescind such legislation so that there can be no doubt as to where Harvard stands today and where it will stand in the future on the question of religious freedom and equality. We believe that any refusal to permit the burial or the marriage of non-Protestant students or officers in accordance with non-Protestant services in Memorial chapel constitutes a rejection of one of Harvard's greatest values. We believe, therefore, that the University should now reaffirm its belief in tolerance and freedom of religion.

After only a day or so of circulation, the letter bore more than fifty additional signatures of members of the faculty and was presented to Pusey at a meeting with him on Thursday, April 17. The letter was delivered to Pusey by a group including many who had drafted it. Because some of the original signers were unable to come to this session with Pusey, it was thought desirable to invite replacements. As a result, some of the most respected and most respectable members of the faculty turned up at this meeting. The two most distinguished attendants were C. H. McIlwain, the political scientist, by then a very old emeritus professor, and William L. Langer, the eminent historian. In addition there were J. L. Adams and Krister Stendahl of the Divinity School, Mark Howe of the Law School, and from the Faculty of Arts and Sciences there were Samuel Beer, Robert McCloskey, Myron Gilmore, I. B. Cohen, John Finley, Perry Miller, and myself. I kept no notes on the meeting, but I do remember that Pusey was both nervous and unyielding. I especially recall Perry Miller's remark about our not liking the pietistic fallout around the Yard. And I remember my saying to Pusey that while his published statements about religion were so inclusive as to make it identical with feeling—something that everyone could do together—his attitude toward the chapel was the height of exclusivism in religion. I came away from the meeting deeply depressed. Pusey remained stubborn, saying only that he would appoint a committee to study the entire matter.

Meanwhile, however, the corporation must have been thinking differently. For at its meeting the following week, it agreed to what it called a modification of its policy governing Memorial Church and abandoned the position that Pusey favored. The University News Office reported this in a release for the morning papers on Wednesday, April 23, that read as follows: "Upon recommendation of the Chairman of the Board of Preachers, the Harvard Corporation agreed this week to modify its policy governing Memorial Church to permit its use on certain occasions for private non-Christian ceremonies conducted by officials of other religions. The historically Christian church had been a center of recent discussion because of the University's long-time policy requiring the presence of a Protestant clergyman for marriages or funerals of non-Christians."

In announcing this modification of policy the corporation stated:

> Throughout its history Harvard has felt obligated to provide a place of Christian worship for members of the University community. In continuing to do so, the University does not intend to assert the validity of the tenets of any denomination or creed. Its services are conducted both in response to a want felt by many of its members and in recognition of the fact that worship has an appropriate place in a community of learning. The form of worship observed in the Memorial Church stems from Harvard's Christian tradition. Though necessarily particular in character, it is nevertheless intended to support the universal values of religion.
>
> It is clearly gain that the Harvard community is today a mixed society. It contains numerous groups with religious loyalties other than those

which gave shape to Harvard's ceremonies of public worship. Generations ago religious worship at Harvard was separated from the secular activities of academic life. Today as earlier, the Christian church within the complex society of contemporary Harvard has a duty while keeping its identity to try to honor the convictions of each member of the Harvard community. Accordingly—in part because the church building is a memorial to all the Harvard men who fell in World Wars I and II—we recognize, as our predecessors did, that Harvard's Christian church ought, whenever it appropriately can, to offer hospitality to members of its community for private marriage and funeral ceremonies.

It is now agreed, therefore, that such private services may be conducted in Memorial Church by an official of an individual's own religion when this is desired, provided he is willing to do so notwithstanding the church's essentially Christian character. As in the past the responsibility for granting permission for the use of the church is lodged with the Chairman of the Board of Preachers.

Once Pusey was reined in by the corporation on the religious issue, he gave up talking about religion for a while, and Harvard was spared a good deal of his theology and philosophy. I think it worth adding, however, that in spite of the great regard in which Pusey held Reinhold Niebuhr, some of Pusey's sharpest critics on the faculty were those I have called "Atheists for Niebuhr." Not only was Arthur Schlesinger Jr. in the vanguard of the anti-Puseyites on the chapel issue, but he thought little of Pusey as a president and believed that the setback he had received might unseat him. It was rumored that Dean McGeorge Bundy had privately condemned Pusey's stand on the chapel and had strongly disapproved of his letter to the *Crimson*. Then there were all those religious professors at the Divinity School who signed the letter to Pusey and who regarded him with less than enthusiasm.

Pusey's stock was low in 1958, but I think it sank lower a decade later, when his actions and his failures to act led to much more disastrous consequences. Unfortunately, many who saw how unwise Pusey had been on the chapel issue did not see his failings in 1969, for during the intervening ten years a number of them who had criticized him in 1958 became his supporters. Why they shifted is a long and complicated story. They were older without being wiser, but something else was involved. I suspect that when Pusey was rebuffed on the religious issue, he shrewdly decided that he would try to win over some of his opponents by luring them into the Establishment in a way that made it difficult for them to abandon him in 1969. In my own case, the reverse was true. I had reached the high point in my influence at Harvard under Conant and Buck in the early fifties, and whatever influence I won after that, I did not win from Pusey. My differences with him over the chapel may explain his unwillingness to approve my appointment to a position at the Harvard University Press for which I had been recommended a few years after the controversy. The story of that has never been made public before.

In 1961 I was asked by Thomas J. Wilson, then director of the Harvard University Press, whether I would accept an appointment as editor in chief of the John Harvard Library beginning in 1962. The John Harvard Library was a series of books deemed to be important for the study of the American past, mostly books that had gone out of print. I said that I would accept, and therefore Wilson sent me a copy of the letter recommending my appointment to the Harvard Corporation on August 31, 1961.

Gentlemen:

I understand that it will be impossible for this Press to have the benefit of Professor Howard Mumford Jones' services as editor-in-chief of the John Harvard Library after 30 June 1962, when his present term in that position expires. The Board of Syndics of the Press has instructed me to recommend to you that Professor Morton G. White be made Professor Jones' successor as editor-in-chief of the John Harvard Library as of 1 July 1962.

Professor White's qualifications for this position are of course obvious and we shall be most fortunate to have him work with us. Furthermore, as a member of the Board of Syndics, he has worked for some years on the special committee of the Syndics to which the Editorial Board of the Library has been responsible.

In order to achieve the maximum of continuity in this important matter, we should also like to have Mr. White serve with the Editorial Board of the Library as a regular member of that Board during the coming academic year, while Mr. Jones is still editor-in-chief.

Therefore, we respectfully request that the President and Fellows make the following appointments:

1. Professor Morton G. White to be a member of the Editorial Board of the John Harvard Library from 1 October 1961 to 30 June 1962.

2. Professor Morton G. White to be editor-in-chief of the John Harvard Library from 1 July 1962 to 30 June 1965, and that Professor White's compensation as editor-in-chief of John Harvard Library be at the rate of $3,000 a year during his period as editor-in-chief. This rate is now being paid to Professor Jones for the same services.

Believe me,

> Very truly yours,
> Thomas J. Wilson
> Director, Harvard University
>   Press
> Chairman of Board of Syndics
> Harvard University Press

I heard nothing for quite a while, but in January I was told by Wilson that a most unusual thing had happened: the corporation had refused to appoint me. Wilson sent me a copy of a letter sent in response to the corporation, otherwise known as the President and Fellows of Harvard College. It was written by a subcommittee of the board of syndics—the faculty committee that had responsibility for the editorial policy of the press. They wrote:

> . . . the Syndics have been greatly disturbed by the refusal of The President and Fellows to approve the Board's first recommendation that Professor Morton G. White be made editor-in-chief of the Library. Many of us interpret this action to mean that the Corporation thought the nomination of Professor White an insufficiently considered one, made without adequate reference to the requirements of the position. This interpretation appears to be confirmed by the informally given explanation that the chief editor of the Library should be a historian or a scholar in American literature whereas Mr. White is a philosopher.
> We assume that, in the interests of good working relationships within the University, The President and Fellows would refrain from overriding the judgment of those whom they have made responsible for the editorial policy of the Press with respect to such a question as this, of scholarly capacity and necessary scholarly qualifications, unless they thought the judgment to be seriously deficient. Thus, we cannot fail to

view the action on Mr. White's nomination as a rather extraordinary expression of lack of confidence in the Board of Syndics.

In response we can do no more than to assure The President and Fellows that we named Mr. White only after full thought and discussion. Though he is Professor of Philosophy in Harvard University, he is also an outstanding historian of American civilization and ideas, recognized throughout the United States for his accomplishments in these fields which are the foundation on which The John Harvard Library is building. In fact, Mr. White's next book, THE FEAR OF THE AMERICAN CITY: From Thomas Jefferson to Frank Lloyd Wright, which the Press will publish in 1962, is a work in American social and literary history that is brilliant proof of his competence and, it seems to us, of the soundness of our original recommendation.

The book to which Wilson referred in his letter had already been accepted by the press. It was written by Lucia and me, and was finally entitled *The Intellectual Versus the City: From Thomas Jefferson to Frank Lloyd Wright.* My own *Social Thought in America* was by then a well-known book in the field of American studies, and I had been for many years a member of Harvard's Committee on Higher Degrees in American Civilization. I was a scholar of standing in the field of American intellectual history, yet I suspected that some specialists in American history or American literature might have resented my appointment and might have protested to Pusey. It was clear that somebody was working against me, as may be seen in Pusey's response of February 6, 1962, to the syndics' letter. A copy of that letter was sent to me by Tom Wilson.

In it Pusey wrote that the corporation's failure to act in the case of the syndics' recommendation was not a "refusal" to appoint me editor of the John Harvard Library and that it was not an expression of lack of confidence in the board of syndics. The corporation, he said, was merely raising a question and encouraging an exchange of ideas about a recommendation for an appointment. Pusey then went on to lecture Wilson on the nature of the legal relationship between the press, the corporation, the board of syndics, and another body called the board of directors of the press. He insisted that the president was the ordinary means of communication between the corporation and the press, that he had the right to ask reconsideration of any recommendation for appointment, and that the corporation had the ultimate responsibility in approving appointments. At the bottom of a copy of this letter, Wilson wrote in his own hand: "Morty—as you will see, this letter completely begs the question—avoids the two most important points—our firm recommendation and their refusal, orally delivered by the President, but absolutely definite as————can testify. Tom." I use a blank in the above because I cannot decipher the name used there. Wilson made clear to me that Pusey was exploiting the distinction between *refusing to appoint* and *not appointing*—in this case a distinction without a difference.

After reading Pusey's letter to Wilson, I concluded that although he was a Christian, he was not as good a Christian as he would have had to be in order to forgive or forget some of my actions. Only once did he seem temporarily inclined to forget our differences; and that was in the summer of 1962, when I was considering an invitation to become dean of the humanities at the University of Chicago. In the academic year 1961–62 Pusey was serving as his own dean of the Faculty of Arts and Sciences, and was therefore obliged to react to the offer that Chicago had made me when I brought it to his attention. I was earning $19,000 per annum at Harvard, but Chicago offered me a university professorship at $30,000, plus an additional $5,000 while I was dean. When I went to see Pusey, he went through a long song and dance, looked up the salaries of other Harvard people of my age, and finally offered me a raise of $2,000, which, he said, brought me to the very top of my age-group in salary. For a variety of reasons, I decided to stay at Harvard, and when I wrote Pusey that I would be staying, he wrote me a note in which he addressed me by my first name, signed himself "Nate," expressed his pleasure over my decision to stay, and said philosophy, the humanities, and the social sciences at Harvard all needed my presence.

I remind the reader that this note was written about a year after Pusey denied me the editorship of the John Harvard Library because I was allegedly not enough of a literary scholar or historian, yet he was now telling me that Harvard philosophy, Harvard humanities, and Harvard social sciences all needed my presence. When I told Tom Wilson about this, he remarked that it was one thing for Pusey to deny me the editorship but another to lose me as a member of the faculty. Tom thought that although Pusey feared that he might be criticized for losing me to Chicago, he had felt little compunction about preventing me from becoming editor of the John Harvard Library, since he knew that I would not be likely to resign over that small an issue.

Although Pusey mollified me when he gave me a raise, I was not to remain permanently mollified, for in 1969 I was once again at odds with him on an issue of far greater importance. When he called the police into Harvard Yard in 1969 (about which more later), I believe he subjected the university to a blow from which it would not recover for years. I hope that my saying this will not be regarded as an expression of personal dislike for Pusey. Naturally, I was affected by his preventing me from becoming editor of the John Harvard Library, since I could hardly be expected to have loved him for that. My objection had to do with his ideas, especially his theories about the role of religion in education. Like Holmes and Dewey, I thought that theories can be the most practical things in the world, and I feared that Pusey's educational theories would harm a great university that had treated me extremely well before he had come on the scene.

Some of my readers may wonder why a nonbelieving, nonobservant Jew was so aroused by the fact that Pusey tried to discourage Harvard Jews from getting married in Appleton Chapel. Indeed, many Jews on the faculty sat out the controversy because they despised those Jews who wanted to be married in a Protestant Chapel; for example, my friend Wolfson took this view and remained totally silent on the issue. I should say for myself that I was not so much upset by Pusey's attitude toward the use of the chapel as I was by what Perry Miller had described as the general pietistic fallout that might smother many who had once flourished at Harvard. For this reason I used my philosophical wits to oppose Pusey's views on religion in education. Not all philosophers engage in this sort of polemic; some avoid it because they have no skill at it, some because they have no stomach for it, and some because they think it beneath them. However, when I lit into Robert Hutchins, Alfred Korzybski, and Stuart Chase in my youth, I was encouraged by the existence of a long tradition in which philosophers took on what were called philosophasters in the seventeenth century. Locke went after Filmer, and Kant went after Swedenborg, and I was proud to follow in their footsteps by taking on Nathan Pusey and later the more famous Reinhold Niebuhr and Walter Lippmann.

Soon after coming to Harvard I began to wonder why some of my friends at Harvard admired some of the ideas of Niebuhr—why they found his views on human nature superior to those of John Dewey, and why they thought Niebuhr had provided a firmer foundation for liberal politics than Dewey had. At about the same time, I began to wonder how the "new conservatives" could admire Walter Lippmann's book *The Public Philosophy* and the weakly defended version of the doctrine of natural law he advocated there. So, when my *Social Thought in America* was about to be issued in paperback, I decided to give voice to my reservations about the ideas of Niebuhr and Lippmann in a new epilogue. I thought Niebuhr's views on human nature, especially those on original sin, might be instructively compared with those of Dewey, and that Lippmann's views on natural law might be usefully compared with those of Holmes. I took the occasion to say that although I had criticized Dewey and Holmes in *Social Thought in America*, I was even more critical of Niebuhr's doctrine of original sin and Lippmann's doctrine of natural law. I emphasized that I did not share Niebuhr's religious faith, that I did not approve of his Hegelian way of dealing with contradictions between his views on original sin and those on free will, and that I deplored Lippmann's second-rate revival of the doctrine of natural law. It seemed "to me a sad commentary on American thought . . . that two of our most popular social thinkers can produce nothing more original or natural than original sin and natural law as answers to the pressing problems of this age."

According to some of my liberal Harvard friends, Niebuhr was aware of man's selfishness and his incapacity to free himself from the effects of original sin, while Dewey was innocently optimistic and unable to illuminate the world of gas chambers and mushroom clouds. Niebuhr, they said, represented tough Christian realism, whereas Dewey was a soft-headed, dreamy, secular child of light in Niebuhr's biblical phrase. With this in mind, I proceeded to examine Niebuhr's view that children of darkness know no law beyond their will and interest, whereas children of light "may . . . be defined as those who seek to bring self-interest under the discipline of a more universal law and in harmony with a more universal good." It seemed to me that on the basis of this definition Niebuhr could hardly find fault with children of light, since seeking to bring self-interest under more universal law and in harmony with a more universal good came pretty close to trying to act morally. And since it struck me as questionable to condemn Dewey for being a child of light according to Niebuhr's definition, I asked whether Niebuhr might instead want to define children of light as (*a*) those who think it *easy* for men to bring self-interest under law, or as (*b*) those who think that they can bring self-interest *completely* under moral law and reach a state in which they never assign weight to their own interests. But I said that if Niebuhr viewed children of light in either of these ways, Dewey could not be called a child of light. Dewey held that social change could be accomplished without the use of violence, but he did not believe that the road to social happiness would be *easy*, and he certainly did not believe that a time would come when *all* human action would be morally right and all tensions resolved. It seemed to me therefore that the difference between Dewey and Niebuhr on human nature could best be expressed by saying that one of them thought that man was better than the other thought he was but that neither of them thought man was perfect. It also seemed to me that however short of perfection men fell, it did not help to explain their limitations by appealing to what happened in the Garden of Eden. In short, I wondered why my liberal friends gave any credit at all to Niebuhr for saying in effect that men were not gods or angels.

For the benefit of Niebuhr's Harvard admirers who inveighed against the idea of historical inevitability, I pointed out that he defended his views on human nature by appealing to a view of history as rigid as any advocated by Marx. After all, Niebuhr asserted the existence of "vast forces of historical destiny," of "inexorable historical developments," and of "inevitability in human history" while arguing that man sinned necessarily. Furthermore, he also said in his *Nature and Destiny of Man* that his belief that men sin necessarily *and* that they are morally responsible for their sins transcended the canons of rationality. I called attention to his admission that "a view which depends upon an ultra-rational presupposition is immediately endangered when rationally explicated" as well as his admission that "the Christian doctrine of sin in its classical form offends both rationalists and moralists by maintaining the *seemingly* [my italics] absurd position that man sins inevitably and by a fateful necessity, but that he is nevertheless to be held responsible for actions which are prompted by an ineluctable fate." Elsewhere, I added, he flatly says that this position *is* absurd—not just *seemingly* absurd. How, then, I asked, did Niebuhr deal with what he thought was an absurdity? It seemed to me that he dealt with it by appealing to a kind of obscurantism that I found appalling, since he held that the doctrine of original sin

> remains absurd from the standpoint of a pure rationalism, for it expresses a relation between fate and freedom which cannot be fully rationalized, unless the paradox be accepted as a rational understanding of the limits of rationality and as an expression of faith that a rationally irresolvable contradiction may point to a truth which logic cannot contain. Formally there can be of course no conflict between logic and truth. The laws of logic are reason's guard against chaos in the realm of truth. They eliminate contradictory assertions. But there is no resource in logical rules to help us understand complex phenomena, exhibiting characteristics which seem to require that they be placed into contradictory categories of reason.

After noting that Niebuhr tried to disarm some of his readers by adding that "[l]oyalty to all the facts may require a *provisional* [my italics] defiance of logic, lest complexity in the facts of experience be denied for the sake of a premature logical consistency," I asked: "How long does he want us to wait?"

and I quoted his unhelpful Marx-like appeal to Hegel: "Hegel's 'dialectic' is a logic invented for the purpose of doing justice to the fact of 'becoming' as a phenomenon which belongs into the category of neither 'being' nor 'non-being'. The Christian doctrine of original sin, with its seemingly contradictory assertions about the inevitability of sin and man's responsibility for sin, is a dialectical truth which does justice to the fact that man's self-love and self-centeredness is inevitable." Mainly with Arthur Schlesinger in mind, I summed up by saying that Niebuhr had not provided a defensible philosophical outlook that could logically sustain a liberal attitude in politics. It was one thing, I said, to vote the same ticket with Niebuhr, but another to admire his philosophy, and so I rejected the idea that Niebuhr had come in triumph over Dewey as a philosopher of American liberalism.

Although my epilogue also referred to Lippmann's views on natural law, I found them so weak that I took the occasion to criticize the views of John Locke and Thomas Aquinas instead. Lippmann's view of natural law was so unpersuasive that almost nobody defended it to me in correspondence. Justice Learned Hand dismissed Lippmann's views in a letter of September 20, 1956, as "a kind of Platonism," and McGeorge Bundy denied that he agreed with Lippmann because he was thanked in the preface of Lippmann's *Public Philosophy*. Bundy wrote me on April 27, 1956, that he had not read the preface, and went on to say that although he liked and respected Lippmann, and had considerable sympathy with some of the practical political judgments in the book, he had advised that it not be published, precisely because its discussion of natural law was unsatisfactory. I don't recall sending my piece in the *Partisan Review* to Lippmann, and I don't know whether he read it. In any case he never replied to my criticisms of his views on natural law, whereas Niebuhr quickly responded in a two-and-a-half-page single-spaced letter on May 17, 1956, to which I replied on June 29 in a letter of about the same length.

Niebuhr thanked me for sending him my piece and, possibly with tongue in cheek, for my great desire to be fair in argument. He added that although I had not always been as fair as I wanted to be, my arguments had "been much fairer than most polemical arguments turn out to be, including [his] own." Immediately after that he criticized a remark that I had made while making a transition between the two main parts of my essay, my statement that "Niebuhr's Augustinian doctrine of original sin is neatly matched by the Thomistic doctrine of natural law in Lippman." Niebuhr objected strongly to my linking him with Lippmann, especially because, as he pointed out, I had acknowledged that he disagreed with Lippmann in certain important respects. But I linked Niebuhr's doctrine of original sin with Lippmann's theory of natural law only because they were at bottom religious views that were opposed to the naturalism and empiricism of Dewey and Holmes, and I don't think that was unfair.

The most interesting part of Niebuhr's first letter to me was his charge that I did not mention what he called his chief criticism of Dewey: "The criticism of his opinion that the 'scientific method' could be applied with the same validity in the historical as in the natural realm, if only, in the warfare between science and religion, a truce had not been made prematurely delivering the historical sciences to the interference of 'State and Church' and therefore condemning them to permanent inexactitude." Niebuhr called this "the root error of modern culture, resting on the failure to recognize the intimate relation between reason and interest and passion in all historical judgments." Then, in an effort to counter my remark that he was "a devotee of the a priori road that begins with a theology based on faith," he protested that he had learned empirically of "the taint of interest upon the purity of reason" and not in an a priori manner. He wondered therefore whether he might have been foolish to call "the inevitability of self-regard in various forms 'original sin,'" since many nonreligious historians and political scientists who agreed with him about self-regard were not criticized as he was. However, he tacitly acknowledged one important difference between himself and his nonreligious colleagues when he said that after coming upon the views of Augustine and Paul, he "began to speculate about the mystery of the universality of inordinate self-regard and the paradox of our feeling of responsibility for our selfishness." Niebuhr added that Augustine's "presuppositions seemed to throw light upon facts that had perplexed [him]," but he did not even try to say in his letter how those "presuppositions" threw light on that mystery or resolved that paradox.

As I reflect on Niebuhr's response, I still think I was right to call attention to his use of nonempirical methods in spite of his insistence that he had learned empirically of the taint of interest on reason. The point is that he tried to *throw light on* or *explain* his empirical belief by appealing to a theory that was *not* empirical, and was therefore subject to criticism that could not be justly leveled against those historians and political scientists who did not try to *explain* their empirical discoveries by appealing to a theological dogma. By contrast, Niebuhr did attempt such an explanation, and that is why I could not understand why my atheistic or agnostic Harvard colleagues had heaped so much praise on his work. Surely they did not need the ghost of neoorthodoxy to teach them that as a matter of fact interest often tainted reason, and surely they could not, as atheists or agnostics, accept the Christian dogma that Niebuhr relied on in his theological explanation of a psychological fact.

Some of this criticism I had expressed in a review of Niebuhr's book *The Irony of American History* that I had published in the *New Republic* in 1952. This same book was reviewed in the *Christian Century* a little later by Arthur Schlesinger Jr., who used the occasion to criticize some things I had said in my review. After saying of Anthony West's review in the *New Yorker* that "it is impossible to believe that Mr. West read Niebuhr's book," Schlesinger wrote: "But Professor White, who is one of the best of our younger philosophers, does show some signs of having read *The Irony of American History*. This makes it all the more difficult to see how he has succeeded in so generally misunderstanding it." I hit the roof hard when I read the phrase "*some* signs" and wrote Arthur a letter on August 30, 1952, in which I expressed my anger. He replied in a brief note that he was sorry to have given offense and that his remark "was intended to differentiate [me] favorably—and not invidiously from other reviewers." The whole thing blew over pretty quickly, since our friendship was strong enough to survive our disagreement. But our exchange reveals one of the fundamental reasons for my publishing "Original Sin, Natural Law, and Politics" four years later. In my reply to Arthur's letter I said that I could not see how an agnostic or atheistic liberal like him, who did not believe in Niebuhr's God, could accept what Niebuhr called the ultrarational doctrine of original sin, and I might have added that I could not see how an anti-Hegelian like him could accept Niebuhr's dialectical resolution of his belief that original sin and blame were incompatible. I granted that Arthur might vote with Niebuhr and other Americans for Democratic Action, enjoy his sermons, seek his advice, and value his wisdom on political matters, but in rejecting Niebuhr's theology he rejected the one belief that distinguished Niebuhr's theory of human nature from that of naturalists like Dewey and Holmes, who also recognized that men were not perfect.

In reply, Arthur wrote: "As for the matter at issue, I fear it is basically a difference between the philosopher and the historian. For you the logical foundations of a faith have most reality; for me, perhaps, the psychological and social. I do not conclude from this that we differ as to the substance of the faith." Our correspondence on this matter ended there, and we have remained good friends ever since, but I should say here that I still disagree with Arthur's appraisal of Niebuhr's version of the doctrine of original sin even though I agree with both of them (and the authors of the *Federalist*

Papers as well as many others) that interest and passion often interfere with our efforts to use reason in inquiries about human beings. I insist, however, that this cannot be *explained*, *clarified*, or *supported* by the doctrine of original sin, and if I am right about that, it is hard to see how an atheist or agnostic can give many points to Niebuhr for his views on human nature. In criticizing Niebuhr as I did, I tried to do what philosophers often do when criticizing philosophasters. And though this may seem a waste of time to some philosophers among my friends, I hope that in doing so I have contributed to the advancement of understanding and to a recognition that philosophy can play a part in the task of critically analyzing general ideas that appear in everyday discussions of religion, politics, and education.

15

English Philosophy at Midcentury
Moore, Russell, and Wittgenstein

Because my interest in the history of ideas, in the philosophy of history, and in what is sometimes called cultural criticism distinguished me from most of my Harvard philosophical colleagues, I could easily avoid stepping on their toes by teaching subjects in which they had little scholarly or proprietary interest; indeed, most of them looked down on those subjects from what they regarded as their lofty perches in pure philosophy. And since I was not overly impressed by the philosophical skills of my colleagues other than Lewis and Quine, I knew those colleagues were not imparting truths that made it unnecessary for me to speak out on systematic topics. Indeed, I sometimes wondered whether I should give up teaching in the history of ideas entirely for teaching in systematic philosophy. Even though I was urged by my well-wishers in American literature and history to teach the former, I ceased doing so after my first year at Harvard. The closest I came to lecturing on things of interest to Perry Miller and the two Arthur Schlesingers was in my course in the history of American philosophy and one in the philosophy of history, where I dealt with such questions as historical explanation and the concept of narration. The latter course was attended primarily by under-graduates, the majority of them concentrators in history, whereas my much more technical Philosophy 154, Problems of Analytic Philosophy, was mainly attended by undergraduate and graduate students of philosophy. I first gave Philosophy 154 in the fall of 1951, when I also gave a seminar on Oxford philosophy devoted to the writings of Ryle, Austin, Strawson, Hampshire, and Hart, philosophers who had been commended to me by Isaiah Berlin in 1949. Berlin had urged me to go to Oxford on my Guggenheim in 1950–51 so that I could find out at first hand what was happening there. I spent the fall at home trying as much as possible to avoid departmental business and then went abroad at the end of March. While I was in England, I was prevailed on to give a talk on the BBC after much doubt about whether I should. I was unsure whether I could expound philosophical ideas for nonphilosophers without at the same time offending professionals. I tried to solve the problem by taking Lucia's advice that I speak as though I were sending a letter to Arthur Schlesinger Jr., so I must thank Arthur for helping me in writing philosophy as well as history.

Although I was to spend most of my time in Oxford, my talk was devoted to the triumph of analytic philosophy as represented by G. E. Moore, Bertrand Russell, and Ludwig Wittgenstein of Cambridge, a fact that is easily explained. When I was asked to give the talk, I had not been in England very long, and so I was not familiar enough with the *dernier cri* at Oxford to report on that in anything like an authoritative way. However, it seemed obvious to me that what was being said at Oxford took off, so to speak, from what Moore, Russell, and Wittgenstein had said earlier, and, what is more important, I knew more about their views than I did about the views of the Oxonians.

I began my talk by saying that profound differences within the analytic movement made it extremely difficult to present one doctrinal platform to which Moore, Russell, and Wittgenstein would subscribe but that there were a number of important common traits in their writings. I noted how hostile to traditional metaphysics all of them were and how often they insisted that philosophy as they conceived it was not a rival of ordinary language or science but rather an activity intended to clarify both. I observed how little concerned they were with advancing a moral philosophy in the sense of a guide to life, and how intensely preoccupied they were with finding out what we mean by or how we use the words "good," "bad," "right," and "wrong." I also observed how analytic philosophy had become absorbed with language, how it treated some traditional problems as the products of linguistic confusion, and how it had drastically revised the formulation of others. I said that English philosophy seemed unlikely to return to the sort of speculation that had preceded the emergence of analytic philosophy and, in a remark that my English friends seemed especially to like, that Oxford, the university Americans regarded as the last haven of idealism, Platonism, Aristotelianism, and moral piety, "was now a philosophical boomtown where linguistic analysis was all the rage."

In passing I made a few remarks about what was happening at home, especially with Harvard in mind. I said, as I thought silently of my senior colleagues' search for a young Royce or Santayana, that we had not yet come to the point where linguistic philosophy had attained the respectability it had in England, but that we had come far in that direction. Almost all our able young philosophers, I said, had been influenced by some form of analytic philosophy—so much so that more traditional American professors, when they chose their successors, were willing to sacrifice something they dismissed as cleverness and ingenuity for something else called vision. American partisans of traditional metaphysics and moral philosophy, I thought, yearned for a bright young philosopher-prince who would come to slay all the positivistic dragons and restore philosophy to its ancient dignity and solemnity. I confessed that I had not met this attitude in England but suspected that there were many traditionalists who patiently awaited the day when the analytic movement would have spent itself.

Because of the triumph of analytic philosophy, I continued, it was no longer possible to speak of it as a single undifferentiated movement; sects and varieties had appeared with the advance of the century. Even the superficial historian, I thought, was likely to distinguish at least three strains, and each of them would probably be identified with one of the three philosophers I had mentioned. Russell was the legendary leader of those who apply the techniques of mathematical logic to the problems of philosophy. No matter how often he might repeat words that resemble Marx's "Je ne suis pas Marxiste," he was the hero of those who build new, artificial languages for the solution of ancient and modern puzzles, whereas G. E. Moore was the patron saint of those who respected ordinary language and who were anxious to examine it in an effort to produce clear synonyms for key philosophical expressions. I then said that Wittgenstein, whose posthumous writings had not yet appeared, abandoned both programs for something that only the most devoted of his disciples were supposed to understand but that had been described as "therapeutic positivism"—the effort to get at the roots of the insoluble problems of philosophy in a way that would make us aware of how we come to ask our strange questions and free us from the need to ask them again. I remarked that the Russellian strain was much less active in England than it was in America, that English philosophical attitudes were much more influenced by Moore and Wittgenstein. In the United States, I reported, there was considerable interest in mathematical logic, both as an independent discipline to be pursued for its own sake and as an instrument for the solution of philosophical problems, whereas in England philosophers had little interest in pure logic or in using it as a tool for philosophy. However, I observed, English philosophers were playing their important and traditional role of warning against the dangers of scholastic verbiage masquerading as science and philosophy. It was pleasant, I said, to report that this was being carried on with great zest and vigilance at Oxford, and encouraging to know that in England free and critical examination of the remote questions of philosophy was still going on.

This talk seems to have been well received, but I should add a story about some political correcting that was done on it by the BBC without consulting me in advance. At the point where I referred to three strains of analytic philosophy, I had in my original text remarked that it would be as difficult and dangerous to summarize the views uniting the philosophies of Moore, Russell, and Wittgenstein as it would be to summarize the views uniting Freud, Jung, and Adler or the principles held in common by all socialists and Communists. However, the producer of the talk removed my reference to the principles held in common by all socialists and Communists, because a general election was going on and therefore the socialists might have said that my lumping socialists together with Communists was objectionable.

This is a convenient place at which to report a nonpolitical change made in a memoir of Moore that I broadcast on the BBC after he died. Upon reading my script, the producer told me that Russell would be speaking on the same program, that he was feeling depressed, and that she wondered whether I could add something a bit soothing after I reported that Moore had felt no obligation, while I was visiting him in 1951, to listen to a talk of Russell's on the BBC. In response to the producer's request, I added a passage in which I said that Moore had once said in my presence that if he had had the difficulties with the Barnes Foundation that Russell had had, he, Moore, would also have sued Barnes. Since this addendum was true, I did not hesitate to include it in my talk, in the good cause of making Russell feel better.

This effort to make Russell feel better was not the only one I have made in my life. I did not really know Russell, but when my book *Toward Reunion in Philosophy* appeared in 1956, I sent him a copy and received the following disconcerting reply:

28 May, 1956
41 Queen's Road
Richmond
Surrey

Dear Professor White:

Thank you for sending me your book *Toward Reunion in Philosophy*. It is full of interesting matter, but I have not yet had time to study it as fully as I hope to do. In so far as it advocates views that are in the direction of Pragmatism, I do not find myself able to agree with what you say. But that will be no surprise to you. I note that you say many things about me and that, in the main, they are such as cannot be displeasing to me. But I find that, in common with most recent English and American philosophical writers, you do not mention anything that I have published during the last thirty years. I should be grateful if you would tell me with complete candour whether this is because you think all my writings during the last thirty years completely worthless or whether it is because you have supposed them not worth reading. A good many of the criticisms that were and are levelled against my earlier writings do not seem to me (though in this I am perhaps mistaken) to be applicable to what I have written more recently. I find, in much recent writing, arguments against views which I long ago abandoned, without any indication as to what I have thought since. I shall be genuinely grateful if you will give me an explanation of this curious fact.

Yours sincerely,
Bertrand Russell

Needless to say, I had a hard time composing my answer to Russell. I did so in the second part of a letter that began with my regretting that he had recently declined an invitation extended by me as chairman of the Harvard Department of Philosophy to give a lecture honoring Whitehead. I wrote:

Dear Mr. Russell:

I was very sorry to hear that you feel unable to give the first Whitehead lecture and I know that my colleagues share my disappointment. We had looked forward so much to hearing you once again.

Having been rushed with examinations, papers, and committee

meetings when your personal letter of 28 May arrived, I am sorry to have delayed my reply to it until the present moment. I can certainly say with complete candor that I have learned a tremendous amount from *all* of your writings, not only those that I discuss in my most recent book *Toward Reunion in Philosophy*, but also your more recent statements of your views. Therefore I can not only say that I have read them but also that I found them eminently instructive and worth reading. I think that by the time you have finished my book you will see that the reasons for my not having considered your later views are chiefly these. Firstly, the plan of the critical part of my book—for better or worse— was to consider three main philosophical movements of the twentieth century: platonic realism (or that I call analytic platonism), several varieties of logical positivism, and several varieties of pragmatism. It seems to me that those views which you (and Moore) expressed early in the century were obviously typical of platonic realism, but that other writers could more properly be taken as representative of positivism and pragmatism, notably Carnap, Wittgenstein, and James. The second, and most important reason, is connected with the fact that two of the major divisions of the book concern the problems of analytic statements and ethics, and these—certainly not the latter—have not been in the forefront of your concern during the last thirty years. What has been most central in the literature on analytic statements has been the view of logical positivists like Carnap, against which I am in reaction. And the so called emotive theory of ethics—against which I am also in reaction—is one which I think you helped originate, but which has been more fully developed by others. . . .

As an expression of my generally sympathetic attitude toward *all* of your views—philosophical and otherwise—I should like to refer you to my book *The Age of Analysis* (Houghton, Mifflin and New American Library, 1955) in which I have a chapter on you. I cannot forbear quoting one sentence about you from that book. I say "No philosopher has had a more salutary influence on the intellectual life of the twentieth century."

Yours sincerely,
Morton White

Russell replied in part:

Plas Penrhyn
Penrhyndeudraeth
Merioneth
21 July, 1956

Dear Professor White,

Thank you for your letter of June 13. I quite understand why, in your book *Toward Reunion in Philosophy*, you concentrated on my earlier views. Thank you also for sending me your book *The Age of Analysis*. I have not yet had time to read either book with careful attention, though I plan to do so before long. What you said about me in *The Age of Analysis* was such as to give pleasure to any author. . . .

Yours sincerely,
Bertrand Russell

Having said something about my talk on the holy family of analytic philosophy—Moore, Russell, and Wittgenstein of Cambridge—I want to say something about my brief visit to the Cambridge home of the Moores in 1951. I described it in some letters to Lucia.

c/o G. E. Moore
86 Chesterton Road
Cambridge, England
May 9, 1951 (Wednesday)

As you see, I have been at the Moores for one night and they've been extremely sweet to me. They both look very well tho Moore *has* aged since we saw him last. He has slowed up physically but his mind is quite as lively as ever. Mrs. Moore tells me that he is very much better than he was about a year ago. His disease is arteriosclerosis and he's had one coronary thrombosis, so that there is a good deal of anxiety about a future attack. They live in a large old house which they once occupied themselves. They own it and rent out two flats as well as a made over stable. This leaves them a large kitchen downstairs (basement) with a bedroom (mine) adjoining, and then on the main floor Moore's bedroom and study. Moore sleeps in the former and Mrs. M. in the latter. They are quite poor and there would be something pathetic about it were it not for Moore's utter indifference to pomp and circumstance. She talks a little nostalgically about the old days but then puts on a certain bravado herself. I was very happy to have your wonderful birthday present which came the day I left so that I could very easily bring the Moores some of the food that had previously come in my family's package—a tinned ham, some bacon, a big bar of bitter-sweet chocolate, and a box of tea. It was very sweet of you to send me your package and I want to thank all you three dears for your kindness. It keeps me well-fed and allows me to be generous.

I spent last night talking some philosophy with Moore and while Mrs. Moore tends to protect him less than she used to, she did suggest that I do the philosophy earlier in the day because he sometimes loses sleep after a night's discussion. He goes to bed at 10:30 so, of course, he can't really get very deeply involved. Tonight John Wisdom, the Cambridge philosopher, is coming to dinner and I shall wait to see whether he initiates the philosophy-talk. There is really much less philosophical activity here than at Oxford. Oxford has 40 philosophers and Cambridge about 7, the point being that at Oxford a man has to take philosophy in two of the courses—"The Greats" (classics and philosophy) and "Modern Greats" (Phil., Politics and Economics)— while at Cambridge you do philosophy all by itself. I suppose I wrote you that the mysterious Wittgenstein has died. The Moores went to his burial and report that a Catholic priest officiated. I wondered whether that meant that he had become a believer again (he was born a Catholic). Many of his most devout disciples are Catholics now—a Miss Anscombe at Oxford, a certain Smithies, a librarian at Oxford— but Moore thinks he did not enter the faith again. On Monday night I had a wonderful time with A. J. ("Freddy") Ayer who is Professor at London. We went to dinner at his club—"The Travellers"—and I was witness to what I had only read about in Trollope and Conan-Doyle. It was very austere but the coffee, wine, and trout were very good in that order. I particularly enjoyed a plaque in honor of Talleyrand, who was a guest at one point. I return to Linton Lodge on Friday for I fear imposing on the Moores in spite of their offer to have me for two weeks.

Love and kisses,
Morty

P.S. (1) The weather's been horrible. Still wearing overcoat!

P.S. (2) Spoke to Popper by phone and his wife is very ill. He sounded unhappy.

After returning from Cambridge, I wrote Lucia from Oxford on May 12, telling about a lovely time with Moore at Trinity College.

Linton Lodge
Oxford, May 12

I arrived late last night from Cambridge (via London) to find your note of May 7 in which you berate the people who sent my food-package. By now you will have had my acknowledgment and my thanks for the wonderful thing. Also my account of having been able to give the Moores some of my food.

The three days with the Moores was really very pleasant. After a while I got used to Mrs. Moore's incessant, compulsive chatter, but it was good to escape with Moore one evening when he took me to dine "in hall" at Trinity College. We were joined by von Wright, the new professor, and I was put between him and Moore. The atmosphere at Trinity was much more easy-going than at any Oxford College. After dinner we went up (Moore and I) to the Combination Room for the fruit and madeira and port and coffee and cigars (Cambridge uses "Combination Room" where Oxford uses "Common Room"). I spent all of my time talking to Moore who was extremely sweet in some of his stories. He told me that he was reading a correspondence between Yeats and his poet-brother T. Sturge Moore, and that it was all about philosophy, indeed about *his*, Moore's philosophy. He chuckled and told me that Yeats complained of him (Moore) that he was so *"British"* a philosopher, emphasizing *"British"* in that way he has of emphasizing the absurd sometime. After dinner we walked home together and he told me that I was going to see a great astronomical spectacle—Venus shining very brightly and quite high. We walked home across a beautiful commons, Moore in cap and gown stopping to admire the great beauty of it every so often. His innocence of spirit was never better illustrated than in his appreciation of simple and clear beauty. He asked me whether I remembered the passage in the "Ancient Mariner" where Coleridge speaks of Venus being in "the nether tip of the Moon" and then pointed out how absurd it was when you looked at the heavens. I asked him whether Coleridge could have been confusing it with another star and he replied "Oh! no! I think he just thought it would look nice and sound nice that way"! On the way back I stopped in London and went to the Royal Albert Hall to listen to Beecham conduct a wonderful Mozart-Haydn program—Mozart Symphonies— "The Paris" and "The Prague" and Haydn's #102 (B flat). Also some Mozart German dances. The latter were incorrectly listed in the program so Beecham *himself* announced that he "was only going to play 5 dances and not ten, that they were opus nos. K600 and K605 but so far as he cared they could be 705"! The crowd roared and people whispered "He's in great form tonight." . . .

> All my love to you and the boys,
> Morty

In a letter of May 14 to Lucia I tell of the BBC talk by Russell that the Moores and I *did not* hear, because of their personal attitudes toward Russell, and also about a paper on Wittgenstein that I heard Ryle give.

. . . Last night I went to Ryle's rooms and heard him read a brief, unpretentious, but well-done paper before a group of about seven dons of his own generation who've been meeting regularly for many years, rotating the place in their different houses and providing a dinner before it. I skipped the dinner altho I'd been invited, and came later to hear the paper. It was a forthcoming BBC broadcast on Ludwig Wittgenstein, the late philosopher. What amused me was one of those English silences after the paper. For almost ten minutes, I swear, there was a stony, impenetrable silence, during which you could have heard an electron perspiring. In my American way I was tempted to interrupt it with a question or comment, but then I thought it would be better for one of the club-members to begin, and one did to my great relief. Over in the States, I think such a silence would have been taken as a demonstration of lack of interest; not so here—it just meant that they were thinking hard.

. . . Russell talks on [the BBC] tonight on "Life in the Atomic Age." Last week, when I was at the Moores', he gave the first broadcast and I got a sense of the Moores' personal animus against him. Mrs. Moore said she didn't *want* to hear him but felt obliged to listen; Moore said he didn't have any feeling of obligation. P.S. We didn't listen, and

I didn't feel like engaging my hosts in a discussion of their reasons. But the rift between Russell and Moore is awfully deep.

On May 16 I made some comparisons between Oxford and Cambridge.

> Linton Lodge, May 16, 1951
> Oxford

. . . I think I wrote some of my impressions of Cambridge though I can't remember whether I made any comparative judgments. I certainly liked Cambridge more as a town and I even preferred the academic atmosphere from what I could gather of it. But Oxford has a charm that hasn't been completely destroyed by the shuffling crowds and the auto industry, and its academic people have many good qualities that haven't been crushed by the need to be clever and cute. I must say that everyone I've wanted to see has treated me with extreme kindness, notably Ryle and Berlin, and while I haven't found out as much about the place's philosophy as I would if I were a student and assiduously attended lectures, I've seen another side from having *talked* philosophy with some of them and from having exchanged ideas. I think the trip has been worthwhile if only because it has initiated some connections and associations which may deepen over the years. . . .

> With all my love to the three
> of you,
> Morty

16

A New York Yankee at Oxford

Immediately upon coming to Oxford from London on Saturday, April 14, 1951, I began a series of letters to Lucia and the boys that reveal a side of me which is very different from what sometimes appears in my book reviews, in my polemical essays, and in my academic battles. They also show how much I enjoyed being at Oxford and getting to know some of the Oxford philosophers.

> Linton Lodge Hotel
> Oxford
> April 14, 1951

I came down to find one letter waiting for me in London and then when I arrived in Oxford today I was delighted to see two more envelopes waiting for me. You've no idea how warming it is to see your words on the envelope. Even the smallest letter is welcome, whether it contains news of mammoth events in Cambridge or not; the merest token of you is delightful to get, so don't hesitate to set some lines down at any moment. As you see, I act on the same principle and I've no doubt that some of my letters are quite uninformative. And yet they help me too. When I write them I *feel* in contact with you sweet darlings.

The train trip to Oxford was very pleasant. After getting about 20 miles out of London the English landscape took over. Broad, low lying fields, covered with green and with only the slightest suggestion of hills. But everywhere the results of the terrific rainfall is evident. Meadows inundated with water, rivers overflowing their banks. Today the sun came out beautifully in the morning but by the time I boarded my train the London clouds took over and I began to despair. But not for long. By the time I reached Oxford the sun appeared for longer than it has since I've come to England. The Drebens told me that I was bringing sunshine with me. In gratitude they served me the most magnificent steak dinner for noon-day meal and meanwhile Burton picked me up on Oxford philosophy. He's enjoying himself immensely and profiting, he tells me. He predicts I will have a profitable stay here too. I was delighted to see someone I knew and it helped me greatly. I suspect that the isolation of London had a good deal to do with my depression there, to say nothing of the chalky gray of the buildings and sky.

The Linton Lodge is an extremely clean and pleasant looking inn. My room is twice as big as the one I had in London and costs about the same. It has one tremendous window looking out on Linton Road, a nice desk, a wardrobe, a simple fireplace (with an electric heater where there would normally be logs), a wash-stand, and also central heat! Having the last is quite wonderful. I didn't have it in London. I learned from Huebsch's friend, Gwenda David (Mrs. Mossbacher) that Harold Guinzburg, the president of Viking Press, was in London, staying at the plushy Savoy, right across the "road" from the Strand Palace. We both remarked on the fact that the two hotels—that of author and that of publisher—nicely reflected the class struggle!

Stevie: Thank you *very* much for your postcard with the pretty girl on it. Your writing is really quite wonderful. I hope you enjoy your TV.

Nicky: Thanks for your letters. Your handwriting is so very clear. I hope the injections aren't too painful after your unpleasant bout with flu and measles. Today I was taken through the grounds of Magdalen (pronounced "Mawdlin") College and saw a herd of deer which they have fenced in. You'll all be interested to know that the British are now eating reindeer meat in the shortage.* I haven't tried any, but people say it's quite good. Next thing you know they'll have it at the Harvard Faculty Club!

I live in a very quiet residential section of Oxford, not very far from what's called the Banbury road, which leads into town by bus. I'm thinking of renting a bicycle as soon as I decide that I can get into the habit of keeping left on the road!

With lots of love and kisses,
Poppa

*I don't think the Magdalen scholars eat *their* deer!

P.S. You might buy a Penguin Guide of "Berks & Oxon" and then follow some of my geographical remarks more easily that way.

In my next letter I refer to a report of Lucia's on a Harvard symposium in which Meyer Schapiro had participated, and I report some experiences in Oxford.

Linton Lodge
Oxford
April 16, 1951

It's odd that on the very day on which I receive your typed letter that I should turn to manuscript, but I'm writing this fairly late and don't want to wake anyone with the rat-tat-tat.

I was delighted to get your letter (the typed one of April 13). It came this morning, testifying to the extraordinary speed of air-mail. Now, when we've both settled down, exchanging letters turns into a correspondence, which is always more interesting, I think, than letters that perpetually cross each other. It's like talking past each other; though make no mistake, I was overwhelmed with joy to get your first letters even when they weren't replies and I suppose my diaries of the voyage may have been fun for you to get. . . .

Your report of the Meyer-symposium sounds a little grim. I wish someone would sit in the audience when Meyer talks and make faces or wave a handkerchief when he starts to overdo it! What other responses were there? I'm sure his new admirer Kay had fits over it, didn't she? And how was the dinner party for him? Write me about that. I also got all the enclosures, for which many, many thanks.

Oxford is so much more like Cambridge, Mass. than London is like

N.Y., that I've begun to lose a sense of being in a foreign land. I haven't seen anyone but Dreben and his wife, who have had me to meals with them 3 times in one weekend—the nice kids. Isaiah is not yet back and term doesn't start until next week.—Today a sweet note came from Mrs. Moore, welcoming me to "the other place," which is how Cambridge refers to Oxford!, and asking me when I was coming over.—Today I took my first stroll through part of the University and was quite overwhelmed by walls towering over narrow winding streets. The University was like a fortress in early days, wasn't it?—Tonight I went, alone, to my first English theatre (I avoided them in London) and saw the Old Vic company do Sophocles' "Electra" and a Chekhov farce called "The Wedding." They did these two absolutely different things with tremendous éclat and taste. The "Electra" is a very moving play—more about it when I have more space. I miss you very much.

Love, Morty

Linton Lodge Hotel
Oxford, April 19, 1951

I have an interesting report to make about the power of music—it has power to soothe the civilized breast too. I had come into my room at about 7:30 after a singularly dull dinner of ham and chips, and gooseberry tart, finished off by a particularly bad cup of coffee, after picking out a poor restaurant. The food is quite good at the Lodge here and there is also a decent restaurant called the "George" in town, but in an exploratory mood I had chosen some dive called "The Rose Café" on High Street (known here as "The High"—Broad Street is known as "The Broad") and had picked a lemon, as we say back home. After several sunny spring days, the weather suddenly decided to get cold again and I came home in the graying part of the day, and when I came into my room, there welled up in me a profound sigh of homesickness and deep sorrow over my separation from you. I suddenly came to feel as I did one day on the boat and on several days in London. The term has not yet begun and my friends the Drebens had gone to Manchester to visit a relative; Berlin is not yet in town and I am not to dine with Ryle (at Magdalen) until Saturday and with Robinson (Oriel) not until Sunday. So I had spent a real bachelor's day with hardly a word exchanged with anyone, sometimes walking, sometimes shopping, sometimes at my typewriter doing philosophy. But I had arranged today to rent a radio and it had been installed in the afternoon. So I turned on the radio and got a BBC recording of "Enoch Soames," a story about a poet of the nineties who is disappointed and depressed about the lack of recognition. He is a diabolist—a worshipper of the devil(!)—and at one point agrees to sell himself to the Devil, who suddenly appears at his side in a Soho restaurant. Completely fed up with this, and even more depressed, I switched the program in desperation, when there emerged the sweet sounds of Mozart—his 39th Symphony (not K.39, but his 39th symphony; I don't know what Köchel listing it is). I cannot communicate to you the joy this brought to me. Suddenly the clouds lifted; I started to sing and beat time; I danced about my room; I was out of my blue funk! I have come to feel, therefore, that we must get a new phonograph one of these days and go back to the fun of listening to music as we used to. Perhaps we can economize on something else. I'm sure the children will love it. I remember how sweet Nicky used to look when he was two, curled up in a big chair on 108th Street, sucking his finger and listening to Mozart and Beethoven, with a transported expression and such rapture.

I meant to tell you that you will be getting at some point a copy of Stephen Spender's autobiography. I lent my copy to the Mossbachers in London and they promised to mail it to you when they were finished with it. I hope it gets there before you leave. . . .

With all my love to the dearest one.

Morty

Linton Lodge Hotel,
April 20, 1951

The sweet letter you wrote while lying on the big couch has just come and filled my day with love and beauty. How I wish I could be there with you . . . ! Today is about the fifth straight day of sunshine and spring appears to have arrived, with all its cruelty. . . .

Today brought a number of harbingers of activity. I got a big mail, which helped. First a postcard from Isaiah from Nice which read: "I have, in fact, visited Israel. Very queer too. En route home I was 'unavoidably' delayed in Nice by my family (very agreeable) and shall be late for term, arriving, in fact, I hope, on Monday afternoon next. My first week is complicated by the arrival of my patron, Mr. Conant, who has ordered me to collect various persons ('interested in administration, etc.' whom ex hypothesi I don't know) to entertain him, etc. So be prepared to be asked to lunch with him on Thursday. Anyhow wd. you telephone me at 3625 on Monday and come to see me at once? I much look forward. *Isaiah*" Then a letter from Hao Wang who says he will be in Oxford on April 30 or May 1, and who will sail on the Queen Elizabeth from Southampton on May 2. And finally another letter from BBC asking again about broadcasting on the Third Programme! And so at last the days of solitude are over and soon I suppose I shall be regretting the beginning of a social storm. And yet right now I look forward to it. I am *not* a lone wolf!

I went walking in a park today, it was so lovely. Daffodils are just about over and if I were a better gardener I would be able to tell you something of their successors, but I can't. I watched a number of university cricketers practising what must correspond to our pitching and batting in baseball. They use a large rubber ball, slightly bigger than a baseball and the pitcher hurls it in quite hard so that it usually takes one bounce before the batter gets hold of it. The batter wears leg-guards and uses a bat which has a queer shape, something like this:

They take some good whacks at it, but so far as I can see, they rarely get any good fly balls out. I must learn the rules of this game, so that I can understand some of this. It's quite maddening to watch and not know what the devil it's all about!

I noticed today something peculiar about the complexion of the English children, especially the babies. They have a queer kind of redness on their cheeks which is almost unnatural. It's not the high color of health but more like the high color of chapping or even rouge which has not been put on well, but left in a kind of blob on the face. Do you know what that could be? Do you suppose it's the result of any food shortage? Or do you think it's got to do with poor heating and consequent chapping?

Well, I have as usual put less down than I wanted to. So I'll stop with mountains of love and as many kisses as there are stars to all of you.

Morty-Poppa

On April 18, I infer with the help of my datebook for 1951, the following note was written by Lucia, thereby helping to start a correspondence between us as opposed to an exchange in which we each received five or six letters at a time.

Wednesday A.M.
[April 18, 1951?]

We just received your first letter from Oxford. With the sun out there, the Drebens, their steak, not to mention Berlin it must be much more enjoyable than London already. But DO YOU WANT ANY MORE SWEATERS, WOOL SHIRTS, AND/OR YOUR NEW OVERCOAT? Perhaps not with central heating in the Linton Lodge Hotel, which does sound very nice, and I hope its food is as much of an improvement over the Strand Palace as the room is.

I hope all my letters catch up with you in the next week or so. I think some haven't reached you yet. I should have numbered them. Did you ever get the one sent care of Thos. Cook?

Your present for Stevie's party, the cable, and your two letters to the boys arrived at exactly the right moments. The cable came at 7:15 A.M. and woke me and then Stevie answered the phone and beamed and giggled as she read it to him. If you want to be sure we get up at the right time just send a delayed cable—they always seem to arrive at that moment. . . . The party was a brilliant success, I wish that you could have been in the midst of it. Ten children was the final count; eight boys and two girls. We had a fairly uproarious game of post office, and then the children went conveniently amok after they discovered their rubber balls at the spider webs, and just before the ice cream and cake. When the television program came on a miraculous peace descended. No, I haven't bought one yet. The extraordinary thing is that the children, left to themselves without any prohibition at this age seem to want only two or at the most three programs of half an hour each day. So perhaps we'll be safe for awhile.

I am going to send this short and snappy letter off to keep you up to date on the news. With many, many kisses from Nicky, Stevie and

Lucia

In reply to this letter, I wrote one in which I first described "my debut into Oxford Society" as a guest of Gilbert Ryle at Magdalen College, and then my evening at Oriel College as the guest of Richard Robinson, who worked in ancient philosophy.

Linton Lodge Hotel, Oxford
April 22/51 Sunday

I thought I would begin by answering the questions in your letter written last Wednesday—I don't really need any sweaters, shirts, overcoats, etc. because the sun has been shining for about a week now and things promise to get warmer and warmer. There was a ground-frost last night but the prediction is for it to go up to 50 or 57 today. Also, all your wonderful letters have caught up with me, including one sent to Thomas Cook (there was only one such, though, wasn't there?). The food here is very much better than it was in London except for one famous fiasco with ham and chips about which I've already written, so have no fear on that score.

I'm delighted to hear that Stevie's party was a success. The power of television to calm the little animals at the party ought not to be advertised, lest they—the T.V. companies—use it in their ads for TV.

Last night I made my debut into Oxford society. Gilbert Ryle very kindly invited me to high table dinner at Magdalen last night, I went, and here is what happened. I went up to his rooms, a very handsome apartment in a building that dates from the 1720's. He served me the predictable but good sherry and we talked for a little while, gossiping in an effort to find out each other's prejudices, I expect, and then he proposed "wandering" over to dinner. He donned his academic dress (over "lounge," i.e ordinary, suit) and we strolled through the cloisters over to a Common Room into which I was ushered. There I saw about twenty or so men, all in gowns, gathered close to the fire, which was on the far side of the room from the door. When I entered there was, fortunately, no elaborate race to meet the guest. On the contrary, everything was carried on as if I hadn't been a new animal in the zoo. Ryle introduced me to two people who were nearest the door—one Oscar Wood, a young man who had spent some time at Harvard in the Fall of '48, (someone I'd met once, as I recall)—the other was a man in his fifties, I should say, whose name I didn't quite get; I think it was "Weldon." He was the fluttery kind of Englishman, giggling and snorting and making eyes; while Wood was the quiet type. Not so with Ryle, however. He is a tall, angular, half-bald man who bears a certain resemblance to Herbert Schneider in his leanness and rough-hewn quality. He is quite homely, but very honest and penetrating. He strikes me as one of the better English academic types, at least the kind I get along well with.

There was nothing but chit-chat in that room, and then at a signal we all started to file out to the dining-hall. When we got there the undergraduates had already been waiting. When the dons got to their places at the high-table at the far end of this high-ceilinged, paneled room, they all stood and waited for the Vice-President (name unknown) to say grace, which he said in Latin. This was only one sentence and we immediately sat down to dinner. Before anything was served, waiters came up to each don and asked for their alcoholic orders. Some ordered wine, but Ryle, who seems to have a great taste for the stuff, ordered us beer—which was served in a wonderful pint-sized silver tankard.

At a certain point early in the game Ryle said to the Vice-President who was at the center of the table (opposite Ryle): "Excuse me, Mr. Vice-President, but I neglected to introduce my guest—Professor Morton White." This was followed by an exchange of polite howdyados. I was at Ryle's left where he put me because he complained of poor hearing in his other ear (he's only about 50 or less). At his right was Wood and at my left was Mr. Weldon (?).

The first course was very unusual and, I must confess, a new experience—snails. I was amused at the banter about this, notably Ryle's, who said: "What on earth are you giving us?" to the jolly, youngish, vice-president. Apparently the vice-president is also steward. "How on earth does one eat them?" asked Ryle in his peasant-manner (I don't think it's affected). The vice-president called attention to the tooth-picks which were being passed by the waiters, and so that settled that. Next course was sweet-breads, and finally a lovely melted Gruyère in a patty.

The conversation during dinner was rather stiff; I exchanged a few pleasantries with Weldon, who had been at Harvard during the war, but talked most of the time with Ryle. I liked all of these people very much and was at ease in spite of not meeting any of the dons other than the three or four I've mentioned.

Since my back was to the undergraduates I had almost no knowledge of their presence until a great wave of quiet had settled over the room; I then realized that they had silently left the hall and the dons remained in solitary splendor at the high-table, perched above the cares of the world and enjoying the best meal I had had since my arrival in England. Soon this came to an end; we rose; something was said again in Latin and they started to file out. At this point I was ushered into a delightfully small room (not the original common room) to have some port, grapes, and nuts. This time there were six of us—Ryle, Wood, the Vice-President, an old man whose name I never learned and to whom I was never introduced, and another middle-aged man with whom my relations were similar.

Ryle sat to one side of the fireplace (right); the old man sat at the left. Then there was a large table on which the wine and fruit sat. Mr. Wood and the Vice-President flanked this, and I sat between Wood and Ryle. You will notice that I have included a fascinating thing I'd call a trolley but I don't know what *they* call it. It was a little inclined plane with two tracks on it. In the tracks there are two little wagons, deep enough to hold a bottle of wine. When the old man was finished serving himself Port he put it into the wagon at the top of the plane, the force of gravity went into operation, and "Zip" it went to Ryle. There was much delight over this and before it was put into operation Ryle cutely said "I hope you've never seen one of these things before!" Now when one wagon went down the plane to Ryle, another empty wagon rode up the plane, since the two wagons are connected by a chain! (When wagon 1 goes down bringing Wine to Ryle, wagon 2 goes back empty to the old boy, so no one ever has to get up in the whole process of passing wine several times around!!!)

The Port was passed three times, and there was much joking over the rules. Apparently for all of their delicacy the English are great ones for observing and openly stating rules about food which more genteel American hosts would be embarrassed to announce. "How many times

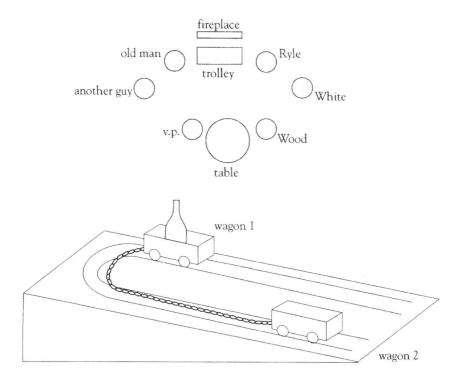

is it passed at Christ Church?" the v.p. asked Ryle, and there was some half-serious report of the rule there. Similarly at dinner there was a candid question about when the snails were served, about how many were allowed. "Six" was the matter-of-fact answer! And also an index of how they can live together peaceably—candor on the one hand and great tradition and rigamarole, which latter can easily be the death of candor if not tempered with good sense.

After I don't know how long in the dessert-room (if I may call it that) I was escorted back to the Common Room, where only a few of the dons recongregrated and we spent about an hour or two gossiping and talking a bit of philosophy. At about 11:30 Ryle suggested we go back to his rooms, which we did, and we started some serious and interesting philosophy. He served me a glass of beer (by this time my bladder was in trouble) and we talked until about 1:00 A.M. Then he kindly drove me home after I feared for the moment that I would have to walk about two miles because the buses had stopped and the porter's office (where the telephone is) had been closed, thus preventing us from getting a cab. By some good chance Ryle had left his car out and he sweetly insisted on driving me home. Since the alternative was a 2 mile hike in the middle of a night when frost had been predicted, I did not protest too violently, and so I accepted, thinking that he wouldn't have proposed it if he didn't mean it, which is a safer rule in England than it is in America!

I have now spun all I can of the details, so I will mail this to you. If my dinner tonight at Oriel introduces anything new in the pattern, I will add that in another letter.

Much love,
Morty

Monday A.M. 4/23

Because yesterday was Sunday I was unable to buy a stamp for this, so I delayed sending it and can now include the account of my evening at Oriel, which was somewhat different from the Magdalen night but in many ways the same.

This time, of course, my host was a man I had never met before and in fact I never learned *why* he invited me. He didn't seem to know my writings and he never made it clear to me how he knew I was in town, etc., etc. One of the results of this was that I spent most of my evening talking to the other people around me, and they were a jolly crew. Robinson, my host, met me in the Oriel Lodge, which is what we would call the janitor's office at Harvard, and in a rather nervous way led me across to the dining hall, not being quite sure whether we were going to be early or on time, and suggesting that we walk slowly, as if coming there a little early might expose some family idiot or skeleton whom I should not see at all costs.

When we arrived at Oriel Dining Hall I had the impression of less wealth than Magdalen (I must confirm this). The dining hall was less magnificent, less somber, and in general the people struck me as more relaxed. The Provost of Oriel (whose proper name I never learned) sat at the head of the high table (rather than at the center), and I was put at his left, and my host to the left of me. Since Robinson and I got there early in spite of his nervous effort to prevent that, I chatted with the Provost. He is a short man with blue eyes and a rather pale expression, much like what a movie would make him out to be. He told me with a twinkle in his eye that once a year the College entertained at dinner the Chief Constable of Oxford (the local chief of police—not the university chief of police) and that this year it was to be tonight. His honor had not yet arrived but I began to worry about having to make conversation with him, as he was going to sit across from me at the provost's right. Well, he finally arrived, a handsome man, over 6 ft. with absolutely white hair, and a very pleasant, outgoing manner. It turned out that he and I and the provost had a fine time together and I was forced to neglect my host (Robinson at my left) almost totally. This I did with small regret as it seemed to me that he was making little effort to put me at my ease, except to say at one point in order to break a long silence "And what did you *do*, today?" My theory is that he had heard that a Harvard professor of philosophy was in town, and since he had lived in America while at Cornell for about 20 years, felt some kind of obligation to play the host. I also think that he expected a somewhat more impressive and dignified elder statesman than myself, so he was somewhat surprised to see someone less than 60. But I may be wrong.

The dinner at Oriel was not quite as good as at Magdalen but the wine service was excellent. I was given some sherry at the beginning and champagne during the meal. We had roast beef and yorkshire pudding, preceded by honey-dew and followed by ice-cream. I should have said that grace at Oriel was said by some student after the provost rapped a gavel on the table. The boy launched into a long Latin speech after which we sat down. At the end of the meal for the dons (the students had left, as at Magdalen) the provost said two words: "Benedictus" followed by some other word, and we started to file out. Again, the same gambit. Across a quad, this time to a small dining room which had the port and the fruit on a table. A steward-don appeared with a list and asked me to sit at his left and the provost at his right. Robinson was, fortunately, no longer near me, so I lost any sense of responsibility to that wet rag, and started to drink port and talk with this steward and the provost. Again, the port went around three times. But on this occasion we were not in a dark room lit only by a fireplace—as we were at Magdalen when we had our port—but rather in a gaily lighted room. One chap, a short, stocky, cross-eyed fellow started to get drunk and he was the object of a good deal of genial banter culminating in a refusal to pass him the bottle for more than the third time.

One of the high-points in the conversation at our end of the table came when we started talking about American slang. Many of them are quite fascinated by this, and they go to our movies and watch our gangsters with rapt admiration (contempt, of course, but genial contempt). The steward gave a wonderful imitation of Humphrey Bogart saying something that had brought the house down in an Oxford "cinema." Bogart had accused his moll of doing something wrong and she started to explain in an elaborate, irrelevant way. At this point Bogart produced a line that shook the Oxonians with laughter: "Never mind da footnotes, give us da text!" The classics-don-steward conveyed this by screwing up his mouth in the most Bogart way and had everyone in stitches around him. At this point I began to tell them a little of American slang and produced for them the famous expression "You're cooking with gas." When he asked me just what that meant, I told the provost that the nearest I could come to translation for him was "You're burning with a hard gem-like flame." This was positively killing and they almost fell and rolled in the aisle—both provost and steward. "Oh dear!" said the provost, "and I wonder what Walter Pater would have said, Pater who had sat at this table so many times. To think that he was being translated in that way" and then again he fell into gales of laughter. The incident ended with both the provost and the steward agreeing that they were going to use that on the boys to show that they had an inside track on American slang, and the provost proposed that the next time he had an excellent paper from a student he would take his hand and say: "You're cooking with gas!"

After the port-room we went into a sitting-room to have coffee, followed by beer, and here I fell into talking with a couple of political scientists and finally a physician. The last was somewhat silly and I think drunk, but he started to talk sensibly about American doctors and praise many of them, including Walter Cannon. This went on for some time until he finally revealed that he was an admirer of MacArthur (the first Englishman I've met of that variety) and that Mac was in the right as against Truman. I was rescued from this by my host, and very soon afterward he helped me get a cab (at about 11) and I sped home after another pleasant evening. Not a word of serious philosophy was exchanged by us.

I am going to send this off at once. Since there may be people who'd like my impressions of Oxford life, you might read this to them; I've neglected to write anything but postcards to Van, Nelson, Arthur, and Henry, since I'm waiting for more evidence of the philosophy of Oxford. These reports may serve to let them know what's happening to me.

With all my love, sweetheart, and hugs and kisses to you and the children,

Morty

In reply to this, Lucia wrote on April 27.

Your wonderful letter about the High Table dinners at Magdalen and Oriel arrived yesterday; it reads like a novel and I am going to carry it about for the delectation of your good friends. I've already read various parts of the other letters about your boat companions, your observations on London and encounters with people there and monuments. Everyone is much taken with all these reports and so are we of course. It's been so heartening to have all these vivid letters and now it's just about one more month when we shall be again with our darling, Morty-Poppa. . . .

Ever so much love,
Lucia

On April 26, just before Lucia had written the above letter, I had sent her one in which I described Isaiah Berlin's luncheon for President and Mrs. Conant at All Souls. The millionairess mentioned by Mrs. Hart toward the end of the description later became Isaiah's wife, Aline. In retrospect, I think the most amusing sentence in my letter is the one about the "mysterious man named Austin, who is supposed to be the ablest phil. here." Why I called him "mysterious" I can't remember. Perhaps it was because his Oxford reputation far exceeded his international reputation at the time.

Linton Lodge Hotel,
Oxford, April 26/51

It's always wonderful to come downstairs and to find your sweet letters waiting for me. Your last one was magnificently full and detailed. . . .

I'm very happy to hear about the nice way in which the Gs, As, and Qs are rallying around; it's what I would have expected. . . . Now that people are back here I have also been the recipient of hospitality. Berlin has started the ball rolling. The other day I lunched at New College with him; next week high-table and tuxedo at All Souls, and today I attended a luncheon of about twenty in honor of the Conants. It was very pleasant to see them and they did look like a couple of Henry James characters abroad. He with his open expression and affability and she with her sweet, girlish smile. I didn't talk very much to them because they were obviously anxious to meet other people, and so was I. But we did chat a little and I asked her to give you my regards when she returned. I think they're leaving here on the 5th or they expect to be home on the 5th—I can't remember. The party was, of course, presided over by Isaiah in one of the dining rooms of All Souls College and characteristically he arrived slightly late. I can't remember all the people, but on my left there was Dr. Enid Starkie, a 50-ish woman who writes about Baudelaire and who is an amiable bore. When she stopped chewing my ear I was able to talk to Mrs. Hart, the wife of a philosophy don at New College. Both of them are quite nice. Then there was Sir Something Henderson and Lord David Cecil, the latter a Fellow or Professor of English at New College, and a friend of Isaiah's. There was also an American expatriate law professor, Mr. Goodhart and his wife, who are both stuffy and bores, I think. I must check with Isaiah because they asked me to come to their house for a drink on the 12th of May. That was so far ahead that I couldn't refuse, but I'm going to receive a card she said, so I suppose I can refuse then if he confirms my suspicions. Then there was a lady who was the head of Lady Margaret Hall (for women, of course) and she was rather bright. Cecil seems nice; and then there was a German refugee atomic physicist named Halban married to a woman who was described as a millionairess to me by Hart's wife, and the "representative of wealth in Oxford." I didn't get to talk with her. A number of them said they would get in touch with me. I have attended a seminar and lecture of Ryle's and they were good. I've met a mysterious man named Austin, who is supposed to be the ablest phil. here, but spoke little with him. I look forward to a good deal of stimulation and conversation, and I've been able to get some writing done on the kinds of questions that are discussed here—Existence, for example. . . . I'm glad that you are not likely to come down with the measles. It would be a nuisance. I miss you as always but the appearance of people has diminished my loneliness.

> With all my love,
> Morty

After having spent my first days at Oxford being wined and dined, I began to attend some classes and lectures, and to develop some reactions to what I was hearing, as my letter of April 28 indicates.

Linton Lodge,
April 28, 1951

. . . I'm delighted to hear that the boys are so well and that they are so helpful. I think of them so much and look at your pictures so often . . . , and sometimes I have visions of hopping a plane back home. Maybe I was silly to plan this heady campaign without any attention to the needs of the body and the heart. I cannot say with Dr. Faustus "Sweet analytics, 'tis thou hast ravished me!" for as yet I have not seen much analytics and even if I did, "ravished" is not the word for what they do to me when I do see them! Thus far Gilbert Ryle has been very cordial and his talk very bright. Yesterday I went to a lecture by O.K. Bowsma, a Nebraska colleague of Werkie's [Werkmeister's] who is all that Werkie is not—bright, whimsical, and something of a clown, but a very clever one. He gave a talk called "Muddling in the flux" or "The Leaky Pot" or "The World is like a Man with a Running at the Nose." These last two titles are allusions to a Platonic dialogue called "The Cratylus" in which, I think, Plato uses these as metaphors. Being something of a disciple of the mysterious Wittgenstein, Bowsma is concerned to know how Plato came to think of the world in these metaphorical terms and so far as I can see the rest of the lectures will be devoted to this theme. The style is highly imaginative, and even poetical, but the emphasis is exclusively oracular. It is something of an irony that the founder of one of the most logical and straight-forward philosophies of the 20th century (I mean Wittgenstein, the founder of logical positivism) should be spawning and encouraging what is really a variety of mysticism. Although Wittgenstein is very popular here, there is a local brand of analytic philosophy, led mainly by Austin and Ryle, which is less oracular. I've yet to see it in fast action, but I'm told that Austin is awfully good. This native brand is very much influenced by W. but more articulate, less metaphorical (tho metaphorical enough) and quiet anti-formalistic. The work of Van and Nelson is respected but regarded as some kind of scholastic machinery which does not fully probe the secrets of the universe. I am being quite vague and am trying to communicate what I sense about the aura of the philosophy. Later, when I find out more about its insides, so to speak, I will write again. By a strange irony your words about "social relations people" feeling "that they have lost something of concreteness, of the expression of individual feeling and conviction" is somewhat the spirit in which certain philosophers here view a good deal of mathematical logic. The point here is that it is not scooping up the life-juices of ordinary language (there's a metaphor for you!). All of this I report without clear understanding of the point. That may come later.

After writing the above I went to a lecture by Isaiah—one of six to be given under the title "Social and Political Ideas of the Early 19th Century." He talked very brilliantly but not originally about the 18th century background and next time will develop what is likely to be more original—his ideas about the German Romantics. I am reminded of a wonderful story which Russell told to Isaiah about what happened when Russell saw the King after he had been granted an O.M. (Order of Merit). The King said: "Well, Lord Russell you have lived a very adventurous life; it wouldn't do for *every*one to live such a life, would it Lord Russell." To which Russell was tempted to reply: "Yes, your majesty, as your brother has so well discovered"!!

I was delighted to get your birthday letter and it came in time. I wish you all will have spent a pleasant Sunday celebrating. By the time you get this I will have passed my 33rd year, by which time Christ had died and founded a world religion. But since I was long ago persuaded that I was not God, I am not surprised that I haven't builded as impressively. Nevertheless the thought of all of you three makes me feel as though we have builded well together and that we have so far made a good deal of our motherly and fatherly talents. I am a very happy man and I love you very, very much. And I feel so sure of your love that I am carried through many a lonely moment thinking on you. . . . If you have never read it, read E. M. Forster's *Howard's End*—it's charming and very instructive about England. It's out in a Penguin which you might be able to get at the Mandrake Book shop if not at Phillips. I am in the midst of it.

> With all my dearest love to the three
> dearest people in the world,
> Morty

My letter of May 1 continues to report favorably on what I had been doing and hearing. In it I speak of seeing Hao Wang, the Harvard logician, of dining with the Oxford philosopher Herbert Hart, and of much activity to come.

Linton Lodge, Oxford
May 1, 1951

Well, here is May Day! And my guide book tells me that in the great tower of Magdalen College (1492) a hymn is sung on May Morning. Needless to add, I did not rise at 5 in order to hear the hymn at six. But there is also a reason besides the hour which is neatly contained in the following piece in the *Times*: "There were falls of snow in the Midlands and the south of England yesterday, and sleet showers and frost were reported in many areas." After a perfectly delightful ten days England has chosen to go normal again; many people say "We've had our spring and summer."

Let me say how delighted I was to here your sweet voices on my birthday. I had gone out to dinner with the Drebens that night. I had decided to celebrate quietly by myself when Dreben came into my room. I offered him a drink and then another and then, feeling warm, I remarked that this was my birthday, and so we all went out to the best restaurant in town. After staying at their house till about 11:30 I came home to my dark hotel and found a little note telling me to call International Radio–London. At first I was a little alarmed, but then I realized what it was. It was so good to hear you. I must say that there was something a little peculiar about the tone of the voices—as if they were coming through a corridor. One felt as if they were taking time to reach one—I mean more time than I would have supposed. Did you have a similar feeling about my voice?

One of the brighter occasions since I've been here was the arrival of Hao Wang yesterday. He stayed with me at the Lodge here for one night and we had dinner together. I took him to the station this morning and he will sail on the Queen Elizabeth on May 2 and should arrive in Boston on the 8th. He brings my love and a little token of my affection. I hope you will excuse my failure to have sent anything for you up to now, but everything I fix on is so heavy that if I were to send it to you air mail it would be prohibitive and, of course, if I were to send it ordinary mail you wouldn't get it until after you'd left the States.

    . . . As soon as I get the food package you mentioned I will arrange to go to the Moores, as I don't want to be put up by them without bringing anything. And, of course, if your package comes late, I can always go to London and buy food in a special place for Americans with dollars—viz. Piccadilly Parcels—so don't worry about that. I may also take a trip to Paris if I hear from you in reply to my request for your views on our traveling to the continent when you arrive.

You will notice from the staccato style that we have lots of things to talk about in a preparatory way, so I hope my next letters aren't too directorial and dull. I can be an awful fuss-budget about doing things in advance! Stop me when I'm overdoing it, please.

Tonight I am to dine with H.L.A. Hart, a philosopher at New College and a friend of Isaiah's. He will arrange a meeting with some of the younger philosophers here, which I look forward to. Yesterday I had a very interesting exchange with Ryle and some of his friends and students in a seminar of his. I find it very instructive. Tomorrow I lunch with Isaiah and some more new people—philosophical and literate. Thursday I dine with Drebens and Ryle. Friday I have invited Ryle as my guest. Sunday I go to High-table at All Souls with Isaiah. It is my hope to go to Cambridge the following week. As usual I will wire you any change of address, e.g. the Moores', when and if I get there. I think this week will be the climax of my Oxford stay. I will arrange a place at this hotel for all four of us on the night of June 9; I will also arrange for space in a London hotel in case the ship comes in very late. We can, of course, alter this if it turns out that we want to go to another part of England or the continent. Meanwhile I will gather advice from the local travelers with experience with children.

Love,
Morty

My next letter to Lucia, of May 2, tells of my plan to go to Cambridge to stay with the Moores and of a luncheon on May 2 given by Berlin, at which Stuart Hampshire was present. This letter also reports on my dinner with Herbert Hart the night before at New College, which was followed by a visit to Hart's house to meet the philosophers Strawson, Grice, and Warnock.

. . . Today I had luncheon as guest of the generous Isaiah, along with an economist Balogh . . . and a philosopher named Stuart Hampshire. I liked H. very much and look forward to seeing him when

I get back from Cambridge. He knows Meyer Schapiro and he regards him as "near genius, but quite mad." Last night I dined at New College with a philosopher named Hart who then took me over to his house, where a little group of philosophers and their wives had foregathered. Strawson and Grice and Warnock were the other dons and they were affable but quite stiff and self-conscious. And also a little on the prissy side and very much aware of their awareness of each other, if you know what I mean. Inevitably a stranger feels that his companions are leaving him out when they know each other well, and I now see the dangers of the Henry-Van banter in the presence of strangers more clearly than ever. . . . I don't mean that I didn't say anything (you know how improbable that is), and as a matter of fact Hart was extremely gracious, but the group was really too donnish for my taste. Not so with Isaiah's parties, however. He is like Arthur Schlesinger in that respect, of course. One of the interesting issues of the evening, however, was an invitation from Grice to have lunch with him tomorrow, after which he will take me to a cricket match. He is a famous cricketer himself and he is also interested (as many Oxford philosophers are) in the nature of *games,* so he is curious to see how I will succeed in discovering the rules of cricket without any instruction, since I know nothing of them! This will be fun for both of us, and it will also help me be more instructive when the boys come over! . . .

My associations with the philosophers I met at Oxford deepened over the years, especially those with Gilbert Ryle, John Austin, Herbert Hart, Paul Grice, and Stuart Hampshire. In 1951 Ryle had us out to his country retreat in the village of Bucklebury in Berks, where we met his twin sister and their adopted daughter on a very jolly occasion. In the same year our family also visited with the families of Austin and Hart, both of whom, like Grice, lectured at Harvard later in the fifties. I had never met so many philosophers that I liked while disagreeing with them. Several of them were civilized men who led me to think that I was not alone in my inclination to apply analytic tools to matters of general human concern.

In 1949 Ryle had published his influential book *The Concept of Mind;* in it he tried to explode what he called the Cartesian myth of the ghost in the machine by presenting what he called the logic of psychological concepts without postulating an immaterial mind in a material body. Although I agreed with much of what he said there, I had reservations about it, which I expressed in *Toward Reunion in Philosophy.* When I sent that book to Ryle, he wrote in May of 1956: "I haven't read it all yet, but I have read a good many bits and pieces in it. I hope you'll be glad to hear that it annoys me a good deal. However, the only annoyance that I'll mention at this stage is with the beastly title; who wants a reunion anyhow?" He also sent his regards to Lucia and to "the gang at Harvard."

I replied on June 11 that I was sure that *my* annoyance at his response would be diminished when I heard the causes of *his* annoyance. I asked him not to pull his punches, and he replied that he disliked the book because "[t]here's nothing that I think is more healthy than that philosophers should be at loggerheads on central matters. No progress is ever made otherwise, so I'd have much preferred a book intended to sharpen and harden the differences between roughly Anglo-Saxon schools of thought. But I don't expect you to agree with this or—to be consistent with what I've said—wish you to." Although I was taken aback by Ryle's comments, I was not angered by them. There was something healthy about his directness that made his criticism easier to take than the carping expressions of disappointment in Ernest Nagel's letter to me about *Social Thought in America*. When I replied to Ryle, I said that candor was contagious and told him that he was excessively preoccupied with the title of my work. I said it was a contentious book in which I attacked many views in order to show that certain disagreements were fruitless, for example, that about whether philosophy is nothing but the philosophy of ordinary language or nothing but the philosophy of science. I went on to say that my desire for the reunion of certain movements was less important than the specific views I advanced on existence, the a priori, and value, and that if he were to turn his attention away from the war waged by the book as a whole to the individual battles waged in the chapters, he would see that I was criticizing those who think there are many senses of "exists" and those who were wedded to dubious distinctions between "analytic" and "synthetic." I did not add, as I might have, that I was in this way aiming at some of Ryle's views.

After a lapse in our correspondence of several years, Ryle wrote me on December 8, 1965, about my *Foundations of Historical Knowledge*, which he said he was enjoying and from which he was profiting. He then asked me why people who write about history don't mention the history of ideas, in which he was then especially interested because he was writing on the development of Plato's theory of Forms. I answered that he would find discussions of the history of ideas, in chapters V and VI, and that I was of course interested in intellectual history. A few years later Ryle asked me to review A. J. Ayer's book on the origins of pragmatism, but I declined because I was doing it for the *New York Review of Books*. Later, in the last letter I had from him, Ryle praised my essay "Why Annalists of Ideas Should Be Analysts of Ideas." Because that was combative in style, he liked it, writing in April 1976: "This is partly to thank (and felicitate) you for 'Annalists of Ideas. . . .' It was high time that someone should say just what you have said. I hope that in the internal combats in which sociologists etc. (like all of us) engage one party will seize on your 'Annalists . . .' as a weapon against rival parties. This is the way in which light tends to be spread, namely as a concomitant of heat!"

In thinking about my friendship with Ryle, I recall one incident that I found very perplexing. While I was in Oxford in 1951, I invited him to be my guest for dinner at the Linton Lodge in Oxford, making an inadequate attempt to respond to his generous hospitality to me. In the course of the evening we talked about many things while polishing off a bottle of bourbon, but just as our talk was winding down and as he was about to leave, Ryle said spontaneously that he had never had as pleasant an evening with John Austin, his colleague at Magdalen. I found this very odd and sad. Of course, Ryle and Austin were the two main figures in Oxford philosophy during the fifties, and I knew that Austin could be very icy, but since Ryle was older and more outgoing, I wondered why he had never taken the initiative in an ice-breaking campaign. I knew that Austin warmed up considerably when he later came to Harvard, but Ryle must have felt it would take much too much heat to warm up a man who, when asked by his military colleagues during the war to use Christian names, responded by saying: "Austin is a Christian name"!

In the U.S.A. Austin was certainly not the iceberg he had been—or had been made out to be—in the U.K. He came to Harvard in the spring term of 1954–55 to give lectures entitled "How to Do Things with Words," and it fell to my lot as chairman of the Department of Philosophy to introduce him. I made a feeble effort at wit by saying that his title at Oxford, White's Professor of Moral Philosophy, should not be taken to indicate that he had been my teacher. "Would that he had been," I added. Then I said, just before turning the lectern over to Austin, that the pragmatic William James would have been delighted to think that an Oxford philosopher had come to Harvard to tell us how to *do* things.

At the beginning of Austin's lectures, the hall was packed, but since they were very technical, they were heard at the end by only a handful of loyal listeners. This was amusing in light of the circumstances under which we had invited Austin to give the lectures. There was a time in 1953, I believe, when as few as five permanent faculty members of the Department of Philosophy were in residence (because several were on leave at the same time), and those five managed by a majority of one to nominate Charles Malik to give the James Lectures. Charles Malik was a Lebanese politician of some importance in the United Nations and had received his Ph.D. in philosophy at Harvard under the supervision of Whitehead. My recollection is that Demos, Wild, and Williams voted for Malik, while Quine and I voted against him. When the recommendation went to the administration in the spring of 1953, it was rejected by Provost Buck, who said that we should appoint a distinguished academic philosopher who might attract only a handful of students to his lectures rather than a Malik who might pack them in. The department reconvened and nominated Austin, who wound up lecturing to a predictable handful while exercising a powerful influence on our best students and on some members of the faculty.

I took advantage of Austin's presence at Harvard by asking him to read some chapters of the manuscript of *Toward Reunion in Philosophy*. He was good enough to discuss them with me, usually after having dined with Lucia, the boys, and me. He wrote me from Oxford on October 10, 1955, to answer some letters of mine, one of them a request for his opinion of my junior colleague, Burton Dreben, then under consideration for a promotion. Austin supported the appointment strongly. In December of 1956, I sent Austin a copy of my *Toward Reunion in Philosophy*. He replied quickly and made clear that he had a better opinion of my book than Ryle had: "I think the book makes solid and excellent reading, and I should expect it must be making a considerable impression. I wish we had had time to discuss some of the later parts of it in detail in the way we did the earlier: I find them most interesting and helpful. Is there any prospect of your coming over here again—next year?"

A couple of years later, during the academic year 1959–60, while I was a fellow at the Center for Advanced Study in the Behavioral Sciences in Stanford, California, I heard the shocking news of Austin's death. I wrote to his widow to express my feelings about him and to say something about his impact in this country. I spoke of his great success at Harvard, of his powerful philosophical impact on both senior and junior members of the department. I said he was admired by linguistic philosophers and by traditionalists, by shy students and aggressive ones. Even our two boys responded to him in an easygoing way, which they didn't always do when distinguished philosophers came to dinner. The Oxford image of him as a cold, impersonal analyst was destroyed in America.

Another Oxford philosopher I came to admire and respect was Herbert

Hart. Immediately on meeting him during my first trip to Oxford, I found him appealing and especially interesting because he worked in legal philosophy—a subject about which I had thought on and off since my undergraduate days and had touched on in *Social Thought in America*. Early in 1956, Benjamin Kaplan, then professor of law at Harvard and later a Massachusetts judge, learned about his writings from me and helped arrange a visiting professorship for him in the Law School and in the Department of Philosophy during the coming academic year of 1956–57. When I sent Hart a copy of *Toward Reunion in Philosophy*, he wrote on May 8, 1956, that he admired a good deal of it, thanked me for the trouble I had taken in fixing up his "Janus-faced activities in Harvard," and said he was delighted with his program. When he came to Harvard, he was a great success at the Law School and in the Department of Philosophy. Soon after leaving Harvard, Hart generously wrote me from Oxford about his colleague Paul Grice, who was about to give the William James Lectures at Harvard:

> Just one word about Paul Grice, who will be coming at the end of January, which perhaps you will not think it wrong of me to write: He is a marvellous dialectician, far better, I think, than anyone here— including even Austin, at least as far as pure, critical, rigorous argumentation goes. He has, I think, got exciting things to say on some central issues on the philosophy of logic, and as long as he is stimulated by finding questions to answer and points of view to criticise, all goes very well. He does, however, rather depend on others to provide the stimulus: he is rather like an engine that needs warming up, and Strawson among others has often played this part. I think, possibly, the success of his seminars would be made more certain if some senior member would go along simply to help in raising topics for discussion and criticism. Possibly some little concerted arrangement beforehand might be good. If you yourself could find time for this I am sure Paul would be both enormously grateful and it would assist him very much. I say all this because he has so much to offer which others of us have not got, that it would be a pity if through lack of this kind of psychological stimulus prop he did not get it all out.

To this I replied: "Grice is doing splendidly and is very much liked in all parts. The Department likes him, students like him, and the crowd at Adams House is enthusiastic. I have been going to his seminar on Meaning and have had some good talks with him. Albritton and I both find him stimulating and,

I should say, more flexible than most Oxford philosophers! There is a kind of indifference to winning arguments it seems to me, and a certain lack of party thinking which I find enormously impressive. He is not, I should say, a debater."

While Hart was teaching at Harvard in 1956, Robert Oppenheimer gave his William James Lectures, and—as I have said earlier—Hart, like several other members of my department, was greatly disappointed by Oppenheimer's discussions of familiar philosophical topics—for example, relativism by contrast to physical relativity. Hart's own seminar in philosophy was very lively, but I did not attend it, because I was too burdened by the duties of the chairmanship. However, I can remember one amusing story about it. It seems that he was often given to using the words "Surely it would be fantastic to suppose that . . . ," followed by some statement that he denied but which people in his class believed. As a result, one would often hear students (and faculty) leaving Hart's seminar mockingly saying: "Surely it would be fantastic to suppose that 2 + 2 = 4." During the year I wrote Isaiah Berlin that I admired Herbert very much but found him somewhat doctrinaire, too much given to repeating the Oxford party line. To my amusement, Isaiah replied that Herbert admired me but found *me* too doctrinaire. This did not prevent us from enjoying each other's company, and when in later years party lines began to blur or disappear, we came to have very cordial relations, philosophical and otherwise. When Herbert and his colleague Honoré brought out their *Causation in the Law*, I published a favorable review of it in the *Columbia Law Review*. On September 20, 1960, Herbert wrote to thank me for this and went on to say: "[A] good deal of the sparkle went out of the air when John Austin died. There's quite a lot of interesting movement and change but nothing to take his special place." Hart also wrote: "What do you think of our emergent Hegelianism and Kantianism in Hampshire and Strawson? I'd love to talk to you about the shifting philosophical scene."

When Hart came to teach for a term at UCLA in 1961, Lucia and I arranged a party for him in Cambridge, which he was to visit on his way home. When writing to accept our invitation, he remarked that he was attending Carnap's seminars at UCLA and finding his defense of the distinction between analytic and synthetic statements "feeble"—a sign, I was glad to see, that the American attack on that distinction was making some headway at Oxford. After returning there, Hart told about seeing the Berlins, who had just come back from India: "Isaiah's imitation of accent, gestures and thoughts (I see, Sir Isaiah, you do not think quite so highly as we do of the late Professor H. Laski—would you please explain why that is so!) are all fantastically funny. He is well but in bed with some minor leg pain. He has just completed the last round of his public quarrel with E. H. Carr." Hart also wrote about the idea for a book on intellectual antiurbanism that Lucia and I were then writing, saying that he had enjoyed reading an article we had published on the subject.

In the fall of 1965 I sent Hart a copy of my *Foundations of Historical Knowledge*, where I used an idea developed by him and Honoré in *Causation in the Law*. Suppose, they say, a man has an attack of indigestion—an event that may be regarded as abnormal in different ways by the man's wife and by his physician. The wife thinks of her husband as normally free of indigestion even though he has ulcers, and therefore she thinks his having eaten parsnips is the cause of his attack. By contrast, his physician, who is professionally interested in diseases or deviations from the normal condition of human beings, regards his patient's having ulcers as the cause of his indigestion. Two analogously different approaches are possible in the case of history, I said. A revolutionary leader who looks at a revolution in his country may say that the cause of it was the activity of the revolutionary party because the leader thinks that the activity stands to the revolution as the eating of parsnips stands to the attack of indigestion in the illustration of Hart and Honoré. The revolutionary leader, observing that his country had previously gone without a revolution while in a revolutionary situation, attributes the revolution to the work of his party. Yet a visiting historian might conclude that the cause of the revolution was the presence of a revolutionary situation, since he sees the revolutionary situation in the visited country as a deviation from the normal condition of countries he has studied for years.

My work in the history of ideas also benefited from Hart's. When he read my *Philosophy of the American Revolution* after it appeared in 1978, he called my attention to the fact that he had written at some length about the relationship of one John Lind to Jeremy Bentham, John Lind having written a work on the Declaration of Independence that I had discussed briefly in my book.

1/11/78

Dear Morty,

I have been reading your book on the philosophy of the American revolution with very great interest and I imagine you might care to see the passages about *John Lind* in the enclosed (pp. 548–56). J.L. was a fascinating figure and plainly Bentham was in love with him. More

important all the philosophical part of Lind's Answer to the Declaration some of which you quote was written by Bentham. This appears as
I say on p. 555 n. 37 from a letter written by Bentham to Lind in Vol.
I of the Correspondence in the Collected Works of J.B. (I:341–44). The
whole story is fascinating. . . .

   Best wishes,

                                              Yours ever,
                                              Herbert

   In the paperback edition of *The Philosophy of the American Revolution*,
which appeared in 1981, I referred to Hart's fascinating discussion of Lind and
Bentham, but I did not see Hart again until December of 1987, when Lucia
and I spent Christmas in Oxford. The Berlins gave a dinner party to which
the Harts and I came, but, alas, Lucia was not feeling well and couldn't come.
It was a hilarious evening at which Isaiah held forth in a remarkably funny
way, but I was quite surprised to find Herbert very stooped and old looking.
Isaiah had told me that Herbert and Jenifer had been in a car accident, but
I learned little of the details until I had a letter from Herbert on May 28,
1989, more than a year later. There he thanked me for a reprint of mine on
the philosophy of the *Federalist Papers* and then told me of an awful thing that
had happened to him and his wife:

> We stagger along not too badly after a rather disastrous car accident in
> which ribs were broken, lungs punctured and Jenifer lost the sight of one
> eye. But we were so lucky not to be killed by the lunatic (driving on the
> wrong side of the road) who smashed us up. These things don't help
> one's creative powers! and I write little. We are about to celebrate
> Isaiah's 80th birthday. He is in remarkably good form and a wonderful
> disseminator of light, warmth and intellectual gaiety here. Our public
> affairs under this horrible Thatcher government are unspeakable so,
> following Wittgenstein, I remain silent about them.

   After receiving this word, I sent the Harts a copy of my *Philosophy, "The
Federalist," and the Constitution* along with a letter in which I commiserated
with them. In reply, Herbert wrote to thank me and to tell me with
characteristic pleasure and friendliness about the celebration of Berlin's
eightieth birthday: "Have the sounds of Isaiah's 80th birthday celebration
reached you in N.J.? They have been most remarkable. The University

celebrated it with a dinner presided over by the Chancellor and a fascinating selection of Isaiah's heterogeneous old friends: there is an excellent 'Profile' of him in the *Observer* newspaper of May 11th and there is to be a great concert with stars like Brendel and Fischer-Diskau playing and singing in his honour. Virtual canonization!; but he remains marvelously unperturbed and in extraordinarily good form—which is good to contemplate." Herbert's letter was written in the summer of 1989 and was the last I had from him. I heard of his death long after it occurred, and wrote a letter of condolence to his widow. In it I recalled Isaiah's telling me at Harvard in 1949 that there was a man at Oxford named Hart of whom I reminded him—an assimilated Jew he called him, married like me to a Gentile and a very popular member of the Oxford community. I said that when I met Herbert, I discovered that instead of not liking this supposed Oxford *Doppelgänger* of mine for being too much like me, I took to him almost immediately. I was delighted, therefore, to join with Benjamin Kaplan of the Harvard Law School in bringing Herbert to our Cambridge for a year so that philosophers and lawyers could profit from his teaching. He was an extremely able and interesting philosopher.

When I think now about my association with Oxford philosophers in the fifties and sixties, I see how pleasant and profitable it was for me. I did not know most of them as well as I knew Hart and Berlin, but I knew all of them well enough to think that I would have been extremely happy to be a colleague of theirs in this country. When I reflect that Ernest Nagel was the only philosopher at Columbia with whom I ever had serious conversations, that at Pennsylvania there was only Nelson Goodman to talk with, and that at Harvard for several years there was only Quine to learn from, I realize how marvelous it would have been to talk regularly with Ryle, Austin, Hart, Berlin, Grice, and Hampshire. Of course, I took pleasure in talking with Berlin about anything, and especially about the nature of history and the history of ideas; Hart would have taught me much about the philosophy of law; seeing Hampshire would have allowed me to discuss with him the many philosophical topics in which we were both interested; and being in touch with Austin, Ryle, and Grice would have helped me much as Moore, Goodman, and Quine had on topics such as meaning, mind, perception, and necessity. In short, my Oxford friends encouraged my interests not only in metaphysics, ethics, and epistemology, but also in the history of ideas and in the philosophy of history, law, religion, and politics. I say this even though sharing these interests with them did not always lead to agreement: witness the negative effect of *Toward Reunion in Philosophy* on Ryle, my disagreement with Berlin on free will, and my separation from most of the Oxonians on the distinction between analytic and synthetic statements.

Some of my differences with *some* Oxford philosophers emerged in a talk I produced in 1957 for the BBC. In it I criticized a volume entitled *The Nature of Metaphysics*, which consisted mostly of talks delivered earlier by Oxford philosophers. Although I praised a piece that was jointly written by Paul Grice, D. F. Pears, and P.F. Strawson, as well as others by Gerd Buchdahl, P.L. Gardiner, and Iris Murdoch, I complained that most of the other pieces were tiresomely programmatic and obscure. On September 17, 1957, I wrote to Berlin: "[I]f you turn on your radio on September 26 at 7:15 P.M., I am told, you will hear me deliver a somewhat blistering attack on a volume called 'The Nature of Metaphysics'—a medley of meanderings by some of your colleagues on a subject for which they have little feeling but for which some of them seem to have developed a nostalgic affection. When the talk is broadcast I shall probably only have three friends left in Oxford: Austin, Hart (who also disapproves of the book, he tells me), and I hope, yourself." Then on November 6, 1957, I wrote to Berlin: "I cannot resist asking you whether you heard any groans about my review of *The Nature of Metaphysics*. Stuart sent me an extremely nice note and made me feel sorry about having been so waspish, but, as Marx said so frequently, 'I have spoken and saved my soul.' Oxford philosophy ain't what it used to be."

Stuart Hampshire, who gave one of the talks I reviewed and whom I liked very much, wrote me on September 29, 1957:

> Dear Morton,
>
> I heard the first two-thirds of your broadcast on metaphysics with Herbert Hart, who happened to be dining with me, and then we were compelled to go before the end, so I do not know whether any relaxation of the strictures, any reprieve was granted to us at the end. Herbert, from memory of the script, thought not. I can only plead that we were told by the BBC to discuss the nature of metaphysics, and not in that unfortunate Cambridge, England phrase—to 'do' any metaphysics, it being rightly thought that 20 minutes on the air is not the right circumstance for 'doing' metaphysics. But I must admit that I am in favor of all philosophers attacking all other philosophers, and so enjoyed what I heard, except the praise of Buchdahl who seemed to me easily the worst of the lot. But like you I thought Iris Murdoch rather good. I also thought that I was rather good, in a reckless sort of way, but I am shaken now.

How are you and what are you writing and why do you not visit England? There *is* activity here, both philosophical and political, the political being on the whole most interesting. There are too many little books of essays in British philosophy, but arguments in Societies and classes are still sometimes quite good. I would be very pleased to hear what you are thinking. There are so many things that I would want to say about your book that I could not say them in a letter: but there will come an occasion. Please give my best wishes to Lucia.

Yours ever,
Stuart Hampshire

To this I replied on October 8, 1957:

Dear Stuart:

How kind of you to reply in such a friendly way to such a waspish review! You confirm my faith in English philosophers, who are so much more inclined than we are to remain friendly in the face of doctrinal differences. My review of *The Nature of Metaphysics,* I assure you, is not a declaration of war against Oxford Philosophers but only the working out of a recurring feeling of boredom with meta-philosophy which I had supposed I shared with many of my Oxford friends. I agree, of course, that one can't *do* metaphysics easily in twenty minutes but a *book* of such twenty-minute talks is another matter and I had hoped that there would be some development. Also I suppose that I am temperamentally (and hence doctrinally) opposed to the classification of the sciences and the philosophical disciplines in accordance with supposedly differ-ent methods. At heart I am a follower of J. S. Mill on this, very suspicious about efforts to delineate different "methods" of establishing what we claim to know, whether it be in metaphysics, physics, logic, or ethics.

Yours ever,
Morton

I think this last remark shows that my views in philosophy were sometimes very different from the views held by my Oxford friends. Nevertheless, I liked and admired them as people and as philosophers. I enjoyed being with them and felt that I could range over almost the whole field of my interests with them in a way that was certainly not possible in the Harvard Department of Philosophy in 1951—or in the Columbia department in 1941. About a half century later it amuses me to recall how Irwin Edman had once put me down by telling me how inferior my table manners were to those of Oxford dons, who, he said, *never* talked philosophy at lunch—a great falsehood. I also recall with pleasure a sharp attack by Herbert Hart on someone at Harvard for *daring*—Herbert's word—to say that Isaiah Berlin reminded him of Irwin Edman. Herbert had met Irwin when Irwin had lectured one summer at Oxford, and Herbert thought it *obscene*—also Herbert's word—to slander Isaiah by speaking of both of them in the same breath. How splendid of Herbert to be so candid and so right; and how nice it would have been to be a colleague of his and of the other Oxford dons I came to know in the 1950s!

17

Isaiah Berlin

A Bridge Between Philosophy
and the History of Ideas

My first contact with Oxford had been by way of Isaiah Berlin. Before the Second World War he had been a rising philosophical star at Oxford, a contemporary of J. L. Austin and A. J. Ayer, but during the war he developed doubts about his ability to do important work in philosophy, doubts that seemed to be strengthened by conversations he had with H. M. Sheffer, to whom Felix Frankfurter had introduced him. Sheffer had advised Berlin that to do philosophy properly one had to be a mathematical logician or a scientific psychologist, so if one were neither, one should forget about being a philosopher. Period. Such advice had a chilling effect on Isaiah, naturally. As he flew back to England after his talk with Sheffer at Harvard, he mulled over Sheffer's grim pronouncements and was convinced by them that he should give up philosophy. What should he do instead? Cultivate his interest in the history of ideas, he seems to have said. He had already published a well-received book on Karl Marx in the Home University Library; he was a voracious reader in the history of philosophy, political thought, and literature; and so he was very well prepared for work in the history of ideas.

When I saw Berlin at Harvard in the spring term of 1948–49, he was lecturing on historical subjects in the Department of Slavic Studies, as I have said earlier. We were introduced by Arthur Schlesinger Jr. but immediately

recalled that we had met earlier in the forties at a meeting of the New York
Philosophical Circle, an imitation of the Vienna Circle whose most prominent members were Ernest Nagel, Sidney Hook, and Meyer Schapiro. Berlin
and I quickly became good friends. I found him a delight to be with because
of his interest in philosophy and the history of ideas, his tastes in music and
literature, his charm, his wisdom, and his sense of humor. In addition, he
admired G.E. Moore greatly. Once at the Harvard Faculty Club in 1949, he
and I and a few other philosophers were joined at lunch by a well-read French
chemist, Philip Le Corbeiller, who was then teaching at Harvard. When the
philosophers began to talk about G.E. Moore, Le Corbeiller told us about
how much Moore had enjoyed the French girls in Paris. Berlin and I smiled
knowingly at each other but waited until after lunch to explode in laughter:
Le Corbeiller had confused our George Edward Moore with George Moore
the novelist!

I was able to communicate with Berlin on almost all levels, both personal
and intellectual, in conversation and in almost fifty years of correspondence
with him. During 1948–49, my first year at Harvard, he spread good news
about me among those who counted there and was, I am sure, very helpful to
me while serving on the ad hoc committee that recommended my promotion
to a permanent position in the Department of Philosophy. When I visited
Oxford in 1951, he introduced me to all of the philosophers there whom I
came to know and like; he reviewed my *Social Thought in America* very
generously; he counseled me about the direction that my work should take;
he wrote in support of my appointment to the faculty of the Institute for
Advanced Study; he recommended that I be asked to edit *The Age of
Analysis*; he encouraged me to think hard about history and free will; and
whenever I saw him, I could have a good laugh with him or cry on his
shoulder.

When I was reintroduced to Berlin at Harvard, he had already resolved to
give up philosophy for the history of ideas but was still quite *au courant* of
what was going on in English philosophy; and since I was then trying to
maintain my interests in both subjects, he was in a position to offer me a good
deal of valuable advice. He did not urge me to give up philosophy but strongly
advised me not to abandon my interest in the sort of thing I dealt with in
Social Thought in America even if I did not teach about it. He pointed out how
unhappy a pure but unproductive philosopher could be, and he urged me to
keep up my work in the history of ideas. He said it would serve me in good
stead when no philosophical ideas were popping into my head, and, indeed,
it would give me pleasure to work in it. Throughout all of these conversations, however, he never discouraged me from continuing to work in

philosophy, and he certainly did not attack it as a subject, as ex-philosophers often do. On the contrary, he praised the work of his Oxford friend and colleague John Austin and was enthusiastic about the developments at Oxford under the influence of Austin. Isaiah Berlin did much more than introduce me to Oxford philosophy: he helped me in my efforts to bridge the gap between my work in philosophy and my work in the history of ideas, to make myself intellectually whole. For many years we talked about collaborating. First we thought we might produce a book in the theory of historical knowledge; then we thought it should consist of letters between us because of the geographical distance separating us; later we thought it would have to consist of letters because of the intellectual distance separating us in the theory of historical knowledge; and finally we thought we might produce a correspondence on free will in which we aired our increasingly wide differences on that difficult subject. In the end, unfortunately, we produced nothing together, but we used every opportunity to talk and to write letters to each other in which we tried to pinpoint our philosophical disagreements. Throughout this period my admiration and affection for him grew steadily in spite of those disagreements.

The Atlantic was the first of the obstacles we had to overcome if we were to collaborate effectively. We tried to overcome it by appealing to two American foundations for support that would enable us to travel across the ocean occasionally and to be free of some of our academic duties, but they turned us down flatly. Yet even if they hadn't turned us down, there were other obstacles to surmount: the death of Isaiah's father, the illness of his mother, the school schedules of my sons, my travels, his travels, my duties as a departmental chairman, and his as president of Wolfson College and of the British Academy. As time went on, both of us—especially Isaiah as he grew more eminent—were unable to find long periods during which we could get together, and therefore the letter became our main means of communication. Our writing to each other had started soon after Isaiah returned to Oxford from Harvard in the spring of 1949. I began by sending him a letter of which I have no copy because I had no secretary then, did not type well, kept no carbons of what I did type, and often wrote my letters in longhand without copying them. His reply to that was dated December 29, 1949 and was sent from New College, Oxford, where he was then a fellow. It was four and one-half pages long, single-spaced, and full of very good practical advice: he told me at what time of the year to come to Oxford and when not to come, when he would be there, and how to apply for money from the Fulbright people, and so on. But his most important piece of advice was that I should come to investigate the new wave in philosophy at Oxford: "Thank you very much for your letter. It arrived at a moment when I was dreadfully exhausted, for some reason, by teaching at Oxford, although the prospectus which I tried to sell you describing the advances we are making [in philosophy] turns out not at all inaccurate; as the non-Zionist said who came back from Palestine impressed: 'all the lies are true.' But of that another time."

In 1950, Isaiah wrote from Italy about his plan to review my *Social Thought in America*:

> I have now read your book in these idyllic surroundings, with the greatest pleasure & interest. As soon as I return I shall try & concoct a review: I apologize for penalizing you—someone not a friend, some good competent stranger would no doubt have celebrated you long ago: what strikes me about your subject is the similarity to Russian intellectual affairs of roughly the same date: but I shan't say that to the readers of *Mind*: it would upset them & strike them as a piece of exotic non-professionalism, a piece of showoff & chichi from which they have a right to feel themselves protected. I shall be v. grave & judicious.

Early in 1951 Isaiah exclaimed, "I am delighted that the die should have been cast!" after I had told him that I had decided to come to England in March of 1951. Answering a letter of mine in which I reported some of my interests at the time, he described the philosophical scene at Oxford, said something about some of his colleagues there, paid me an undeserved compliment, and made a comparison between philosophy and the history of ideas that would often turn up in our correspondence. He wrote:

> I could not agree more strongly with you [about] the appalling difference between the sufficient but shallow waters of Geistesgeschichte as against the deep dark wells of philosophy proper. Indeed, I feel a weakling and a poltroon for leaving the latter for the former. Philosophy is a fearfully difficult subject, more so with every advancing year. One needs, I am sure, a singular capacity for shutting out irrelevant interests and love of variety with which I am sadly afflicted, and, believe me, you are a far more effective writer than I shall ever be; you seem to combine a capacity for phi and psi with civilized subjects in a most enviable manner, and this I shall duly say some time in "Mind."

On the eighth of February 1951 Isaiah sent me a postcard in which he tersely reported: "Wittgenstein is said to be dying slowly in this town: Ryle is fuller of beans than ever. I am really delighted you're coming." At the end of March 1951, I went to Oxford and, as the reader knows, stayed abroad with Lucia and our two boys into the summer of 1951. After I returned to Harvard in the fall, Isaiah wrote me again on October 4, 1952, about doing a joint work on the philosophy of history:

> I think we could produce a book on the philosophy of history and I think what we ought to do is to write letters to each other on the subject. . . . Certainly no such thing has ever been done before, novels have been written in the form of letters and philosophers have answered 1st and 2nd Objections, but a formal correspondence on a selected topic entitled, say 'Letters on the Philosophy of History' or the like has never been perpetrated to my knowledge, only imaginary ones like Lowes Dickinson's Letters to John Chinaman, and things by Diderot and the like. I really do not see why not, do say what you think. I would be prepared to start early in the spring.

All of Isaiah's letters were full of sparkling observations about ideas and about the virtues, foibles, and problems of people. On March 4, 1953, he commented on something I had written to him about my impending jump to a full professorship over the head of Henry Aiken. I must have expressed uneasiness of the kind I report in an earlier chapter, and so Isaiah wrote: "It is splendid about your full professorship, but seemed to me . . . certainly very obvious and irresistible and to be taken for granted. Your feelings about Henry Aiken I can understand all too well. That is the kind of thing I know all about and am infinitely sensitive to and understanding about (though I say it myself). Of course you had to go through these frightful convolutions and of course it would be madness to wait. Sooner or later he will get his full professorship, and after all he is a nice good man."

With a letter from me to Isaiah written on January 18, 1954, my extant correspondence with him assumes the form of an exchange, since that letter is the earliest of mine of which I have a copy. I was answering one from Isaiah in which he reported his father's death, its effect on his mother, his need to stay with her in England and to be there while probate of his father's estate went on. He was also worried about whether to accept the headship of a newly formed college in Oxford—Nuffield—and on top of that was burdened by his failure to keep his promise to join me at the Institute as a fellow visiting member in the second, or spring, term of 1953–54. In my reply of January 18, I offered my condolences to him, assured him that everyone would understand why he could not come to the Institute, and gave him some of my news. I reminded him that I was, like him, an only child and the son of a businessman, so I fully appreciated the situation in which he found himself. I said that I went into scholarship in sharp reaction to business and that I remembered the pain with which I used to face working "from the bottom up" while selling shoes. Later I reported that I had finished writing thirteen chapters of *Toward Reunion in Philosophy* and had about four or five more to go. But I added that the controversial nature of philosophical ideas led me to pine for the kind of rich, thick brew that pleased historians when I talked about Holmes, Beard, and Co. I recalled that when young Arthur Schlesinger heard from Perry Miller that I was writing a "metaphysical work" at the Institute, he wrote me that for that I was too old or too young.

On the twenty-eighth of January 1954, Isaiah issued a report on Quine's visit to Oxford as the Eastman Professor—a report that showed how poorly Isaiah's informants understood Quine's philosophical position vis-à-vis Carnap.

> I wish I could give you detailed notes about Quine. He had dinner with me and was delightful and charming as always, Austin treats him exactly like a Marshall Plan ambassador, not to be affronted on any possible grounds; the complaint against him is that he is splendid on his logic, but as far as philosophy is concerned is saying the kind of things that Freddie Ayer used to say in 1937—that it is still the same ancient Carnap analysis. I don't know how far this is just: it would obviously be disastrous if a real rift opened between him and us, but I think that will probably be averted through much good-will and tact. He is clearly enjoying himself a great deal, he has dined out quite a lot and is obviously having what is called a good time.

Isaiah then described meetings of an Oxford philosophical discussion group that were run "by Austin with the authority of a Stalin—Ryle is a kind of second-in-command, Zhdanov or Malenkov, all offices are divided between them, Austin is on all committees, Ryle on about three-quarters, and poor Price sits there like an old Menshevik, not actually in person but clearly an obsolete figure who is not to be employed in any capacity."

On February 27 I sent Isaiah a long letter in which I described an outburst of mine against the literary critic Francis Ferguson, whom I had recently met at a dinner at the Institute. Ferguson had delivered an ill-tempered attack on logical positivism that made me furious in spite of my not being a positivist; I couldn't stand his unfairness and ignorance. Isaiah answered on

March 15: "Forgive me if I do not write a proper letter in answer to your splendid, spontaneous, disinterested, excellent, enjoyable, admirable one." My onslaught against Ferguson, of course, was not about politics, but Isaiah in his response captured the spirit and structure, so to speak, of my attack by writing of a similar exchange between him and a group of intellectuals collected by Robert Hutchins at a London conference.

> I know very well the feeling you mean—here was I who really feel bitterly unsympathetic to the left, far more so than you do, with far more of a penchant of a "disreputable" kind towards all kind of romantic views, but when faced with Adler and Hutchins during [a] notorious meeting of the Ford Foundation in London I developed a most tremendous, violent, fanatical defence of leftist practices, which distressed everyone at the table but was, it seemed to me, the only thing to do. I feel myself to be on the extreme Right Wing edge of the Left Wing movement, both philosophically and politically, and rightly regarded with suspicion by the orthodox members of the Left Wing movement; but when faced with people conspicuously outside it who wish to attack it as such, there is nothing to do but man the walls, behave as in war and adopt a hundred per cent position. We absolutely agree about that. To compromise then is ignoble, and is the suppression of the real truth in favour of some kind of formal, moral alibi.

On March 23, 1954, I assured Isaiah that I understood his decision not to come to the Institute that spring, and went on to tell about the state of my work on *Toward Reunion in Philosophy* and about my plans for *The Age of Analysis*. I was especially concerned to get his views about the latter, since he was the unofficial general editor of the Mentor Philosophers series. I spoke of some difficulties I had in deciding "*what* philosophers to immortalize for typists, soda-jerks, commuters, and subway strap-hangers." I also spoke about the problem of organizing my philosophers. I had decided not to divide them into the schools that they represented, such as the conventional ones of realism, positivism, and pragmatism, and I mentioned two other approaches. One would be to divide them by focusing on the disciplines in which they had made their main contributions, for example, metaphysics, morals, or logical analysis. Another approach would be to divide them in accordance with the science, concept, or aspect of life that most engaged their attention—logic, organism, common sense, society, or natural science. What, I asked Isaiah, did he think? His reply was quick and to the point. He wrote on April 8 to recommend that I "play for safety," urged me to ignore his views if

I found them unacceptable, and ended by saying that "we shall certainly write our book together. I feel convinced about that now."

On the twenty-seventh of April 1954, after about five years of talking about that book on the philosophy of history, Isaiah wrote about a suggestion of mine that we try to get a foundation to help us finance work on our book: "I have not the slightest guilt about asking foundations for money for our collaboration—this will be one of the least speculative and unsound ways in which any of them will ever have spent the relatively tiny sums involved." We both devoted a good part of 1954 to trying to get a measly $10,000 from a foundation, a sum that would enable us to be together in one place for a few uninterrupted months. Some might say that the foundations were prescient when they turned us down: they knew that we'd never write the book, and were wise enough not to waste their dollars on us. Maybe. On the other hand, their failure to support us might well have contributed to our failure to produce the book. What we hoped to do was described in a draft of a letter that I sent to Isaiah before sending it on to the Rockefeller Foundation and to the Ford Foundation:

> Among the questions we hope to discuss are: the nature of historical knowledge, the relation between history and the social sciences, the role of value judgments in historical research, the nature of historical explanation and causation, the character of historical language, the similarities and differences between history and the natural sciences, the nature of an adequate historical description of a given culture, period or event, and kindred questions. We have not yet determined the exact form of the book which we hope will issue from these studies but we have been considering the possibility of publishing a philosophical correspondence in which we exchange and examine each other's views in a consecutive way. Alternatively, we may, of course, put down the results in the more usual kind of collaborative work.

When I sent this to Isaiah for his approval, he wrote to me on October 4, 1954:

> . . . I agree with your programme, as you know, and should only like to add this:
> On your last page (page 3) you give a list of the topics it is hoped to discuss. To this I should like to add what is, in my mind, one of the most important of these, namely, the nature of historical understanding—that

is to say of what is meant when it is said that historians understand a period well or badly, that they are good historians or poor, or profound or shallow, or that their accounts are plausible or unconvincing. You partly cover this by your term, "historical explanation," but not perhaps quite. I have been lecturing on this subject at Oxford, and have had very interesting reactions to the view which I have expounded, which is somewhat different from official Positivist views, from historians who have come to these lectures, and, in particular, from the eminent Professor of Latin—just retired—Eduard Fraenkel, who explained to me why it was that he had declined to write the life of Mommsen when requested to do so by Wilamowitz, and taught me a great deal about German historicism in the process. He came to all the lectures and generally took a great deal of lively interest in the whole thing. The nature of the logic of the human studies, in general, for example, the reconstruction of the historical past, the technique of emendation of historical and literary texts, and inference, as used, for example, by paleographers, seems to me to be highly relevant to our study.

When we were turned down by the Rockefeller Foundation, Isaiah wrote on November 30, 1954, after meeting with a representative of theirs in Oxford: "I would really rather have nothing to do with him if possible. If Ford comes through well and good, if not, do not let us repine and [let us] continue to communicate from a distance." On December 30 I wrote, after the Ford Foundation turned us down: "Now that we have tried to extract funds for a worthy cause, and now that we have been rebuffed, I suggest that we . . . leave these shabby people, and write our book as scholars have for ages and ages—without foundations."

The end of 1954 brought a practical problem for me in connection with *The Age of Analysis*. On December 3 I reported to Isaiah that Blackwells, the publisher of Wittgenstein's *Philosophical Investigations*, refused to give me permission to print a passage from that work unless I printed the German text along with the English translation. After much consultation with Victor Weybright, the publisher of the series, it was agreed that Wittgenstein's German should be printed in an appendix. Since Weybright had asked Isaiah to look at the whole of my manuscript, he dutifully wrote me a letter about it on January 11, 1955, to which he attached six single-spaced typed pages of remarkable notes, writing, to my great relief, that I had made an "admirable selection," that he was glad to see nothing of Heidegger in the book, and that he was proud that I had used his metaphor of the Hedgehog and the Fox at some point in my discussion. Soon afterward, we exchanged several long letters about *The Age of Analysis,* beginning with mine of January 27, 1955. I said there that my deadline prevented me from taking into account some of his comments on my manuscript: in particular that I was forced not to follow his recommendation that my volume not include selections in ethics, because I felt that Dewey's main contribution was in moral theory. On February 2, 1955, Isaiah urged me to make a few changes in my sections on Husserl and Sartre. And on February 23, 1955, I assured Isaiah that I would be able to do something about Husserl and Sartre, and went on to describe J. L. Austin's arrival on the scene at Harvard to give the William James Lectures in philosophy.

> The big news around here in which, of course, you will be interested, is the arrival of Austin. He lectures under the amusing title "How to Do Things with Words," gives a seminar on *Excuses,* conducts a small informal class on Saturday mornings for some faculty and advanced graduate students, and is prepared to talk philosophy indefinitely and with anyone. I am delighted with him and think that he is really making quite an impact on the young people. I find him ever so much brighter than most Oxford philosophers, if you will permit me to say that, and exceedingly unlike some of the doctrinaires under his influence. Unlike them he seems not to have some kind of "line" and is willing to listen to arguments from whatever quarter. Even my colleague Williams, who is so old-fashioned and, in general, hostile to linguistic philosophy, has taken quite a shine to Austin. I am amazed at how controlled Austin can be in the face of Williams' inveterate tendency to inject irrelevant political emotion into arguments about the smallest remote, technical points. I have the feeling that Austin's philosophical life *is* conversation and exchange and that he enjoys this so much that he will never produce a book except under duress. Such duress we may have supplied in the case of the William James Lectures. It is hoped that they will be published and I gather that Austin is prepared to cooperate and, indeed, seems to think of himself as bound to produce a book. If nothing more comes of his visit I shall be happy. But something else has come and is coming even for the general public. I must say that more people are staying on (he has now given three lectures) than I had supposed originally.
>
> I had a rather good time at the opening lecture where, as chairman, I was obliged to introduce Austin. I made much of the fact that he was the first Oxford philosopher ever to give these lectures after mentioning

some of his predecessors like Dewey, Lovejoy, Russell, Gilson, and Popper. I then pointed out that William James would have been delighted at the irony in an Oxford philosopher coming to Harvard and telling us how to *do* anything—even to do something with *words*. I also joked about his being "White's Professor of Moral Philosophy" at Oxford, and pointed out that whereas I admired him and his work he had not been *my* Professor of Philosophy. He responded to all of this in a very witty and charming way, far more so than I thought was likely in the light of my memory of him as a dry, pedantic, pinched but clever man when I knew him at Oxford—by dint of great effort or by virtue of the fact that he is *au fond* not like what I thought he was at all. . . .

On April 7, 1955, I wrote a long letter that expressed the fatigue I felt after reading proof for *The Age of Analysis* and finishing the manuscript of *Toward Reunion in Philosophy*. I said that I felt a great urge to go back to history and social and political philosophy, and would in the following year offer a course of lectures called the Nature and Function of History in an effort to make the subject respectable at Harvard. I thought this might be interpreted as apostasy by some of my colleagues but had given up worrying about their views of me. I said that Austin was the only philosopher to whom I had spoken recently and that I found him very stimulating, but not stimulating enough to make me change my mind about teaching philosophy of history. I also wrote that Arthur Schlesinger Jr. was "a breath of fresh air in Cambridge. He laughs at the right people and is bored by the right people. . . . I know of no one else to whom I can speak with utter candor and yet remain on friendly warm terms with."

After receiving my letter of April 7, Isaiah wrote me two and one-half single-space pages on May 2, which began with his asking to be forgiven for writing a letter "rather briefer than usual," no doubt because he thought he was about to produce a brief one by his standards. He went on to speak hopefully about "our book" on the theory of historical knowledge after mentioning *The Age of Enlightenment,* his own volume in the Mentor Philosophers series, and he agreed that Arthur Schlesinger was a very good character, very noble hearted, and the most reliable foul-weather friend he could think of. On June 23, 1955, he wrote that the manuscript of his *Age of Enlightenment* had gone off to Weybright, that the manuscript of Stuart Hampshire's *Age of Reason* was about to be sent off, and that "the public may really roll off to the triumphant sound of Harvard Oxford trumpets."

In the summer of 1955, when Lucia, the boys, and I were all at the Salzburg Seminar, I tried to arrange a meeting with Isaiah somewhere in Europe in

July. At one point it was decided that we should all meet in Lucerne—the four of us, Isaiah, and his mother—but, alas, Mrs. Berlin broke her leg, and so that meeting had to be canceled, and Isaiah and I saw each other briefly in London. He put me up at the Reform Club for a couple of days while Lucia and the boys took a trip into the English countryside. When they returned, we all had tea at the Hyde Park Hotel, and it was there that Isaiah and I agreed (once more) to write our book on the philosophy of history. In a letter of November 16, I summarized what I had said to him in London about our proposed book, and produced something like an outline of my *Foundations of Historical Knowledge*, which I published ten years later:

> . . . I will repeat my proposal, made outside the Hyde Park Hotel last summer, that we distinguish at least four types of questions: (1) The logic of establishing single, singular statements about the past. Not a very interesting question in my opinion, but a manageable one. (2) The logic of establishing causal statements—"so"-statements, "since"-statements, "because"-statements, "therefore"-statements. (3) The logic of judging the adequacy of narratives. To me the central problem, where a narrative is conceived as a total historical work about a period or place, etc. (4) The logic of judging large, Toynbeesque, Hegelian, Marxist, Spenglerian "theories" of the process of history or civilization.

In March of 1956, I sent Isaiah our very best wishes on his marriage to Aline, and on May 8, I received a communication from him about a draft I had sent on May 1 of my review of his *Historical Inevitability*. The review appeared in the summer 1956 issue of a literary magazine called *Perspectives USA*, published by James Laughlin. In it I was enthusiastic about parts of his piece but presented a criticism of his views on free will and determinism that is close to what I would still say today, and he wrote me an answer to my criticism that I believe he accepted to the end. One issue that separated us for years was our disagreement about the status of the principle that "ought" implies "can." In disagreeing with me, Isaiah said in effect that "You ought to have done that" is "logically incompatible" with "You could not have done that." Later he said that the principle connecting "ought" and "can" is a "conceptual truth," whereas I held that it is a moral principle, which is not a conceptual truth. I maintained that it could be rejected or revised, whereas Isaiah thought otherwise and later said to me that it was a synthetic necessary principle.

On May 1, 1956, I also sent him the manuscript of my attack on Reinhold

Niebuhr and Walter Lippmann in my article "Original Sin, Natural Law, and Politics," and wrote him a covering letter in which I remarked in passing that Mac Bundy had described him to me as an ideal candidate for a university professorship at Harvard, and that the administration hoped he would accept one if it were offered. One week later, on May 8, I had a reply from Isaiah in which he admitted that his view that determinism is logically incompatible with saying that a person ought not to have performed a certain act might be the result of an invalid extrapolation from his own personal mental habits. To this day I continue to think that this extrapolation created *the* basic flaw in his position.

Isaiah went on to say:

> Your other piece about Niebuhr and Lippmann is altogether admirable and I quote it (with the greatest approval) in my latest piece—one on Equality written for the Aristotelian Society, to be read there next Monday as part of a symposium with Wollheim, although I do not say much about his piece. As soon as I have an off-print I will send you one. The only thing wrong with that piece of yours is that it is too short—surely even Arthur cannot defend "Reinie" for placidly accepting logical contradictions as part of the mystical dialectic of man and Nature? When theological persons say "In religion we accept these contradictions" usually with triumphant pride, one ceases to have any common language with them. That is worth emphasizing over and over again.

To the above I replied on June 30, 1956.

> Dear Isaiah:
> Your letter of 8th May came to me just as I was in the middle of the most horribly rushed period of our term, but now I am free, reading a weird assortment of books and tending to my garden—literally. I have had such a horrible year, apart from having brought out my two books, that I find it almost impossible to do anything serious for the longest time. In any case, Lucia is so completely recovered that we are both in a state of incomparable bliss, the kind of special bliss that comes after one has come out of a nightmare. I am really glad to be in the unusual (for me) condition of not going anywhere for the summer. Neither Japan, nor Austria, nor—I blush to say—England. Not even Connecticut, for we have sold our little cottage there and are experiencing the

great relief of owning only one house. We shall probably take little trips into the New England countryside. Sometimes we toy with the idea of a flight to England for, say, two weeks, but this is sheer silliness and playfulness. Only if I could be persuaded that you and I might expedite the writing of our book in a really serious way would I begin to think of such a trip.

Speaking of books, I must say that your *Age of Enlightenment* is excellent. I disapprove of nothing but the snippy selections from the off-beat people like Hamann and Lichtenberg, especially when they are listed in the table of contents as being treated in chapters which have the same official status as those devoted to, say, Hume. Also the brevity of the Voltaire selection is disconcerting. Everything else is splendid. I am much relieved after all of your dour predictions and your doubts about the wisdom of "collaborating" with Marcus [Dick]. As usual, you are likely to underestimate the standards you do attain in your writing.

One philosophical word. As you will no doubt see when and if you ever plough through my *Toward Reunion in Philosophy,* I am always suspicious of talk about what is or is not "logically impossible," but I am convinced that the statement "You may blame a determined act" is not "self-contradictory," whatever that might mean in this context. . . . I say that it's not like the mistake of saying "5 is odd and 5 is not odd," i.e., not a logical mistake. "You are wrong but you couldn't have chosen to do otherwise" is subject to different kinds of criticism. At best it's like saying that determined acts are not in the category of the blameworthy, that is to say, neither right nor wrong. But this "discovery," I hold, is not a simple one about our use of language. What we want to say is that we *should* not describe such acts as right or wrong, and the great problem is: "What kind of 'should' is this last one?" I say it's very close to a moral "should." At any rate, I am sure that we don't get the right answer here simply by doing logic in any ordinary sense. . . .

Your reaction to my piece about Niebuhr and Lippmann cheers me. Most radicals, atheists, and Jews approve, except that I have received some strange reactions from Perry Miller and Judge Wyzanski, both of whom regard "Reinie" as a heavy thinker. Arthur, in his loyal way, remains an atheist for Niebuhr. I have spoken at last to Niebuhr and found him charming. . . . I should say that he is philosophically no more acute than Professor Butterfield, who has just spent June accepting honorary degrees all over America. Mr. Pusey, naturally, agrees with Reinie, but told me at a dinner the other night that the debate should go on. He reminds me of the king in Hamlet.

I quite agree that my Niebuhr piece is too short, but it will appear in an unabridged form as the epilogue of a paperback edition of my *Social Thought in America* next year (also in an Italian translation [!] of the same). Do send me your Aristotelian Society offprint. I belong, but must wait till the bound volume appears to get my own copy.

I have a letter from Russell . . . about my *Reunion* book, . . . asking me why I—like other young philosophers—do not refer to anything he has written in the last 30 years. He asked me to be candid and I think I wriggled out honorably without offending him. . . .

I sent a letter of congratulations to Isaiah on April 22, 1957, on his having been elected to the professorship of social theory at Oxford; and in the same letter I wrote about Oppenheimer's William James Lectures at Harvard, about their effect on the philosophers—especially on our visiting professor, Herbert Hart—on Billy James, son of *the* William, and on the hordes who came to hear the lectures:

Now, at last, I write to you to send our warmest congratulations on your professorship. We are delighted and, as my mother might say, wish you long years in it! Lucia and I cabled you as soon as we heard about it but, alas, it's only now that I find myself with a free moment just before going to hear Director O's third William James Lecture. No doubt you've been reading about the brou-ha-ha created by his appointment, what with a special committee of alumni, called the "Veritas" committee, setting itself the job of "getting to the bottom of things." Thank God, there were no demonstrations at the first lecture, or at the second, so we can go about reading our theses with a certain amount of composure. He was, I must admit, his usual fuzzy self in his first lecture but responded admirably to my suggestion that he talk less about pragmatism and "cognition," so that the second lecture had lots of competent and interesting stuff about science and super-novae. As you might expect, some of the fiercer philosophers, e.g. Herbert Hart, were outraged by the first one, lacking, I think, that kind of charity and even sense about what a first lecture on such a foundation is supposed to be like. . . . Fortunately, Billy James loved it and Director O., so that I thought the first lecture was a success for that alone. Oppenheimer was given a most moving ovation when he was introduced by Pusey. There were 1,200 in Sanders Theatre and 800 more listening to him in New Lecture Hall, into which his words were piped.

Now: tell me about yourself. What will you do in the chair? How is your work going: Does this mean that you and I shall never write our book together: Maybe we should shift the subject to political philosophy rather than do the philosophy of history. How is the Oxford Movement? I find myself agreeing to do a review for the BBC of the collective volume on metaphysics. Did you put Gregory up to asking me? And I have just done a friendly review of Freddy Ayer in *Encounter*. I really like the book. Do you?

This is my last month in my chairmanship and I *pine* for the day of my release. How I stood it for three years I don't know. It's like being the keeper of a lunatic asylum.

Sometime in the spring of 1957 (in a letter of which I have no copy) I once again congratulated Isaiah, this time on his recently acquired knighthood; and on July 19 he sent me almost three single-spaced pages of candid reflections about what he and some of his friends felt about his becoming Sir Isaiah, as well as some touching remarks about how his old mother "virtually burst into tears" when he suggested to her that he might refuse the honor. In a postscript he wrote: "It really was very nice of you to write to me on this occasion. I am more grateful than I can say for reasons which I need not explain at all. There is that common element which we share which makes it unnecessary to explain what I felt and why I am grateful."

In my September 17 reply to this letter, I reported:

> Our personal news is rather simple and in some ways sad. Lucia is feeling very well but yesterday we took our older son, Nicky, to Exeter Academy where he will be enrolled for the coming three years. This is a great wrench for both of us and I cannot write very fluently about it. The boy is now 15 and, if I may say so, very handsome and very gifted. He is an excellent scholar, a first-rate athlete, and plays both the violin and viola very well. The irony is that the very qualities which make him so lovable and which make us miss him so are the ones that are obliging us to send him to as good a school as Exeter. We can only hope that his own happiness will be so increased by this venture as to diminish somewhat the sadness we feel about his going away. His younger brother is still with us and he is also a wonderful boy (I hope you will forgive the crowing about my children. If one cannot do it with good friends, with whom can one do it?).

Most of my brief correspondence with Berlin in 1958 had to do with a proposal of mine, first made on March 17, after getting John Rawls's agreement, that Berlin join me and Rawls, then teaching at Cornell, in discussions of political philosophy that would take place in Cambridge, Massachusetts. Unfortunately, Isaiah could not participate but said that he "would love to sit down with you and Rawls and do exactly what you propose. The subject does need revitalising—it is a sad thing that undergraduate societies constantly invite me to talk to them about why the subject is so dead."

To Isaiah's declination I replied on May 6, 1958:

> What a pity that you cannot make it. . . .
>
> I have just concluded a seminar on political philosophy and feel that if the best that can be done is the collection of essays published by Laslet then political philosophy *is* dead. Somehow I think it was indecent of Laslet to bring out such a body, and to deliver a funeral oration over it. Perhaps the thing to do is not to "revitalize" the corpse but start in some altogether different direction, where I do not know. Let me say here that your paper on "Equality" was much appreciated by the seminar. I think you should consider bringing together a number of your pieces like this in a volume. It is a pity to have it buried in the grim, unread pages in *Proceedings*.
>
> Do write me again soon. We have heard from you all too infrequently this year. Have you been reading about our controversy over religion at Harvard? Too big to narrate at the present moment. Suffice it to say that our President's devoutness has at last gotten him into an unpleasant row with the faculty, and the faculty won a decisive victory. No doubt you will be hearing about it from visiting Americans soon. Arthur, Perry Miller, and I were in the thick of it, not to mention other good friends of yours who performed valiantly.

The next letter from Isaiah that I find is a very long and very funny one dated February 6, 1959. In it he tells of his being unable to stomach Richard Nixon, whom he had met at dinner; of his very different feelings about Stravinsky, the "small, dry, heartless, wonderfully elegant, self-sufficient and competent man of genius"; of his urging the BBC to get me to participate in a symposium on Moore; of how Freddie Ayer had been elected to his Oxford professorship over the objections of Ryle and Austin (but with *his* support); and of his refusing to review a book by Hannah Arendt. He wrote: "I found it absolutely unreadable, and all the rot about the Greeks not liking work and the Jews liking it and men being alienated first from God and the Renaissance and now from mother earth herself—the desire to go to the moon being a deep metaphysical anxiety for flight from one's roots and origins—that is in the first forty pages—I found absolutely awful."

To this letter I replied at some length but without any interesting gossip, since I was, after all, away from home, in California. I spoke of my growing impatience with Oxford philosophy and of being bored with Harvard; also, I said that in spite of my great spiritual kinship with Isaiah, my differences with him might make it hard to collaborate. These observations are more negative than I remember myself feeling at the time—but there they are, in black and white, anticipating a number of things that happened much later, among them my departure from Harvard and, alas, my failure to write a book with Isaiah.

March 27, 1959

Dear Isaiah:

Your letter of 6 February was so wonderfully full and, as always, so interesting, that I have been unable to write for fear that I could only repay you in the most niggardly way. Then your *Two Concepts of Liberty* arrived and that put me under another debt. I have at last read the latter and think it excellent. I agree with you completely and think that this is a wonderful time for saying what you say: the one-hundredth anniversary of Mill's essay *On Liberty* and a period in which we need more and more protection from parentalism and from those who tell us to be free through recognizing necessity. How are you being received? I saw Arthur's review and Annan's, the latter being a little too mushy for my taste.

Speaking of reviews, I enclose one of my book [*Religion, Politics, and the Higher Learning*], because it says that *you* are the hero of my book! I hope you do not feel too upset about this role. Meanwhile I hear of coming reviews that may be interesting. One of them will be Stuart Hampshire's: he's doing it for *Partisan Review*. I have written him that I am braced for a volley in reply to my handling of that *terrible* book in which he has an essay, *The Nature of Metaphysics*. But maybe he will find things to like about my book in spite of my growing impatience with Oxford philosophy. . . .

On the other hand I find myself incapable of adopting party lines in any subject, perhaps because of the way I was burned in my twenties: by Marxism, positivism, pragmatism, and all of the other bureaucratized currents swirling around New York in my youth. Hence my ambivalent attitude toward Oxford in my last two books, which makes me suspect, I am sure, in the eyes of some of my English friends. This also explains my great pleasure at Freddy Ayer's election. In 1951 I treated him, as so many of us did, as old hat. But now, after almost ten years of Ryle, Austin, and *Mind*, it's good to have Freddy in the middle of things. . . .

Speaking of Moore, I have already recorded my talk for Miss Kallin, and by now you may have heard it. I think it is a tiny bit sentimental at the end, but many people have liked it and I feel good about having done it. Let me know what reaction to it there is—if you hear of any. You know, of course, that Bertrand Russell and Leonard Woolf will also be heard on the same program.

My life has begun to circulate around memorials, I'm afraid, and this is a sign of age. Not only have I had to do something on Moore, but this is the hundredth anniversary of Dewey's birth, and so I've been besieged by all kinds of organizations. So far I've agreed to do only one or two talks and congratulate myself on my strength of character. Believe it or not, but there is a Committee, consisting of New York characters like Sidney Hook, James T. Farrell, Ernest Nagel, Horace Kallen, et al., whose purpose it is to stimulate people all over the world to hold regional conferences in celebration of the occasion! This seems like madness to me and suggests how little these poor people are capable of moving on their own steam. Something about life in the cities brings people into pathetic little groups, whereas one would have supposed that it might encourage independence and freedom from this. . . . I admire the English freedom from all of it. Harvard is also relatively free of it. For example, we have been attacked by countless people for forgetting to "do something" about Royce's centennial in 1955. . . . It is all part of the need to identify, I suppose. And my own recent history has been one long effort to be myself and free of religious, political, doctrinal sectarianism. I suppose it stems, ultimately, from having been an overprotected only child, as the chaps in our Social Relations Department would say. . . .

I have read Zhivago and enjoyed it enormously, partly because of this mood. It represents such a wonderful effort to say things which one thinks are true without wondering what their effect will be. The opposite tendency is what horrifies me about so many people around here. Our new Henry Ford Professor, David Riesman, whom I like in *some* way that I cannot fully understand, is given to saying "I would say this in this company but not in that company," and so on. My God, how

I can remember the same thing coming from Stalinists. What one does not say in front of children, servants, Gentiles! Phooey!

No doubt you can see that I need a year's leave in California. Harvard has treated me well and I have treated it well in return. But I am bored with it and irritated with parts of it in a way that suggests the need for travel. I find myself thinking the hedgehogs too vapid and the foxes too trivial. So I fly to California, hoping for a bit of vacation from all of this. I shall work on my history thing and if it seems at all like the kind of thing that will not bore you, I shall send it along. I feel great kinship with you on the large, spiritual issues of our time, as you know, but somehow we manage not to see eye to eye on details in a way that might make it hard to collaborate. What we need is talk together. Maybe we can rig something up somewhere after I do my California thing. . . .

Do write me again. Your letters are wonderfully cheering.

Lucia joins me in love to both of you.

Ever,
Morton

On December 6, Isaiah sent me a postcard on which he wrote, among other things, that he would arrive in New York on New Year's Day or thereabouts, go to Washington for a few days, and then be back in New York on January 6, when he hoped we could see each other. I replied at once, briefly saying something about my forthcoming review of Ernest Gellner's controversial book *Words and Things* in the *Scientific American*. I said I had been following the brouhaha over the book and thought Ryle had made a dreadful mistake in refusing to review it. I also said that Gellner was right on several points, though exasperatingly wrong on several others. I added that I found myself in the position of liking much and disliking much in "linguistic philosophy" as it was then developing.

We did meet in New York, and soon afterward I wrote Isaiah that my article "New Horizons in Philosophy" had been accepted by the *Saturday Evening Post*. I said I regretted slipping into journalism but that I could hardly pass up such an assignment while paying for one son at Exeter and another at Harvard. I added that my consolation was that I had not appeared in *Esquire* or *T.V. Guide*. My letter crossed one from Isaiah of January 27, 1960, in which he reported that John Austin was dying. In passing he repeated a familiar thought about our proposed work on the philosophy of history, begging me "not to doubt (a) the seriousness of my desire to write this book with you; (b) my capacity for organizing my life with sufficient firmness and reliability to carve out adequate time."

In reply to Isaiah's account of Austin's illness, I expressed shock and sadness, remarking that, like Isaiah, I had always thought of Austin as both nice *and* brilliant, and that when he was at Harvard, he was so unferocious and so winning that I felt we had succeeded in uncovering the real Austin, whereas Oxford knew only the cold suit of armor. I recalled that during his last stay in Cambridge (after leaving Berkeley) the department gave him a gala dinner and that I could see how touched he was and how he glowed through the evening. I said he could draw out and be liked by people as different as Demos, Firth, Dreben, and me. I also remarked that when the time came at which I could be sure of enough votes, I would try to bring Austin to Harvard permanently. Somehow I thought that although Berkeley failed, we might succeed. On February 12, 1960, I heard from Isaiah about Austin's death. He wrote:

> Austin died two days ago, being I gather in no great pain since he was heavily drugged. He had been wandering in his mind for some time before that, although there were lucid intervals in which he talked coherently to his wife. I enclose the Times obituary which was certainly written by Ryle and which, although it brings out certain things, does not bring out a) that he was probably the most influential philosopher, at the time of his death, in the English-speaking world; and b) his humanity, his charm and general sweetness of character, and the devotion which he inspired in you, in me, in Burton [Dreben], and all the graduate students up and down America. Also the fact that the vivid examples he used in his lectures were sometimes carried away by a pupil who had only heard him lecture once and then went on using them endlessly in their own lectures on this and that and this applied to physicists as well as philosophers. I have tried to stimulate Herbert Hart to add to the obituary in The Times and also Marcus Dick will write on what it was like to be his pupil. Perhaps that will be enough so far as Oxford is concerned; but if you and/or Burton both wrote little letters to The Times of a form—"Professor X of Harvard writes," or "a friend writes," or "M.G.W. writes," it would I am sure give his wife pleasure and also to all his friends. So do it if you feel inclined; it will not be too late if you write when you receive this. The funeral is tomorrow and will be attended by no more than a dozen intimate friends; there will be a memorial service later no doubt. There is really nothing to say: we know

each other's feeling for him. I think that someone will have to write a notice about him for the British Academy, perhaps George Paul, if it appears I will endeavour to send it to you. I wonder how long it will take for the edifice that he built more or less unaided in Oxford to crumble. . . . I wonder what next. Not Ryle, not Quine, something more romantic, possibly more woolly, but also closer to answers to problems which people are oppressed by. I think that an inflationary spiral is due; with mathematical logicians going their way; while the others will talk in less and more humanistic language. I am not sure that this is a good thing: (in fact I think, on the whole, very much *not*) but I have a feeling that it is what will happen.

If you do feel inclined to do something more about J.L.A. besides a letter to The Times (about which I am bullying you), do send a letter to Mrs. Austin repeating how much he was admired in America.

As the reader knows, I did write to Mrs. Austin; but on June 3, I had to write of my own bad news to Isaiah: my father had just had a heart attack. Isaiah wrote in reply a week later: "I lived under a similar sickening cloud with regard to my own father for nine months—I do hope your cloud lasts much, much longer than that; after a bit it dissipates. When elderly people with heart attacks look after themselves very carefully they sometimes, as you know, live longer than they otherwise might. At any rate I hope it will be so in your case."

Soon a plan was hatched by the Department of Government to bring Isaiah to Harvard in 1962, and I wrote to him that I would be happy to give a seminar with him on the philosophy of history. He came to Harvard in September 1962, but, as things turned out, I did not want to surrender a sabbatical leave that I would have lost if I did not take it that year. Therefore I took the leave and went to the Institute as a visiting member when Isaiah came to Harvard. He wrote me in January 1962: "I am very sorry to hear that you will be in Princeton at about the time when I am at Harvard—but nevertheless I think we may organise meeting somehow. Perhaps we shall write two books, one each on this topic as a result of discussion. I still feel passionately interested in the subject, as I am sure you are, and Carr's book merely whetted my appetite."

I did not answer for several months. My remarks about Ernest Nagel in my letter are not incompatible with what I have said about him in an earlier chapter. They briefly touch on one aspect of the question of value-free history, a subject I was later to discuss at length with Isaiah.

June 5, 1962

Dear Isaiah:

Last night . . . I realized that I had been meaning to write you for weeks, first of all to apologize for not writing for months before that, and secondly to tell you how much I approved of everything you had said about Carr—both in your review and your letters. That subject, you will recall, occupied us much in our exchange this winter. My own views on it came into print a few weeks ago in the *New Leader;* a tear-sheet is enclosed. You will observe that I say nothing with which you will disagree. I wanted to be more waspish but my hand was stayed by memories of Carr's being my cordial neighbor at the Center for Advanced Study in the Behavorial Sciences in California. I am no longer as fierce as I was in my twenties, laying about with the conviction that every destructive act could be justified by the "knowledge" that one was preparing the way for better things. Every awful negative thing one said seemed to be a prelude to a great, positive good. Time was when I would have gone after Carr as I used to go after Jacques Barzun, Mortimer Adler and Stuart Chase in the pages of *Partisan Review* circa 1939. But I really do like being gentler, even though some of the young (and old) think I am going soft.

Needless to say, I still bare my fangs when attacked. The other day I did so in defense of a long paper I had read at a conference on philosophy and history, run by Sidney Hook. It was held in New York, where I met many of my old friends and teachers like dear Meyer Schapiro and not so dear Ernest Nagel. My paper was, if I do say so, quite good on this (our) subject. One of its points was that a narrative could not be evaluated simply on the basis of the truth of its component statements; hence a value-judgment of memorability had to be made by the historical critic. I elaborated this point—a rather obvious and mild one I thought—and said many other things that you would have agreed with, I think. But no sooner did I sit down than I was exposed to a very confused, very emotional "question" from my teacher, Nagel, who seemed to think that I was opening the gates for the black hundreds by suggesting that there were considerations that transcended the evaluation of truth in the total evaluation of a historical narrative. Alas, I then had to fight under unfortunate circumstances: to knock him out as I pulled my punches. Witnesses tell me I succeeded, but I was quite upset afterward. Not by the intellectual exchange but by the appearance of Nagel in what my colleague Donald Williams picturesquely called "rancorous disarray." . . .

I will not go on much longer, except to say that we have finished reading galleys—Lucia and I—on our joint work, entitled "The Intellectual Versus the City: From Thomas Jefferson to Frank Lloyd Wright." Some people think it is a good book, and it has gotten a lot of advance publicity. The other day the *Chicago Sun-Times* reprinted an article by us, one in which the theme of the book had been announced about a year ago. I think I sent you a reprint of that . . .

Love from Lucia and me to both of you,

Yours ever,
Morton

On September 4, 1962, I received a card from Isaiah in which he urged me to delay my departure for Princeton until September 21 and said that he would "reward me with a cornucopia of gossip if I did." Fortunately, Lucia and I did delay our departure; Isaiah had dinner with us on Thursday, September 20, and we left for Princeton the next day. In 1963 I must have written *something* to him, but I find copies of nothing by me, though my folder for that year contains two letters from him. *What* letter of mine he is referring to in his of April 17, 1963, below I do not know. I do know, however, that I was not sympathetic to his advice that I not be afraid of betraying science or of falling into acceptance of the doctrine of natural law. Indeed, his advice raised further doubt in my mind whether we would write a book on the philosophy of history together—meaning one to all of whose statements we could subscribe jointly. First Isaiah wrote on April 17 and later on September 3. In the second letter he spoke of possible titles for *Foundations of Historical Knowledge*, the manuscript I had written on my own.

17th April, 1963

Dear Morton,

 . . . Don't subjugate yourself to the covering theory model too much! I may have gone too far in the other direction—I now think I have—but I am sure that what people like Hempel say is far from true and that all discussions of things like free will, action, intention, etc. are bedevilled by a terror of betraying science in some way, just as in legal discussions the terror of natural law petrifies people unnecessarily—

there are these monsters standing at the door of the cave from which one must emerge, ready to smite unless one acquires huge protection against them, which I do not believe to be necessary. But don't let me preach—I am about to commit myself to scientific method in the form of an operation in about twelve hours, so don't let me decry it too much. This is only a brief note to say how pleased I was to get your letter and how much I should like to receive another one. . . .

Yours,
Isaiah

3rd Sept. 1963

Dear Morton,
    . . . As for your book—not "Logic of History," I do see that, nor "The Language of History," that at least is intolerable now, owing to Hare and such. "Foundations of Historical Knowledge?" is all right, particularly if you include the question mark, but why not just "Historical Knowledge"? I am reading Schopenhauer on freedom of the will—it is very good and very wrong—but at least we might make an anthology of books which are good and wrong as opposed to books which are bad and right . . . the majority of articles in Mind seems to me to have reached an absolute nadir. But do come to New York in the second part of December and let me know, and I shall set aside time and we might even talk about "The Foundations of Historical Knowledge." . . .
    Love to Lucia.

Yours,

Dictated but not signed by
Isaiah Berlin

These letters were followed by a significant exchange in 1964 about the relations between analytic philosophy and the history of ideas. Although the exchange took place in the sixties, most of the worries in it harked back to our joint concerns in the fifties, worries I have had to deal with throughout my intellectual career. It began with my reporting to Isaiah that I had finished

Foundations of Historical Knowledge, which I had dedicated to him and Arthur
Schlesinger Jr.

All Souls College
Oxford
23rd November.
[Postmarked 1964]

Dear Morton,

I have just had another operation—hernia—I seem to have them
about once in two years; I do not really mind, as I enjoy the convales-
cence so much, nor is physical pain what frightens me most: I mind
"guilt" far more than that—all to do with one's early education, I
expect.

I am very glad you have finished your book on history—while you
write original works one by one, I am merely pottering with hermeneu-
tic exercises about the books of others: with the greatest shedding of
blood, I finished a long essay on Herder, which is to appear in a Johns
Hopkins collective volume—this is my lecture of last spring; then I
must get on to the book on Vico, Hamann, de Maistre; then on to the
Yale Lectures, etc.—all of which are about other people and mere
commentary, interpretation, etc.—I cannot bring myself to set sail into
the open ocean, as you rightly do; I hug the shore and do a lot of
hideous coasting which does neither me nor my authors nor the
reviewers any good.

Thank you very much for the dedication: I feel genuine pride. I forgot
that an essay by me on Churchill has just appeared as a kind of
coffee-table Christmas gift, in stiff covers; I shall not send you a copy as
I am ashamed of the whole transaction—I am merely telling you in case
you wonder why: until I write something serious I shall send you
nothing, for I cannot bear to.

I am very glad also that you are writing about Austin. You are right
about the arguments versus the conclusions—his originality consisted
in the actual views, that bold shifting of the framework in which
problems were seen, not in the arguments themselves, which are mainly
designed to win, and are sometimes a trifle unscrupulous, as you rightly
perceive. Still, "poor Moore" was just as unfair to others, e.g. Mill and
Russell, so that's nothing new in philosophy.

I am coming to America next March, in order to deliver the as yet completely unprepared lectures on the origins of Romanticism—yet another book—more about other people, I suppose, in some sense—this is just search for security on my part, I suspect: perhaps this is all post-illness depression. I shall arrive in New York in mid-March, stay for a day or two at the Carlyle before delivering the first lecture on Sunday at the National Gallery, where they keep on asking me whether I want slides—but how bogus can one be? I cannot talk about painting, and will not—it will all be about philosophy and politics and the like, and all those old ladies will scatter after the first lecture and I shall talk to two people at the maximum for the remaining five (you note that my depression continues). At any rate, will you send me a message about where you are to be reached after March the 15th, and we shall get together somewhere, and more than once, I hope: I shall be in the United States for six lectures, which brings me more or less to Easter. . . .

My love to Lucia, and from Aline—she too is a grandmother—and let me know from day to day what happens to you.

Yours ever,
Isaiah

To this I replied as follows:

November 30, 1964

Sir Isaiah Berlin
Headington House
Headington
Oxford, England

Dear Isaiah:

I am terribly sorry to hear of your operation and hope that all has gone well and that you are now convalescing comfortably.

I also hope that by now you have shaken off the post-operative depression that must have been behind some of your self-deprecation in your letter to me. Although I am sure that one can *explain* the idea that out-of-the-blue analyses of space, time, matter, good, bad, history and law are intrinsically superior to analyses of the views of other *people*, it does seem silly to me. I find it ironic in an age when "original philosophy" itself has become analysis of the meanings of words and interpretation. Why, then, I ask, is it more important to analyze what a street-car conductor means when he says "I see a pipe in my hand" than it is to analyze, place in its historical context, and evaluate what Kant means when he said "Ought implies can," to say nothing of finding out whether he *did* say so?

Which brings me to Austin, who was the big "out-of-the-blue" original thinker of your generation at Oxford. It is extraordinary to see how much of his writing was historico-critical. Where would he have been without the texts of poor Ayer, Moore, and Nowell-Smith to seize upon? True, he said some profound things about all of them. But where, I ask, except in his William James Lectures—and they are not his best production, in my opinion—does he set sail into the ocean, as you put it, rather than hug the shore? Curiously enough, if one treats a *contemporary* writer one is thought to be original, whereas if one treats a far greater figure of the past, one is thought to be derivative or parasitical, or what have you. Nonsense, I say.

It is also worth remarking that there is a simple way of transforming a historical work into a "pure," "original" work. One writes the first, with references to other people, pages, chapters, verses, expounding them and criticizing them; then one goes over the manuscript, carefully eliminating all the inverted commas and references, and starts talking about the theory of the ghost-in-the-machine or category mistakes or traditional dualism, etc., etc. Immediately one ceases to be Byzantine and becomes Greek, thereby becoming original and unparasitical. Nonsense, I say.

Finally, I remind you that I too have written a good deal about "other people" and don't think that when I do, I am doing something inferior to what I do when I sail jauntily into the ocean. On the contrary, whatever one may say about the relative merits of the *enterprises,* I suspect that my historical productions are probably more valuable than my transoceanic voyages. Maybe that's a sign of limitation in me but I refuse to say so. And I am absolutely sure that the world is far better off because of your brilliant *pages* on Marx, Hess, Herzen, De Maistre, et al., than it is on account of the silly, sophomoric essays on the ontological argument that have caused me to pile up my copies of *Mind* without opening them, to say nothing of the equally silly *treatises* on similar subjects.

So there is my apologia—although I don't think one is needed except in moods like yours when you wrote your letter—for your vita and mine. This is the "pep-talk," as my dear friend Harry Wolfson calls it, that all of us need sometime. Wolfson is really precious. As you may know, he's a great movie-goer, and once loved Westerns. But today's Westerns he finds too high-brow, so he said to me the other day: "Today, you take ah psychopet and pud 'im on ah hoss—and dot's ah Vestun. Ah! I tell you!"

We both send love to both. We are thrilled by our granddaughter, as is our son and his wife. That son—Nick—is turning his attention from Greek and Latin literature to Greek philosophy, so you see, my family *needs* arguments of the kind I have previously offered for the value of talking about great minds of the past! But they are good arguments, so we are happy. You get happy too, and please send me your piece on Churchill now that you see that I am not so pure as you think I am. I love to read about people. Some of my best friends are.

Affectionately,
Morton

In reply to my letter, Isaiah wrote on December 14:

You are a very good and very true friend. As you realised, my self-deprecation was absolutely genuine and not an attempt at either false or genuine modesty, but extreme depression about what I am and do. And yet, I think that what Austin and Quine and you and Hart do *is* more valuable than historical interpretations—particularly in the un-footnoted, imprecise way in which I do it. Still, I feel, as Henry James once said after meeting Winston Churchill in 1915 and being insulted by him—remind me of that story and I will tell it to you in detail, it is very funny—"much bucked." So back I plunge into the darkness of the eighteenth century—and it is dark, no historian worth his salt even attempts an answer—it is a commonplace by now, I suppose, to say that nobody has made a serious effort to explain why the Renaissance happened—in however mechanical, Marxist, materialist, causal sort of way—but nobody has. All that people do is to try and say that there wasn't a Renaissance and that it all started in the 12th century and was very gradual and that the whole thing is a kind of historical hallucination—when we all know perfectly well that some-thing happened in the fifteenth century quite different from what

happened before and after, and unique and earthshaking. Similarly with
the Romantic movement. Why should the second half of the eighteenth century suddenly be filled with waves of irrationalism, women
with stigmata, somnambulists, peasants in fields suddenly prophecying,
Freemasons and Rosicrucians, and a tremendous retreat of all those
triumphant rationalists of the 1740's and '50's—all ending in a huge
outburst of German romanticism. Meyer, whom I naturally asked,
immediately referred me to articles ("which of course you have read")
by Hautecoeur in the "Journal de Beaux Arts" of 1911, or it may have
been 1903, ascribing it all to financial bankruptcies in the 1770's, and
also complained that the one novel dealing with this situation in
Germany had been bowdlerised in English because the bedwetting
episode had been left out by the English translator of 1902; he also
referred to Eric Erikson.

The story about Wolfson is a rare and precious gem, which I shall
never forget. Thank you very, very much indeed for your letter: if you
haven't a place in heaven, this alone will earn it. I have always loved
you deeply but never as much as at this moment.

Yours, with the deepest
gratitude,
Isaiah

P.S. O.K., I shall send you Churchill, but with feelings of false shame
nevertheless.

I was deeply touched by this second letter from Berlin, and I was very
pleased with my way of linking the history of ideas and analytic philosophy
in my letter to him. For many years since then I have moved back and forth
from the history of ideas to systematic philosophy under the aegis of the
notion that a central task of both disciplines is that of analysis, though my
view of analysis underwent serious changes in this period. During my
twenty-two years at Harvard, from 1948 to 1970, I was primarily concerned
in my courses with the sort of philosophical analysis that is reflected in
Toward Reunion in Philosophy and *Foundations of Historical Knowledge,* but I
managed on the side, so to speak, to bring out *Social Thought in America* and
to collaborate with Lucia on *The Intellectual Versus the City: From Thomas
Jefferson to Frank Lloyd Wright,* published in 1962. However, when I joined
the faculty of the School of Historical Studies at the Institute for Advanced

Study in 1970, I felt that by accepting my professorship I committed myself to working primarily in history, so my main books between 1970 and my retirement in 1987 were historical, namely, *Science and Sentiment in America* (1972), *The Philosophy of the American Revolution* (1978), and *Philosophy, "The Federalist," and the Constitution* (1987). Yet throughout those years, I wrote articles on topics allied with free will, and in 1993 I brought out *The Question of Free Will: A Holistic View*. My interest in that topic was aroused in great measure by my reading of Berlin's lecture *Historical Inevitability* (1954), which shows that in his letters to me of 1964 he overestimated the degree to which he had been hugging the shore of history in his work. Besides, as I tried to persuade him, hugging that shore in the age of analysis did not differ as greatly as he might think from sailing the ocean blue. That was my way of making peace between the two souls at war in my breast (*pace* Goethe).

I must say that the peace in my case has been only a temporary one. On June 18, 1990, almost thirty years after Berlin and I exchanged letters on this subject, I wrote as follows to him:

> Sometimes I am haunted by the idea that I made a mistake forty-odd years ago when I decided—partly under your influence—to "do" the history of ideas along with philosophy, thinking that I've spread myself too thin, that I'd have done better work if I'd been a narrow, Moore-like philosopher who never touched subjects like the philosophy of the American Revolution or social thought in America. And sometimes I feel satisfied with having followed my double-bent, as it were, to do just what I've done, however poorly; at having ranged beyond "*p* implies *q*," sense-data, universals, the analytic and the synthetic. You are the only person I know who can judge me here for only you, as Mill might have said, have also lived this double-life.
>
> My aim, I must confess, has been to imitate my intellectual grandfathers—Dewey, Russell, James—rather than my intellectual ancestors of a later generation—Quine, Nagel, Goodman. I have always thought that I could and should combine logic-chopping with the bigness and breadth of the old-time luminaries. And I have thought of you as a sympathetic luminary who, whether you know it or not, encouraged me to move in this direction. The danger of moving in this direction is obvious: by trying to be *both* an historical hedgehog and a philosophical fox one may wind up being some sort of lonely hybrid who lacks intellectual companionship precisely because there are so few similar hybrids. And yet I am sure that I am happier as a lonely hybrid—with

you as a fellow-hybrid—than I would have been if I had spent my life writing notes in *Mind* about "ifs" and "cans."

To this Berlin replied on March 4, 1991:

> I am quite sure, having re-read your letter, that you chose wisely, and that so did I. I do not believe that if I had gone on with, as it were, Austin, Ayer, Strawson, Herbert Hart and all the local luminaries, that I should have made much of it. I was never a first-rate philosopher, I was a perfectly competent teacher at New College, but I do not think much more than that. Writing *Karl Marx* excites me far more than writing papers for the Aristotelian Society. Your case is somewhat different: I think you really were inspired by Quine and Moore—but even so, the history of ideas is what you have done nobly—better than anyone else—and the same is true of me, though it sounds boastful, in the case of Russian and some other ideas as well. The other half of our lives, the purely philosophical one, was indispensable. One thing which is certain is that historians of ideas who haven't done philosophy don't know what they are writing about—unless one knows what it is to be puzzled, indeed, agonised by a philosophical problem, the idea of writing the history of such problems and their would-be solutions is an absolutely mechanical affair. There is the monstrous example of most histories of philosophy, from Kuno Fischer: first Kant, then Fichte, then Schelling, then Hegel, with only the faintest links between them—but even if you supply the links it's no good unless you really know what it is to be a philosopher. So I think we needed our philosophy to do best what I think we are both best at. Nevertheless, there are certain problems which do torment me—not as much as in the past, but nothing does, that's just old age or even senility.

As I reflect on Berlin's reply, I think that he might have achieved more inner peace on the subject than I have, since he seemed to have rid himself of his worry about hugging the coast of history instead of sailing the ocean of philosophy. By contrast, I am still worried by my tendency to hug the coast *and* to sail the ocean. Although my argument that the history of ideas and philosophy both involved analysis might have led Berlin to feel happier about working in the history of ideas alone, it probably led me to think that I could simultaneously work in both disciplines and therefore to spread myself too thin.

18

Choosing Scholarship over Power
I Decline to Become a Dean

Although I did not think when I wrote them that my books in the history of ideas or my essays on religion and education would give anyone the impression that I wanted to become a university administrator, it may well be that their "breadth" by comparison to my writing on, say, the paradox of analysis prompted the University of Chicago to invite me to become dean of the humanities there in 1962. After a good deal of reflection I declined that invitation, and in the light of what happened on American campuses in the sixties, doing so was probably one of my wiser and luckier acts.

Sometime near the beginning of June 1962 I received a telephone call from Edward Levi, then provost of the University of Chicago and later attorney general of the United States. Levi urged me to come out for a visit so that Chicago could have a "chance" at persuading me to accept the deanship even though I had, in an earlier exchange with him, indicated no great interest in the job. A day or so after Levi's call I was also invited to visit by Professor Edward Kracke, a sinologist who was chairman of the faculty committee to find a new dean. Although I had been less than lukewarm in my response to Levi's most recent invitation, I had, by the time I had spoken to Kracke, become a little more interested, and so I told Kracke that I would let him know in a day whether I would travel to Chicago. This more encouraging response of mine was immediately relayed by Kracke to Levi, who called to renew his urging. After all of these telephone calls, I decided that it would be embarrassing not to visit Chicago, so I agreed to turn up there on Friday, June 8. I arrived in the morning after bouncing across a good part of our land by train, and soon found myself in the glass Saarinen building of the Chicago Law School at about 10 A.M.; that was where Levi's office was, since he was dean of the Law School as well as provost of the university. I stumbled around with my heavy bag in the big boxy hall on the first floor until I finally located Levi's office.

After fifteen minutes or so Levi appeared—a hunched, shuffling figure who was fifty but who looked younger than that to me. He wore glasses, his complexion was fair, and his eyes were bright and dancing nervously. He extended his hand only after I had offered mine; he looked very uneasy. For my part I was relieved that I didn't need or very much want the job for which I was being interviewed, so I resolved to let Levi try to sell *me*. This he certainly tried to do. He gave me a long account of the university's structure, its needs, problems, and aspirations. He told me something about the possibilities, advised me that I should begin the life of an administrator at forty-five (my age then) if I wanted to be one, that Chicago was moving ahead, that the job was a great challenge, that I would have great power, and that I was wanted. He reminded me of my interest in urban affairs and candidly told me that a dean would have to raise money. We talked about many subjects, including legal philosophy. We dropped names to each other, and when I alluded to something in that morning's *Times*, Levi told me that his *Times* was not promptly delivered in spite of his wife's being a Sulzberger.

At noon Professor Kracke came to Levi's office in order to lead me to the luncheon meeting of his committee. Kracke was very tall, very thin, very shy, and very nice. He had wispy fair hair, a large mouth, and an extremely pleasant smile. He was a son-in-law of the Harvard philosopher William Ernest Hocking and a friend of Ed Reischauer and Bob Hightower, my Harvard colleagues in Far Eastern studies. In every way Kracke seemed the model of a reserved, withdrawn scholar of Asian languages. Together we strolled across the midway to the International House, where lunch was being served because the Quadrangle (Faculty) Club was very busy that day. It seemed that I had come on Commencement Day, or, as I think it was called there, Convocation Day.

Before lunch began, I was introduced to some members of the committee: a professor of German, one in Romance languages, one in English, and Hugh McLean, a professor of Slavic whom I knew when he had been a junior fellow at Harvard. Except for the engaging McLean, I felt that I was meeting a depressed, frightened, demoralized part of the Chicago faculty, especially when I was introduced to a professor of English who had suffered greatly during the regime of Robert Hutchins and who couldn't leave that subject alone. The committee was very cordial to me and reported their formal approval of the appointment to Levi before the day was out.

After getting the okay of this committee on the deanship, I was asked to meet with another one that was to pass on my credentials as a scholar. I think it was called the Committee on Policy of the Division of the Humanities, which had to have its say even though I was assured that the interview with them would be purely *pro forma*. By then I had come to feel that a good deal of the vaunted "democracy" of Chicago was ritualistic, that forms were being gone through by a group of men who were, and who wanted to be, led by the administration. Among the members of this committee, the most impressive man was a red-faced medievalist with piercing eyes and a charming smile, a forceful man who was eager to persuade me to see the opportunities and possibilities of the deanship. He assured me that a new library would soon be built, that many new appointments would be made, that more money would become available, and that in general I would be able to carry on in a handsome way. A fat, bald scholar guided me through the intricacies of the bureaucratic structure of Chicago's Oriental Institute, all of which I immediately forgot, and at this point I began to wonder what I was doing there. I became more and more aware of my lack of interest in university administration, and I began to feel guiltier and guiltier about coming out and wasting their time. Still, I had had *some* interest in the job before coming, and after Levi's importunate telephone calls I would have had to be very rude to refuse to visit them.

At last I was rescued by Professor Kracke, who came to take me to the incumbent dean, my possible predecessor, Professor Napier Wilt. The name Napier reminded me of logarithms and rapiers, but no two associations could have been more wrong. He was neither mathematical nor sharp. He was a very genial, bald, baggy-necked professor of American literature who wore spectacles and who inhabited a gloomy office that reminded me of some that I had known fifteen years earlier at the then indigent University of Pennsylvania. Curtains with holes in them, threadbare rug, dark-making Gothic windows, pale and frightened secretaries. All of this was in sharp contrast to Harvard. It was also very different from the glassy opulence that surrounded lawyer Levi and from the Nebraskan freshness of biologist George Beadle— then president of Chicago. Wilt, I thought, was wilted. He told me of his troubles in the deanship, of his terrible times under Hutchins, of his high regard for my *Social Thought in America*, of his hopes for the young Chicago philosophers. He strongly advised me not to work in the job for more than nine months in the year, and I left him with relief and sorrow. The more I thought of the whole situation—gloomy dean and cranky professors—the more I felt sorry for the humanities at Chicago and unequal to the job of improving them.

After the visit with Wilt, I was escorted by Kracke to Levi's office. There Levi introduced me to the chairman of the board of trustees of the university, a Glenn Lloyd, if I caught the name correctly. He bore a striking resemblance to my colleague Harry Sheffer, but no two men could have been more different: the one a formidable tycoon and the other a mad logician! Lloyd did not stay for more than a few minutes, and soon after his departure Levi took me to my hotel, where I was to rest until evening and then dine with Levi and President Beadle. While in my room I had a phone call from Richard McKeon, the philosopher and one-time occupant of the deanship for which I was being considered. At the behest of Levi, he offered to tell me more about the situation at Chicago, but I declined his offer because I had found him rather boring on previous occasions and because I was exhausted. I could not help recalling how awesome an academic potentate he had seemed to me when I was a graduate student, awesome and objectionable because I disapproved so much of his philosophical and educational ideas. Yet here he was, twenty-five years later, trying to help the Chicago administration persuade me to take his old job. I must say, however, that in spite of my differences with McKeon, he did seem like a large figure by comparison with some of his colleagues; and I think I said something like that to Levi. Unfortunately he relayed what I had said to some of the younger Chicago philosophers who were in revolt against McKeon—some of them my former students—and when my mild praise of McKeon reached their ears through the indiscreet Levi, they were upset. Still, I am sure that I was right. The devilish McKeon had to be given his due as an academic figure.

In the evening Levi picked me up at the hotel and took me to the office of President Beadle. An interesting bit of byplay began right after I was introduced to him. Levi asked Beadle whether we should go to the Tavern Club (whatever that was—I did not and do not know). Beadle at first declined to make the decision but then allowed that while the Tavern Club was higher-class, "more tony"—I remember his words—Morton's Restaurant was closer and did have good food. Levi seemed to prefer the club, but Beadle won out, and Morton was taken to Morton's, where we began with very good

Martinis. Levi then told us that although he had once given a poor grade to a relative of the restaurant's proprietor, the proprietor was now his great friend. As if to confirm this, the waitress said that the proprietor wished to buy us our second drink. Because it was Convocation Day, the place was in turmoil, full of graduates and their parents, and it reminded me of a well-known restaurant in Brookline, Massachusetts, called Jack and Marion's— mammoth menus, noisy eaters, brash waitresses. It soon became evident to me that Levi had known that this was the atmosphere of the place, and that that was why he was pushing for the Tavern Club. However, Beadle was not in the least bothered by the delicatessen-like noise and excitement. He was a biologist and a farm boy, and he seemed to have none of Levi's nervous worries. That was why I felt very much at ease with him, the all-highest at the university.

I can remember little of the conversation at dinner. Beadle and Levi talked about the low morale of the humanists; they complained about their lack of self-confidence by comparison to the natural scientists, the people in the professional schools, and the social scientists. I could see what they meant as my mind wandered back to the committee meetings of the earlier part of the day. On the other hand, I felt that neither Levi nor Beadle could understand the personalities of the literary scholars or philosophers under their command. It seemed to me that Levi was a remnant of the Hutchins era in which he had grown up, incapable of sympathizing with the new analytic wave in his philosophy department. As a scientist, however, Beadle was far less respectful than Levi was of Hutchins and Mortimer Adler, and at one point spoke with great scorn of the latter as the Rasputin of the Hutchins regime. Throughout the dinner Beadle seemed to like me, and I liked him.

After dinner Levi drove me to his house, where we continued our conversation long into the night. As the evening wore on, I came to like him more and more. He seemed to become less nervous, and I began to have second or third thoughts about my negative judgment of the whole idea of going to Chicago. These further thoughts were encouraged by the money that Levi proceeded to offer me, and so I boarded my train the next day thinking that I could not honestly say that I had no interest in the job. It was this glimmer of interest in it that led me to tell Pusey about Chicago's offer on June 26, 1962, almost three weeks after I had been in Chicago, and to think I would accept it if Harvard were to do nothing in response. I talked endlessly to Lucia about the whole business, and we examined every aspect of the thing with care in early July on the sands of Wellfleet, where we were renting Herb Wechsler's house that summer. Levi, still on my trail, phoned me occasionally, and I finally made up my mind not to accept, for the reasons given in the following letter:

Wellfleet, Mass.
July 12, 1962

Provost Edward H. Levi
Office of the President
University of Chicago
Chicago 37, Illinois

Dear Mr. Levi:

I do not think that I can conscientiously keep you waiting any longer, for I do not think that I am going to change my mind in the foreseeable future, and you must surely want to get moving once again on the problem of finding a Dean. Therefore I must say—with what great difficulty I will not be able to describe in detail—that I cannot accept your University's offer, on such generous and attractive terms, of the Deanship of the Division of the Humanities.

I may be making a great mistake, but my reasoning is as I have described it to you on the telephone. I have decided that I am not yet ready to take up administrative work, since I feel that I have a number of books in me that I should like to get out in the next five or ten years. I realize that someone else might be able to continue his research and writing while he was Dean, but I think that my own tendency to throw myself wholeheartedly into whatever I do would make it impossible for me to carry heavy water, as it were, on both of my shoulders without dropping some from each. I would not want to be an inferior Dean and an inferior scholar, nor would Chicago want to have me if that was my future in the job.

As I told you on the telephone, my financial sacrifice in not coming will be heavy. And more than that there is the missed attraction of being in a position at Chicago to influence the course of higher education at a great center of learning. That too I must forego, to say nothing of the opportunity to participate in Mr. Beadle's and your campaign to improve a great University.

You see, then, that I know what I am giving up, and that I give it up with great difficulty. But I have come to the conclusion and there is no sense in keeping you waiting, nor in keeping myself and my family in a state of tension on the subject.

You have asked me to suggest names for the post and I will do so at a later date, after I have recovered a bit from my own decision.

I cannot close without expressing once again my great appreciation to you personally for all your kindness and all your thoughtfulness. I should be very happy if I were able to think that I am as good as the invitation implies. Will you be good enough to convey my deep regret to Mr. Beadle, as well as my appreciation to him for his efforts and words? And please convey my regret to Mr. Kracke, to his committee, to Manley Thompson, and to the Department of Philosophy.

> Sincerely,
> Morton White

In reply Levi said that he was not surprised by my decision but regretted it. He added in a nice way: "[Y]our moving letter convinces me even more that you are the right person for us. I wish there were some way we could get you." He also said that he was much interested in my "Reflections on Anti-intellectualism," which had recently appeared in *Daedalus*, adding that the dean of the humanities division should be dealing with that sort of question.

My telephone exchanges with Levi were not to end with my declining the deanship, for on July 23 he called me once again to ask whether I would accept a so-called university professorship at Chicago at a considerable salary *without* being dean. I should have said earlier that the original professorship offered was also a university professorship—one that would carry special honor in addition to a special salary, and that would involve a reduced teaching load. Now I was being asked to take such a professorship without the administrative burdens that I had shied away from when I wrote my letter of declination. What was I to say now? I said that I was exhausted by the questions I had been forced to face that spring and summer, and that I was not ready to respond to his most recent generous offer. I then proposed, with Levi's approval and agreement, to leave the matter as follows: When and if I should be interested in such a university professorship, I would get in touch with him. He and I agreed that his proposal on the phone was not to be construed as an official offer, but it was to be understood that I could draw an official offer if I were to signify my interest in the near future.

By the end of the summer, however, I had given up all idea of going to Chicago. I hadn't wanted to become dean because I hadn't wanted to give up scholarship; and I didn't want to become a university professor at Chicago because, I concluded, I was not ready to leave the East. Nick and Steve were there in school, and my parents were ill in New York. Lucia and I would therefore be flying back constantly to see all of them, and the cost of travel might well eat up a good part of my increase in salary. I must say, too, that I was made uneasy by going to Chicago at a salary well beyond that paid to the most senior professors in the university. I knew what kind of envy and hostility that could create, and I wasn't inclined to risk it. The reader will recall that I had experienced such trouble at Harvard when I had been promoted rapidly in the 1950s, but there the difference in salary between me and my jumped-over colleagues had been small in comparison to what it would have been at Chicago. In the end I was convinced that I would be happier in Cambridge than I would be in Chicago—if only because I would have better students and better living conditions there. Chicago was a place where one did not walk the streets at night in the vicinity of the university.

By declining the deanship at Chicago I gave up my first and last opportunity to become an influential executive in the academic world. I had cast my lot with scholarship over academic power, and I was proud of that. In retrospect I see that I did, as I said I might in my letter to Levi, produce a number of books in the years that followed the offer, and I am sure that most of those books would not have appeared if I had become a dean. Moreover, I would probably not have been invited to join the faculty of the Institute for Advanced Study in 1970 if I had not written those books. In addition, I would not have made a good hatchet man, ready and willing to fire or discourage some of those under me; I would not have been able to raise the money Levi would have expected me to raise; and I would not have been a very effective leader of the university during the student revolt that lay ahead. I have indicated that my disenchantment with Harvard and Cambridge began in the sixties, but my decision to stay there and to resist the blandishments of Chicago shows that my serious doubts about Harvard must have begun sometime after 1962. For in 1962 I was prepared to stay at Harvard in spite of being denied the editorship of the John Harvard Library, in spite of being put off by Pusey's religiosity, and in spite of my growing anxiety about how I would combine my many different intellectual interests.

Had I become a dean at Chicago, I would probably have had to face turmoil there, as all administrators did in the late sixties, but I did not avoid turmoil at Harvard, as the reader will soon see. I had foolishly agreed to become acting chairman of the Department of Philosophy so that the chairman, Rogers Albritton, could take a leave of absence in the spring of 1969, when all hell broke loose in Cambridge. Not even a prior leave of absence at the Princeton Institute in calendar year 1968 gave me the physical and spiritual strength I would need to weather what came to be called the bust at Harvard that spring.

19

The Spring of 1969
The Bust at Harvard

During my year at the Institute, the political situation at Harvard had become as tense as it had been earlier at Berkeley, Chicago, and Columbia. The students had become more restless and more militant in their opposition to the Vietnam War; the faculty had become more divided about methods of dealing with the students; the administration was losing support among the faculty; and even students who were not radicals were pushing for drastic reforms. From the day I returned to Cambridge in January 1969, I heard people speculating about when a university building might be occupied, and the time finally came on April 9, 1969.

A group of students entered University Hall, where Franklin Ford, the dean of the faculty, had his office, and they brutally forced him and various members of his administrative staff to leave. Some reports had it that about 250 demonstrators occupied the building, and at 4:15 P.M. I saw Ford mount the steps of Widener Library to make an announcement. Through a bullhorn he said that Harvard Yard would be closed until further notice, that only freshmen (all of whom lived in the Yard) could come back after leaving the Yard, and that all those who did not leave University Hall within fifteen minutes would be subject to prosecution for criminal trespass. I immediately left the Yard, but Ford's announcement did not lead any students to abandon

University Hall; indeed it was soon occupied by more of them. About twelve hours later, at about 4 A.M. on April 10, some four hundred policemen entered the Yard at the request of President Pusey. Soon they were joined by state troopers, and at 5:30 A.M. University Hall was cleared out. A teaching fellow who witnessed the bust reported to me that there was a good deal of indiscriminate beating of bystanders by the police, and that he was himself chased by a bat-swinging cop up the stairs of a nearby residential hall. I stayed up all night, anxiously listening to radio reports of what was happening. There was a good deal of violence when University Hall was emptied by the police and the troopers.

Because I was acting chairman of the Department of Philosophy, many of whose students, graduate and undergraduate, were militant, I was in a very difficult position. Like many of my colleagues, I was caught between what I regarded as two objectionable extremes: a bungling administration and a lot of confused radical students. And because so many graduate teaching fellows in philosophy were leftists, their offices on the top floor of Emerson Hall—which housed the Department of Philosophy—became a center of leftist activity. The radical newspaper *Old Mole* was distributed from an office on the top floor of Emerson Hall, which, like many other parts of the university, was a scene of chaos. Graffiti covered the walls of the corridors; posters were pasted up everywhere; noisy students milled about after a strike had begun on April 11. All parts of the university were affected by the strike. Some professors held their classes outdoors in the Yard itself; some classes were interrupted; some students wore red armbands to express their sympathy with the strike. Filth was strewn throughout the Yard, its grass turned into dust.

My direct involvement in the events began when I received a telephone call from President Pusey's office at 9 A.M. Tuesday, April 15. His secretary said that he wished to see me that morning at eleven o'clock, and I agreed to see him. When I met him in Massachusetts Hall, he said that he wanted to talk about two matters. The first had to do with an effort on the part of the Department of Philosophy to bring the philosopher Israel Scheffler into closer budgetary contact with us. He was a member of the Faculty of the School of Education who did some teaching for us without being on our budget, but there were, Pusey said, problems connected with our desire to transfer him to our budget even in a partial way. Pusey and I had a brief exchange on the matter before he turned to the subject that was probably uppermost in his mind. Pusey asked me: "Is the third floor of Emerson Hall cordoned off?" I emphasize that his exact phrase was "cordoned off." I answered that it was not, and added that I had just been there and had walked around it because I had anticipated that something like that might have been on his mind. I went on to say that the third floor was certainly not in a normal state but reminded him that no part of the university was in a normal state during the strike. My memorandum of our conversation contains the statement "He did *not* ask me to take any action," and I left with the impression that he had believed me when I said that the third floor was not cordoned off. Still, I thought, if Pusey could have asked that question, other members of the faculty might also ask it at the special meeting that was to be held that afternoon, and so I gathered together a number of my colleagues to discuss the matter at length. Among those I consulted were John Cooper, then a junior member, and my senior colleagues Roderick Firth and John Rawls.

I valued their counsel and support during those awful days because they took what I thought were sensible, centrist positions on major issues. Flanking us on the right were Van Quine and Nelson Goodman, both of them conservative on the issues of the day; to the left of the centrists were Hilary Putnam and Richard Boyd; and somewhere off the chart was Burton Dreben, who had become the parliamentarian of the faculty and who therefore felt obliged to be neutral on many issues. When I met with Cooper, Firth, and Rawls just before the faculty meeting on the afternoon of April 15, it was agreed that if a question should be asked at the meeting about the situation in Emerson Hall, I would after quick consultation with them rise to answer it. I was to describe what was happening in Emerson Hall—not an easy job—and, of course, to deny that the top floor was "cordoned off." For most of the meeting I waited tensely, hoping that Pusey would not raise the question, and he did not. But then the question did come up. Toward the end of the meeting, Professor Bruce Chalmers made a motion on ROTC that the administration did not like. Dean Ford responded as follows, according to the transcript sent to me by the Harvard registrar, Robert Shenton, on March 16, 1970.

Dean Ford: Mr. President, I had hoped it wouldn't be necessary, or even appropriate, for me to speak this afternoon, but much as I respect the motives which have led Professor Chalmers to make these proposals, I think it *is* important to remind this Faculty of the situation with which it is now confronted. Today, circulating in the Yard, are pamphlets which simply say, "WE'RE GONNA—G, O, DOUBLE N, A—SHUT HARVARD DOWN." A part of a University building is still occupied, and from it are issuing a variety of documents, some of them still dependent on the rifling of my office's files last week. We are not sitting here discussing in complacent self-assurance, after a crisis is over, how to approach some of the substantive issues which clearly still do confront us. But we are meeting here, with the university still in grave danger of destruction. And to start at this point saying that every issue that this Faculty has discussed in the last few months has suddenly become a new issue, because a building is seized, seems to me to confuse completely the priority of issues.

Because of Ford's statement that part of a building was still occupied, my nearby philosophical colleagues began to signal me that it *was* time for me to speak. Professor E. Bright Wilson asked the first question in the exchange that follows, though the person who prepared the transcript attributed it to me. A question mark indicates that a speaker was unidentified.

Question: What building has been occupied, Mr. Dean?

Dean Ford: I did not say any building had been occupied. I said part of a building is—

White: What part has been occupied, Mr. Dean?

Dean Ford: Well, I think perhaps your department could speak to that. If I'm not correct, say so.

?: Yes, we will.

White: Mr. President. The use of the word "occupied" is what I am questioning. In the normal discussions of these matters in the university these days, the word "occupied" has a very powerful and direct significance—it means that something has happened comparable to what, in fact, did happen in University Hall. I believe that if the Dean is giving the impression that this is in fact happening in Emerson Hall, that is not true. There is no barrier to anyone entering Emerson Hall at this moment. There is no difficulty whatever in going to the third floor in Emerson Hall, and walking about as you choose. Therefore I wish to make perfectly clear that although I do not in the least sympathize with—and in fact deplore—what happened in University Hall, I wish to make a plea, simply on the basis of fact, that this body not get the impression that something is happening in part of Emerson Hall which in fact happened in the whole of University Hall. This is simply not true. [APPLAUSE]

Dean Ford: If I had meant to imply that Emerson Hall was at present in the state that University Hall was, last Wednesday afternoon until Thursday morning, I would have said "forcibly occupied" or "forcibly seized." I did

not say that. [PROTESTS FROM THE AUDIENCE] But let me nail down a small
point of fact. You say that there is free access to Emerson Hall including
the third floor. Yesterday—early yesterday afternoon—mid-afternoon—
out of curiosity—because I'd heard reports about the third floor—I
walked into Emerson Hall freely, asked if there was any restraint on
moving around, and was told by two, I *assume* students in this university,
"Anywhere but the third floor."

White: I do not believe that this is sufficient evidence to arrive at a
conclusion to the effect that part of Emerson Hall is "occupied," Mr.
Dean. [APPLAUSE]

Immediately after this meeting, which closed soon after my exchange with
Ford, a number of colleagues and I went quickly to the third floor of Emerson
Hall to see what its condition was. Events could move so swiftly that some
wild men might well have "occupied" it in an effort to embarrass the centrist
"liberals" while I was making my statement. Fortunately that had not
happened. The third floor was its disheveled self, but access to it and through
it was free, and a number of other faculty members were also inspecting it
while we philosophers were. I felt an enormous sense of relief.

I was also pleased when I read the following report in the *New York Times*
the next morning:

A Bitter Exchange

The session became bitter during an exchange between the dean of
the faculty of arts and sciences, Franklin L. Ford, and a member of the
philosophy department, Morton G. White.

Their clash was over the use by dissident students of the philosophy
building, Emerson Hall, for their headquarters.

Professor White rose on a point of order to make it clear, he said, that
an implication by Dean Ford that the students had occupied the
building was incorrect.

"What part of the building has been occupied?" he asked the dean.
"There is no barrier to anyone going to Emerson Hall at this
moment . . . and going anywhere [in it] they choose."

Dean Ford said that he had gone to Emerson Hall himself early
yesterday afternoon. "I walked into Emerson Hall freely," he said "and
was told by two, I assume, students in this university that I could go
anywhere but the third floor."

Professor White said "I don't believe this is sufficient evidence" to conclude that the building is occupied. Loud cheers followed his statement.

Newsmen have been permitted freely into Emerson Hall, including its third floor. They met no resistance to their entry.

On the same morning the *Boston Globe* also attested to the truth of my statement that there was free access to and through the top floor of Emerson Hall:

> As the meeting was drawing to a close, Dean Ford stressed the fact that the illegal takeover must remain the key issue, and mentioned that part of a Harvard building Emerson Hall, was even then "occupied" by students.
>
> This drew a sharp rebuke from Philosophy Professor Morton White with an office in that building who said there was completely free access. Newsmen had no trouble in circulating in any part of Emerson Hall.

The relief I felt after reading these morning newspaper reports came to an end when I was told on the same morning that Franklin Ford had suffered a mild stroke and was in the hospital. I had always liked Franklin and had had friendly relations with him for a number of years, and so I was sent into deepest gloom by this latest bit of bad news. On April 17 I wrote his wife how sad I was to hear of his illness and to express my hope that his recovery would be speedy. In a cordial reply, Ford said it was a time of tension, and that there could be no more striking proof of that than the bickering of two such solid friends as he and I were over the operative definition of "to occupy."

Ford's reply was handsome, and I appreciated it. I must say, however, that in my view we were not bickering over the meaning of a word, since Pusey called in the police when University Hall was declared occupied, and therefore the interpretation of "to occupy" was no trivial matter. I was told that after my exchange with Ford, Pusey asked someone: "Why is Professor White quibbling over the meaning of a word?" But Pusey did not intervene at the meeting of April 15 to report that he had asked me that morning whether the top floor was "cordoned off," that I had said that it was not, that he had not asked me to take any action, and that he had not disputed my account of the situation on the top floor. Instead, he maintained absolute silence on the matter at the meeting, and Ford later told me, when I informed him that I was contemplating leaving Harvard, that Pusey had not told him of his (Pusey's) exchange with me on the morning of April 15. The administration's claim that I was "bickering" or "quibbling" was also reflected in an article called "The University—April 1969," which appeared in the publication *Harvard Today, Spring 1969, News of the University—Special Edition*. Speaking of the faculty meeting of April 15, the author wrote: "Toward the end, there was an acrimonious exchange between Dean Ford and Professor Morton White, Acting Chairman of the Philosophy Department, over the Dean's remark that the third floor of Emerson Hall— designated as strike headquarters and giving office space to the Old Mole— had *in effect* [my italics] been occupied" (p. 14). I have italicized the words "in effect" because they give the impression that Ford didn't say flatly that the third floor of Emerson Hall was occupied, and by scaling down Ford's assertion in this way the author made it easier for his readers to accuse me of quibbling. I repeat, however, that when Pusey asked the crucial question of me on the morning of April 15, he asked me whether the third floor was "cordoned off"; and the fact that Ford implied that he could not go up to the third floor of Emerson Hall indicates that he too thought it was "cordoned off."

My critics who said in 1969 that I was quibbling were gentle by comparison to the journalist Roger Rosenblatt. In his 1997 book *Coming Apart: A Memoir of the Harvard Wars of 1969*, he gives the following account of my part in the exchange with Franklin Ford: "Morton White, a professor of philosophy who later left Harvard for Princeton's Institute for Advanced Study, stood in the center of the room and, in a shrill voice, called Franklin Ford a 'liar' for having reported a takeover of the third floor of Emerson Hall, the philosophy building. Ford's report was accurate, but White called him a liar in front of his colleagues anyway. 'Mr. Dean, you are a liar'" (p. 52). But I did not say that, and the transcript I have quoted earlier shows that I never uttered those words or any other words in which I accused Ford of lying. My disagreement with Ford began when he told the faculty that "part of a building [Emerson Hall] is still occupied," meaning that it was in that condition even after University Hall had been cleared out by the police. And, as the transcript shows, when Ford cited what he took to be evidence for this, I replied that he could not conclude that the third floor of Emerson Hall was occupied merely on the basis of being told by two unnamed persons on the first floor that he could not go up to the third floor. But I certainly did not accuse Ford of lying when I said that the third floor was not occupied; I did not say or imply that Ford deliberately and deceitfully misrepresented the condition of the third floor.

Had I been a more astute politician or a clever debater, I might have done myself a service by reporting my earlier exchange with Pusey when I spoke before the faculty. But I did not, partly because I thought that reporting it would not have been in the best interests of the university, and partly because of the great emotional pressure on me. In any case, I am not sure that many of my critics would have changed their opinion of me had I told about my exchange with Pusey. Indeed, some of them might have hated me even more for rocking the boat even harder. One of the most pervasive features of faculty thought, speech, and action in those terrible days was the idea that the Harvard faculty must not be split as other university faculties had been in the face of similar disturbances. This was in turn reinforced by Harvard clubbiness. Never had I witnessed a more vivid expression of the feeling that loyalty to Harvard—often identified with loyalty to Pusey and Ford—must take precedence over everything else. Closing ranks in defense of them was even thought by some of my contemporaries on the faculty to take precedence over speaking the truth, and when I chose truth, I suffered the consequences.

One of those consequences came about because the meetings of the faculty were then broadcast throughout the Boston region over the Harvard radio station, WHRB. As a result, I received a number of very hostile anonymous telephone calls, one of them a threatening one. "Why don't you stop murdering my university?" asked one of my callers. When I tried to explain why I had said what I had said, and asked him to write me a letter conveying his criticism of me, he replied: "I'll do more than write a letter to you if you don't stop murdering my university; I'll do to you what you're doing to it." I might add that some of the most unpleasant calls did not come after the acrimonious meeting itself but after the report of events appeared in *Harvard Today*. That report did nothing to prevent the reader from inferring that the Department of Philosophy officially designated the third floor of Emerson Hall as strike headquarters, and that the department gave office space to the *Old Mole*. That, of course, was not true. Whatever space was given, was given by individual members of the department, usually teaching fellows, and not by the department itself. The most circumstantial account of the situation appeared in a statement prepared by the Department of Philosophy entitled "Political Activity in Emerson Hall," which was circulated to the faculty after my exchange with Ford. The document reported that at the departmental meeting at which the subject was discussed, nobody thought that people could not walk freely through the corridors on all floors of Emerson Hall. Investigation by a departmental committee had shown that one office in the building had been used as a distribution point for *Old Mole* but that the paper was neither edited nor assembled in Emerson Hall. Moreover, no member at the meeting of the Department of Philosophy thought that there had been any illegal activity in the building or that documents stolen from University Hall had ever been kept in Emerson Hall.

I have now reported many of the details concerning my part in the events at Harvard during the spring of 1969, most of it having to do with my exchange with Dean Ford on the floor of the faculty meeting on April 15 and some of it with my dealings with President Pusey. When writing to Registrar Shenton on March 27, 1970, I asked that the minutes of the meeting of the Harvard Faculty of Arts and Sciences contain the full verbatim account of my exchange with Ford or, as an alternative, that they report Ford's defense and my rebuttal of his claim that the third floor of Emerson was occupied. But by the time the minutes appeared, I was no longer a member of the Harvard faculty, and the minutes were not sent to me. In any case, a reader who wishes to learn what was actually said during the exchange can find out only by examining the transcript. Since I was not a member of the Harvard faculty when the minutes were approved, I could not vote on their approval. Although that was unfortunate from my point of view, I was confident that someday I would set it all down in some such account as the present one, thereby giving people a better chance to understand and evaluate my behavior.

Time has helped *me* understand my behavior better and to see what bothered me most during that period in my life. The more disturbing facts were simple. After my speech I was snubbed by many people who had previously given me the impression that they were my friends, and some of them failed to live up to ideals I had thought they espoused. I felt the force of ostracism for the first time in my life, and I came to see how one might become depressed when ostracized. Of course, I do not wish to give the impression that everybody at Harvard behaved in that way. There were many who behaved admirably, some of them people whom I hadn't known well or for a long time. What disturbed me most was that so many of my so-called friends behaved so badly that I wondered how on earth I could ever have thought that they were my friends.

In retrospect one of the sadder pictures that comes to my mind as I go back to 1969 is that of the historian Robert Lee Wolff, another man whose name I forget, and Robert McCloskey of the Department of Government, all seated next to one another in the Loeb Theater during a tense and exhausting faculty meeting. Ken Galbraith called the group "the Mountain" as he pointed them out to me: Wolff, with his bearlike shoulders hunched as he leaned forward and looked daggers at any liberal or leftist speaker; the second man furiously working his jaws; and McCloskey with a very pained expression on his face. Within a year, McCloskey was to die of a heart attack, and Wolff was to have one of the attacks that ultimately killed him. I cannot help thinking that their illnesses, like Ford's, were precipitated by the pressures of the time. I myself suffered from a peculiar, undiagnosed malady that I associate to some extent with the events of 1969. For more than two years afterward I had a sore tongue and palate, though no doctor or dentist could ever find any lesion in my mouth. I believe that the tension I felt, especially during my speech to the faculty, played a part in producing or exacerbating this pain. During much of this period I had troubled dreams and would often wake up in the middle of the night with a dry mouth and in a state of panic.

Another of the stories I remember had to do with a member of the faculty whom I prefer to leave anonymous. On a day in February before the bust, I met him coming out of Widener Library on a blustery, snowy night, and since my car was parked beside the library building, I offered to give him a lift. He asked me to do no more than take him to the bus stop in Harvard Square, from which he would then take a bus to Belmont, where he lived; but when I got to the bus stop, it seemed perfectly clear that the poor man might freeze before the next bus came, so I drove him all the way home. He was extremely grateful, and I was happy to have done him a good turn. But after the bust he certainly did not respond in kind when, on a very rainy day in May, I was standing on the corner of Coolidge Avenue and Mt. Auburn Street, waiting for a bus that would take me to Harvard Square. At that corner a red light forced this scholar and his wife, who was driving their car, to stop. He saw me and I saw him, and I noticed a quick exchange between him and his wife during which, I am sure, they decided *not* to offer me a lift.

Things like that, and much worse, were happening all the time. Not only faculty members, but their wives and even the widows of former professors were caught up in a wave of animosity. For example, the widow of Perry Miller broke off relations with us, and I can remember the icy stares we would receive in the Faculty Club. In surveying the history of our social connections at Harvard, Lucia and I came to think that somewhere in the middle of our stay there—which means around 1960—a great transformation had come over the place. Before that time Cambridge was associated in our minds with Arthur Schlesinger Jr.; with Isaiah Berlin, who, as I have indicated, often visited Harvard; with Robert Lowell and Elizabeth Hardwick, who had lived in Boston for a couple of years in the fifties; with Perry Miller, who was a friend in spite of his differences with me over the views of Reinhold Niebuhr;

with Henry Aiken as he was when we first came to Cambridge; with Van
Quine during the same period; with Jack Sweeney, Lucia's friend during her
New York days; and even with Mac Bundy, who, in spite of our sharp political
differences, was a friendly companion. Some of these people had left to go to
Washington with Kennedy in 1961; some died; some left Cambridge; some
stopped visiting Harvard. The effect of their disappearance was to diminish
the ranks of our generation and to cut down on the number of people who
were interesting to us even when we did not share their views on politics. By
the time they had all left Cambridge, we had far fewer friends whose company
we could enjoy.

I continued to be a regular attendant at Wolfson's Table in the Faculty
Club in the spring of 1969, but most of my luncheon companions were at best
tolerant and did not try to drum me out of the club. Sam Thorne (the legal
historian), Van Quine, Sidney Freedberg (the art historian), and Dick Baxter
(the law professor) were politically conservative, and I think they regarded
my speech at the faculty meeting with more disapproval than they ever
expressed to me. Like some of their more agitated colleagues, they probably
felt that loyalty to Harvard should have led me to withhold or moderate my
criticism of the dean even though what I said was true. I have heard that it
was only when Quine learned of my prior conversation with Pusey and of my
failure to report that conversation on the floor of the faculty that he
developed any sympathy for my position. I don't think he was at the faculty
meeting at which I spoke, but I'm sure he disapproved of my stand. I do not
know how much his disapproval diminished when he heard of my conversation with Pusey. By contrast, a few colleagues were good enough to congratulate me on my behavior at the faculty meeting of April 15: James Watson, the
biologist; John Kenneth Galbraith, the economist; and Zeph Stewart, the
classicist. And during the night on which I was receiving hate calls from all
over the Boston area, the distinguished composer Earl Kim was kind enough
to phone me in order to say how much he admired what I had done.

Once when I remarked on the degree to which I was being attacked or
avoided by members of my own generation on the faculty, my colleague
Roderick Firth tried to comfort me by pointing out that older colleagues who
disapproved of my stand would leave the faculty before those who admired it
would. That was a helpful remark, but it did not gainsay the fact that I was
isolated from most of the people I had known during my twenty-two years at
Harvard. And although some of my junior colleagues in the Harvard
Department of Philosophy sympathized with me because they too opposed
the bust, they were not close friends of mine. I did not have enough contact

with sympathetic colleagues to compensate for the alienation I felt, and that is one reason why the spring of 1969 was the beginning of the end for me at Harvard. I am sure that I would have accepted an appointment at the Institute for Advanced Study even if the bust had not taken place, but it is fair to say that the bust had a profound influence on my decision to accept the appointment when it was offered in 1970.

One scene from those hard times is worth mentioning here because it provides an ironic picture of what was then going on at Harvard. The member of the faculty who had accepted a lift from me in the snowstorm and then declined to offer me one in the rainstorm moved successfully that during all meetings of the faculty a big crimson banner with white letters reading "Veritas" should be displayed in the Loeb Theater. When it was put up, however, it was attached to a stage curtain *behind* the back of the president and his administration, who therefore could not see it.

20

Last Days at Harvard

While I was deciding in the spring term of 1969–70 whether to leave Harvard, I thought much about the Department of Philosophy, which I had helped transform over a period of more than twenty years. I don't know how I shall be judged for what I did, but I played a part in bringing Firth, Dreben, Albritton, Cavell, Rawls, Putnam, Scheffler, and Goodman into the Harvard philosophical community, and I felt especially pleased when Goodman was finally invited, because I thought that justice had triumphed after years of vain efforts in his behalf. But even though so many fine philosophers and interesting people were on the scene, I felt like a disappointed revolutionary, not altogether happy with the change I had helped to bring about. By the time I left Harvard in 1970, the department was thought to be one of the best in the country, one that commanded much more respect in the councils of the university than it did when I entered it in 1948. Links with Government had been forged by Rawls, with Classics by Owen and Albritton, with Education by Scheffler, with Psychology by Goodman, and with English Literature by Cavell. The logicians Quine, Putnam, and Dreben continued the department's long-standing association with Mathematics; and I was in close touch with History and the Committee on American Civilization. All of my colleagues were decent, able, highly intelligent men who were respected in other parts of the university. What, then, troubled me about the department?

One of the main reasons for my dissatisfaction was its failure to become an intellectual community. Well before the spring of 1969 I made efforts to revive the Philosophy Colloquium so that faculty and students might have a congenial setting in which to exchange ideas outside the classroom. Since some of our colleagues rarely published, I thought that a colloquium might provide an opportunity for the rest of us to find out what they were thinking as well as a forum in which all of us could try out our ideas. The few who did not publish much were very good in discussion, and I thought they might be encouraged to become more productive if they could present their ideas to a friendly audience. Although we had gambled on them when we invited them to join the department, I was still betting that we had gambled rightly, and thought that if they were to present papers to their colleagues, those papers might turn into distinguished articles. But my efforts at reviving the colloquium were utterly unsuccessful. Apparently those who did not write articles or books didn't want to read papers to their colleagues. Nor was Quine, our most eminent and most prolific colleague, enthusiastic about reviving the colloquium or forming a group consisting only of faculty members, probably because he felt that it would take too much time from his research and writing.

To show how much communication within Emerson Hall had declined, I will tell a story that speaks volumes. After the department had persuaded me to give an introduction to systematic philosophy in 1964 or 1965, I sent the following letter to many colleagues who had strongly urged me to give the course, but I did not receive an answer from *any* of them:

Widener U
Cambridge, Massachusetts
November 5, 1964

Dear

This is a cry for help. As you probably know, I have decided to concentrate on the notion of compulsion in Phil. 3 this Spring and am now casting about for readings. At the moment, I think of the course as divided into four main parts, each of them to receive, say, three weeks of treatment. They are as follows, though not necessarily in temporal order. (I) Causal necessity: law; explanation; free will; determinism, etc. (II) Logical necessity: rationalism vs. empiricism; a priori knowledge, analytic and synthetic; the nature of philosophical analysis, etc. (III) Obligation: the right and the good; natural law; moral obligation and legal obligation; ethical reasoning, etc. (IV) Political Constraint and Liberty.

Now for my problem. I need good and interesting readings that are accessible in editions that won't be too expensive. Would you do me the great favor of jotting down any ideas that you may have and send them to me? Use the other side of this sheet, if that will speed things up.

Also, please let me know if you have any reactions to the idea or to the general outline. For example, other "species" of compulsion may have escaped me, or I may be picking too many, etc., etc. Do let me have the benefit of any easily recorded knowledge and wisdom you may have on this subject. I shall be eternally (and necessarily) grateful.

Yours ever,
Morty

The department was not only unwilling to talk philosophy but it had very little interest in getting together socially. Lucia and I did our best—especially when I was chairman—to gather people together in our home, but many of those who accepted our invitations would rarely invite us to their places. In my most paranoid moments I thought that there was a lively social life going on behind our backs, but I finally realized that *nobody* in the department was seeing *anybody* else in the department after the shop closed down. Each of us may have been living jolly social lives, but rarely in the company of fellow philosophers.

In our earliest days at Harvard we saw very little of some colleagues and their wives because our views and our outlook on life were totally different from theirs. But in the late sixties the members of the department had become more philosophically sympathetic to each other, and many of us seemed to be good friends. What, then, was keeping us apart? It was said that some colleagues were so busy trying to produce important work that they did not have time for sociability, but we could not take this seriously, and we soon retreated to the sad conclusion that the department was a scene of alienation, an example of what was going on in the world around us: "the eclipse of community" as it was then called by sociologists. Not a full explanation, but I think close to the truth. Only the Quines would invite us to parties like those to which we invited them, but often they did not seem to invite other philosophers, probably for the same reasons that led us to give up trying. The result was that we saw fewer and fewer philosophers or their wives even before Harvard broke apart over the issues of 1969; and the irony was that all of this took place in a department that, I assumed, had every reason to make up a friendly social group. Relying on this assumption, I thought that most of my colleagues would support me by speaking out in public after my sharp exchange with the dean, but that did not happen. Consequently I felt like a leader whose troops were abandoning him in his time of great need. Apart from producing the document "Political Activity in Emerson Hall," my colleagues did little in public to support my speech to the faculty even though some had encouraged me to intervene. I was distressed by their silence, and my distress made me wonder whether I wanted to remain at Harvard.

I began to think seriously about leaving it when my very thoughtful colleague Firth told me that he was thinking of leaving. During lunch one day he allowed that he was troubled by the behavior of some of our colleagues before, during, and after the crisis. I can remember his saying that he thought that he had withdrawn too soon from active participation in the administration of the department on the mistaken assumption that younger colleagues would take over and act wisely. Firth was a very conscientious man and a good philosopher who had served as chairman even longer than I had; and he was a decent man with whom I had always had cordial, though not very close, personal relations. He was a Quaker, not likely to express his emotions very much, but they were strong. During the Second World War he had been interned as a conscientious objector, and he had spoken out courageously but somewhat ineffectually against the bust. So when *he* began to speak of the possibility of leaving Harvard, I began to think that it was not out of the question for me either. He spoke with feeling about how nice it would be to go to a place where one would have a light teaching load and where one would be free of the need to direct Ph.D. theses by second-rate graduate students. He remarked on how much he envied a friend who had managed to get a lot of writing done under such circumstances, and he gave me the impression that he was then negotiating for just such a job. For my own part, I began to think of the Graduate Center at CUNY, where I had given an enjoyable seminar in the fall of 1968–69.

After talking with Lucia, I decided to explore this possibility with my always helpful friend Arthur Schlesinger, the Schweitzer Professor at CUNY, where he had gone instead of returning to Harvard after his stint in Washington. I had lunch with him in New York on June 23, 1969, and we talked at great length about the possibilities. Characteristically, Arthur said he would do everything he could to get the Graduate Center to offer me something for which I would leave Harvard. And so quickly did he do something that on July 2, 1969, I received a letter from the provost of the Graduate Center, and later its president, Mina Rees, which began: "Arthur Schlesinger has suggested to me that you may be willing to explore with us the possibility of your accepting an appointment as a professor at the Graduate Center of the City University of New York. We are, of course, greatly interested in this possibility." Since *I* was greatly interested in that possibility, I came down to New York from Vermont in the latter part of July and talked with Dr. Rees.

Soon after that, I was to go through some of the most harrowing experiences of my life: my mother died on October 27, and my father died on December 5. For many years my father had been seriously ill, and my mother had been his faithful nurse. In the year 1959–60—while I was at the Center for Advanced Study in Behavioral Sciences in Palo Alto, California—my father had a heart attack, and that was the beginning of the decline of both of my parents. He was about sixty-eight at the time; my mother about sixty-seven. Soon after the attack it was discovered that my father also had cancer of the prostate, and that began a drawn-out period of almost ten years that ended with his death. He and my mother struggled bravely against heavy odds. They continued to live on the Lower East Side of New York, making occasional trips to Cambridge to see us, their two grandsons, and their great-granddaughter, Jenny, my son Nick's daughter. I often traveled to New York to see them, always with feelings of great pain. They were old, sick, and poor, but they were courageous and as cheerful as circumstances allowed. I helped them financially by supplementing the pittance they had from Social Security. They had no other source of income and no savings.

Early in the fall of 1969 a crisis developed. My father was in greater and greater pain as his cancer spread, and he became seriously incontinent. We arranged to hire a housekeeper for him and my mother. Up to that time they had insisted that they could manage by themselves, partly, I think, because they did not like the idea of a stranger in their small apartment, partly because they valued their independence. Soon Lucia and I became convinced that they would either have to come to live with us or go to some kind of nursing home. We began to build an apartment for them in our Cambridge house, but their health deteriorated so rapidly that we felt it necessary to propose that they come to live in a nursing home near us. They resisted that strenuously. I can remember reminding my father that they had often said that they wanted to live near us, and that now, if they came to Boston, they would see much more of us, their grandchildren, and their great-grandchild.

My father, hardly of a philosophical or religious turn of mind, replied that even though they were far away from us, they would continue to live with us in spirit! So they returned to New York after vetoing the idea of a nursing home: they would have none of it. When they returned to New York, my father entered Mt. Sinai Hospital. He behaved badly there, breaking a window with a cane that he had thrown at a roommate who, he said, had insulted him. He was therefore discharged, and he returned to his apartment, where my mother was herself having a hard time.

During all of this period she had been complaining of her health and was typically seeing one doctor who insisted that there was nothing wrong with her and another who said that although she had heart trouble, he could keep it under control. Soon after my father returned from the hospital, I received a phone call from him in the middle of the night. While sobbing, he told me that my mother had collapsed and had been taken by ambulance to the nearby Beekman Downtown Hospital. It was Sunday, so their housekeeper was off. I called a very helpful and generous cousin in New York, Helen Steinberg, who, with her physician husband, Myron, arranged for a nurse to come to my father while Lucia and I rushed to the Boston airport. Before we reached New York, Myron decided that my father should enter a hospital once again, so he was taken to a hospital in upper Manhattan whose name I can't remember. When we got to La Guardia Airport we called the downtown hospital and were told that my mother was resting, so we went uptown to see my father, planning to visit my mother after we visited him—presumably the more serious case. After seeing him, we went by cab to my mother's hospital, and when we arrived, we learned that she had just died.

Lucia and I were overcome with grief and exhaustion. Only the fact that many things had to be done quickly kept us from collapsing. We decided that my father could never go back to his apartment. We therefore arranged to give it up and in one day emptied it of a lifetime accumulation of clothing, jewelry, books, letters, medicines, furniture, and countless papers, including several worthless stock certificates that he had saved in the futile hope that their value would some day revive. Meanwhile he lingered near death in the hospital, constantly asking about my mother and begging to see her. His doctor said that he should not be told of her death, but he would keep asking his nurse to read him obituary pages—where, of course, I had not announced my mother's death—since he suspected what had happened. Soon he developed pneumonia and died. Within a period of six weeks Lucia and I had arranged two sad services in New York, but we took consolation from the fact that my mother and father had finally been released from great pain and misery, and that each had been mercifully spared the news of the other's death. We were overwhelmed by what we had gone through.

It was in the middle of all this that I heard, on November 11, from Dr. Rees about the situation at CUNY, and the news helped to divert me. Dr. Rees wrote: "We want very much to have you join our faculty, and both the philosophers and the historians would welcome you." She also proposed that I come to New York in order to talk with her and a number of people on her faculty, including Arthur. That conference with philosophers, historians, and administrators went well, and soon I was offered a very handsome job as distinguished professor of humanities. I was to begin at about $35,000 in the first year, 1970–71, go up to $36,275 the next year, after a general raise was to go through, and then continue at their highest salary, whatever that might be. In addition, Lucia would be my half-time research assistant at $5,300 in 1970–71 and $5,700 in 1971–72. If she wanted to work more than half-time, her salary would be increased proportionately. A grant of $1,000 would be made to cover my moving expenses; I would have all the secretarial help I needed; I would have an office at the Forty-second Street Center, which would take all of my books; and so on and so forth. Never did an institution try harder to get me.

At once I began to think very seriously about the offer, and drew up a memorandum in the manner of Darwin in his *Autobiography*. One page had two parallel columns headed "Pro-Harvard" and "But"; the other was the same in form, except for having columns headed "Pro-CUNY" and "But." They read as follows:

Pro-Harvard	*But*
Phil. colleagues	Little contact with them.
Better grad. students	Their politicization a problem for me. The scramble and competition for them. All of us teach similar things. Besides I *have* turned out a lot and can knock off.
Better undergrads	Not sure I want to teach lecture courses, which is main and typical way of reaching undergrads.
Cambridge living easier; safety greater; less wear and tear	No buts!
Cambridge society?	Our generation depleted; haven't gotten to know many younger people.

| More influence via | Undeniable, but CUNY may permit more writing, hence greater influence that way. |
| Prestige | Don't care. |

Pro-CUNY	*But*
Hist & Phil teaching	No buts; not likely at Harvard and besides don't *want* membership in Harvard Hist. Dept. as now constituted.
Only grad. seminars	No buts, and besides, can teach undergrads when I want to.
Money	Higher costs in N.Y. because of more lures; big rents. *But* maybe live in Princeton, which might be cheaper—esp. if Institute cooperates. Also if we keep 28 Coolidge Hill Road, we'll get big rent for it.
More lively (?)	Getting to see people in N.Y. harder—cab problem—safety problem.
Greater freedom about what I do with my time	Few buts; except that I *might* have to worry about membership in *two* depts.
Big fish in small pond	Not a consideration.

After Lucia and I went through these various reflections, I began to talk to my philosophical colleagues and others at Harvard. A number of them were distressed to hear that I was thinking of leaving, and their concern moved me. Yet several of them knew what I had been thinking about Harvard, so they weren't altogether surprised by my taking the CUNY offer seriously. I must say that I was deeply touched by the feeling for me expressed by several of my colleagues when they heard I might leave. So, after talking with Lucia, I came to think that it would be unwise to take action too quickly and decided, with CUNY's and Harvard's consent, to go to CUNY as a visiting professor for one trial year in 1970–71. This decision put my mind to rest *for a while*. In order to assess the merits of teaching at CUNY independently of the possible demerits of living in New York City, I arranged to rent a house in Princeton from the Institute for Advanced Study; and the Institute's director, Carl Kaysen, was kind enough to say that he would also arrange a nonstipendiary membership for me that would permit me to have a study at the Institute. Naturally, I was delighted to hear this and grateful to him. I had gone down to Princeton to talk to Kaysen and to my friend the classicist Harold Cherniss before deciding about the CUNY offer, since I thought they might give me advice that would be more objective than what I was getting from interested parties at CUNY. Both of them encouraged me to accept a trial year at CUNY rather than to accept or reject the permanency there at once.

Meanwhile other thoughts were forming at the Institute. Once some of my friends there, especially Cherniss and the historian of science Marshall Clagett, realized that I might leave Harvard for good, they rightly concluded that I would rather leave it for the Institute than for CUNY, so they helped form a plan to bring me to the Institute as a professor. On December 17, 1969, Cherniss wrote to ask me whether I would accept such an offer if it were made, and I replied *at once* by telephone, saying that I would certainly accept. But, of course, Harold could not predict with certainty how things would progress from that point on.

It happened that I was scheduled to leave for Carleton College in Northfield, Minnesota, on January 2 in order to give a series of eight Cowling Lectures there in a period of four weeks, so Lucia and I had to leave for that frozen land without any clear idea of how things would develop at the Institute. In fact, I received no further word about that until the second week in February, when I was told that the School of Historical Studies had finally voted to recommend that I be invited. But since my informant was Harold, my suspense was not entirely removed. Being extremely cautious, he pointed out that there were other hurdles to be jumped, especially those that might arise during the open season in which the *whole* faculty would mull over the nomination in order to raise whatever questions and objections they might have about it. Because of the slowness of the Institute's operations, Lucia and I spent not only all of our four subzero Minnesota weeks wondering about our fate, but also the whole month of February and a part of March in Cambridge. On March 23 Kaysen finally wrote me a letter of invitation. To make matters more agonizing, there was a postal strike at the time, so I went down to Princeton to receive the letter by hand and to reply on the spot! I couldn't bear the suspense any longer.

Naturally, I had already alerted the CUNY people about my negotiations with the Institute, but I was now faced with the difficult task of informing them of my final decision. They had been kind enough to keep their door open to me until the bitter end, so on March 26, in a letter that was exceedingly hard to compose, I wrote them of my decision not to come to CUNY. I received no acknowledgment of this letter from Dr. Rees, which led me to fear that she had been deeply offended. Arthur Schlesinger, of course, was very disappointed but it was like him to sum it all up by asking: "How could anyone refuse a job that requires no teaching?"

I found it easier to write my letter of resignation to the new Harvard dean, John Dunlop, with whom I did not discuss the matter at all. I hardly knew him personally, and what little I knew of him I did not especially like. In the hectic days after the bust he was a leading member of the so-called Conservative Caucus of the Faculty, and during some negotiations between that caucus and the Moderate or Liberal Caucus, to which I belonged, I was struck by his toughness and by a general manner that suited his role as a labor arbitrator. I felt no obligation to see him or Pusey personally, so I resigned from Harvard by mail, curtly ending twenty-two years of service at an institution to which I had come happily and where I had been happy for a long time. Some of the best days of my life and Lucia's had been spent in Cambridge with our family. Our two sons had been educated there; I had made many friends there; I had taught many students there; I had helped rebuild the Department of Philosophy there. However, I had also lived through very troubled times there, and I was glad to be leaving it for a place I had always admired enormously.

I regret that one episode connected with my leaving might have offended my Harvard colleagues. After much reflection and much conversation, Lucia and I decided not to accept the department's proposal—made very late, I must add—that it give a farewell dinner in our honor. Somehow that didn't seem appropriate to us. The university and the department were still feeling the effects of the bust, we were not in a mood to celebrate, and I doubt that the department was either. Such a dinner might have been appropriate in the case of a retiring professor but not, I thought, in the case of one who deliberately leaves his colleagues in midstream. What would I say to them in a farewell speech? Could I speak the whole truth without giving offense? I knew I could not issue the glowing sentimental remarks that might be expected of me, so I declined. I suspect that some of my colleagues were offended, but I think I was right to ward off what might have been an anticlimactic and possibly unpleasant evening. If I gave offense to my colleagues, I am sorry, but I think I was right to do what I did. Our friends Raya and Burt Dreben, in a spirit that we greatly appreciated, gave an informal dinner for us to which they invited some of our oldest and best friends in the department. At the end of it, Burt offered a generous toast, to which I responded with gratitude. It was better to leave my friends that way, I think, but maybe even that much fanfare should have been avoided.

Harvard had created a bitter taste in my mouth, and the same feelings that had led me to decline a farewell dinner led me to see to it that my colleagues did not follow an old custom by coming to my last lecture. They expected me to give it on a Tuesday, so in order to be certain that none of them would come to it, I gave my last lecture on the Thursday before, not announcing until the beginning of it that it would be my last. At the end of it I was applauded by a class that had listened in a stunned state, since I was publicly mentioning my resignation for the first time. After acknowledging the applause, I sadly closed my folder of notes and with it one of the most important chapters in my life.

A short time later I recalled an incident that showed that sad and complicated leave-takings were not unusual in the Harvard Department of Philosophy. One night, many years before I had left Harvard, I was giving a seminar in my house at 28 Coolidge Hill Road in Cambridge, when, at the end of the meeting, Ronald Dworkin, then my undergraduate tutee and later Professor of Jurisprudence at Oxford, asked to make an announcement. I consented, and he proceeded to tell us that Professor H. M. Sheffer would be giving his last class the next day. Dworkin urged us to come to that class, which he was attending, and to spread the word to others. The class was given in the seminar room on the first floor of Emerson Hall, and the next morning a large group of students and faculty gathered together there, hoping to walk into Sheffer's classroom just after his class had begun. The seminar room had two doors, one that allowed entry from the corridor and another—a sort of back door—permitting entry from the large lecture hall, Emerson D. So a group of us lined up in Emerson D, preparing to enter Sheffer's seminar room by the back door. At the head of the line was Henry Aiken, followed by me, followed by a dour-looking C. I. Lewis, followed by the less than enthusiastic Quine, and by many others. Brave man that he was, Aiken opened the door and walked over the threshold with me close behind. At that point Sheffer looked up from his notes through his very thick glasses and the two—yes, *two*—students in the class turned their faces toward the intruders at their rear. The always nervous Sheffer was very perturbed and fiercely shouted, "What is this? Get out!" Aiken protested feebly but was finally forced by Sheffer's commands to turn on his heel, followed by me, followed by Lewis, followed by Quine, and so on down the line. Our efforts to be nice to the unhappy man had been foiled. He didn't *want* to be treated nicely on that day after many years of not having been treated nicely at Harvard.

I tell this story because on my last day of teaching at Harvard I had feelings *like* those of Sheffer on his, though I can hardly claim to have been as unhappy in my last few years at Harvard as he had been for decades. Yet, like

Sheffer, I did not want to be cheered while feeling as I did. At my last lecture at Harvard my mind went back to my last lecture at Columbia. Then I was being let go, and now I was quitting, but in certain respects the occasions seemed very much alike to me. I was sad both times, but this time I could console myself by thinking of the delightful situation I was about to enter at the Institute.

21

Explosives in Paradise

When I was appointed to the faculty of the Institute I was ecstatic. I had known its charms ever since I had been a visiting member there in 1953–54 and writing my book *Toward Reunion in Philosophy*. On a second visit to the Institute in 1962–63, I produced a major part of *Foundations of Historical Knowledge*, and I began work on *Science and Sentiment in America* during my third visit in 1968. From the moment I first came to the Institute in 1953, I longed to be there forever. The idyllic surroundings, the conveniently close residential quarters, the company of distinguished colleagues, and ideal working conditions made it seem like an academic heaven.

There was a time when the stuffiness of the town of Princeton was very forbidding to a city boy who, when asked how he liked Harvard, said that he wished it were in Central Park. But the deterioration of New York and Boston made them less attractive than they had been in 1953, and the explosions in American universities during the sixties made the Institute yet more attractive. Even when I had been happier at Harvard than I was in 1969, I would have left it for the Institute, so nothing stood in the way of my accepting an appointment there when it was offered. The disturbance at Harvard had seriously interrupted my research and writing, and I yearned to get back to them under the conditions provided by the Institute—a large salary by academic standards, a full-time secretary, a research assistant, a handsome study, a generous travel fund, no teaching duties, a period of required residence from late September to early April, a house that I could buy with the help of a mortgage at a very low rate of interest. Only someone with a passion for teaching and for the confusion and dirt of Cambridge or New York, or a fear that he had nothing more to say, could turn down such an offer. If I wanted to see good philosophers, there were several in the Department of Philosophy at Princeton University whom I had known as students at Harvard; and if I yearned to teach, I could do so at the university if invited. But the great attraction of the Institute was that I could read and write there without interruption while maintaining contact with mature visiting scholars and with distinguished faculty members at both the Institute and the university.

While thinking about whether to move to the Institute, I came to realize that I was less sociable than I had once thought I was, and recalled that my contact with students during the trouble at Harvard had become minimal. Rightly or wrongly, I concluded that my ruling intellectual passion was literary and that I would relish writing and reading all day. When I settled in at the Institute during the summer of 1970, I immediately began to work full-time on *Science and Sentiment in America, Documents in the History of American Philosophy*, and a volume of essays to be published under the title *Pragmatism and the American Mind*. I also wrote some philosophical papers, had occasional philosophical conversations with Kurt Gödel, and lunched regularly with Harold Cherniss, Marshall Clagett, and Kenneth Setton. I saw less of my other colleagues, and I saw more of Carl Kaysen, the director, in my first year than I did later.

Before I say why I came to see less of him, I should say a few words about my remote connection with the discussions of who should succeed Oppenheimer as director of the Institute as well as something about my relations with Kaysen shortly after he was appointed. In 1965 he was under consideration for the directorship of the Institute while he was a professor of economics at Harvard. Presumably because I had been a member of the Institute, a trustee of the Institute came to call on me to discuss the question of replacing Oppenheimer, who had recently submitted his resignation. The trustee was Barklie McKee Henry, who visited me in my study in Widener Library in October of 1965, accompanied by Kenneth Auchincloss. I had met Henry at a party in Princeton during the academic year 1962–63, but I had not met Auchincloss before; I believe he was then secretary of the Trustees' Search Committee, of which Henry was chairman.

In the course of my conversation with Henry and Auchincloss, I responded quite favorably to Henry's question about expanding the faculty of the Institute to include more than professors of mathematics, physics, and historical studies as then conceived. But, as I recall, he did not mention the possibility of founding a school of social science, nor did he mention Kaysen. After the meeting, Henry wrote to thank me on November 3, 1965, but I heard nothing further about the matter until I learned a few months later that Kaysen had been named director. I wrote him on February 14, 1966:

> My warmest congratulations to you on your new post!
>
> Having spent two happy and profitable years at the Institute, it occupies a large place in my heart, and so I am very pleased to think that it will now be in such capable and sensitive hands as yours.

To this note he replied politely, remarking that he hoped we could talk about the Institute in the near future so that he might get the thoughts of "an alumnus."

My next contact with the Institute came in January of 1968, when I began a year's membership there. My relations with the new director were cordial at the time, and I can remember speaking sympathetically with him about his plans for establishing a school of social science. When I came as a professor to the Institute in 1970, Lucia and I saw a fair amount of the director and his wife, who did many things to make our early days in Princeton comfortable. I remember writing him with pleasure when I had heard that he was not appointed to the presidency of Harvard even though he had been described in the newspapers as a strong candidate for the job. I was glad that he would be staying at the Institute.

All of this good feeling was to disappear by Christmas of 1973, during the third year of my professorship; and in order to say why, I must tell a sad story of mounting tension, suspicion, and mistrust at the Institute—a story whose climax was the director's recommendation to the trustees that they appoint as a professor someone who had been voted down by a majority of the faculty. When I began to take lunch regularly with Cherniss, Clagett, and Setton in the summer of 1970, we engaged in very little serious talk about academic politics, but there were innuendoes, hints, and suggestions that showed that not everything was rosy at the Institute. My luncheon companions worried about whether the new West Building and the recently formed Program in Social Science would drain the coffers of the Institute too much. Because the director had not succeeded in raising much new money, they feared that the cost of the building was coming out of the Institute's general funds. To understand why, one must realize that professors in the School of Historical Studies had always been more anxious about the Institute's finances than some of their colleagues in mathematics and physics. Those disciplines had always been lavishly supported by governmental agencies, whereas the School of Historical Studies was almost exclusively dependent on Institute funds for its support.

I could see that my historical colleagues' attitudes toward the administration were much more edgy than they had been during my earlier years at the Institute. Generally speaking, the previous director, Oppenheimer, had had strong support from the historians, who admired him for being sympathetic to their recondite historical research and as a highly cultivated man who knew a lot about painting and literature; they also liked him personally. But Oppenheimer was cordially disliked by some mathematicians, whom the historians regarded as perverse and difficult for that reason. However, in my first year as a member of the faculty I detected a change in relationship between some mathematicians and my friends in the School of Historical Studies. The two groups seemed to be drawing closer to each other inasmuch as my historical colleagues seemed less and less inclined to view their mathematical colleagues as misguided obstructionists. For example, they now spoke of Deane Montgomery as a wise and shrewd critic of the administration rather than as a comical ancient mariner who would stop anyone who was willing to listen to him speak of the director's limitations. I can remember the surprise I felt at my first faculty meeting in October 1970, when I witnessed an exchange between Montgomery and the director that showed me that the director was not admired by all of his faculty. At one point Montgomery asked the director to clarify the status of a mathematically oriented social scientist who was a visiting member in the Program in Social Science, the predecessor of the School of Social Science. Mincing no words, Montgomery condemned the field in which this member worked as unsuitable for the Institute because it lacked intellectual weight, as he put it. He added that if the whole faculty had been asked to review the invitation of that member, the Institute would have been spared the embarrassment of his having been invited.

It was clear from Montgomery's remarks and tone of voice that he disliked the director, that he did not think well of social science, and that he was especially contemptuous of work in social science that used the machinery of mathematics. This attitude, common among mathematicians at the Institute, led me to fear that nonmathematical social scientists of lesser intellectual distinction might be proposed just to avoid criticism by the mathematical purists. Unfortunately, however, I could never persuade Montgomery of this danger; he was too bent on seeing to it that no social scientist of lesser mathematical attainments would embarrass our mathematicians by winning an appointment at the Institute. Unlike Montgomery, I did not oppose or despise social science, nor did I fear, as he did, that appointing a first-rate mathematical economist would open the Institute's gates to second-raters. On the other hand, I admired his tenacity in trying to keep up intellectual standards at the Institute and to avoid spending too much money on the construction of buildings. I also liked him as a person, and I believe that my friendship with Montgomery and with his colleagues Armand Borel and André Weil helped form connections between the mathematicians and historians that proved very important, as we shall see.

I watched the beginnings of this united front in a more or less detached way during my earliest days at the Institute. I had, after all, just come from a university in political chaos, and I had no stomach for participating in another struggle against an administration. Yet I could not help recalling Kaysen's disparagement of certain work in the School of Historical Studies while I had been a visiting member in 1968. He would often refer to what he called the "mindlessness" of certain work done in classics, and he was much closer to the modernists among my colleagues than he was to Cherniss, Clagett, and Setton, my classical and medieval friends. In my first interview with Kaysen after my appointment to the faculty, he told me that the immediate task was to find replacements for the modern historians Gilbert and Kennan, who, he pointed out, were close to retirement. I knew, however, that Cherniss in ancient philosophy and Meiss in art history would retire in the same year as Kennan, that retired professor Benjamin Meritt's successor in classics had not yet been appointed, and, indeed, that Gilbert's retirement would come after those of Cherniss, Kennan, and Meiss. When I asked Kaysen therefore whether the replacement of Cherniss was not a pressing task, he said something like: "Oh! But Harold is irreplaceable, so I don't think that we have to worry about that." Lacking any great interest in the study of ancient philosophy, Kaysen was, I feared, willing to forget about replacing Cherniss but eager to stock the school at once with two new modernists who might even vote to abandon the study of ancient philosophy. I took note of this but said nothing. I continued to remain silent when he remarked to me that the charter or the bylaws gave him a great deal of power over appointments to the faculty. He told me that some members of it were opposed to his plan for a school of social science on the erroneous assumption that the

Institute could not afford it, and he assured me that the Institute's funds were sufficient not only for maintaining the present faculty but also for maintaining the generation of its grandchildren.

I kept these things in mind as I watched my luncheon companions step up their disapproval of the director's policies. Some of them were excessively cruel in their comments on the prose style and grammar of the director's memoranda; others lampooned his tendency to lecture when he sat with us at lunch. I am sure that they would have preferred not to have to do battle with him, but I think they felt that they might have to do so if he pressed them very hard. I continued to say to myself that I *must* not allow myself to become involved in academic politics as I had been in Cambridge. I also retained a feeling of gratitude toward the director for his kindness to me when I first arrived at the Institute, and at times I really felt sorry for him. He was obviously under great pressure to do something splashy but was not getting much financial support from the trustees, or from anyone else except his friend Bundy at the Ford Foundation. At lunch, he would occasionally assume a sad expression that would make almost anyone feel sorry for him.

Many of my colleagues' negative attitudes toward the director were triggered in 1971–72, my second year at the Institute. At one point Kenneth Setton, the chairman of the Library Committee, complained that the director had, without any of the required consultation with the committee, taken over a large part of the lowest floor for books in social science. At another point, Cherniss reported that the director had asked him why he had voted in a faculty meeting against a motion favored by the director, so Cherniss threatened to move at the next meeting that we cast secret ballots and appoint a teller. At yet another point, Clagett criticized the director for trying to evade a prior commitment regarding how many permanencies we would have in our school. All of this, however, was as nothing compared to a blowup in the fall of 1971 over an attempt on the director's part to get a psychologist, whom I shall call Professor X, appointed to the faculty.

Professor X had been a visitor at the Institute for some time, and evidently the director had a very high opinion of him. It seems that the director had been encouraging him for some time to think that he would soon be invited to become a professor, but X had become tired of mere encouragement and wanted quick action because he had been on leave for a long time from his university and would soon have to let it know what his plans were. Pressed in this way, the director, in spite of many statements that he would not propose an appointment in X's field until such time as new endowment funds were available, joined Professor Clifford Geertz of the Institute's Program in Social

Science in formally nominating X in a letter to the faculty. The director added that he would later let the faculty know what the financial "basis" for such an appointment would be.

The forthcoming nomination of X had been reported in advance at a meeting of the so-called Faculty Advisory Committee, which consisted of representatives of all the schools and the director, and upon hearing of it, the two representatives of the School of Historical Studies grew worried. They feared that the director was nominating X without fresh funds, contrary to his previous promises. They therefore gathered together all the members of our school, who decided, at the suggestion of one professor, to send via their executive officer an "aide-memoire" to the director in which they expressed their unwillingness to support such a nomination in the absence of fresh funds:

> The members of the Faculty of the School of Historical Studies, after hearing the report of their representatives on the Faculty Advisory Committee, have asked me to let you know informally that they are not satisfied, from what they now know, that the financial support for a new professorship in the Program in the Social Sciences is sufficiently assured to protect the interests of the existing schools, and that they would not feel themselves justified, in these circumstances, in supporting the nomination of another professor in that Program. This is wholly aside from the question of the scholarly qualifications of the nominee in question.

The director, after telephoning some members of our school, decided to withdraw the nomination, but he called a meeting of the whole faculty in order to explain the situation. At that meeting Setton spoke forcefully about the number of occasions on which the director had promised not to do what he had done in his letter of nomination. To his friends Setton had already pointed out that the so-called financial basis for the appointment was *no* basis: there was no new money for it. Other members of the faculty also voiced their opposition to considering the nomination of X in the absence of new funds, so it was finally decided at that meeting that such a nomination should not be considered at that time. This was a severe blow to the director, and it brought the Institute to a state of considerable agitation. Setton had not only led the charge in our school but had also talked persuasively to mathematicians who had long been critical of some of the director's policies.

They, like the historians, were up in arms; and it was clear that the director had provoked and united his critics in mathematics and history.

Another factor in the faculty's revolt against the nomination of X was the director's handling of a discussion of an appointment to a professorship in the School of Historical Studies. This appointment had been discussed by my colleagues before I had come to the Institute and was taken up again soon after my arrival. Three professors were appointed to a search committee and they came forward with someone I shall call Professor Y. While they were deliberating, however, the director had been collecting opinions about Y, and at one of our meetings produced negative letters about him from outside scholars in what was said to be a departure from custom. Outside authorities were usually consulted only *after* the school had made up its own mind, and so the director was criticized for having injected himself into the affairs of the school in an unusual and unacceptable way.

It should be pointed out here that the director had been appointed a member of our school, not by a vote of the school, but by a ukase of the trustees. He had made it a condition of accepting the directorship that he be made a professor, and they, without asking our school, complied by making him—an economist—a professor in the School of Historical Studies because there was no school or program of social science at the time. For this reason, some of my colleagues thought that his collection of adverse opinions about the candidate proposed by our school's search committee had been doubly intrusive: he was not a historian but an economist, and, as director, he should not have participated as he did in our discussions of candidate Y. They thought he could have used his power as director to *veto* our proposal of Y once we made it, but he should not have tried to torpedo it in advance by collecting adverse opinions of Y. His doing so, I am sure, led some members of our school to veto his nomination of X for a professorship in social science. When it was later moved at a meeting of the whole faculty that the nomination of X not be considered, because of an insufficiency of funds, many historians voted for the motion, in other words, to reject the director's idea of bringing another social scientist to the faculty. Tit for tat.

Soon after this rebuff, the director declared at a meeting of the School of Historical Studies that the trustees had brought him to the Institute to start a School of Social Science and that during the negotiations that preceded his appointment the trustees had been thinking of closing down the Institute or merging it with Princeton University. The implication was that he had prevented this from happening by accepting the post. Indeed, he allowed that he did not know that the possibility of closing the Institute was out of the question at that very moment, and added that should that happen, he would urge that all professors of sixty or over be treated by the trustees in a satisfactory financial way but that younger ones be allowed to fend for themselves. In an effort to be feebly humorous I said that I hoped he would lower the age limit to fifty-five, that being what I would be in April of 1972.

Shortly after the rejection of his candidate X, the director paid a call on me in my office. It was on November 30, 1971, the day of a meeting at which the school had elected its members for the coming year; he came at around 5:30 in the evening. He began by expressing his disappointment over the school's rejection of some applicant and went on to say that leading opponents of this scholar had also led the charge against his candidate X. I really felt sorry for him when he repeated what he had told our school about the board's closing down the Institute or merging it with Princeton University, for I realized how distressed he was by the defeat of X. He said that the board was firmly committed to establishing a School of Social Science, that most trustees selected during his directorship had been tested for their sympathy with this aim, and that they would back him to the hilt. Nevertheless, I wrote the following optimistic words in a journal: "I must say that while this unpleasant saga shows that there is trouble in this scholarly Paradise, such trouble does not seriously disturb me. It is like a thunderstorm, a brief interruption of a very pleasant day. When it passes, the pleasantness reappears, and I forget the noise and the streaks of lunacy. Unlike Harvard, the Institute easily returns to normalcy after one of these storms."

At the time, I felt enough sympathy with Kaysen to give him some advice. I urged him not to throw his weight around so much in our school meetings. I told him that I thought he had made a mistake in the affair over the historian Y and that a good part of the historians' opposition to social scientist X derived from resentment of the director's torpedoing of the appointment of historian Y. I said that his action might well have fostered and encouraged an alliance he might regret between some of the mathematicians and some of the historians. I also said that although he had blocked Professor Y because Y was not broad enough or brilliant enough, a search committee of our school was considering other scholars whom he, the director, might oppose on similar grounds. He agreed that these scholars were no better than Professor Y from his point of view but added that he would not be able to attend the next meeting of our school because business would take him out of town. He also said that my theory would have a chance to be tested at that time, meaning my view that it would be good for all of us if he did not push into our affairs as much as he had been pushing.

My theory was tested, I am sure. The school met without the director present and voted for a candidate whose credentials were different from those favored by him. A few days later the school met once again—also in the absence of the director—and unanimously voted for the appointment of still another professor of whom the director might have been critical if he had attended the meeting. The cat was away and the mice were playing furiously. In those days Mickey Mouse might have commanded a favorable vote in our school if the director were known to be critical of him. Clearly, the school liked the idea of the director's being away, but he didn't; and I suspect that he may have thought I was the architect of this new revolt even though I was not. After all, I had urged him to stay away, and what happened? Two appointments were voted without his having any opportunity to stop them at meetings of the school. Events like that presaged more dramatic events ahead.

22

Avoiding the Simplest Course

At the beginning of my third year at the Institute, on September 25, 1972, the director informed the faculty that he and the anthropologist Professor Geertz proposed to nominate the sociologist Robert N. Bellah—I use a name here because the nomination later became a matter of public record—for a professorship in the social sciences program. The director, no doubt because he remembered his difficulties over the nomination of social scientist X a year earlier, concluded his memorandum with these cheerful words: "There is no problem about the financial basis of this appointment. We have now completed the whole of the Ford Matching Grant program, giving us nearly $4 million in new money for the Social Sciences Program. This provides a basis for at least two new permanent appointments." This time he did not have to worry about money; it was all in the till, and there was nothing to think about save getting the faculty to agree.

Almost immediately after the nomination I read Bellah's book *Beyond Belief* and began to make a number of informal inquiries of outside scholars who might be expected to know something about his work. Because Bellah was interested in Japanese religion, I called up two specialists on Asian matters who, I thought, might be helpful. One of them spoke well of Bellah, whereas the other did not. I then spoke to a sociologist who applauded

Bellah's humanistic tendencies, but his favorable opinion was counteracted by the negative views of two other scholars I called. These adverse critics reinforced certain doubts about Bellah's work on Japan as other critics reinforced doubts about his writings on American society. Since he had been touted by his nominators as a specialist on religion in America as well as in Japan, I had sought the opinions of two distinguished American historians and of two distinguished historical sociologists; all of them were less than favorable about the nomination. Of course, I am fully aware of the difficulty of estimating the standing of scholars in sociology, and I am quite prepared to grant that Bellah's critics might have underestimated his work and his scholarly powers. But, as the reader will soon see, his work and his powers quickly ceased to be the issue. Once the director had dug himself in to defend the nomination, and once a majority of the faculty had adopted a negative view of it, the issue ceased to be Bellah.

After Kaysen and Geertz had made the nomination, the next step was to select an Ad Hoc Committee that would examine it. At the first meeting of the Faculty Advisory Committee, which was charged by the rules to choose the external members of the Ad Hoc Committee, the nominators of Bellah played very active roles, a fact that I found peculiar in the light of what I knew about the formation of such committees at Harvard in my time there. The nominators did not hesitate to propose some scholars who had close ties to the nominee, though they also rejected others because they were too close to him. After this meeting I wrote two letters to Kaysen in my capacity as my school's representative on the Faculty Advisory Committee—one on October 5 and another on October 17. In the first I complimented the nominators on their wise rejection of certain scholars who were much too close to Bellah, notably his teacher Edwin Reischauer. In my second letter I made explicit my concern that the Ad Hoc Committee not be weighted in Bellah's favor. I also suggested the name of Ernest Nagel, pointing out that he would be good to have on the committee because so much of Bellah's writing was methodological, and because Nagel represented a point of view in the philosophy of the social sciences that differed from that of Bellah.

I never received a written reply to either of these letters, but the second of them led the director to invite me into his office. He reported that he had talked to Geertz and that they had agreed that it would be a good idea to have a philosopher on the committee but doubted the wisdom of having Nagel on it because he was so committed to the view that the social sciences should use the methods of the natural sciences, a view that Bellah did not share. Therefore, Kaysen said, he and Geertz wondered about asking a different philosopher to serve, one that Kaysen mentioned. I replied that I preferred Nagel because Nagel had done more writing on the method of the social sciences than the philosopher Kaysen had mentioned, and I left open the possibility that I would propose Nagel at the next meeting of the Faculty Advisory Committee.

That meeting, like the first one, was attended by two mathematicians, by two physicists, by me and a colleague in historical studies, and by the two nominators of the candidate. A well-known sociologist whose doctrinal affiliations in sociology were close to those of Bellah was immediately accepted by all of us, and when the name of a sociologist who specialized on Japanese society was suggested by one of the mathematicians, I responded warmly to the idea, as did Kaysen and Geertz. Unfortunately, however, he could not serve and was replaced by Edward Shils, a Chicago sociologist. When Reischauer's name came up, neither I nor anyone else pointed out that he was Bellah's teacher and hence might be biased in his favor. I did not want to veto Reischauer, simply because I did not want to jeopardize my chances— by pushing too vehemently against a favorite of the nominators—of getting Nagel on the committee; I was willing to let them have as many sympathetic members as they wished so long as they would appoint *somebody* whose views differed from Bellah's.

When I proposed Nagel, I received a negative response from Geertz, who did not stress, as the director had, that Nagel favored the use of the methods of natural science in social science, but rather that Nagel was so critical and polemical that he would not view the candidate's ideas with enough sympathy. With my Harvard experience in mind I could not help thinking how surprising it was for a nominator to be participating so actively in the selection of the Ad Hoc Committee, and even to be telephoning people such as Eliade of Chicago to ask whether they would serve on it. In any case, I continued to push hard for Nagel without success. For a moment I was encouraged when one physicist said that he did not see why Nagel should be vetoed for the reason given by Geertz, but he did not press his point, and my proposal of Nagel was finally killed. After some further discussion, we wound up with Bellah's teacher Reischauer, with Shils, with another sociologist who was sympathetic to Bellah's views, with a philosopher whom I respected, and with a student of comparative religion. In short, with a majority of outsiders who were likely to be predisposed in Bellah's favor.

Although I was distressed by the way in which the Ad Hoc Committee was formed, I hoped that it would work satisfactorily. I also hoped that internal members of the committee would ask probing questions of the specialists about the candidate's work and that the specialists would answer them in a helpful way. I innocently believed that if the faculty were to conclude that the candidate did not merit a professorship at the Institute, the director would not forward the nomination to the board of trustees, and I was even naive enough to suppose that if the director did forward such a nomination, the board would not accept it.

On December 3, the Ad Hoc Committee gathered—the six internal members, the five external members, and the director, our chairman. The meeting had its bizarre aspects. For one thing, the chairman was an advocate of the candidate; for another, Reischauer and the two sociologists were plainly in favor of the appointment, and because they were, they locked horns with internal members who did not favor it and with internal members who had their doubts about it. It seemed clear that the three external members who favored the nominee were taken by surprise when they were forced into this position. Familiar as they were with the very different procedure of Ad Hoc Committees at Harvard, I am sure they had not expected that they would have to defend the nomination against internal members. They had probably not done as much homework as they would have done if they had known that they would be called upon to debate with Institute professors who were very well prepared—indeed, loaded for bear— on the subject. Since Geertz was present for only a part of the meeting as a witness, and since the director, as the chairman, did not speak in behalf of the nominee, it fell to Reischauer and the two sociologists to act as though they were nominators of Bellah rather than consultants to the faculty. I did not envy them, and I regretted the unpleasantness that characterized the ex-changes between them and some of the internal members.

After a vigorous discussion, the Ad Hoc Committee was disbanded by the director without a formal vote, and its external members were asked to mail their views of the nomination to the director. But after the committee broke up, the internal members gathered together informally to discuss the signifi-cance of what was said at the meeting. They passed no motions, but they unanimously agreed that after reading the nominee's writings and listening to the statements by the external members of the Ad Hoc Committee, they did not think that the appointment would be a good one. One of the internal members—a physicist—was especially careful to refrain from saying how he would vote at the forthcoming faculty meeting, because, as he put it, everything would depend on the exact wording of the motion. He said that if he were asked to endorse the nominee categorically on the basis of what he had read and what he had heard at the meeting, he could not do so. In other words, the motion would have to be framed appropriately to get his vote. As it turned out, there was an effort at the full faculty meeting to formulate the motion so as to accommodate his qualms, but I do not want to run ahead of my story.

Before I describe the full faculty meeting, I want to deal with a few preliminary events. When the director circulated what he called the minutes of the meeting of the Ad Hoc Committee, he said that he had condensed the remarks of the internal members more than he had condensed those of the external members. This gave rise to a correspondence between me and the director that turned out to be somewhat unpleasant. He objected to my saying in a letter that his method of unequal condensation was unfair because the more condensed views of the internal members were less favorable to the nominee than those of the external members. In his letter he took the occasion to say: "It was not part of my task to summarize your own views, which you have already expressed widely and will have ample opportunity to repeat." In my reply, I tried to mollify him by saying that I did not regard our differences over the nomination as personal and hoped that he felt the same way. I was determined to keep calm and to extend something of an olive branch to him, but I never received a reply to my letter.

Although the director said that I would have ample opportunity to repeat my views, that is, repeat them at the forthcoming faculty meeting, it became clear to me that I could not speak to the faculty without presenting a carefully considered statement of my reasons for voting against the nomination. I therefore began to write my thoughts down. Soon I realized that my remarks were becoming very extended and that I could not deliver a speech of that length before a group of roughly twenty-five people, some of whom would also wish to speak at length. Consequently, after returning to Princeton at the end of the Christmas recess, I prepared and sent to the faculty a shorter statement entitled "Remarks on the Nomination of Robert Bellah"; and at the meeting I circulated four letters about Bellah's work that I had received from four outside scholars. In doing so, I felt fortified by the fact that the director had presented outside reports about Professor Y at a meeting of my school. I requested that all the copies of the four letters I had distributed be returned to me at the end of the meeting. I did not want them to circulate publicly, and, as we shall see, I turned out to be wiser than I knew.

By way of preface to my comments on Bellah's work I made a few preliminary remarks. First, I said that I was heartily in favor of there being a School of Social Science at the Institute. I added that some of the candidate's interests were somewhat similar to my own. He had written on the history of social thought, as I had; he had written on the nature of religion, as I had; and he had written on the methodology of social science, as I had. I went on to say that the meeting of the Ad Hoc Committee showed that even those external members who praised Bellah's work did not successfully defend it against various objections that had been leveled at the meeting. At the end I said: "I regret to say that after carefully reflecting on a great deal of the evidence, I have come to the negative conclusion to which all of my colleagues who were internal members of the Ad Hoc Committee came just after the meeting of the Ad Hoc Committee. It saddens me to think that this belief separates me from my colleagues in the field of social science, and I assure you that I wish that I could agree with them. It is always painful to have to disagree with colleagues, especially colleagues with whom one lives at such close quarters as we do with each other." My written "Remarks" had been available to the faculty for a few days before it met on January 15, 1973.

At the start of the meeting there was some predictable disagreement about how the nominating motion should be worded. Geertz moved that the views of the members of the Ad Hoc Committee, as reported in the summary of their meeting and their subsequent letters, on balance supported his and Kaysen's judgment in nominating Bellah for a professorship in the social science program. Geertz used the phrase "Ad Hoc Committee" so that it referred only to the outsiders, but if it were used to refer to the insiders as well—as it was at Harvard—the reference in the motion to the views of the Ad Hoc Committee was incorrect. Anyone who insisted that the insiders were not on the Ad Hoc Committee might have been referred to a communication of the director of December 9, 1972, entitled "To the Faculty Representatives on the Ad Hoc Committee," in which we were plainly regarded as being on the committee.

The issue about the constitution of the Ad Hoc Committee was minor compared to the one for which the reader is now prepared. The motion as first presented was framed so as to accommodate the qualms of the physicist of whom I have spoken earlier. So when someone asked why the faculty should not vote on the simple categorical motion that Bellah be appointed, that physicist candidly allowed that he could not vote affirmatively on it, because his decision to approve the appointment would be based entirely on the opinions of the favorably disposed outside experts.

It is important to take into account the views of this fastidious physicist, whom I shall call Number 1, because he did abstain when the motion was amended to read categorically: "This faculty accepts the nomination of Bellah for a professorship in social science." A less fastidious physicist, whom

I shall call Number 2, said that he agreed with Number 1 about the formulation of the motion, but then voted for it. The best that Number 3, another physicist who voted for the motion, could say for the appointment was that it was not financially hazardous or intellectually disastrous. Number 4, a physicist who was one of the internal members of the Ad Hoc Committee, felt that the importance of Bellah's relationship to Geertz in his work was sufficient to warrant voting for the amended motion. Number 5 was a physicist who supported the motion but said nothing at the meeting. Number 6, a historian who voted for the amended motion, said nothing about the nominee's scholarship; neither did Number 7, a historian who voted for the motion *in absentia*, according to the director. Number 8, another physicist, was all for the motion; indeed, he seconded it as originally worded. Only his vote and Geertz's vote for the motion were unequivocally based on their own favorable opinions of the nominee's scholarly accomplishments. That is to say, only two of the eight favorable votes were based on an assessment by the voters themselves of the candidate's work. I stress this because one trustee later pointed to the physicists' support of the candidate as counting heavily in the candidate's favor.

The final vote on the amended motion was thirteen against, eight for, and three abstentions. The negative vote of thirteen consisted of five in the School of Historical Studies and eight in the School of Mathematics. The affirmative vote of eight consisted of one in the Program in Social Science, five in the School of Natural Science, and two in the School of Historical Studies. Of the three abstentions, one was in Natural Science and two were in Mathematics. It should be noted, moreover, that toward the end of the meeting it was successfully moved that the nomination *not* be forwarded to the trustees. The vote on this motion was fourteen affirmative, six negative, three abstentions. Interestingly enough, one of the physicists who had voted for the earlier motion in support of Bellah later voted for this last motion; he had been persuaded by the end of the meeting that it would be unwise to proceed with the nomination.

During the discussion of the nomination, no supporter of it responded to my circulated remarks. One said that he would not respond to them because he did not think it would be appropriate to do so at the point in the meeting at which he was then speaking. His silence, he added, was not to be taken to indicate that my remarks were not answerable, and the director said that "the strongest arguments against the appointment were based on an incomplete understanding of what Bellah is about, and an analysis of his work that would not stand up."

To my pleasure, the logician Gödel said at the meeting that he agreed with my circulated evaluation. He added that the recommendations of several of the outside experts seemed to be influenced considerably by their reluctance to oppose Geertz, whereas it was their independent opinion of the candidate's qualifications that the faculty was entitled to hear. He also pointed out that many scientists of great intelligence, originality, learning, and influence have produced completely wrong theories, for example, Stahl, the inventor of the phlogiston theory of heat. No one of the outside experts, he complained, spoke of the truth or likelihood of Bellah's views. But Gödel's speech was of no avail. The director commented that the simplest course would be for him to say that the bulk of the faculty did not support the nomination and that therefore it should die. However, he continued, he would not take that course. Instead he would take a very grave step that would cause him great personal difficulty and undoubtedly create serious questions within and about the Institute. He was going to recommend to the trustees that Bellah be appointed for a number of reasons. The most important of these was that he remained intellectually convinced by the argument for the appointment and was also convinced that the argument against it was based on a standard that the faculty had not consistently applied in the past. Amusingly enough, a professor in my school who supported the nomination thought that *he* was the target of the director's remark about the faculty's past failure to apply its highest standards, whereas I was equally convinced that *I* was the one the director had in mind.

Four days after the meeting of January 15, the director sent the faculty a letter in which he offered a defense of the nominators' failure to rebut criticism of their nomination at the meeting. This letter was circulated on the afternoon before the trustees were to meet on January 20, and it was primarily directed at them. The director said that the reason why the nominators did not reply to criticism was that "we immediately became embroiled in a procedural discussion." He meant, of course, that the faculty had engaged in a discussion that led to the amendment of the original motion and to its defeat as amended. The director said nothing about why the faculty had been forced to engage in that discussion, nothing about the formulation of the original motion so as to make possible an affirmative vote by those like physicist Number 1 who were *not* convinced by their own independent inquiry that the candidate merited appointment and who therefore sought the protection of the appeal to expert authority contained in the original motion.

In addition, the director disputed what he called my claim to special qualification to judge Bellah's work. Most of my work, he said, had been "devoted to an analysis of the development of ideas, explicating texts and showing the intellectual relations among the systems of different thinkers, etc." (I like that "etc.") "This," he said after his summary of my work, "is in a deep sense exactly the opposite perspective from that appropriate to the sociology of ideology, religion, or culture." Of course, I found it strange that the director should have thought that a sociologist of the development of ideology worked from a perspective that was in a deep sense—whatever that meant—*exactly opposite* to that of a philosophical student of those ideas. Didn't the director think that if Bellah wished to discourse sociologically on the origin and impact of, say, Protestantism, he would have to know what it was, that he would have to understand it? Therefore, it seemed to me that far from being opposite in perspective to that of the sociologist of ideas, the perspective of the philosophical scholar who tries to find out what those ideas are and to understand them must be adopted in some degree by the sociologist of ideas.

The director did not content himself with questioning my claim to any special qualification to judge Bellah's work. Anyone familiar with what Gödel had said at the meeting of January 15 would see that the director, after having criticized my views as well as mentioning my name, criticized Gödel's without mentioning his. Since Gödel had complained at the meeting that the outside experts did not focus on the truth or likelihood of Bellah's theories, the director made this pronouncement: "Enough has been said about the nature of the field and the inappropriateness of the question as to whether, for example, Bellah's view of the role of religion is 'right' or 'wrong' to make it clear that there is no single meaningful answer to the question 'Is what Bellah says right?' We must rather ask, 'Has he given a more persuasive interpretation of the social process he studies than competing ones?'" The director seemed to be saying that Gödel was mistaken in thinking that our outside experts should have evaluated the truth or likelihood of Bellah's theories rather than their persuasiveness or influence. The director thought that the basic question was whether Bellah's "work has been a major influence in shifting the generally accepted view of how we understand what happened in Japan in the last century or so." In other words, the director, in criticizing the views of one of his most distinguished faculty members, seemed to say by implication that a scholar could be given a professorship at the Institute primarily on the basis of having persuaded or influenced a group of sociologists to change their views. "What if those sociologists were second-rate minds?" Gödel asked me after the meeting.

At the meeting, Kaysen left it to his fellow nominator to deal with the more substantive parts of my criticism of the nomination, so Geertz suggested that "perhaps" my inability to understand a certain view of Bellah's was brought about by my "general neglect" of James's *Principles of Psychology* in my work on James. In a rejoinder that I managed to produce before the trustees' meeting, I pointed out that my book *Science and Sentiment in America: Philosophical Thought from Jonathan Edwards to John Dewey* contained a chapter on James in which I discussed his *Principles of Psychology* at length. My rejoinder had to be prepared very hastily because the nominators' reply came to the faculty on the afternoon of Friday, January 19, one day before the trustees were to meet in special session to consider a last-minute oral plea by some members of the faculty. I recall the frantic efforts of secretaries to type my rejoinder and the equally frantic efforts of sympathetic colleagues to collate and staple together its various parts; they reminded me of the Paris taxi drivers who rushed to bring reinforcements to the front during the First World War.

To what avail? To no avail, as it turned out. Those of us who went before the trustees opposed the appointment on scholarly grounds; we complained about certain aspects of the procedure; and we warned the board of the dire consequences of approving the director's recommendation—in his presence, since he attended as an *ex officio* member of the board. We urged the board in the strongest terms *not* to approve the nomination, but they said absolutely nothing—except, as I recall, to ask for repetition of an inaudible remark by one of us. As soon as all of us had finished, the chairman of the board simply said, "Thank you very much, gentlemen," and we departed in a state of fury.

Much later, many explanations of the trustees' silence were offered. It was said that they were so angered by what some of us had said that had they had lost their powers of speech. In particular, one of us seems to have angered them beyond measure by comparing the action that he urged them not to take with one taken at the Norwegian universities during the Second World War. He never mentioned the Nazis; he merely referred to the fact that in 1941–43 certain people were added to the faculty of the University of Oslo against the wishes of the faculty. Then he pointed out that no member of the legitimately appointed faculty ever spoke to these people and that he feared that something similar might happen if the nominee were appointed. The trustees were especially wounded by these remarks, and they were said to have thought that some of my remarks resembled those of a prosecuting attorney. They were also upset by the advice of one professor that they mind their own business by raising money and building buildings, while they left the appointment of professors to us.

This, of course, they did not do. Under the date of January 20, 1973, the chairman of the board sent a memorandum to the faculty in which he reported that the board had resolved to approve the director's recommendation that Bellah be appointed a professor. And on January 30 the chairman sent us almost three typed single-spaced pages in which he described the basis for the board's decision. The chairman said that the board relied primarily on the director's advice, on Geertz's advice, and on the advice of the Ad Hoc Committee, which the chairman, like Geertz, identified with the five outsiders and not with the total committee. He argued that three of the five external members who were most directly qualified to evaluate Bellah— Reischauer and the two sociologists—gave strong support to the nomination. He added that a substantial segment of the faculty (eight out of twenty-four) supported the nomination, "either on the basis of their own views as to its merits or the evaluations of those more expert." Then he went on to describe the board's commitment to the establishment of a School of Social Science and its attachment of great weight to the director's judgment that the proposed appointment was crucial to the further development of the fledgling Program in Social Science, and to his view that failure to move forward would be a threat to the survival of that program. The board's statement was a valiant effort to marshal whatever arguments it could for its decision, but in relying on outside experts, it showed little awareness of how those experts— the external members of the Ad Hoc Committee—had been selected. And while the chairman of the board put great stock in the fact that the eight faculty votes for the nomination were based on the voters' "own views as to its merits *or the evaluations of those more expert,*" he made no mention of the fact that only two of those eight votes reflected the voters' *own* views of the merits of the candidate's work. He added one more consideration: the director's incorrect prediction in 1973 that failure to add Bellah to the faculty would destroy social science at the Institute—incorrect because social science exists at the Institute today.

After the board defended its decision of January 30 to approve the appointment of the nominee, fourteen professors asked the board to join with the faculty in appointing an outside commission to evaluate the director's stewardship of seven years. On February 13 the board declined to do so, but the chairman did appoint a committee of the board, "not including the Director," to meet with the fourteen. On February 19 the fourteen reiterated their request for an external commission and asked that the committee of the board frankly discuss with them the merits of forming such a commission. On March 8 the chairman of the board's committee indicated that it was ready to hear the views of the fourteen "on all aspects of the governance of the Institute, including the value of an outside commission," but that concession was made only after the story had hit the newspapers.

On Tuesday, February 27, Israel Shenker of the *New York Times* came down to Princeton and interviewed a number of us at great length. On Friday, March 2, an explosive piece by him was printed in the *Times*. I saw it first at about 6:30 in the morning, when I was appalled to see through sleepy eyes that Shenker had referred to some of the letters written to the administration. I remembered that when he had interviewed me, he had said that he had acquired all the documents; I also remembered that when I had asked whether he had in his possession the letters sent to the administration, he allowed that he had. When I remarked to him, however, that I supposed he would not quote from them without the permission of the authors, he laughingly said that would be like asking for permission from authors who are quoted in the Pentagon Papers. As I read what was quoted from the outsiders, I was relieved to see that none of the letters that I had collected on my own were quoted; this showed me that *they* were not in Shenker's hands and that I had been wise to retrieve copies of them at the end of the faculty meeting at which I had circulated them. In my opinion, the effect of Shenker's piece was to support the faculty's side in the controversy, as did Shenker's follow-up piece on Sunday, March 4. The faculty's cause was soon helped by three additions to the fourteen original dissidents, and so on March 24 there were seventeen dissident faculty members who met with the board's committee— seventeen out of a faculty of twenty-seven—to discuss the tense situation.

At the end of the spring of 1973, Bellah was formally appointed by the board but did not accept the invitation. Kaysen was reappointed as director and remained at his post until the end of the academic year in 1976, after having announced in the spring of 1975 that he would leave in a year. During the period in which the director hung on, the Institute was an extremely unhappy place. Some professors boycotted social functions to which they had been invited, and some refused to take lunch in the dining hall, preferring to bring sandwiches and coffee to their offices, where much of the discussion concerned the crisis. André Weil, the mathematician, once cracked: "Of course, we could go on strike, but who would know?"

Mentioning Weil leads me to stress that I have reported events in a way that is more appropriate to an autobiography than to a history. Consequently I want to say that during the battle a number of my colleagues, notably Weil,

Armand Borel, Deane Montgomery, and Harold Cherniss were far more influential participants than I was. My main contribution was made during the part of the controversy that concerned the nominee's scholarly attainments. It was enough of a contribution, however, to lead someone to say that I was leading the School of Mathematics by the nose, a remark that caused a great laugh at a meeting of what Shenker called "the dissident majority," since anyone who knew my mathematical colleagues in 1973 would find it hard to believe that anyone could lead them by their collective nose.

Another canard of the day was that it was I who supplied Shenker with the documents he used in the *Times* piece. I have already pointed out that Shenker never quoted from the four letters about the nomination that I had distributed at the faculty meeting, and I want to repeat that I was not Shenker's source. I had occasion to point this out in a letter to the *Atlantic Monthly* of April 1974, where I was responding to a piece on the quarrel that had appeared in the issue of February 1974. I wrote as follows:

February 8, 1974
The Editor
The Atlantic Monthly

Sir:
In the article on the Institute for Advanced Study by Landon Y. Jones, Jr., (February, 1974) there is a sequence of three paragraphs on page 46 from which some of your readers might infer that I, as one of the opponents of an appointment to a professorship, participated in passing out or in a decision to pass out to reporters confidential letters appraising the scholarship of the candidate. This is not true. I did not give to any reporter confidential letters appraising the scholarship of the candidate, nor do I know of any decision on the part of the professors in the so-called dissident majority to do so. I should appreciate your giving me the opportunity to say this publicly. I also wish to say that I regard the publication of any part of those letters as deplorable.

I should like to add that an examination of the Late Jersey edition of the *New York Times* for March 2, 1973, when excerpts from five letters first appeared, will show that four of the quoted comments were favorable to the candidate and only one adverse; and therefore it is not likely that those who opposed the appointment would have been interested in their dissemination. Another edition of the *Times* of that day, in which the report is slightly different, also contains a preponderance of favorable quotation from outside scholars.

Copies of the letters in question were, of course, not only in the possession of the professors in the "dissident majority" but also in the possession of every other professor, of each trustee, and of the Director. Furthermore, the minutes of the faculty meeting at which the nomination was considered show that I had circulated at that meeting copies of four other letters from outside scholars which were written to me personally and which—except for copies to be attached to the minutes—I took pains to collect precisely because I did not wish them to be floating about. Those letters were *not* excerpted in the newspapers or otherwise published.

Yours truly,
Morton White

In addition to the charge that I gave the *Times* the letters from which it quoted, there was a ludicrous one that my critics circulated—the charge that I was seeking to become director. This was supported by citing the gossip of a professor's wife who recalled a supposedly relevant incident at the director's swimming pool. He and his wife had invited me and my wife to use the pool while they were out of town for a few weeks; they had also invited the gossipy faculty wife and her husband to use it. The supposedly significant incident was this: At some point during one afternoon I had jokingly exclaimed that the pool was so wonderful that I could even imagine accepting the directorship just to use it! For a long time I thought that no one would believe that this remark of mine showed I was gunning for the director's job, but then I learned something that might have been combined with it to support the idea that I was plotting to unseat the director so that I could replace him. After the trustees had conducted the search that led to their appointment of him, they issued a report in which they indicated that I had been recommended for the post by three members of the faculty. After I read a copy of that report, I could see why someone with a very fertile mind and no love for me might have argued from the poolside story *and* that report that I was seeking to replace Kaysen. If I were, however, I certainly did not do anything that was calculated to win the support of the trustees. PS, I was never offered the job; and, PPS, I wouldn't have touched it with a ten-foot pole if it had been offered to me!

In April 1975, when the director submitted his resignation, to be effective at the end of June 1976, he wrote the faculty that he had resigned primarily in order to return to scholarly work, that ten years of academic administration and entrepreneurship had been enough, and that he wished to spend the next decade or two in more agreeable ways. He said he believed that he had accomplished one of the chief things he had set out to do: to create a first-rate School of Social Science worthy of taking its place in the Institute.

What else can I say? Much more, but I will content myself with saying this. My discussion of the director's role in the controversy will of course seem excessively harsh to him and his admirers, whereas, of course, my account of my own role will seem prejudiced to them. This is to be expected when one writes about a controversy that generated so much passion. But during the quarter of a century that has gone by, my own passion about it has diminished, and I should not be surprised to hear that the same is true of the former director. Today I am even willing to say things that might be thought by some to excuse his actions: for example, that his disappointment over not being able to expand his School of Social Science because of the faculty's rejection of Professor X in 1972 led him to ram through the nomination of Bellah as quickly as possible in 1973, mistakenly thinking that everything would soon blow over. Indeed, at a faculty meeting in November 1974, he came close to admitting such a mistake. In the past he said—in an obvious reference to the blowup—when he had not acted with deliberation and when the board had not acted with deliberation, it helped neither of them.

Even if one were moved to forgive or excuse Kaysen because he acted out of fear that social science at the Institute would collapse, one would have to acknowledge that his opponents were disturbed by actions of his that they thought would destroy or seriously diminish the academic standing of the Institute. I suppose that a very detached student of the battle might conclude that both sides were passionately pitted against each other in a conflict over which it would be folly to take sides today, but I confess that I find it difficult to be so Olympian even though I feel sorry for Kaysen. I think that he failed to act with sufficient deliberation in 1973 and that he should have instead taken what he had described as the simplest course: "to state that the bulk of the faculty does not support this nomination and, therefore, it should die." Fortunately, the Institute continues to live and prosper as I write these words, many years after I added very painful wounds to those I had suffered at Harvard in 1969.

23

Reflections of a Bridge Builder

My involvement in the acrimonious academic battles I have described reveals a trait of mine that has brought me a good deal of pain as well as satisfaction: pain for reasons that should be obvious to the reader, and satisfaction because I think that I have for the most part fought for worthy causes in my writing and during the academic controversies in which I have participated. Paradoxically, some might say, I have been a contentious separatist as well as a bridge builder, but I think I am more inclined to find or build bridges than to bomb them, as is evident in my long-standing interest in pursuing both the history of ideas and philosophy as well as in my desire to apply philosophy to issues arising in history, religion, politics, and education. The very title of my *Toward Reunion in Philosophy* of 1956 was intended to convey my belief that metaphysics, epistemology, and ethics should be carried on together and that certain divergent movements in twentieth-century philosophy could profitably resolve some of their differences of doctrine and emphasis. In that same book I argued—and still believe—that the traditional epistemological split between the testing of statements about what is and what ought to be, like that between analytic and synthetic statements, can and should be bridged; and I tried my best to do so in *What Is and What Ought to Be Done* in 1981 as well as in *The Question of Free Will* in 1993. I have sometimes wondered what there is in my history and makeup that sends me in that direction, but before I try to answer that question, I want to point out how much I have distanced myself from methodological dualism and other forms of intellectual segregationism.

This tendency of mine is evident in one of my first papers, "Historical Explanation," published in *Mind* in 1943. There I argued that since history as conceived by professional historians is primarily concerned with man's social behavior, historical explanation is not fundamentally different from sociological explanation; and a little later, in "The Revolt Against Formalism in American Social Thought of the Twentieth Century" of 1947 and in my book *Social Thought in America* of 1949, I worked simultaneously in philosophy and the history of ideas while examining the methodological and moral aspects of the work of five American social thinkers. I called special attention to *their* bridge building by labeling a common element in their work "cultural organicism," meaning their tendency to use the results of other disciplines while working in their own. I pointed to Holmes's interest in legal history as well as in law, and to the fact that he was the hero of what was once called sociological jurisprudence; I noted Veblen's concern with the anthropology and sociology of economic institutions; I called attention to Dewey's interest in what he called the cultural matrix of thinking and his effort to link the history of philosophy with a study of class divisions in the history of society; I pointed to James Harvey Robinson's view that history was not merely an examination of things as they really are but an effort at explaining how they came to be, which appealed to generalizing social science; and I emphasized that Beard was both a political scientist and a historian who said that in the place of an economic man, a religious man, and a political man, we must "observe the whole man participating in the work of government."

In 1950 I sounded a bridge builder's theme in "The Analytic and the Synthetic: An Untenable Dualism," which foreshadowed my rejection of a hard-and-fast positivistic distinction between philosophy viewed as a set of analytic statements that cannot be denied or revised by appealing to experience and science conceived as a set of synthetic statements that can be. This idea paralleled my view that analytic ethics should not be sharply separated from substantive or normative ethics, a view I defended in an article of 1952 called "The Social Role of Philosophy," where I criticized the notion that philosophers are forbidden by the very definition of their calling to be concerned with the substantive problems of moral criticism.

In 1955 I even tried to span the great divide between the deflationary analytic methods of Anglo-American thinking and the more expansive concerns of Continental philosophy while making clear in *The Age of Analysis* that although my methodological sympathies were with the analytic and linguistic philosophers of the Anglo-American world, I shared the substantive humanistic concerns of certain Continental thinkers. With this in mind I urged that the techniques of analysts and linguistic philosophers be applied to matters of interest to those Continental thinkers—for example, history, religion, and freedom—as I had tried to do in some of my own work. In *The Age of Analysis* I wrote that as long as the analytic techniques and the continental concerns

> are kept separate, as long as the custodians of philosophical technique develop axes with which to sharpen other axes, they risk developing a sense of weariness and emptiness in themselves and in those who read them. As long as the more literate and more cultivated devotees of philosophy persist in ignoring the great achievements of Russell, Moore, Carnap, and Wittgenstein, in forgetting that the giants of the old days to whom they look back nostalgically—Plato, Aristotle, Descartes, Locke, Hume, and Kant, for example—were tough, technical thinkers as well as men of feeling and vision, they will impede the revival of philosophy's strength. What Hegel saw in a Gothic dream and conveyed in a myth was a little close to the truth. For while a philosopher is not obliged to make himself an expert in all fields, and to produce dull or bogus summaries of all knowledge in the manner of Herbert Spencer or Hegel himself, he should be trained to discover the important similarities and the important differences between the chief activities of man. Knowing, as Bergson insisted, is not everything, and there are interesting general facts about feeling and doing which a philosopher might well relate to knowing—his main traditional concern. Should he heed the call to examine them without becoming a charlatan he will have done a great deal to bolster the strength of philosophy. We live in dreadful times, when a world in conflict seeks and despises that combination of technique and vision for which the great philosophers are justly famous; their successors should not shirk the responsibility to carry on with equal respect for logic and life.

As I have pointed out earlier, my interest in intellectual bridge building received a powerful boost when I came to see the wider significance of Pierre Duhem's idea that physicists test whole systems of belief rather than isolated beliefs. This idea was sharpened and extended by Alfred Tarski and by W. V.

Quine when they said that an experience that defies a prediction can lead even to the revision or abandonment of logical principles. A major consequence of their extension of Duhem's idea was the closing of a traditional epistemological gap between logic and natural science, but I pushed the idea even further by trying to close the gap between normative ethics and descriptive science in *Toward Reunion in Philosophy*, in *What Is and What Ought to Be Done*, and in *The Question of Free Will*.

My antiseparatistic interest in combining philosophy with the history of ideas grew stronger when I transferred from Harvard to the Institute for Advanced Study and shifted from a professorship in philosophy to one in historical studies. In writing *The Philosophy of the American Revolution* and *Philosophy, "The Federalist," and the Constitution* there, and thus examining the philosophy that was explicit or implicit in two documents that were not written by philosophers—the *Declaration of Independence* and *The Federalist*— I resumed the kind of boundary-crossing work I had done in *Social Thought in America*. I approached the views of nonphilosophers like Jefferson, Hamilton, and Madison as I had earlier approached the views of nonphilosophers like Beard, Veblen, and Holmes—in both cases trying to delineate their methodologies and their moral views. Although I am aware of the difficulty and danger of working in both philosophy and the history of ideas, and although I know that some of my critics think I have spread myself too thin by running all over the shop, so to speak, I think there has been an underlying unity in the medley of things I have done in my lifetime. I have never written two books on exactly the same subject, but I doubt that I would have written about so many different things—from analyticity to the American city—if there weren't some psychological trait or interest that tended to unite my seemingly divergent interests.

Why do I see bridges when others do not, and why do I try to build them when I think they should be built? Why have I gone on spanning or closing so many divides? I think the answer has something to do with why I went into philosophy. Like so many young people, I believed it would provide me with a guide to life. From earliest childhood my life was filled with so many disparate and discordant elements that I *had* to bring order and organization into it in order to achieve inner repose and freedom: variety may be the spice of life, but I could not live on spice alone. Since there was nothing in my childhood that I would call a religious impulse and since I had no serious religious training, I sought some other centripetal force that would hold things together for me. I realize, of course, that every young person may need something like that, but I think I needed it especially badly. I was an only

Jewish child who was separated from most other children in my predominantly Italian neighborhood because my parents, unlike those of my contemporaries, were born in America and were not immigrants; they had more
education (small as that was) than their neighbors, and what I had absorbed
from them set me apart from my schoolmates. It helped me skip through
elementary school in five years instead of eight, but each skip increased my
isolation from my classmates in size, physical strength, and sexual maturity.

When I entered high school at eleven in 1928, I attended classes with
many Jews whose parents were immigrants, whereas in elementary school I
had usually been the only Jew in my classes. There seemed to be no avoiding
estrangement and isolation. In 1932 my father went bankrupt, and so I came
to know what it was to be poor as well as lonely. I managed to get a job as a
runner on Wall Street during the summer of 1932 but lost it when I bothered
my immediate superior with too many smart-alecky questions about the stock
market that he could not answer. After I lost that job at fifteen, I developed
an acute anorexia that our family doctor could not understand or cure, so I
would gobble my food at supper in order to keep my parents ignorant of an
attack and to get out of the house as quickly as possible. When I tried to
escape my wretched surroundings altogether by going to an out-of-town
college, my parents informed me that they were unable to support me
financially and that I would have to go to the then free City College if I were
to go to any college at all. It is fair to say, then, that my life was in something
of an adolescent mess when I did enter City College in 1932. After a rocky
beginning in my freshman courses, I took one in philosophy during my
sophomore year that I liked. I did well in it and began to think that studying
it would help me sort things out for myself. I soon discovered, however, that
although I enjoyed what little philosophy I learned, it would not do very
much to bring order into my chaotic life. My teachers were more interested,
as one of them said, in leading students out of the intellectual desert than
into the promised land or even, I might add, to a map of that land.

When I was eighteen, in 1935, and about to begin my senior year at
college, I became a Marxist, partly to put some structure into my life and
partly to escape loneliness by meeting other young people, especially girls. In
doing so I may have unconsciously acknowledged that my Marxism was a
substitute for what others saw in religion and, as Dewey had said so often, that
religion arises from a human need to share experiences. Although I never
formally joined any of the radical student groups at City College, I accepted
a goodly part of their system of ideas, which seemed to answer almost every
large question that I might ask. It offered dialectical materialism to a

philosophical novice who had no more than a smattering of metaphysics and epistemology; it offered historical materialism as a theory that would bring order to the tangled confusion of the past; it supplied a *déclassé* boy with an ethical theory that said that a right action was one that would hasten the triumph of the working class into which he had fallen; it professed to explain why we had economic crashes and depressions and how to avoid them; it reinforced my budding atheism by persuading me that religion was the opiate of the people; it even offered the rudiments of an aesthetic doctrine. In short, it seemed to provide me with tools for solving most of the problems that filled my juvenile head and with a social life to boot. It told me where I came from, where I was, where I was going, and where I should be going; and in its Stalinist form it assured me that the big battalions of the Soviet Union would push everyone in the direction of a classless society.

Marxism continued to exert a hold on me even after I had developed enough philosophical sense at nineteen to see the absurdity of dialectical materialism and enough political sense to realize that Stalinism was a form of tyranny. At twenty I became a fellow traveler of an anti-Stalinist Marxist splinter group that imposed no philosophical orthodoxy, but soon after that I separated myself from most of the Marxian doctrines upon which I had seized in my attempt to find friends and to pull myself together. In my late twenties, during my two-year stint in Philadelphia, my distaste for those doctrines was made more acute by contact with provincial dogmatists who thought their version of Marxism would save the world. When I abandoned my Marxist views, however, I did not abandon my interest in bringing things together; I merely came to realize that Marxism could not do that job satisfactorily for me. I went on thinking philosophically about history, law, ethics, politics, and religion but did so under the aegis of the positivistic idea that a philosopher should study the language used in the different disciplines that Marx called parts of ideology and also under the aegis of the *anti*positivistic idea that philosophical beliefs are not tested in a manner completely different from that in which we test beliefs in history and the sciences. I was more and more attracted by the cultural organicism of my American rebels against formalism, but I did not realize that their organicism had been indirectly preparing me for the epistemological holism that I came to accept under the influence of Tarski and Quine.

In 1985, while preparing my Neesima Lectures at Doshisha University in Kyoto, I happened on a passage of Duhem's that led me to recall that in *Social Thought in America* I had labeled Beard, Dewey, Holmes, and Veblen organicists well before Duhem's holism had seriously affected my thinking. I came to see a connection between his holism and the sort of organicism I had talked about in *Social Thought in America*, since Duhem had said—in a passage to which I had paid no special attention when I first read him as an undergraduate—that physical science was an organism and not a machine. I also noticed that Duhem's organicism was connected with a view of Herbert Spencer's, a philosopher who had influenced some of my rebels against formalism and who had once written in his *First Principles*: "Every thought involves a whole system of thoughts, and ceases to exist if severed from its various correlatives. As we cannot isolate a single organ of a single body, and deal with it as though it had a life independent of the rest; so from the organized structure of our cognitions, we cannot cut out one, and proceed as though it had survived the separation" (p. 121). Learning of this similarity between the organicism of Spencer and Duhem, and recalling the organicism of my rebels against formalism, brought home to me a previously unnoticed link between my earlier historical work in *Social Thought in America* and my later philosophical work in *Toward Reunion in Philosophy*, *What Is and What Ought to Be Done*, and *The Question of Free Will*. I came to see that there was more intellectual continuity between my early historical work and my later philosophical work than I had realized. I came to see that my earlier study of the revolt against formalism had prepared the way for my later acceptance of holism, and to see how antiformalism and holism were related to my Marxism.

However, because my experience with Marxism had been disappointing, my later bridge building became more intra-intellectual and intra-academic in character. My interest in linking my philosophy with political action declined, and instead I linked it more and more with action in the academic world by throwing myself passionately into the 1958 chapel controversy at Harvard, the 1969 battle at Harvard, and the 1973 battle at the Institute. This retreat is in retrospect a source of disappointment to me because I have come more and more to think that nations, races, ethnic groups, religions, and classes are arrayed against each other in a way that demands more contact than ever between philosophy and society. In my earliest years I had turned to philosophy primarily to unify my personal life, whereas later, when I had become more convinced than ever that it should help improve the world, I found myself using my philosophical wits to make little Harvard and the littler Institute better places, or at least to prevent them from becoming worse places. Without doubt the failure of democratic socialism had something to do with my retreat, but I console myself by telling myself that I have struck a few good blows for freedom in the grove of academe, that my bridge building may have done something to make philosophy and history better disciplines, and that I have encouraged some students to apply the tools of philosophy to humane subjects and others to study the connection between the history of philosophy and the wider history of thought—in short that I have crossed, and have encouraged others to cross, bridges I have discovered or have tried my hardest to build.

24

East Side, West Side, All Around the World

My opposition to intellectual segregationism extended to my teaching inasmuch as I taught all kinds of students in philosophy and in the history of ideas, both here and abroad. I did not limit myself to teaching graduate students even though I was an active researcher and writer. As a teacher of Harvard undergraduates I not only lectured to large freshman classes but was sought out as a tutor of seniors because I had (rightly or wrongly) acquired the reputation of being a good coach of thesis writers—for example, David Souter and Ronald Dworkin—and as their supporter in faculty discussions that determined what honors they would receive upon graduation. I also encouraged graduate students like Stanley Cavell, Burton Dreben, and Marshall Cohen, who successfully applied for junior fellowships in the Society of Fellows with my support. In addition to moving up, down, and across the educational spectrum at Harvard, I made many trips abroad, where I also roamed widely. In the same spirit, when I came to the Institute as a professor of historical studies, I did not limit myself to sponsoring specialists on Peirce, James, and Dewey but also supported applications from experts on Locke, Descartes, Hume, Berkeley, Kant, Leibniz, Husserl, and even Heidegger.

I do not wish to exaggerate the extent to which my teaching different kinds of students both here and abroad was the product of my having been born and reared on the polyglot Lower East Side, but I think my life in New York prefigured to some extent my later willingness to travel to foreign lands. Rubbing elbows with many different kinds of people while walking the streets, attending school, and selling shoes in my father's store prepared me in some degree for that. At about nine or ten I once tried desperately to fit house slippers on a Chinese woman with bound feet; I remember a Greek restaurant on Madison Street whose front window bore Greek letters that I deciphered with difficulty as meaning "café"; and I knew native Irishmen who spoke with a heavy brogue. I remember a Russian tailor's shop less than a block away from us; I can recall Poles buying shoes from my father; and I can clearly picture the leader of a small group of Lower East Side Spaniards vociferously arguing with him about politics. I was often taken to Lüchow's, a famous German restaurant on Fourteenth Street, to an Italian restaurant on Catherine Street called the Florence, to a Greek-owned ice-cream parlor on Park Row called the Elite (we pronounced it "the Ee-light"), and to Chinese restaurants on Mott, Pell, Doyers Streets and the Bowery—some of them in dingy basements, others divided into private nooks that one entered through curtains made of strings of shiny glass beads. Because of this cosmopolitan childhood—my mother once called an especially variegated collection of our customers "a regular League of Nations"—my foreign travels held fewer terrors for me than they might have if I had not lived on the Lower East Side.

I felt more at home when I visited London and Bellagio in later years than I had felt earlier in Rapid City, Tensleep, or Reno, where Lucia, I, and the boys stopped en route to a philosophical conference in Monterey, California. That trip to Monterey in 1950 was soon followed by my 1951 trip to England, and in 1952 Lucia and I made a trip to Japan that inaugurated the series of our many journeys to that country. Then in 1953–54 the whole family went to Princeton so that I could take up my visiting membership at the very international Institute for Advanced Study; and in the summer of 1955 we all turned up at the Seminar in American Studies at Salzburg, Austria, where I taught philosophy to an odd assortment of Europeans. After that, an unusually long time elapsed before I went off on a yearlong junket to the Stanford Center for Advanced Studies in the Behavioral Sciences in 1959–60. But immediately after that we flew from the West Coast to Japan, where I gave a seminar in the summer of 1960, and two years later I was back at the Institute for Advanced Study for the academic year 1962–63. In 1965–66 I took leave from Harvard in order to serve as a full-time consultant to Educational Services Incorporated on a project to revise the American high school curriculum. In the spring of 1966 I used my vacation from that job in order to conduct a seminar in Tokyo for a number of Japanese professors whom I had earlier taught in their own country or in Cambridge. I spent the spring term of 1967–68 and the fall term of 1968–69 at the Institute for Advanced Study on the last of my Harvard leaves; this was the last of my visits to the Institute before becoming permanently connected with it. After transferring to the Institute, I went abroad to lecture again in Tokyo as well as in Oslo, Zagreb, and Madrid, and I spent a month at the opulent Villa Serbelloni in Bellagio, courtesy of the Rockefeller Foundation.

In passing I should say that my travels from Harvard to distant parts of the world were the subject of much humor and resentment, as were those of Quine. I was once told that the Harvard Corporation passed a rule limiting leaves of absence because of our peregrinations, a rule that some called the Quine-White Rule. A Boston journalist who complained about how the Harvard faculty was away an awful lot reported that it wasn't the well-supported scientists who were the greatest sinners, but rather two philosophers, of all people, who managed to be away more than anybody else on the faculty. Some critics had a way of forgetting that some of my traveling had been done during my summer vacations; that I had been asked at a relatively young age to take over the chairmanship of a department when an older person should have done so; that the administration had put me on an unusually large number of time-consuming committees; that I gave a great deal of energy to teaching in General Education; that I directed a goodly share of the Ph.D. theses in my department; and that unlike most full professors I even gave a so-called freshman seminar. Furthermore, I used several of my leaves to work on books that I published and was therefore not particularly embarrassed by having been away from Harvard; my trips were seldom vacations.

Even in faraway Tokyo I could put some of my East Side cosmopolitanism to work. Although I knew of the great differences between the Japanese and the Chinese, I overcame some of my anxieties in Tokyo by seizing on whatever similarities I could see between the Japanese there and the Chinese I knew, in order to make myself feel more at home during my first visit Japan in 1952. I was there to teach at Tokyo University in a program of American studies under the auspices of a committee of professors at Tokyo and Stanford Universities, and with the financial support of the Rockefeller Foundation. Five American professors from different fields in the humanities and the social sciences went over as a team to teach during the summer. In that year, economics, history, and political science were represented by Stanford professors, while I taught philosophy and my Harvard colleague Perry Miller taught literature in graduate seminars that met daily for four weeks. This trip to Japan was followed by several others that Lucia and I described at length in *Journeys to the Japanese: 1952–1979*.

My next foreign trip, to Salzburg in 1955, was more closely linked with my East Side past because my father's father had emigrated to America from the Austro-Hungarian Empire, but when I contemplated the wide variety of students I taught in Salzburg, I knew at once from my experience as a shoe salesman on Catherine Street that the now deceased American administrator of the seminar was not treating his customers properly. Far from representing a side of American life that I thought the Europeans should see because they saw so little of it, the director fit the unfortunate stereotypes of Americans to which European students were only too accustomed. He was a heavyset, red-faced man of fifty with a pronounced lisp, very dark horn-rimmed spectacles, and an extraordinary capacity to rush into things like a bull. He behaved like an auto salesman, and instead of getting the Europeans to see that Americans were not all mechanical materialists, he encouraged that stereotype in the students' minds. He issued an elaborate brochure of rules on the first day and then, to make matters worse, mentioned those rules constantly during meals. Oddly enough, he seemed to realize that he was interrupting us with announcements that he could have made in a less annoying way; he would almost always preface his remarks with some highly self-conscious and self-derogating comment about how he couldn't prevent himself from speaking and how we must have been tired of hearing him. To make matters worse, he would ring a dreadful gong before each announcement and was soon jeered at and scorned by the entire group when he rose to ring and speak.

His opening speech was a remarkable example of what not to do under the circumstances. He informed the students that the seminar was poor, that it was giving the students much more than they paid for with their tuition fees, that the professors were sacrificing themselves and working for no pay because of their dedication to the cause of education. Often he gave the students the impression that they were charity cases, and would make matters worse by telling them not to plug in extra electrical appliances, not to awaken the castellan after twelve, and not to make unnecessary noise. I could not help thinking as I listened to him how much better the speeches of my American director in Tokyo had been. They too were tedious, of course, but our man in Tokyo was able to speak in a way that did not feed fuel to the prejudices of the students, that did not confirm their notions of the American as a soulless machine who was interested only in gadgets and money.

Although some of my experiences in Salzburg put me in mind of my life in New York, some of my students were not represented very conspicuously on the streets of my New York. For example, I had never met a Yugoslav in school or in my father's shop, but in Salzburg I met a very intelligent Marxist from Zagreb University who worked primarily in metaphysics and epistemology. He wore dark-rimmed glasses with thick lenses, his complexion was slightly sallow, and his expression alternated between a dull stare and one that suggested great pain. However, when I asked him whether he was married, he said yes with a big smile, and when I asked him whether he had any children, he said yes with an even bigger smile. He had two children and was an assistant at Zagreb, and I had broken the Balkan ice by using a device that I had seen my father use—by getting him to talk about the wife and the kids he obviously loved. This Yugoslav was the late Gajo Petrović, whom I came to know very well in later years. He visited Harvard while he was traveling through the States in 1962, and he impressed me as a highly intelligent and decent human being. He was an editor of the journal *Praxis* and was thought to be one of the best Yugoslav philosophers of his generation. When I saw him while he was a visiting member of the Institute in 1975, I could share neither his views on Marx and Heidegger nor some of the philosophical ideas he had developed after his Salzburg days, yet I encouraged him even though my catholic support of him was not appreciated by some of my analytically oriented friends and colleagues.

That catholicity may have been fostered by my own small-c catholic childhood, which in turn may have fostered not only my globe-trotting but my propensity to cross conventional boundaries in philosophy and in life. I was a Jew who fell in love with, married, and for more than a half century lived happily with a Gentile; I was a philosopher who worked in history and who denied that there is a sharp distinction between the analytic and the synthetic; and I united my interest in technical philosophy with the history of ideas, the philosophy of history, of religion, of education, of law, and of politics. I saw a lot of boundary crossing along with a lot of interethnic salesmanship and politics in my father's store. Even though I was a merchant's son who did not want to become a merchant, the store prepared me to some extent for international travel, for interdisciplinary travel, and for teaching different kinds of students. My travel continued after I joined the faculty of the Institute for Advanced Study, whose founders may have provided travel funds to professors under the indirect influence of Descartes. In his *Discourse* he spoke well of his visits to courts and armies, his intercourse with men of different dispositions and ranks, and the variety of experiences he had while testing himself in the different situations into which fortune had thrown him. Although I did not visit courts and armies in 1976, I did use my funds to travel to Italy, a country about which I had heard much when I lived on Catherine Street.

Herbert Hart had once spoken enthusiastically to me about a conference he had attended at the Rockefeller Foundation's Villa Serbelloni on Lake Como. He described it in 1960 as a fantastic place, a mixture of American gracious living and English country house, and I confirmed this when, in the summer of 1976, Lucia and I spent a month there in the company of about thirty scholars, writers, and their spouses. The director of the villa supervised it with the help of his spouse, and it was as remarkable as Herbert had said it was. It was situated high above the little town of Bellagio and had lovely gardens, extremely comfortable living quarters, individual studies in the surrounding woods, an excellent table and good wines, a tennis court, and excellent views of the lake. Residents were served breakfast in their rooms; they came to a fine luncheon at midday; and at supper they were wined and dined in high style after enjoying cocktails and splendid views of the lovely lake beneath them. Those who liked to walk could explore the ruins of a nearby Roman villa or could wend their way down and up the steep hill leading to the town. Even though Bellagio was very different from Sicily— the birthplace of most of the Italians in my old neighborhood—I felt very much at home with the northerners who lived near Lake Como. Their gestures, their looks, and their ways of talking and walking seemed unmis- takably Italian to me no matter how contemptuous of Sicilians they might be, and I felt that the waiters, the gardeners, and other members of the villa staff were more attractive and more fun than the more elevated staff at Serbelloni—in part because of my humble origins and in part because Lucia felt that we were treated as she had been at boarding school when we were told by the director that we could not leave the villa for more than a day trip.

That order did not sit well with us, nor did the formal arrangements at the dinner table. The evening meal was the chain that tied residents to each other intellectually, and "chain" is just the right word. Our seating was arranged by the director's wife, who put place cards at the long banquet table every night and who for some reason often seated me next to someone who was not a philosopher but who kept trying to engage me in conversation about the philosophy of Whitehead. Since Whitehead was a thinker I had not seriously studied, I was embarrassed by my inability to understand or answer my companion's queries and would unsuccessfully try my damnedest to change the subject. I came to dread the prospect of sitting next to her at dinner, a prospect that made the lunch without place cards a happy occasion before which I rushed around madly to find a seat near people I could stand and understand.

There was one resident of the Villa whom I found absolutely delightful and whom I would sit with any time, and that was V. S. Pritchett—"Victor" as he asked to be called, never "Sir Victor." He was then seventy-six years old, a remarkably easygoing and "regular guy" in the language of New York; it was always a pleasure to be with him. Most often we would talk about people we both knew, for example, A. J. Ayer, who was Victor's neighbor in London; Isaiah Berlin, his fellow specialist in Russian literature; my colleague at the Institute, George Kennan; and Lionel Trilling. After leaving Bellagio, I read Pritchett's autobiography—*A Cab at the Door*—and was intrigued to learn that as a young man he had worked in the leather business, something very close to the business in which I had spent my childhood. Maybe our backgrounds in leather helped me feel at home with him as much as I did. Ironically, he was an English knight whom I enjoyed being with because his background resembled mine on the Lower East Side. My theory about the relation between my childhood experience and my latter-day travels was more than confirmed when I met someone at the villa who knew the difference between Russia calf and Vici kid!

My next foreign adventure, which was very different from the one in Italy, occurred when I lectured in Norway in 1978 under the auspices of my one-time Harvard graduate student and sometime colleague there, Dagfinn Føllesdal. He was professor of philosophy at Oslo and a great mediator between Norwegian philosophers who looked to the Anglo-American world and those who looked to Germany for leadership. Unfortunately, he was not in Oslo during most of the time I was there but rather at Stanford, where he also taught regularly. If he had been at all five of my lectures instead of two, the discussion would have been as lively at all of them as it was at the two he attended. They were entitled "Existence, Necessity, and Value" and were heard almost exclusively by graduate students, who were much more sympathetic to my way of thinking than the more senior members of the Department of Philosophy, most of whom did *not* hear them. From Føllesdal I learned that the two most senior philosophers—he was the third—were heavily influenced by German idealism and that *three* courses on the German philosopher Fichte were being given in the department that year.

While I stayed in Oslo under the auspices of the Norwegian Research Council, I was treated cordially by Nils Roll-Hansen, who was interested in the history and philosophy of biology, and by Jon Elster, an able philosopher of social science who chose to accept a post in the Historisk Institutt rather than one in the Institutt for Filosofi because he was put off by the dominance of German thought in the Department of Philosophy. I should emphasize, however, that Føllesdal did not oppose the study of German philosophy, since he is one of the most sympathetic analytically oriented students of Husserl that I know; and I should add that Elster made some very acute comments on one of my lectures, which were devoted to clarifying some of the ideas I had advanced earlier in *Toward Reunion in Philosophy*. In Oslo I was led to rethink and reformulate those ideas in a way that is evident in my later book *What Is and What Ought to Be Done*, where I use a holistic or corporatist theory of knowledge to question the sharp distinction between the way in which we test descriptive and normative statements. While in Oslo I tried to carry out my promise in *The Age of Analysis* to use Anglo-American analytic techniques to deal with some of the concerns of nonanalytic Continental thinkers, and despite my less-than-enthusiastic comments about Husserl in that book, I like to think that my efforts in this direction were not unlike Føllesdal's attempt to link the work of Husserl with that of the analytic tradition.

Føllesdal made his usual world-girdling trip from Palo Alto to Oslo two weeks before our departure and while in Norway invited us to dinner at his home in Sandvika, a suburb of Oslo. Before driving us home, he generously gave his entire day to us. He drove us all over Oslo, taking us not only to Holmenkollen, the great ski jump outside of town, but also to the Munch museum. These places, we thought, represented the two very different Norways—the outer, dazzling, daylight, ski-happy land and the inner, dark, psychotic screaming one of Munch's subjects. Seeing these two sides of the country on the same day rounded out a visit during which I thought I was observing two analogous tendencies in Norway's philosophers: their interest in logico-analytical Anglo-American thinking and their very different one in the philosophy of Fichte. Though I was a unionist in philosophy, I did not envy Føllesdal in his desire to heal this breach in his country's thought.

Upon leaving Oslo in the spring of 1978, we set out by rail for Zagreb, to which Gajo Petrović had invited me almost twenty-five years after I had taught him in Salzburg. During the intervening years he had established himself as an internationally known Marxist thinker as well as a sympathetic student of Heidegger. I had seen him on a couple of his visits to the States, and I continued to like and admire him personally even though I had long since lost my interest in Marxism and had never been interested in Heidegger. Petrović and his charming wife, Asja, were absolutely marvelous to us.

Gajo insisted upon picking up checks at restaurants and paying for taxis; he even tried (unsuccessfully) to pay for books that I had bought in a local store and introduced me to the Zagreb publisher of the Serbo-Croatian translation of my *Social Thought in America*. His name was Josip Malić and his firm was Školska knjiga, one of the largest in Yugoslavia. He was a husky, blunt, aggressive fellow who had greatly improved his firm's list and its standing among readers. He reminded me of the pictures of the young Tito: stout, imposing, handsome. He wore a brushlike moustache, was fair of complexion, and stood close to six feet tall. In our Middle West he might have been taken for a miner or a steelworker.

When Gajo Petrović picked me up to take me to Malić's luncheon party for me, Gajo was accompanied by a tall, suave, beret-wearing man, Vjekoslav Mikecin, editor of the series in which the translation of my *Social Thought in America* later appeared. His main intellectual interest, according to Petrović, was "the sociology of culture, Italian style," whatever that was. However, he spoke French, and that was the language in which he and I communicated. Mikecin was extremely deferential in the presence of Malić, whom he always called M. le Directeur, but even the brave Petrović showed inordinate deference to Malić, who had published some of his books. Petrović told me that Malić had begun his career as a schoolteacher and that he had once attended a large logic course given by Petrović, who, although he did not remember Malić as a student, had discovered by looking at his records that he had given him a rather poor grade. Malić, Petrović told me with some amusement, never spoke to him about their connection in the past, and Petrović was equally silent about it.

After picking me up at the hotel, Petrović and Mikecin walked me to Malić's office, which was being renovated. We were greeted by a receptionist-secretary who dutifully asked the director whether he would see us. When she gained his assent, she led us into his office, where he invited us to sit down at a coffee table in a high-ceilinged dusty room that was filled with books. Malić apologized for its condition, remarked acidly on the renovation going on, and asked us to pay no attention to the carpenters who kept entering and leaving the room. After his secretary served us some fruit juice, the director, who spoke no English and did not venture to speak French or German, began to talk with me through Gajo, who served as interpreter for both of us. After showing me some of the books he had published, Malić proudly presented to me a copy of *My Inventions*, by the Yugoslav electrical engineer Nikola Tesla, who came to America at the end of the nineteenth century and worked with Edison.

After this introductory session we ambled over to a grottolike restaurant called Split, where the conversation over lunch was disconnected, not only because of the alcohol we consumed but also because I spoke no Serbo-Croatian, the director spoke no English, and Mikecin insisted on speaking French. After I recovered from that Yugoslav counterpart of a New York publisher's lunch by resting all afternoon in the hotel, my cicerone, Petrović, led me to a lecture hall in the University of Zagreb, where I was to give a paper to the Croatian Philosophical Society. When we entered the building, we were greeted by a cloakroom attendant, a figure I had not seen in an American university since the thirties and forties. After he relieved us of our raincoats and umbrellas, we mounted a flight of stairs and entered a large seminar room that was completely filled with students and faculty. There was an air of excitement about the meeting that reminded me of left-wing meetings in the New York of my youth. It was attended by almost as many women as men, which was certainly not the case at my Oslo lectures. A goodly number of senior philosophers turned out, and Petrović was very happy about this. Before the meeting began, he introduced me to two young men who spoke English very well; one of them was to be my interpreter, and the other was writing a thesis on the logician Gottlob Frege. The interpreter asked me to summarize my lecture to him and, on the basis of my summary, he decided to translate sizable chunks of English at a time, not to translate sentence by sentence. The interpretation, he said, was mainly for the benefit of the older members of the audience, since the younger ones all knew English. Because I was suffering from a cold, I decided that I would not read a paper but deliver a brief extemporaneous talk based on a written lecture I had delivered in Oslo. Once again I advanced the holistic view that in science we test conjunctions, rather than single statements, against experience and that we do the same thing in ethics. I defended this view with more verve than I could muster in Oslo because I was more stimulated by the interest shown by all the philosophers of Zagreb.

After my lecture I was complimented by some in the audience, but when Lucia asked Petrović the next day how the lecture had gone, that usually phlegmatic man said: "It was fantastic" or "It was fabulous." I thought he was exaggerating, but I also thought that, even after discounting his generous remark, I would wind up with pretty good grades. When Gajo and Asja Petrović walked me back to my hotel, they expected that we would all have drinks together, but I was really exhausted and declined with apologies. I also felt that Lucia had been alone for too long nursing her cold in the hotel, so I left my companions and took the elevator up to our room. I sighed a sigh of relief and rejoiced in the thought that my lecture was over. I could not easily link Yugoslavia with the New York of my childhood, and what little contact I had with it did not prepare me for the violence that has since emerged there, violence, I regret to say, that was supported and justified by a philosopher in Belgrade who had often visited America.

In 1981 I published a defense of my ethical views in *What Is and What Ought to Be Done*, and soon after that was invited to lecture in Madrid by Victor Pérez-Díaz, a sociologist whom I had come to know in 1975–76 when he was a member of the School of Social Science at the Institute. I accepted and decided to talk about some problems I had discussed in my book. Victor and his wife, Marina, had lived in our house in Princeton during the second term of 1975–76, when I was on leave; they had become good friends of ours, and so we were very glad to fly to Madrid in 1983 in order for me to give a lecture to Victor's seminar in May. Soon after arriving in Madrid we dined at the apartment of Victor and Marina, and we learned of their disappointment with a socialist government that was then too authoritarian for their tastes. They had courageously risked a great deal as youthful opponents of Franco, but what they now faced, they said, was very different from what they had fought for. A familiar story, we thought. After dinner, Victor drove us to our hotel, and we tumbled into bed, reeling from a combination of jet lag and good Spanish wine, and depressed by the political disappointments of our friends.

On Tuesday, May 17, at five o'clock in the afternoon, I gave my defense of my holistic view of ethics. The comments and questions after it turned out to be more interesting than I expected. One man said that the expression "human being" in the statement "No human being ought to be killed" was not descriptive, as I believed, but normative. I defended my view that it was descriptive on the grounds that a moral principle like "No human being ought to be killed" could not be applied to actions unless we could *describe* what actions were said by the principle to be obligatory, namely, actions of not killing a human being. Ethics, I said, would become totally divorced from the world if we could not say in descriptive language just what actions were prescribed or proscribed. The next speaker claimed in a related vein that my antidualism with regard to normative and descriptive statements required a rejection of *any* distinction between normative and descriptive statements. To this I replied that I held that whereas some statements described actions and others said they ought to be performed, these two kinds of statements were *not tested differently*. Therefore, I said, I was not rejecting *all* distinctions between the descriptive and the normative.

After the lecture our hosts took us to a restaurant, where I talked with the very bright, very witty, and very amiable Angel Rojo, a high-ranking economist at the Bank of Spain whom we once jokingly called "Uncle Rocco" because his name sounded that way to us when we were first introduced to him. He told some amusing stories about Karl Popper, whose seminar at the London School of Economics he had once attended. One was quite funny. Evidently one of Popper's books had been reviewed unfavorably in a philosophical journal, a copy of which Popper waved as he shouted: "They have attacked me again. You Watkins, and you Lakatos, I will give you one hour to refute this!" Whereupon, said Rojo, the two acolytes left the seminar and returned with their "refutations." These the master dismissed as incorrect, so he proceeded to refute his critics himself. On the whole I found Spain much more interesting than I had expected it to be. It was culturally removed from what I had known in a New York that had not yet been populated by Latin Americans. I was, both literally and figuratively, traveling in really foreign territory from my point of view. There were few cultural straps I could hold onto in the subway train, so to speak, and therefore I concentrated my energies on expounding my philosophical ideas. Some of the responses to my lectures showed me that many in my audience agreed with me that certain distinctions in philosophy were as objectionable as certain political, ethnic, and religious divisions in the world. I was therefore led to think that I had not wasted my time by trying to disseminate a philosophy that questioned indefensible intellectual divisions that lent support to morally indefensible social divisions. This attitude of mine I associated with the egalitarianism and with the small-d democratic cosmopolitanism that I had known as a child on the sidewalks of New York. I had come a long way from Catherine Street, which had in some respects, but not all, prepared me for a life of intellectual bridge building.

25

Luck in the Grove of Academe

> Athens, the eye of Greece, mother of arts
> And eloquence, native to famous wits
> Or hospitable, in her sweet recess,
> City or suburban, studious walks and shades;
> See there the olive grove of Academe,
> Plato's retirement, where the Attic bird
> Trills her thick-warbled notes the summer long.
> —John Milton, *Paradise Regained*, bk. iv, line 240

Luck or good fortune played an enormous part during my rough ride from Catherine Street, especially my luck in meeting friends or admirers who helped me overcome seemingly insuperable obstacles along the way. Since I had seen so much brutality at the corner of Madison and Catherine Streets, I hoped and believed that life in the grove of Academe would be very different from what I had known on the streets of the Lower East Side. Of course I witnessed less physical cruelty when I entered the academic world—since students and professors rarely beat each other up in those days—but I was naive enough to suppose that I would meet almost no cruelty at all among professors, and how wrong I was! Their brutality was more refined than what I had known in the First Assembly District of Manhattan but no less painful. I experienced nastiness and meanness at the hands of academic teachers and colleagues, and I regret to say that I was sometimes nasty and mean myself. I can see this in my earliest book reviews, which I now read with sympathy for my victims. The belligerent tone of my writing harmonized with much of what I read in radical magazines of the thirties and forties, and when I wrote for them, I was often moved to elevate the brutality of Catherine Street to what Hegel would have called a higher level—higher, of course, in a Pickwickian sense.

Although academics administered beatings that were no less cruel than those administered by Lower East Side bullies, academics were on the whole less courageous than those bullies. Professorial meanness may have been a spiritual form of the beating my boyhood friends engaged in, but professors did not usually have the moral courage that is the counterpart of the physical courage I saw in the streets. Though it is sometimes said that physical bullies are cowards who will run when they are struck, I did not find this to be the rule on Catherine Street. Most of the tough guys I knew did not run away from physical danger or from each other's blows, but I cannot say the same thing about the academic bullies I knew: more often than not they were moral cowards, as I learned bitterly during the academic battles in which I have fought. I might add that the most bullying book reviewers I knew were the most frightened and upset by hostile notices of their own books. I recall—only with a little amusement—the reaction of the combative Sidney Hook to my adverse review of his book on John Dewey in the *Partisan Review*, especially Hook's whining complaint that Dwight Macdonald should not have given the book to a mere stripling like me! I also recall how shaken Ernest Nagel—perhaps the fiercest philosophical reviewer of his day—was when his book *Gödel's Proof* was sharply attacked by two distinguished logicians in their reviews of it. As we used to say on Catherine Street, Sidney and Ernest could dish it out, but they couldn't take it.

My readers know of course that professors who become academic administrators often lack moral courage or practical wisdom. Several of my bosses often lacked the qualities I thought they had when I looked up to them in my innocent youth; they lacked the sagacity they would have needed to get elected sheriff, as Lyndon Johnson once said of some of his academic advisers. Or, as my father used to say, they often lacked the brains to get themselves arrested, and I was unlucky enough to have been passengers of theirs or to have served on their crews in very stormy seas. Even McGeorge Bundy, one of the brightest academic administrators I ever served under, lacked some of the savvy that my father would have regarded as indispensable in a politician, whether academic or not. A story will illustrate my point. When Paul Tillich became university professor at Harvard, Dean Bundy asked me, when I was chairman, whether the Department of Philosophy would invite Tillich to teach a course for it, since the administration could not appoint him to do that without departmental approval. Like most of my colleagues, I did not think much of Tillich's philosophical firepower, but unlike them I thought he was a charming man, and I knew that the students would fill his classroom to the rafters even if he were to give a fuzzy course on post-Kantian German idealism, something that no member of my department could or would teach. So I went to my colleagues and persuaded them to invite Tillich to teach one course for us. When Bundy asked me to thank them for doing what he had asked them to do, I said to him that he was crazy if he thought that I had told my colleagues that *he* had instigated the plan to appoint Tillich, adding bluntly that if I had told them *that*, they would never have let Tillich teach the course. To his credit, Bundy roared with laughter.

I should admit that my need for luck was not only made necessary by the failings of some of my teachers and leaders but also by my own outspokenness and lack of tact. I must have done something to cause my superiors at Columbia to let me go after they had awarded me their highest academic prizes, something to arouse the animosity of some of my colleagues at Penn, something to irritate Pusey and the Harvard professors with whom I disagreed during the chapel controversy and the bust, and something to make some trustees of the Institute for Advanced Study wish I had never set foot in the place. I was once told that when Pusey heard about my role in the big battle at the Institute, he said I was up to my troublemaking again; and only recently an ex-trustee of the Institute told me that in 1973 I was the biggest thorn in the board's side. So, although my need for luck was partly my own doing, I like to think that my colleague André Weil was right in telling me that during the battle at the Institute my outspokenness was attracting as many admirers as detractors. If it did attract admirers, I count that as another piece of luck.

When I ask myself how I ever managed to escape from Catherine Street and the Lower East Side, I tell myself that several unpredictable events prevented me from becoming a shoe salesman or a Tammany political hack. One of the most important of these of course was my meeting Lucia in 1938. She lived most of my life with me, helped me recall much of it while writing this book, and carefully edited much of what I have written here. She had been helping me in this way for almost fifty-six years when she died after a long illness on March 29, 1996. Our marriage was a very improbable one, but we managed to upset all the pessimistic predictions that people made about its future. How, then, did we manage to live together so happily for so many years? The truth is that our different religious backgrounds did not divide us, because we had both given up religion; conventional morality did not divide us, because we were not morally conventional; and money did not divide us, because we had no interest in luxuries that someone of her background might have had. Our understanding and love of each other was reinforced by a half century of intellectual collaboration except when she was felled by bouts of depression, which plagued her throughout her life. During these episodes I tried to help her in a way that complemented what she did for me, but it is ironic that she taught me how to live in society even though her shyness often made her uncomfortable in it, and equally ironic that I, whom she tutored in the ways of society, would often have to protect her from it.

Soon after I met Lucia, I was lucky enough to take a summer course with W. V. Quine at Harvard; another stroke of good fortune came when Herbert Wechsler appointed me as his NYA assistant at Columbia; a third came when the Second World War brought G. E. Moore and Tarski to these shores; yet another came when in 1942 a job in the Columbia Department of Philosophy opened up for me at the last minute; and one more was my meeting Henry Aiken while we were both teaching at Columbia. His presence there was itself improbable, and when he later went to Harvard, he quickly began a dicey campaign to bring me there. Another piece of good fortune led me to an interest in the history of social ideas and to B. W. Huebsch's publication of *Social Thought in America*. After it appeared, I got to know historians of American life at Harvard who became loyal supporters of mine. That was a bit of luck because philosophers with my analytical inclinations rarely worked in the history of social ideas, and I know that my work in that subject accelerated my rise at Harvard. Luck also played a part in my meeting Isaiah Berlin there in 1949 and in his appointment to the Ad Hoc Committee that voted my promotion. The collocation of all these miraculously intervening events helped me move from unemployment when I married in 1940 to an associate professorship at Harvard in 1950, and my good fortune continued when Harold Cherniss led the campaign to bring me to the Institute in 1970. I call this good fortune because a philosopher and historian of ideas with my views and interests was not very likely to attract the support of a classical philologist who worked on Plato and agreed with him—as I did not.

Of course, my benefactors were influenced by their respect for my ideas or my writings, but I think that there was more to their support than that. If I had not been lucky enough to gain their affection, I would not have escaped philosophical servitude in New York or banishment from the profession. Readers of *The Intellectual Versus the City* know that I do not dislike New York, so they will not view what I am about to say as a bit of antiurban prejudice. Though I loved my native city, I did not take wing until I left it. During my years at Columbia, from 1936 to 1946, I certainly did not charm or wow those who had my academic future in their hands. So if it weren't for my loyal supporters, I might never have gotten the jobs I got after leaving Columbia, no matter what philosophical talent or historical learning I might have had: I could have worked like a dog and gone nowhere without the support and encouragement of my friends. I don't underestimate my own part in all of this out of false modesty, but luck played a great part in my escape from the mud gutters of Catherine Street. Luck has also played a part in my coming to know my lovely wife, Helen, to whom I was married on June 30, 1997. She has brought me happiness I never dreamt I would have in my eighties.

Although it is debatable whether luck led my sons to become scholars, their distinguished work and their charm, decency, intelligence, generosity, and wisdom have made me very proud of them, and I believe that if they had been *very* unhappy about what they had heard from me about the academic world, they would not have entered it; they entered it in spite of having heard some pretty grisly tales about it at the kitchen table. I never urged them to become scholars, but I did worry at times about whether I shouldn't have persuaded them to avoid a profession so heavily populated by prejudiced and unfair people, a profession in which standards, especially in the humanities, are so subjective and so heavily influenced by ideology, religion, race, and politics—a profession in which the sins of their father might well be visited on them. So strongly have I felt about this that I once thought I would call this book "With Apologies to My Sons for Not Warning Them" until someone reminded me that business, law, and medicine are not full of angels. In spite of what Nick and Steve heard from me at the kitchen table, they were brave enough to become professors, so I hope that when they reach my present age, they will be at least as pleased as I am about having done so and able to say that some people had helped them as much as I have been helped by Herbert Wechsler, Henry Aiken, B. W. Huebsch, G. E. Moore, Nelson Goodman, W. V. Quine, Arthur Schlesinger Jr., Harold Cherniss, and Isaiah Berlin, to mention only a few of my guides and my supporters. Plato is said to have warned those who wished to enter his Academe to avoid it if they were not mathematicians, but my advice to young scholars is that they not enter today's Academe unless they find that some of its residents are as warm-hearted and as well disposed toward them as my well-wishers have been toward me.

Appendix: Nelson Goodman, W. V. Quine, and Morton White

A Triangular Correspondence in 1947

The correspondence that follows* began with my writing a letter to W. V. Quine that accompanied the manuscript of a note that I later published in *Philosophy and Phenomenological Research* in December 1948 under the title "On the Church-Frege Solution of the Paradox of Analysis." The paradox, propounded by C. H. Langford, is that if true, a statement such as (1) "The attribute of being a brother is identical with the attribute of being a male sibling" says or expresses the same thing as the truism (2) "The attribute of being a brother is identical with the attribute of being a brother." The claim is that if (1) is true, we may substitute the expression "the attribute of being a brother" for the expression "the attribute of being a male sibling" in (1) to get (2), thereby showing that (1) says the same thing as (2). The Church-Frege solution of this paradox is to say that the sense, or meaning, of the expression "the attribute of being a brother" is different from that of the expression "the attribute of being a male sibling," though these two expressions denote the same attribute, and therefore (1) is not synonymous with (2).

This solution requires us to assert not only the existence of intensions such as attributes but also the existence of intensions that are the senses of the names of attributes. In commenting on this solution I said that it was generated by assuming the existence of attributes, and also that Nelson Goodman had remarked to me that it would appear arbitrary to assume the existence of enough intensional entities such as attributes to generate the paradox, and not to assume enough intensional entities to remove the paradox. This remark served as Quine's "springboard" in his letter to me of June

*The letters of Professors Goodman and Quine are printed with their kind permission.

3, 1947. I sent a copy of Quine's letter to Goodman, who then formed the triangle. In that letter, Quine diverged from his view on page 117, above.

> 7737 Mill Road
> Elkins Park 17, Penna.
> May 25, 1947

Dear Van:

I am enclosing something which I have just finished and which is almost ready to be submitted for publication. I must confess that I am more confident about the first part of it than I am about the second. The second, you will observe deals with some of your views, and I would be very happy to get your reaction to and criticisms of it. Indeed, if you should think it irrelevant to your views or wrong I hope you will tell me. One of the things I say on p. 5, viz. "on Quine's view the predicate has the same meaning in all contexts" is gathered not from anything you've written but rather from a letter from you to me of May 7, 1945. This interpretation, you will see, is crucial to the second part of the paper.

I would also be grateful to you for a bit of advice after you've read it. If it's worthy of publication at all in your opinion, do you think I ought to send it to the *Journal of Symbolic Logic*? Normally I'd think of it as too "philosophical" and would send it to *Mind,* but I'm wondering whether the new policy of JSL is calculated to invite contributions of this general style, so to speak.

> Sincerely,
> Morty White

P.S. After June 1 my address will be: Yelping Hill
>>> West Cornwall
>>> Conn.

> Akron, O.
> June 3, 1947
> (Soon back in Cambridge)

Dear Morty,

I think papers of the style of yours are decidedly suited to J.S.L. I find nothing to object to in the details of your discussion, but I should like to express my general attitude on the problem. Best springboard is your reference to Nelson on your last page. I don't think the "paradox of analysis" is wholly attributable to the excessive ontology. Phrased without that ontology, the paradox is, I take it, essentially this: An "analysis" has the form $\ulcorner \zeta = \eta \urcorner$, where ζ and η are synonymous; therefore the whole analysis is synonymous with, or translatable into, the triviality $\ulcorner \zeta = \zeta \urcorner$.

Resolution of the paradox: Distinguish between *intensional* and *structural synonymy*. The distinction is made, I believe, by Carnap in *Meaning and Necessity*; also in effect by Lewis, *Analysis of Knowledge and Valuation*, p. 199.

Intensional synonymy is the basic kind of synonymy; Carnap has called it "L-equivalence," and Lewis "sameness of intension." It is the kind of synonymy that underlies analyticity; also it is the kind that would determine identity of attributes, if there were attributes. It is the kind of synonymy that I have lamented the lack of a behavioristic criterion of. (Carnap and Lewis are unconscious of this lack, for their vision is obscured by excessive ontology.)

Structural synonymy is a narrower relation. Lewis simply calls it synonymy, but derives it from what he calls "analytic meaning"; "structural" is Carnap's word. (In the final version of *Meaning and Necessity* the word may be different; I haven't the book here.) In effect, the definitions of structural synonymy on the basis of intensional synonymy in Lewis and Carnap are substantially alike. No special ontology is really needed, and the definition is straightforward (once intensional synonymy is given), apart perhaps from some minor patching.

The distinction between the two synonymies is needed not only for the "paradox of analysis" but also for paradoxes of indirect discourse and translation. (E.g., since all mathematical truths are intensionally synonymous, substitute an abstruse one for '1 and 1 are 2' in 'Children know that 1 and 1 are 2' and get an absurdity.) These are really all the same paradox; the point is merely that a relation narrower than intensional synonymy, and closer to structural synonymy, underlies indirect discourse and translation. Thus an "analysis" $\ulcorner \zeta = \eta \urcorner$, though intensionally synonymous with $\ulcorner \zeta = \zeta \urcorner$, will not in general be structurally synonymous with $\ulcorner \zeta = \zeta \urcorner$; hence not properly *translatable* as $\ulcorner \zeta = \zeta \urcorner$. Intensional synonymy with $\ulcorner \zeta = \zeta \urcorner$ is analyticity, but not triviality. *Structural* synonymy with $\ulcorner \zeta = \zeta \urcorner$ *does* impute triviality.

It's bad that we have no criterion of intensional synonymy; still, this frankly and visibly defective basis of discussion offers far more hope of clarity and progress, far less danger of mediaeval futility, than does the appeal to attributes, propositions, and meanings. Frege, Church, Carnap, Lewis, and the rest seem to derive from those shadowy entities the same smug illusion of clarity that Toletus did from his substantial forms, and Moliére's physician from the *virtus dormitiva*.

Sincerely,
Van

My reply on June 5 to Quine contains on the top of its first page a message from me to Goodman, after which the reply comes. I had also enclosed my note that was later published, and Quine's letter to me of June 3.

Nelson: Here is my note and a letter by Van and a reply of mine. *You* are asked a question in the last (which may be regarded as a letter to *you and* Van); it raises what I think is an important question about the relation between nominalism and *synonymy*, or rather between nom. and Van's theory of synon. See you 6/13,

Best,
Morty

Yelping Hill
West Cornwall, Conn.
June 5, 1947

Dear Van:

Thanks for your letter and thanks for taking the trouble to read my piece. I find myself quite sympathetic (with reservations indicated later) to your way of going at the "paradox of analysis" and therefore ought to explain my connection with the Church-Frege view on this point. My interest in the puzzle was awakened by Langford and Moore. It seemed to me then that the puzzle *was* due to ontological commitment to intensions; certainly in the form in which they debated it. I came to regard the puzzling consequence as itself reflecting the errors of intensionalism; revealing, so to speak, a result of a basic infection. For this reason I debated with Black in *Mind* a "solution" which he proposed and which was still to retain attributes as entities. My purpose was to show that Black could not solve the paradox in his way, the implication being that he failed because he continued to postulate intensions. Along came Church with his review of my controversy with

Black, to show conclusively that we can solve the paradox provided we admit *more* intensions, i.e., senses of names of senses. I was forced to surrender my conviction that intensionalism was involved in a *contradiction*, and then I came to believe that perhaps Church's solution was *fake*, out of a feeling that attributes might exist but that I had no room in my ontology for the senses of names of attributes. Nelson convinced me of the arbitrariness of this, and so I came to feel that Church solved the puzzle by using a vaster supply of intensions than were dreamt of in *my* philosophy at any rate.

Just at this point I came to realize that a kind of puzzle could be reinstated which could only be eliminated by appealing to another Fregean bit of machinery, viz. oblique and ordinary occurrence of names. In a sense this seems to me to weaken the Church solution, for it reveals the need for even more "unnatural" assumptions (unnatural for an anti-intensionalist by disposition and an embryonic nominalist). I do not draw this conclusion in the article for I felt the need for doing this thoroughly in some other place. For this reason I leave the matter untouched.

I am much interested in your belief that the paradox of analysis is not wholly attributable to excessive ontology, for now, if "the same" paradox may be generated without assuming the existence of attributes, we may solve it along the lines you point out in your reference to Carnap and Lewis. This suggests that where one gets one's version of the puzzle by assuming intensions ontologically one must solve it (a la Church-Frege) by assuming *lots* of intensions; where one gets it without ontological commitment one solves it without having to increase the amount of that commitment. I take it that you would argue, too, that the fact that we can generate "the same" paradox without assuming intensions, reveals the superiority of your way of stating the paradox and hence your way (Lewis-Carnap) of solving it.—But when we come to this point, as you point out, we are left with *intensional synonymy* as basic and as admittedly defective, without the behavioristic criterion you seek, for example.

Now, although I should rather see the problem "unsolved" in this state than "solved" in the teeming universe of Frege's intensions, I must ask this question: *why* are we better off? Since I am sending a copy of this to Nelson I must ask him now whether *he* can make a decision as to the relative merits of two views which he deplores. I know that he finds all kinds of "synonymy" vague and objectionable, and certainly nominalism entails a rejection of intensions as entities. But would you, Nelson, be willing to say that a system based on "intensional synonymy" and *awaiting* behavioristic criteria is *preferable* to the Church-Frege one? I realize that *qua* nominalist your answer might be that the Church-Frege view is objectionable, but nominalism of itself could not support the Lewis-Carnap view. My feeling is that one's aversion to intensions ought not to lead one to support the Lewis-Carnap construction as reported in Van's letter. So far as I can see the strongest argument that can be marshalled in defense of the Lewis-Carnap view by one like Van (who deplores the state of "synonymy" right now) is the fact that it avoids the Platonism of (the?) Church. While I *incline* toward Van's view in this regard, and while Nelson had done a good deal to "nominalize" me, I confess that my aversion to Platonism is not great enough to lead me to accept the ontologically OK but admittedly defective construction reported in Van's letter. Nelson will remember a conversation in which he seemed to agree that his position was "a plague on both your houses"; of all three positions I come more and more to feel that maybe this is the most comfortable, but this, we must remember is no *solution*, but rather a rejection of the problem.

With kindest regards,

Morty

Schwenksville R.D.
Penna. June 8, 1947

Dear Morty and Van:

Just to get in my angle of this triangle:—

(1) First, to answer Morty's question, I should certainly consider Van's treatment of the so-called problem better than Church's; to accept Church's is to feel no need for further study of the problem; to accept Van's is to accept the obligation to make a further study, and the outcome of this further study might be in part a reconception of the problem. You might compare our views to differing religious attitudes: Church believes devoutly and unquestioningly in the gods; Van finds the conception of God unclear but can't cast Him off and hopes to find a meaning for God in human life; I think we'd better recognize that we are going to have to get along without. The end results of Van's efforts and mine might be pretty much the same: what he finds in his search for a meaning and what I find in my efforts to get along without the notion might not be very different.

(2) My skepticism about Van's hope for a behavioristic criterion of

synonymity stems from the fact that I feel that the lack of any behavioristic criterion (or even the dimmest suggestion as to how one might be set up) is a sign that we are not at all clear as to what it is that we have to define. If we had any idea of the meaning of the term, it seems to me we could outline a rough behavioristic criterion at once. I know roughly how to test whether "huksa" in Calubrian applies to the same things as "mrowch" in Calubrian or "cat" in English; but having obtained a positive result, I would not know how to test whether the three terms are synonymous because I don't know what the question means—I wouldn't know what the hell I'd be testing for. The inability to sketch any sort of test and the inability to understand what a term means seem to me all of a piece. Thus it seems that when Van uses a term and hopes for a behavioristic criterion he can't vaguely outline, he is employing a meaningless mark or noise on the ground that he needs it (like "God") in his life and hopes that a meaning will be found for it. My position differs just to this extent: it seems to me that it is sounder policy to try to solve our problems in terms of meaningful marks and noises; while we may not be able to solve them all immediately, such progress as we do make will be more solid than solutions which depend upon proper use of noises we don't understand—upon use, that is, that is in accord with a definition that we don't have and may not be able to get.

It also seems to me that some of the supposed problems disappear as soon as we renounce these meaningless notions. I am not at all ready to admit that the rest are hopeless. The situation with regard to direct discourse no longer presents any difficulty anyway, of course. I have the feeling that sufficient analysis will enable us to deal clearly also with indirect discourse. It is optimism on this, quite as much as pessimism with regard to the line Van takes, that inspires my view. One question occurs to me with regard to Van's letter on the Lewis-Carnap view: why not turn it upside down? Just as one may define extensional identity (overlooking difficulties now) in terms of interchangeability in all—except certain kinds of—contexts without resultant change of truth value, why not define, say, structural synonymity in a similar fashion; i.e. two sentences are ss if either can be put for the other in all contexts of the form "x believes that . . ." without changing the truth value of the whole? This direct definition in terms of truth values does not presuppose a definition of intensional synonymity, and seems perfectly clear. A parallel definition of intensional synonymity might run ". . . if either can be put for the other in any context of the form

'————follows from ....'" (where any sentence is put for '————'
and one of the two sentences in question appears for '..........'). This
latter definition, however, would be unclear because the term 'follows
from' is about as unclear as what we want to define. This merely
strengthens my suspicion that intensional synonymity is meaningless;
but I'd be willing to take anybody's word that some definition which
does not involve such dubious words in it, but is as straightforward as
the one above given for ss, expresses what he means by intensional
synonymity. It seems to me interesting, however, that ss can be defined
in terms of truth values without introducing anything more obscure
than "believes that" or maybe even "says that"; for we presume from the
beginning that we can determine the truth of such sentences, otherwise
the paradoxes under consideration would never arise. Naturally the
kind of definition I here propose would have to undergo careful revision
and reformulation.

Probably the preceding paragraph will convince you both that I am
missing the point entirely, and that's quite possible. I am no specialist
on this problem, and have sometimes the feeling that my views on it are
the result of insufficient familiarity with it rather than just unwillingness to accept certain theses. However, maybe on this basis of the above
revelation of my confusion you can straighten me out.

Regards to all. See you both soon.

Nelson

13 Ware Street, Apt. 8
Cambridge 38, Mass.
June 30, 1947

Dear Morty and Nelson,

I regret having let weeks pass.

In our controversy over synonymy I can be brief, for my attitude
toward your letters isn't very controversial. The great gulf is rather the
one that yawns between me (or us) on the one hand and Church, Frege,
Lewis, Carnap, Black, etc. on the other.

What is perhaps the main plank in my platform has been rightly
stated by Morty: "So far as I can see the strongest argument that can be
marshalled in defense of the Lewis-Carnap view by one like Van (who
deplores the state of 'synonymy' right now) is the fact that it avoids the
Platonism of (the?) Church." To put it another way: Problems of

meaning, analysis, analytic truth, necessity, etc. are, in the literature, intimately bound up with two kinds of things which I deplore: Platonism and intensional logic. My purpose (in what concerns synonymy) has been to separate the above-named problems from Platonism and intensional logic; to isolate them so that they may be talked about nominalistically and extensionally. Thus isolated, the problems take the form essentially of a single problem: behavioristic definition of intensional synonymy. I don't say this problem can be solved; what I say is that this is the way the problems under consideration should be conceived, if at all. And that I can't understand such things as the philosopher's (e.g. Carnap's) concept of "analytic truth" unless this problem be solved.

My attitude may be further clarified by a remark on Nelson's proposed definition of structural synonymy in terms of belief; viz., interchangeability in contexts of the form 'x believes that . . .'. For me such a definition is unsatisfactory precisely because I am not clear on the conditions of such interchangeability. Would Nelson, in declining to acknowledge a problem here, grant the unclarity of 'believes that . . .' (or of 'belief', as relating persons to statements) and therefore renounce this notion altogether?

Belief is, indeed, a bigger problem than structural synonymy; clarifying the latter would be a necessary but not sufficient condition for clarifying the former. Clarifying the latter would tell us only what statements are interchangeable as objects of belief, and not what ones are believed.

However, as I have said, I think structural synonymy presents no serious problem over intensional synonymy. As for intensional synonymy, Nelson proposes a definition in terms of 'follows from'. But 'follows from', or 'analytic consequence', is precisely my problem. It is interdefinable with intensional synonymy, and with analytic truth. Explain any of these in clearer terms (behavioristic ones, as I am wont to put it), and I ask no more.

Nelson says that he feels "that sufficient analysis will enable us to deal clearly . . . with indirect discourse." I venture to say that this, if it can be done, will yield as by-products some strong hints as to how to define synonymy.

Nelson says "The inability to sketch any sort of test and the inability to understand *what a term means* [my italics] seem to me all of a piece." Would he go further and say that when the "tests" for two terms are the same then "what the terms mean" are the same? Then he has already taken a step toward a definition of synonymy such as I'd like to see; I merely want a clear and complete definition. At any rate he doesn't seem in this passage to be "renouncing these meaningless notions."

Or take, again, the lexicographer. There should be some satisfactory formulation of the synonymy relation which his whole empirical enterprise is devoted to cataloguing.

I agree with Nelson that synonymy is in a sense meaningless. Meaningless in the sense in which "confirmation" and "probable", in inductive logic, are meaningless. I think the same kind of philosophical problem of analysis or clarification is involved in both cases: in the Carnap-Hempel program on confirmation and in the problem of synonymy.

Morty: Thanks for reprint on social thought. It contains the *bon mot* of the year: "Antiformalists . . . call upon social scientists in all domains, ask them to unite, and urge that they have nothing to lose but their deductive chains".— I look forward to seeing you in Cambridge. I'll be around except for a week in late July.

Nelson: A fair typist is already tintinnabulating on nominalism. I inserted a long explanation of our definition of "Proof"; also your footnotes; and I revised the comment on ancestral as you suggested. We can give it a final going over after it is typed.

Best regards to selves and wives.

Yours,
Van

July 2
Pigeon Cove, Mass.

Dear Van & Morty:

I read it and wept. Seldom has there been a mixture of so much agreement with so much misunderstanding. The most serious misunderstanding seems to me to be that revealed in the paragraph beginning at the bottom and running on to the top of page 2 of Van's letter. The definition in question I proposed only to reject immediately on just the score that Van explains; I did not offer this definition as a way of getting anywhere, but rather to show that while structural synonymy could be defined in terms more likely to be behavioristically explicable (e.g. "Believes that" or "says that"), a similar attempt for intensional synonymity gained no such ground, but left us with "follows" which is about where we started. This I considered an added reason for my feeling that: intensional synonymity is probably meaningless, whereas structural synonymity seems less hopeless. I don't mean that we have behavioristic criteria available for "believes," but at least what is in question here is a psychological state and I can imagine reasonable investigations being carried out to arrive at behavioristic criteria, while I have no idea how to define intensional synonymity in terms of psychological states.

To clarify my position further:

1. When I say I don't understand the meaning of "analytic" I mean that very literally. I mean that I don't even know how to apply the terms. I do not accept the analogy with the problem of defining, say, confirmation. I don't understand what confirmation is, or let us say projectibility, in the sense that I can't frame any adequate definition; but give me any predicate and (usually) I can tell you whether it is projectible or not. I understand the term in extension. But "analytic" I don't even understand this far; give me a sentence and I can't tell you whether it is analytic because I haven't even implicit criteria. As I have suggested before, the problem of defining "analytic" seems something like the problem of defining absolute motion. If you can show me a large group of sentences that are clearly analytic, and another large group that are clearly not, as I can show you a large group of predicates that are clearly projectible and another of predicates that are not, I will not only agree—as I now cannot—that the two problems are similar, but probably I will be impelled to seek for a definition. But I can't look for a definition when I don't know what it is I am defining. I am sorry that Van did not comment on what I think is the heart of my letter: the illustration drawn from the Calubrian language.

2. I deny the charge of inconsistency when I use such phrases as "what a term means". A term can be defined by any number of exten-sionally equivalent phrases, and my only plea is for complete democracy among these. Any of them gives a meaning of the term; in this sense, a term has several meanings rather than one, but thinking of extensional equivalence as the (strictly a) criterion of identity of meaning, we can also speak of any of these phrases as giving the meaning of the term, (whereas certain other phrases will not give the meaning). There is no implication of intensionality in my use of such language. What I am inveighing against is the intensionalist's notion that one or a few of the

phrases give the meaning while others are only accidentally extension-ally equivalent. Thus Van's case of the lexicographer seems to me clear. The l. is trying to find for each term an expression that has exactly the same extension. What is supposed to be a criterion of essentiality operating in his choice seems to me rather to be criteria of reliability; that is among various phrases he chooses that which he feels most unlikely to differ in extension from the definiendum. Since he seldom has the complete extensions of both available for examination, he has to use all the means at his command to guess about the application of the terms to the unknown (including future) cases. (Among the things he will take into account is what he knows of the course of word usage over a period of time). What I deny is that one of the means at his command is a mere "analysis of meanings" which is something different from the [guess?] about inductive process. The nearest I could come to a definition of analyticity would be something like this: "The phrase said to express the analytic meaning of a term is that one which of all considered is least likely to diverge in extension from the term." But this, even supposing there is one least likely, will hardly satisfy the intensionalist for: (1) The analytic meaning will vary according to the evidence available, and will not remain constant. (2) The phrase which gives the analytic meaning at a given time may not actually be extensionally equivalent with the term.

I might go on, but these are the main points. I am left in the embarrassing position of not grasping a problem which apparently seems to both of you quite as clear as others which I do grasp and am eager to solve. Although as you say, the big gap is between us and the others, I wish this little gap could be closed.

Morty: I gave Peter your phone number and suggested he call you. If he hasn't, might be a good idea to call him, Flushing 3-9173.

Van (and Morty). About the Ms being with the fair typist, I wish you analyticists would explain how it happens that while all fair typists are fair, many fair typists are not fair. Fiction apparently supposes that all typists are fair and that the large majority are fair, even though some are very unfair. I hope that our typist is fair and fair but since you will have all dealings with her it is not important to me whether she is fair and fair.

So long,
Nelson

Yelping Hill
West Cornwall, Conn.
July 3, 1947

Dear Nelson and Van:

Dance 6 from the Three-Cornered (Old?) Hat

My impression of Nelson's reply to Van is that Nelson did indicate that he thought "believes" furnished a better foundation for proceeding behavioristically than did "follows," and that he ought not to be interpreted as one who is convinced of the clarity of "follows."

But it's also my impression that Nelson in using the phrase "what a term means" (seized upon by Van as suggesting an inconsistency) suggested an interest in finding the meaning of a term which resembles that of some of the analyticists. His reply, however, (and conversation in Philly) reveal that he thinks this does not commit him to more than a spectrum of extensional equivalences one of which *may* be singled out as the basis for discovering what the analyticists call a necessary connection. I take it that he urges us never to claim (as philosophical definers) that we are giving *the* meaning of a term but always to speak of giving *a* meaning of the term. And I suppose that *a* meaning of a term is given by *an* extensional equivalent of the term. For those of us who still are interested in finding a unique meaning he has a sop, a sop which he recognizes, however, as incapable of satisfying a violent intensionalist. Thus far I *understand* him. To what he has to say I want only to add that the philosopher, like the lexicographer, usually limits himself to one natural language, thereby limiting the number of candidates in Nelson's democracy of extensional equivalents. He even limits himself further as a rule by specifying (most often the lexicographer does this) the domain of human thought and activity in which the definiendum is used. So, for example, "work" is given one everyday definition and one mechanical definition. Now I suspect that where the philosopher and the lexicographer impose enough limits of this sort they tend to feel secure in picking out *one* extensional equivalent as giving *the* meaning. What we must guard against, of course, (the philosopher and the lexicographer) is setting these limits in a question-begging way. We must not define "work" as "force × distance" by indicating that this is proper for the context in which people say that "work" means "force × distance," but rather in an "independent" way

(I'm worried now that I've introduced the notion of *independence*—am
I begging the question?).

It seems to me that this stipulation of language and domain is
continuous with a stipulation of the date or era. If we could pile up a
number of these qualifications without going *ad hoc*, we might then
have a matrix like this: x is *a* term which of all considered among those
used in the USA at time t_1 is least likely to diverge in extension from
the term to be defined, y (where x and y are distinct and have other
relations usually included among the formal conditions for definition).
Notice that this matrix might be satisfied by no x's (for some y's). In
that case we'd even have a sop for the"unanalyzabilists" like Moore
(except that here they'd best be called "unanalyzedists", for obvious
reasons). I must admit, however, that I cannot give Nelson all the
qualifications necessary, and for this reason am at his sceptical mercy.

But now comes the major problem. I am inclined to feel that there's
a serious difference between all of us (perhaps the difference is greatest
between Nelson on one side and Van and me on the other) on the
question: "What terms are candidates for philosophical definition or
analysis?" The most liberal position is taken by no one of us, namely, *all*
terms. The next one in strength requires that the terms be understandable. This embraces Van and myself, I think. The strongest condition
imposed thus far is that of Nelson, in spite of his claim that he too uses
understandability as a requirement for candidacy. His condition is: a
term P (let's make it a predicate) is understandable if and only if, given
any x I can tell you whether the sentence beginning with the name of
the given x, followed by "is," followed by P, is true (I started to be exact,
but I'll skip further nicety; you know what I mean). He sticks in
"usually" before "tell" but let's not quarrel over that. Now I think that
this condition is too strong, and the only way I can defend my point of
view is to select some terms which were selected as candidates for
philosophical analysis in the past, and which did not have Nelson's
property. The first one, and I don't need to present others, is "true."
Given *any* statement Nelson could not usually tell whether it is true
(nor Aristotle, nor Newton, nor Einstein, nor . . .). And yet it has
been selected by Tarski for a treatment which all of us think, I take it,
was worth his (and our) while. Now I am not quibbling about Nelson's
not being an encyclopedist. Even if we put "science" in place of
"Nelson" in the definiens of "understandable" we would rule out "true"
as non-understandable. Nor am I arguing about the verb "tell"; I don't

require that science be able to tell me in a flash; I will give it all the time and equipment it needs.

Nelson might reply that he need not insist on science or Nelson telling whether the given thing has the property expressed by the understandable predicate (forgive the Platonism). But then what does the condition for understandability come to in the case of "analytic"; simply that given any sentence it is either analytic or not. Just like the traditional analogue for "true." And just as the existence of statements whose truth-value we don't know didn't faze Tarski so I shouldn't be fazed by the wholly analogous situation in connection with "analytic."

Nelson may rightfully ask me what I mean by "understandable" and I suppose he might ask this of Van too. I have no clear answer; I only have vague intuitions. I do know that I understand a lot of sentences in the writings of Goodman and Quine, and very few in the writings of Fichte and Schelling. I know that some people (mainly philosophers) use the words "analytic" and "synthetic" and sometimes I think I understand what they mean. I think they are clear enough to merit further clarification. I feel that Nelson's criterion, if acted on consistently, would eliminate my interest in certain predicates which are used with apparent ease and consistency by philosophers who usually speak clearly. I keenly feel Van's objection to Carnap's attempted definition of "analytic," but like him I want to press on for a better one. I am interested in going along the lines suggested by Nelson's proposal; in other words I'm not a violent intensionalist. With it I have another difficulty. It obliges me to carry on an inductive study which I hadn't supposed necessary before in the detection of analyticity. My conception of inductive science involves test-tubes, research, questionnaires and a lot of the stuff prated about by my (and Nelson's) colleagues. If we're going to be inductive, let's do it right, but I must admit that I (like Nelson) don't know where to begin.

> Dixi et salvavi animam meam
> (Is that right Van? I
> mean the Latin),
> Best all around,
> Morty (a typist who is fair but
> not a fairtypist—and
> who will not have any
> dealings with any typist
> who is fair, says Lucia.)

P.S. I have just reread Nelson's letter and I see a misunderstanding on my part. I understood Nelson to say, when I wrote the above, that an understandable predicate is one whose correct applicability he can detect, given any object. A term that is not understandable I took to be one whose applicability he could not detect in some cases. This, of course, is the case with "true." But now, as I reread, I suspect that he rejects "analytic" as incomprehensible because he can find *no* sentence (or large group of sentences) which he knows is analytic, or can tell is analytic, whereas, clearly, there are sentences whose truth he can tell. My reply to this weakened criterion is different. I cannot reject this as a necessary condition for a comprehensible predicate, but I must say that there are sentences whose analyticity I can tell, e.g. "everything in New York State right now is in New York State right now." Granted that all pineapples are not apples, and that all fair typists are not fair. But these are Nelson's pets which illustrate the difficulty in establishing *some* attributions of analyticity: I bow before the perplexities they present and hope that the ultimate definition of "analytic" will handle them. But let us remember that there are statements whose truth is difficult of detection, too, and that we are not in a position to say "how to go about finding out whether they are true" except to say "Be careful, experiment, use laboratories, etc."

Pigeon Cove, Mass.
July 5, 1947

Dear Morty and Van:

Morty's letter seems to me to put the case so well that I am about content to let the matter rest. There are only a couple of words I would add:

(1) My rough criterion of understandability was not determinateness of all cases, as Morty recognizes in his P.S.; nor is it determinateness of at least one case, but rather determinateness of an appreciable group of cases. I wouldn't attempt to be more precise than that.

(2) Morty's choice of a sentence he knows to be analytic seems to me as unfortunate as Moore's famous choice of the fake ceiling window. The quoted expression he gives is false if we take it very literally, for some of the things that were in New York State when he typed the first occurrence of "right now" had moved out by the time he typed the second occurrence. Of course he can change the example and eventu-

ally get something which I will admit has a very high degree of likelihood of being true, but it seems to me that it is this and only this he is doing—rather than finding a sentence that is "analytic" in some divergent sense.

(3) I am of course open to—indeed have advocated—the idea of dealing with "analytic" along the lines suggested near the top of Morty's page 2, except that if one is willing to go this far it would seem quixotic not to go the whole way with me and agree that analyticity is a matter of degree. The fact that Morty cannot give all the conditions in his proposed definition along this line seems to me a minor matter. If he takes the single step of modifying the definition so that analyticity is a matter of degree, his position then seems to me indistinguishable from that I have argued for this winter. In that case the rest of the discussion becomes purely academic.

Morty's letter convinces me more strongly than ever that he is the man to do a survey article on the whole problem. If Van feels the same way, perhaps he will help me urge it.

Regards to all and when will we be seeing you?

Sincerely,
Nelson

13 Ware Street, Apt. 8
Cambridge 38, Mass.
July 6, 1947

Dear Nelson and Morty,

I'm sad about having missed Nelson's satire. The reason for my obtuseness was that the definition of structural synonymy in terms of belief (which, I take it, Nelson *did* intend seriously) isn't appreciably more satisfactory to me than the satirical definition of intensional synonymy in terms of logical consequence.

Nelson's position, as I now see it, is as follows: (1) There is some hope of making sense of structural synonymy; as much, perhaps, as of confirmation in inductive logic. (2) There is no such hope for intensional synonymy (nor, therefore, for analyticity).

When Nelson comes out flat-footedly for extensional equivalence as a standard of synonymy, it ill becomes me to take issue; for I have always been all for extension, with the world against me. When Nelson says he doesn't know how to apply "analytic," much less define it, I agree with regard to myself. This is a very iconoclastic view—the doctrine of the essential unclarifiability of analyticity—but maybe it's the right one. In any case the status of my doctrine of intensional synonymy remains unchanged insofar as expressed in the long paragraph of the first page of my letter of June 27.

However, I would still question the preferential status accorded to structural synonymy in (1). I'm not clear on belief and indirect discourse. If in fact a satisfactory definition of structural synonymy were at length attained (without help of intensional synonymy), I'd have renewed hope for intensional synonymy itself; though I can't yet suggest how a definition of the latter in terms of the former might run.

As to typists, it has been my experience that they fall into nine slightly overlapping classes: good typists who are good, good typists who are fair, good typists who are poor, fair typists who are good, and so on. My present typist is a good typist who is good, fair, and poor. But

If she be not fair to me
What care I how fair she be?

Van

13 Ware Street, Apt.8
Cambridge 38, Mass.
July 7, 1947

Dear Morty and Nelson,

I agree with Nelson that Morty's account of July 3 puts the problem in the right light. My only misgiving is over the analogy drawn between 'true' and 'analytic'. In cases where I don't know whether a given statement S is true, I can still either (a) determine, from an examination of S itself, a method of trying to decide its truth; or (b) direct my empiricistic objections upon certain terms inside S. But in cases where I don't know whether S is analytic, I don't know where to begin finding out; nor can I pass the buck to terms inside S, in any way similar to the case of 'true'. Morty's suggestion at the top of page 2 is a step toward an answer to this problem; and it is such steps as this, and not the analogy to 'true', which I think should carry weight.

I think it would be a swell idea to talk Morty into doing a survey article on all this.

Yours,
Van

Pigeon Cove, Mass.
July 8, 1947

Dear Van and Morty:

I think our triangular correspondence has about accomplished its purpose, and I am not trying to prolong it by the present epistle, but only using an odd half-hour to jot some further reflections on the topic in question. Replies are not expected unless the spirit moves.

(1) Van's paragraph 3 reminds me that while I have always been extensionalist-minded, it was talks with Van that led me to my present conviction that the problem of analyticity is a bogus one; so it indeed "ill becomes" him to take issue. I am glad to see that he is little inclined to do so, as I had feared lately that he was becoming too much infected with Carnapean tolerance.

(2) I agree with Van's dissent to Morty's comparison of "true" with "analytic." I was unwilling to accept it when I read it but at the same time not able to produce any adequate counterargument. I am not sure that Van's will convince Morty, but I feel that further discussion would bear Van out.

(3) While I have been posing as an extensionalist for the purpose of this discussion, I should like to repeat what Morty knows from conversations this winter and Van from my paper on definition at the Harvard colloquium some years ago: That actually I think that extensional equivalence is not too weak a criterion of synonymy (as the intensionalists would hold) but rather too strong a one, and that we must drop extensional equivalence in favor of the weaker criterion of isomorphism. Strangely enough this still weaker criterion, since it seems to depend on structure looks in one way like a return to a more intensionalistic position, even though it is a step still further away.

(4) I don't think that intensionalists are likely to be satisfied with any interpretation of analyticity that construes it in terms of degree of reliability because as I understand them they feel it is a matter rather of the nature of the grounds on which the judgment is made, analytic

sentences being those whose truth can be determined quite apart from any experience. I think they confuse themselves here. The judgments they call analytic are usually judgments which can be made without knowledge of instances of the sentence in question but: (a) many judgments they would not call analytic are of this kind—e.g. "There are no live elephants inside Mt. Rainier", "All the marbles produced by that machine but not observed by me are red" (when I have observed 5 million random cases out of a possible 5 million and one). (b) Judgments of this kind are not made independently of experience but only independently of experience of their instances. Often they are analogic rather than analytic. In the kind of case most frequently pointed to the situation seems to me something like this: we find by experience of their instances that many sentences of the form "all r things are r" are true and we project this principle to judge that the sentence "all red things are red" is true. Our experience underlying this is not necessarily experience of red things, but rather experience of the reliability of similar sentences. When we discover exceptions—e.g. that red politicians are not red, we tend to discount them, preferring to maintain the truth of our induced general principle. That is we tend to try by force to maintain the truth of the principle "all sentences of such and such a form are true" and we make question-begging reservations to maintain it. Sentences honored by such solicitude are called analytic.

(5) Note that in order to show that a given sentence is not analytic, we ordinarily try to show that it is not true. The intensionalist feels vindicated to a degree if he can find a principle of any generality that we cannot show to be questionable—i.e. perhaps untrue. But the anti-intensionalist need not deny that there are some sentences whose truth he does not question. When Morty concocted the sentence about New York State as an example of an analytic statement, I wonder whether he was actually not merely trying to find a sentence having a non-trivial number of instances that he felt willing (unwisely in this case) to commit himself to wholeheartedly?

(6) If Van agrees that he not only doesn't know how to define "analytic" but doesn't know how to apply it either, what is it that he is hoping to find a behavioristic definition for? Certainly not the mere sound, in which case the definition would be quite arbitrary. Rather he is looking for a behavioristic definition for which the test of adequacy will presumably be in accordance with a usage which he doesn't have before him. It seems to me he is then in the same position that he would

be if he were to set out to define the Calubrian word "phwanischk." But in view of his latest letters, I gather he feels about the same amount of hope in both cases, so that the only difference between us is perhaps over the illusory aid and comfort he seems to give the enemy.

This is too damn long.

Sincerely,
Nelson

Morty: (not on Van's copy)

Heard from Peter about latest developments and your phone call. Guess things are likely to remain dormant until Fall.

Hope you can make the Fisher concert. It now seems very likely we'll be there, and it would be nice to see you afterwards. In fact Margaret mentioned that if you come you'll be included, along with us, in an invitation to a buffet supper at the studio in the evening. I think we all might have a good time.

You will have to do that survey paper on the non-existent problem.

Index

Made in the USA
Lexington, KY
13 September 2015